Architektur | Zentrum | Wien

5. Wiener Architekturseminar
5th Viennese Seminar on Architecture

6. Wiener Architekturseminar
6th Viennese Seminar on Architecture

Der leere Raum 94

Der öffentliche Raum 95

11 internationale Projekte / 11 international projects

The Empty Space 94 **The Public Space 95**

SpringerWienNewYork

Das Wiener Architekturseminar und dieses Katalogbuch werden aus Mitteln der
Geschäftsgruppe Stadtentwicklung, Stadtplanung und Außenbeziehungen der Stadt Wien dotiert.

The Viennese Seminars on Architecture and the accompanying catalogues are financed
out of the budget of the business sectors Urban Development, Town Planning and Foreign Relations

5. Wiener Architekturseminar / 5. Viennese Seminar on Architecture
Architektur Zentrum Wien
Konzept / Concept: Boris Podrecca, Dietmar Steiner
Koordination / Coordination: Karin Ivancsics, Kurt Plöckinger, Ruth Wetschnig

6. Wiener Architekturseminar / 6. Viennese Seminar on Architecture
Architektur Zentrum Wien
Konzept / Concept: Boris Podrecca, Dietmar Steiner
Koordination / Coordination: Katharina Katzelmayer, Kurt Plöckinger

Der leere Raum 94 — Der öffentliche Raum 95 / The Empty Space 94 — The Public Space 95
Ausstellung / Exhibition
Architektur Zentrum Wien, Burggasse 1, 1070 Wien
Inhaltliche Betreuung / Concept: Katharina Katzelmayer, Kurt Plöckinger
Gestaltung / Design: Scott Ritter
Graphik / Graphics: Atelier Unterkircher Jankoschek

Katalog / Catalogue
Herausgeber / Editor: Architektur Zentrum Wien
Redaktion / Editorial staff: Ines Mitterer; Mitarbeit / Team: Katharina Katzelmayer, Kurt Plöckinger
Gestaltung / Graphic design: Atelier Unterkircher Jankoschek
Übersetzungen / Translations: Marinos Agathocleous, Brigitte Eisenberger, Anneliese Lindner,
Christoffer Lindner, Christine Plunger, Sigrid Szabó, Regina Thaller, Michael Zobel
Verlag / Publisher: Springer-Verlag Wien New York
Druck / Printing: Seitenberg, Wien

Das Werk ist urheberrechtlich geschützt.
Die dadurch begründeten Rechte, insbesondere die der Übersetzung, des Nachdruches, der Entnahme von Abbildungen, der Funksendungen,
der Wiedergabe auf photomechanischem oder ähnlichem Wege und der Speicherung in Datenverarbeitungsanlagen, bleiben, auch bei nur
auszugsweiser Verwertung, vorbehalten.
This work is subject to copyright.
All rights are reservend, whether the whole or part of the material is concerned, specifically those of translation, reprinting, re-use of
illustrations, broadcasting, reproduction by photocopying machines or similar means, and storage in data banks.

© 1996 Architektur Zentrum Wien und die Autoren

ISBN 3-211-82895-8 Springer-Verlag Wien New York

Inhaltsverzeichnis / Contents

Hannes Swoboda	Vom Experiment zur Institution / From the experiment to the institution	6
Ines Mitterer	Angewandte Pluralität / Plurality in practice	8

5. Wiener Architekturseminar / 5th Viennese Seminar on Architecture

Boris Podrecca	Stadtlandschaft zwischen Paradies und Abstandsfläche / Cityscape between paradise and neglectingspace	12
Luc Deleu	**A strange attractor in Vienna**	14
	Orbanes Planungsmanifest / Orban Planning Manifesto	16
	A strange attractor in Vienna	20
Adriaan Geuze	**A yearning for authenticity**	26
	Sittin' on the dock of the bay	28
	Die Sehnsucht nach Authentizität / A yearning for authenticity	32
José Llinás Carmona	**Strips**	38
	Das ungewohnte Umgehen mit freiem Gelände / About the unusual treatment of empty space	40
	Strips	42
Mark Mack	**Manifest for controlled chaos**	48
	Architektur der Körperlichkeit / Corporal architecture	50
	Manifest für das kontrollierte Chaos / Manifesto for controlled chaos	54
Ippolito Pizzetti	**Dialogue between man and tree**	60
	Kommt der Genius Loci geflogen / The genius Loci comes flying	62
	Zwiegespräch zwischen Mann und Baum / Dialogue between man and tree	64
Martha Schwartz	**Napoleon did not sleep here**	70
	Vernachlässigte Landschaften / The landscape of neglect	72
	Napoleon hat nicht hier geschlafen / Napoleon did not sleep here	76

6. Wiener Architekturseminar / 6th Viennese Seminar on Architecture

Boris Podrecca	Räume, räume / Spaces, spaces	80
Mariano Bayón	**The scale as scale**	82
	Vom Prinzip des minimalen Aufwands / On the principle of minimal effort	84
	Der Maßstab als Maßstab / The scale as scale	88
Ben van Berkel	**Organization of structure**	94
	Körperliche Kompaktheit / Corporal compactness	96
	Organisation der Struktur / Organisation of structure	100
Michelangelo Pistoletto	**Progetto Arte**	106
	Kreative Zusammenarbeit / Creative collaboration	108
	Progetto Arte	112
Fabio Reinhart	**Vielschichtig verwobene Sequenzen**	118
	Bedeutungen schaffen / Creating meanings	120
	Vielschichtig verwobene Sequenzen / Multi-layered interwoven sequences	124
Dagmar Richter	**Experimente zur adäquaten Raumfindung im öffentlichen Raum**	130
	Die Kunst zu kopieren – Manifest eines ex-zentrischen Subjekts / The art of copying – Manifesto of an ex-centric subject	132
	Experimente zur adäquaten Raumfindung im öffentlichen Raum / Experiments for adequate spaces creating in the public space	136

Symposium „Der öffentliche Raum" / "Symposion The Public Space"

Thomas Held	Alle Architektur ist öffentlich / All architecture is public	142
Jos Bosmann	Zwei Strategien für die Neugestaltung des öffentlichen Raums / Two strategies for the re-designing public space	146
Kay Friedrichs	Architektur auf der Infobahn / Architecture on the data highway	151
Mariano Bayón	Über den öffentlichen Raum / On public spaces	156
	Übersetzungs- und Bildnachweis	160
	Teilnehmerliste	161

Vom Experiment zur Institution: Die Wiener Architekturseminare

Hannes Swoboda

Das junge Wiener Architekturseminar hat bereits Tradition. Das anfängliche Experiment, StudentInnen und junge ArchitektInnen aus der ganzen Welt die Möglichkeit zu bieten, mit internationalen und renommierten ProfessorInnen Projekte für Wien zu entwickeln, ist zu einer Art Institution gewachsen.

Das Wiener Architekturseminar wurde zu einem wesentlichen Bestandteil der „Architekturstadt Wien", die in den letzten Jahren offen und neugierig einer zeitgenössischen Interpretation von Stadt und Gesellschaft Raum zur Entfaltung bot. Die Ideen von Außen, die sozusagen fremde Sicht der Stadt in den Projekten der Wiener Architekturseminare, hat auch die interne Sicht der Stadt befruchtet. Und noch etwas ist geschehen in diesen Jahren, das niemand vorhersehen konnte. Es hat sich inzwischen eine informelle internationale Gemeinde der „Architekturseminaristen" gebildet, bislang 600 StudentInnen und 47 ProfessorInnen, die auf gemeinsame und vergleichbare Erfahrungen zurückblicken können und so eine ganz besonders kenntnisreiche und qualifizierte Gruppe von „Botschaftern" Wiens in der Welt bilden.

Die Themenstellungen des 5. und 6. Wiener Architekturseminars waren für mich persönlich besonders spannend. Die Beschäftigung mit dem – provokant bezeichneten – „leeren Raum" der Landschaft Wiens und die folgende Hinterfragung des „öffentlichen Raums" hat wichtige Probleme der Stadtplanung in das Zentrum der Aufmerksamkeit gerückt.

Unbestreitbar hat Wien dem grünen Raum, der Landschaft, den Parks – von den historischen öffentlichen Stadtgärten bis zum Wienerwald und zur Donauinsel – immer große Aufmerksamkeit geschenkt. Neue, zeitgenössische Formen und Typen für die Grünräume in den neuen Gebieten der Stadterweiterung zu entwickeln, ist dabei genauso wichtig, wie neue Erholungsräume in den dichtverbauten Stadtregionen zu erschließen.

Große Anstrengungen wurden in Wien auch für die Neudefinition und Neugestaltung des öffentlichen Raums unternommen. Viele Fachleute behaupten, der öffentliche Raum finde heute nur mehr medial und telekommunikativ seinen „Ort". Dem hat Wien mit vielen medialen Angeboten und Projekten, auch im Internet, entsprochen. Aber dennoch bleibt der konkrete und reale öffentliche Raum, die Straßen und Plätze der gebauten Stadt, eine soziale und kulturelle Aufgabe mit allen politischen Problemen der Umsetzung. Denn gerade hier zeigt sich immer wieder, wie sehr sich Wünsche und Projektionen von betroffenen und engagierten BürgerInnen zu oft widersprüchlichen Argumenten bündeln. Autofreie historische Plätze werden begrüßt, solange nicht der eigene gewohnte Abstellplatz davon betroffen ist. Wichtige Mahnmale und Denkmäler werden prinzipiell befürwortet, sie sollten aber lieber woanders errichtet werden.

Das 5. + 6. Wiener Architekturseminar hat zu diesen Problemen und Fragen wichtige Anregungen entwickelt. Dafür sei hier den Leitern, Boris Podrecca und Dietmar Steiner, dem Team des Architektur Zentrum Wien für die effiziente Durchführung, den engagierten ProfessorInnen und den ambitionierten StudentInnen und ArchitektInnen für ihre Beiträge zur Wiener Architektur- und Planungskultur gedankt.

Dr. Hannes Swoboda
Amtsführender Stadtrat für Stadtentwicklung,
Stadtplanung und Außenbeziehungen der Stadt Wien

From the experiment to the institution: The Viennese Seminars on Architecture

Hannes Swoboda

Although it began not long ago, the Viennese Seminar on Architecture has already assumed a traditional character. The initial experiment which consisted in allowing students and young architects from all over the world to develop projects for Vienna together with international professors of great renown, has become a kind of institution.

The Viennese Seminar on Architecture is now an integral part of the „Architectural City of Vienna". With great openness and interest, Vienna has provided the necessary space for the expression of a contemporary interpretation of city and society. The ideas from outside, in a sense the foreigner's perspective of the city, reflected in the projects presented at the Viennese Seminars on Architecture, also enriched the inhabitants' views of their city. Something else happened in these years, too, something nobody could ever have predicted. In the meantime, an informal international community of „Vienna Architecture Seminarists" has developed, consisting so far of 600 students and 47 professors who can look back to common, comparable experiences, forming worldwide a well informed and qualified group of „Ambassadors" for Vienna.

Personally, I found the topics of the 5th and 6th Viennese Seminar on Architecture very exciting. Debate on the intentionally provocative issue of "empty space" in Vienna's land-scape and the subsequent discussion over "public space" has helped focus attention to important problems of urban planning. In Vienna, green spaces, landscape, parks - from the historical municipal parks to the Wienerwald and the Donauinsel - have always played a significant role in the city's life. Developing new contemporary forms and types of green spaces in the new urban areas is equally important as creating new areas of recreation in the existing, densely built regions of the city. Vienna has also undertaken great efforts to redefine and reformulate public space. Many experts believe that public space today is a "site" to be implemented only through media and communication. Vienna was quick to adapt to this new form by presenting numerous media events and projects, even Internet homepages. Yet the real, tangible public space, the streets and squares in the existing urban environment remain a social and cultural issue with all the political problems involved in its implementation. This is exactly where we repeatedly see how the wishes and projections of affected and active citizens are reflected in completely divergent arguments. Everyone, for example, welcomes plans for a car ban at historical sites as long as one's own favourite parking lot is not endangered. In principle, people support the erection of important monuments or memorials, yet they would rather have these erected somewhere else.

The 5th and 6th Viennese Seminar on Architecture has developed significant stimuli to these questions and issues. I would therefore like to thank the directors of the seminar, Boris Podrecca and Dietmar Steiner and the team of the Vienna Architecture Centre for its excellent organization, as well as the committed professors and ambitious students and architects for their contributions to the Viennese culture of architecture and planning.

Dr. Hannes Swoboda
Municipal Councillor for Urban Development,
Urban Planning and Foreign Relations of the City of Vienna

**Stadtraum Remise – Veranstaltungsort des 5. und 6. Wiener Architekturseminars /
Stadtraum Remise – venue of the 5th and 6th Viennese Seminar on Architecture**

Angewandte Pluralität Ines Mitterer

Ausgangslage. Sommer 1994, 1995. Zweihundert Architekturstudenten aus vieler Herren Länder – von Argentinien bis Kroatien und von Südafrika bis zu den Niederlanden – brechen zum 5. und 6. Wiener Architekturseminar auf. Und sie wissen, was sie tun. Denn trotz des immer noch vorherrschenden Pioniergeistes, ist das Wiener Architekturseminar – dank der erfolgreichen Durchführungen 1 bis 4 – zu einem Fixpunkt auf dem europäischen Architekturkalender geworden, dessen grundsätzliche Vorgaben und Arbeitsmethoden weithin bekannt sein dürften:

Annäherung. Wien ist Ausgangspunkt aller Überlegungen: für allgemeine, zukunftsweisende, visionäre Stadtplanungs- und Architekturdebatten genauso wie für konkrete Projekte an konkreten Orten - Stadtrandgebiete, terrains vagues, ehemalige Industrieareale, zentrumsnahe Bereiche, ehemalige Vorstädte; Problemzonen, die in Wien wie in jeder vergleichbaren Großstadt einer entsprechenden Aufarbeitung bedürfen, aber aus Zeit- und Ressourcenmangel im Planungsalltag nicht berücksichtigt werden können.

Partner. Andere Studenten - andere Schulen, andere Denkansätze, Sprachen und Traditionen sowie hochqualifizierte Gruppenleiter, nach deren Anregungen Konzepte zu den Themen „Der leere Raum - Der öffentliche Raum" erarbeitet wurden. Die Präsentation der Projekte erfolgte gruppenweise am Ende des Seminars.

Baustelle. Eine alte, denkmalgeschützte Straßenbahnremise mit riesiger Halle, intakten Schienen und romantischen Säulen, in der man die Sommertage abseits des üblichen Arbeitsumfeldes diskutierend, planend, zeichnend und modellbauend verbringt. Inzwischen kann der Ort schon historisch gesehen werden, steht er doch dem Wiener Architekturseminar ab Sommer 1996 nicht mehr zur Verfügung (derzeit als Halle für Rollerblader adaptiert - weitere Nutzung ungewiß).

Ergebnis. Ein Reflexionsreservoir zu relevanten städtebaulichen Fragestellungen - mit positiven Begleiterscheinungen für alle Beteiligten:
* für die Stadt Wien, die jederzeit auf dieses professionell erarbeitete und ohne jeglichen - funktionellen, finanziellen, politischen, ökologischen - Druck entstandene geistige Material zurückgreifen kann.
* für die Studenten, die vom Erfahrungspotential ihrer Professoren profitieren, ihre eigenen Ideen anhand konkreter Beispiele auf Umsetzbarkeit testen und die erarbeiteten Konzepte als urbanistisch / architektonisches Vademecum mitnehmen können.
* für die Gruppenleiter, deren Berufscredo und Arbeitsmethoden hierzulande Verbreitung und Anerkennung finden - eine vorzügliche Voraussetzung für jede Berücksichtigung bei zukünftigen Planungsaufträgen.

Realisierungsphase.
20/08 - 11/09/1994 und 26/08 - 17/09/1995 ... wobei sich wieder einmal herausstellt, daß man - bei aller Vorinformation - nie wissen kann, was tatsächlich geschieht.

Umsetzung. Die Pluralität der persönlichen und professionellen Hintergründe von Professoren und Studenten spiegelt sich in der Pluralität der Heran-

Plurality in practice Ines Mitterer

Point of departure. Summer 1994, 1995. Two hundred architecture students from all over the world – from Argentina to Croatia and from South Africa to the Netherlands - come to join the 5th and 6th Viennese Seminar on Architecture. Mind you, they're well aware of what they are doing. Despite the pioneer spirit that dominates this event, the Viennese Seminar on Architecture has become a fixed point on the European architecture calendar and its main objectives and methods are well known, not least because of the first four successful seminars.

Approach. Vienna constitutes the starting point of all considerations: for general, trend-setting, visionary urban planning and architectural debates as well as for concrete projects on concrete locations - suburban areas, terrains vagues, former industrial sites, near-city center sectors, former suburbs; critical areas that not only in Vienna but in any other comparable metropolis need to be reconsidered, yet cannot be given any attention by planners due to a lack of both time and resources in their everyday routine.

Partners. Different students, different schools, different approaches, languages, and traditions and highly qualified seminar professors, whose suggestions lead the groups to develop concepts on the topics „Empty space - Public space". Presentation of the projects is done in groups at the end of the seminar.

Building site. An old tramway garage under preservation order, featuring a huge hall, intact rails, and romantic columns, where one can spend a summer day discussing, planning, drawing, or building models, away from the ordinary workplace surroundings.
In the meantime, this site has already assumed a historic perspective, since it will no longer be available for the Viennese Seminar on Architecture by the summer of 1996 (it has now been adapted to accommodate inline skaters - its future use is still unknown).

Outcome. A reservoir of opinions on relevant issues of urban planning with positive side-effects for all participants:
* for the city of Vienna that anytime has access to this professional material which was developed without any functional, financial, political, or ecological pressure.
* for the students who could learn from their professors' experience, test the feasibility of their own ideas on concrete examples, and bring back home the concepts they

gehensweisen und Lösungsansätze, wie zum Beispiel:
- Luc Deleu und seine Studenten überraschen mit ihrem kompromißlosen Projekt der kompletten Verbauung der Donauinsel.
- die Gruppe Martha Schwartz stellte mit Hilfe des Stadtgartenamtes eine Wiese auf die Schienen der Remise.
- der Spanier Mariano Bayón setzt mit seinem Team auf Pragmatik. Alle arbeiten an einem Projekt, das Realisierbarkeit zum Ziel hat und es auch erreicht.
- unter den, in Kleinstgruppen aufgeteilten Studenten Dagmar Richters, wird vornehmlich theoretische Diskussionsarbeit geleistet
- der Niederländer Ben van Berkel besteht auf Einzelarbeiten und Selbstverantwortlichkeit.
- die Gruppe Michelangelo Pistolettos gibt sich geheimnisvollen Vorbereitungen hin (keiner darf das Werk sehen, bevor es vollendet ist), um am Ende eine künstlerische Architekturinstallation zu präsentieren.

Klima. Bei denkbar ungünstiger Großwetterlage - der Sommer hält sich in beiden Jahren nicht an die Spielregeln, und man friert bei knapp 10 Grad Celsius in der unbeheizten Remise - resultieren die unterschiedlichsten Mikroklimata aus der jeweiligen Konstellation der Seminarteilnehmer:
- anfängliche Skepsis löst sich in Wohlgefallen auf: einige Studenten, die vorerst durch den konzeptiven Ansatz eines Michelangelo Pistoletto (der erste an einem Wiener Architekturseminar teilnehmende Künstler) irritiert sind - sind am Ende froh über die neugewonnene Perspektive.

developed as an architectural/urban vademecum.
- for the guest professors, whose professional credo and work methods will become known and acknowledged in Austria, meaning that they will be more likely to be taken into consideration in future planning contracts.

Implementation phase. 20/08–11/09/1994 and 26/08–17/09/1995 ..yet it seems that despite all the information you gather, you can never know what will actually happen.

Realization. The plurality of personal and professional backgrounds of both professors and students is reflected in the plurality of approaches and solutions, for example:
- Mariano Bayón from Spain and his team are adherents of pragmatism. They all work on a single project with the objective of realizing it, and they actually succeed in doing this.
- the students of Dagmar Richter are divided into very small groups in which they mostly discuss theoretical concepts.
- Ben van Berkel from the Netherlands focuses on individual work and self-responsibility.
- all preparations of Michelangelo Pistoletto's group are done under a veil of secrecy (nobody is allowed to see the work before completion) in order to present an artistic architecture installation in the end.

Climate. The weather being generally awful – the summer hasn't behaved as such for the past two years, so work in the unheated garage at 10°C is not necessarily comfortable – the

**Stadtrat Hannes Swoboda /
City councillor Hannes Swoboda**

- umgekehrt verwandelt sich ursprüngliches Interesse in Unsicherheit und Ablehnung – so erlebt in der Gruppe Dagmar Richter. Spannungen, die sich sprichwörtlich „über Nacht" in einem kleinen kreativen „Sabotageakt" entladen:

Kunst am Bau. Eine Rieseninstallation aus zusammengenagelten Holzbrettern hängt von der Decke der Remise, Schienen und eine Säule leuchten in orangem Lack. Unglücklicherweise ist das Gebäude denkmalgeschützt und eine Holzkonstruktion der vorgelegten Art ein gewisses Sicherheitsrisiko, weshalb das Kunstwerk keinen Bestand hat und der Kreativitätsschub der Richter-Studenten dazu verurteilt ist, in einer stundenlangen, mühsamen Demontage- und Putzaktion zu verebben.

Exkursionen. Architekturführungen durch Wien (inklusive Kanalnetz und Gasometer) sowie Ausflüge in die Umgebung zu Bauten von Adolf Loos in Böhmen und Preßburg rufen hingegen ausschließlich positive Reaktionen hervor. So wie überhaupt das Interesse der Kursteilnehmer für Wien weit über touristische Neugierde und die gestellten Aufgaben hinausgeht und wohl nicht mit der Abreise der Seminarteilnehmer abrupt endet....

Folgeerscheinungen. Das Seminar ist vorbei, das Spiel geht weiter - soviel haben die Ereignisse der letzten Jahre schon gezeigt:
- eine „internationale Gemeinde" von „Wiener Seminaristen" breitet sich langsam über die Welt aus.
- Beiträge finden Eingang in Diplomarbeiten, die von den Studenten an ihren Heimatuniversitäten vorgelegt werden.
- das intensivierte Zusammenarbeit zwischen ausländischen Universitäten (bisher vor allem Spanien, Italien, Kroatien) und dem Wiener Architekturseminar.
- Architekten bestätigen den Erfolg des Seminars, indem sie die Wien-Arbeiten als wichtige Projekte ihrer architektonischen Entwicklung in ihre Publikationen aufnehmen, so bei Adriaan Geuze, Wiel Arets, ...
- spätere Kontaktaufnahmen von Architekten und Architekturstudenten außerhalb des Seminarkontextes besiegeln das Interesse an neu entstandenen Beziehungen: Jennifer Ann Luce, Assistentin von Martha Schwartz, etwa, trifft „ihre" Studenten zu einer Arbeitswoche in New York.
- einigen Seminarteilnehmern gelingt es, sich durch ihren Arbeitseifer und ihr Können als Mitarbeiter in den Architekturbüros der jeweiligen Professoren wiederzufinden.
- und nicht zuletzt verlassen zweihundert hochmotivierte Architekten und Architekturstudenten die Stadt mit dem Gefühl, drei Wochen lang hart gearbeitet, viel kennengelernt, Spaß gehabt und etwas Besonderes geleistet zu haben. Gut für Wien.

different constellations of participants at the seminar create most divergent microclimates.
- the initial skepticism turns into approval: some students who are at first irritated by the architectural approach of Michelangelo Pistoletto (the first artist to participate at a Viennese Seminar on Architecture) are glad to have a new perspective enriching the seminar's work.
- in the reverse case, students filled with enthusiasm are gradually overcome by a feeling of insecurity and rejection, something we experience in Dagmar Richter's group. Tensions that are released virtually "over night", resulting in a small creative "act of sabotage":

Art in architecture. A huge installation of wooden boards nailed together is hanging from the studio ceiling, the rails and a column are painted in a fluorescent orange color. Unfortunately, the building is under preservation order and a wooden construction of this kind bears a certain safety risk. This piece of art will therefore not last long, the creative spirit of Richter's students being doomed to go down in hours of arduous disassembling and cleaning.

Excursions. In contrast to this, architectural guided tours in Vienna (including the sewer system and the gasometer towers) and excursions around the city or to buildings by Adolf Loos in Bohemia and Bratislava are echoed with positive reactions. But the participants' interest for Vienna goes far beyond tourist curiosity and their project duties, and does not abruptly disappear after embarking on the journey back home...

Follow-up. The seminar has finished yet the game goes on - an experience we made in the past years:
- an "international community" of "Vienna Seminarists" has slowly begun to expand all over the world.
- the contributions at the seminar are often included in students' thesis presented at their universities.
- cooperation between foreign universities (so far especially Spain, Italy, Croatia) and the Viennese Seminar on Architecture is strengthened.
- architects like Adriaan Geuze, Wiel Arets and others underscore the importance of the seminar by including the Vienna projects in their publications, referring to them as being an essential part of their personal development.
- later contacts between architects and architecture students outside the seminar context are a proof of the interest in new relationships: Jennifer Ann Luce, assistant of Martha Schwartz, for example, meets with "her" students for a working week in New York.
- as a result of their diligence and skills, some seminar participants succeed in finding employment in their professors' architecture studios.
- last but not least, two hundred highly motivated architects and architecture students leave Vienna with the impression that for three weeks they have worked hard, learned a lot, had a lot of fun and achieved something exceptional. Good for Vienna.

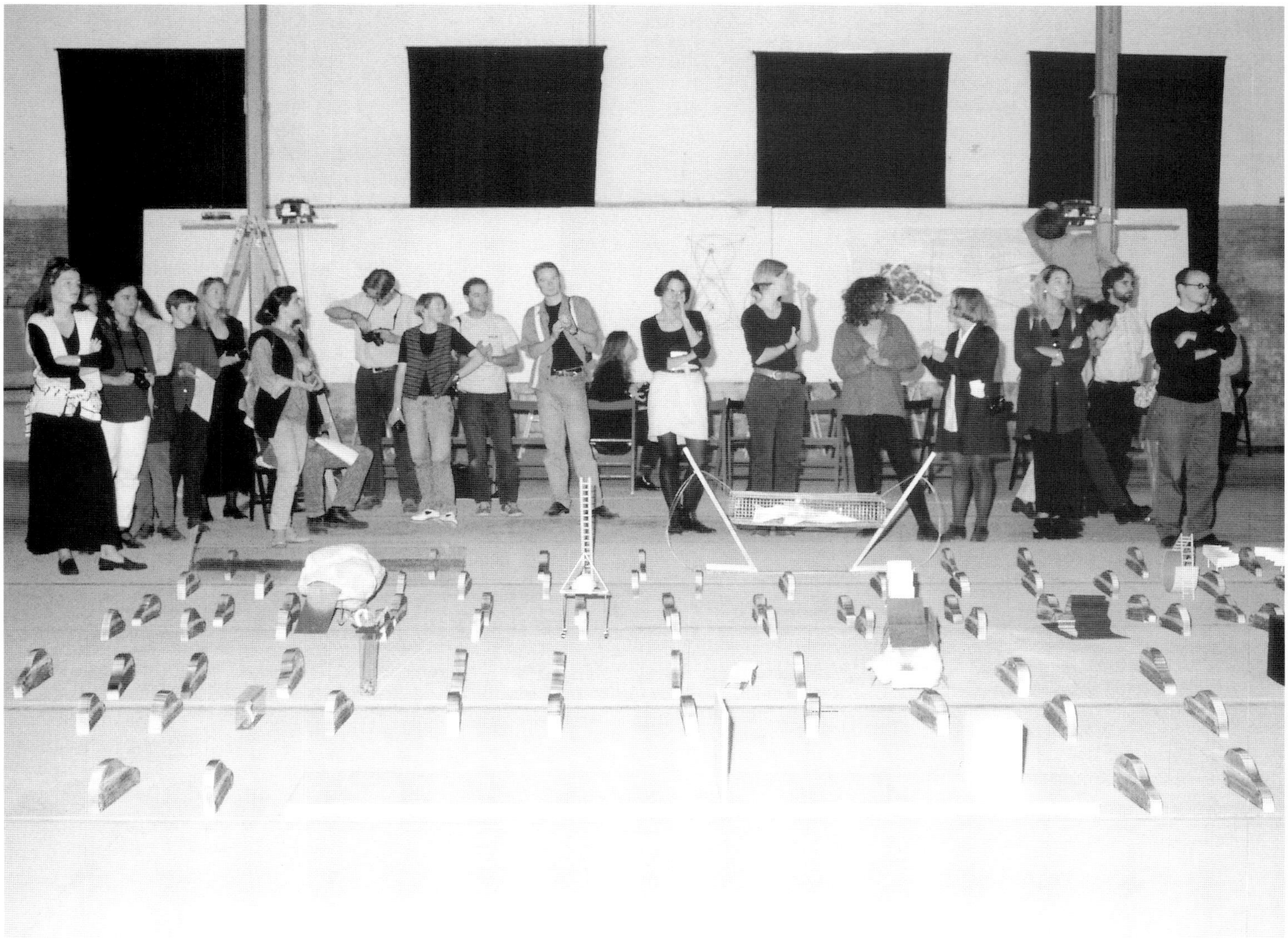

**Abschlußpräsentation /
Final presentation**

Boris Podrecca bei der Abschlußpräsentation /
Boris Podrecca at the final presentation

Stadtlandschaft zwischen Paradies und Abstandsfläche Boris Podrecca

Der öffentliche Diskurs über den Landschaftsraum Wien wurde in den letzten Jahren mit New-Age-Etiketten wie Vernetzung, System, Struktur, Virtualität überschwemmt. Doch die angestrebte Qualität des Freiraumes wurde in den meisten Fällen nach sogenannten Richtwerten beplant, sodaß hier eher Begriffe wie Flurbereinigung, Abstandsfläche, „Ware" Landschaft, Grünkompensation angebracht gewesen wären. Ernsthafte, großkonzipierte Projekte konnten sich nicht über den Denkanstoß von Kommissionen hinausemanzipieren.

So blieb die Organisation des Landschafts- und Freizeitraumes Wiens auf einer bloßen Projektionsebene angerissen. Beispiele hierfür wären die Reparatur und Ausstattung des Donaukanals im städtischen Bereich - der zentrale Mistkübel für unerwünschte Aktionen im bewohnten Milieu, die ungenützte Chance einer Verklammerung des Wienerwaldes mit den Prateraüen durch einen linearen großstädtischen Park und die Loslösung von einem monopolistischen Diktat hinsichtlich merkantiler Substrate und Kunstintegration an der Donau. Seit den zwei internationalen Gartenausstellungen im letzten Jahrzehnt wurde bisher kein großstädtisch angelegter Park konkret angedacht. Vor allem sind jedoch das Konzept für die Pflege der städtischen biologisch und ökologisch sinnvoll geführten Landwirtschaft sowie die Atomisierungsgefahr ihrer Wohn- und Arbeitskerne kaum verbindlich bearbeitet worden.

In der allgemein geführten Diskussion über den transdanubischen Raum hat es sich als schicksalshaft gezeigt, daß der Entwicklungsprozeß Stadt - Landschaft eine Grüngürtellösung als Sicherung des städtischen Freiraumes gewährleisten muß, falls es parallel zum Bebauungsprocedere gelingen sollte, die Wunschvision der geträumten neuen Stadt mit den analogen austrocknenden Finanzstrategien zu überlappen.

Alljährlich entsteht in der Remise hochwertige Qualität und Vielfalt an Architektur. Diese Ideen und zugleich Herausforderungen wurden von der Stadt bisher leider allzu peripher verwertet. Unser Architekturseminar in seiner anti-akademischen und stadt-praxisorientierten Haltung, versucht trotzdem weiter auf Unerledigtes Antworten zu finden.

Um einer bloßen Ästhetisierung der Alltagswelt entgegenzusteuern, hat das 5. Wiener Architekturseminar Experten aus den benachbarten Disziplinen wie jener der Landschaftsgeschichte, der hybriden Gestalt, der Freiraum-Kunst und der Stadtraum-Architektur versammelt und sie auf heiße und intensiv zu bearbeitende Orte hingewiesen. Die Ergebnisse der überdurchschnittlich engagierten Arbeiten sprechen für sich und warten hoffentlich diesmal nicht vergeblich auf das Echo der Stadt.
Euch, den Lehrern und Studenten gebührt unser aufrichtigster Dank.

City landscape between paradise and spacer areas Boris Podrecca

The public discourse on the urban landscape of Vienna has been inundated with New Age labels such as networking, system, structure, virtual reality in recent years. But, in fact, the desired qualities of the free space were planned in most cases according to so-called standard values so that it would be more appropriate to use terms such as field amalgamation, spacer areas, landscape as merchandise, green compensation. Serious, large-scale projects were not able to go beyond the usual impulses set by commissions.

Thus, the organisation of the landscape and recreational areas of Vienna merely remained a sketch at a projection level. Examples are the repair and design of the Danube Canal in the built-up area – the central waste bin for undesirable activities in a residential environment, the lost chance of linking the Vienna Woods and the Prater meadows by a linear, metropolitan park and abandoning the monopolistic dictate regarding mercantile substrates and art integration along the Danube. Since the two international gardening shows organised in the last decade, no concrete thoughts have been given to creating a park with a metropolitan design. But, above all, the concept for maintaining urban agriculture in a biologically and ecologically sensible way as well as the threat posed by the fragmentation of its living and working cores have hardly been dealt with in a committed way.

In the general discussion on the transdanubian area, it proved to be fateful that the development process of city – landscape has to ensure a green-belt solution for safeguarding urban free if, in parallel to the building procedure, the vision of the new city dreamed of could successfully be brought to overlap with the corresponding, draining financial strategies.

Year by year, high-quality architecture is created in a great variety at the *Remise*. But unfortunately, these ideas which, at the same time, are also challenges have been exploited by the City in an all too marginal way. In its anti-academic orientation to urban practice, our architecture seminar, nevertheless, continues to try to find answers to unresolved issues.

In order to counter a mere aestheticism in every-day world, the 5th Vienna Architecture Seminar brought together experts from related disciplines such as landscape history, hybrid design, free-space art, and urban space architecture and drew their attention to hot spots requiring intensive work. The results show above-average commitment and speak for themselves. This time, we hope, they will not wait for an echo by the City in vain. We owe our most sincere thanks to the City, the teachers and the students.

Architektur | Zentrum | Wien

Projektgruppen mit Architekten

Architektur des leeren Raumes
5. Wiener Architekturseminar
Landschaft Wien

Project groups with architects

Architecture of the Empty Space
5th Viennese Seminar on Architecture
Landscape Vienna

Seminarleitung / Seminar Coordinators

Boris Podrecca
Dietmar Steiner
Wien

20|08 – 11|09|1994

Projektgruppen mit / Project groups with

Luc Deleu
Berchem-Antwerpen
Adriaan Geuze
Rotterdam
Pepe Llinàs Carmona
Barcelona
Mark Mack
Los Angeles
Ippolito Pizzetti
Rom
Martha Schwartz
Boston

**Projektgruppe / project group
Luc Deleu**

Assistent: Jan Verheyden

Susy Baasel

Martin Benner

Joachim Bilger

Barbara Bisch

Maxi Bötsch

Markus Busch

Julia Carstens

Lieven De Boeck

Thilo Folkerts

Marie-Paule Greisen

Stefan Höher

Nel Janssens

Isabella Marboe

Marin Prümm

Eva Rupprecht

Ursula Schneider

Alexander Schranz

Manuel Schweizer

Luc Deleu Berchem-Antwerpen

1944 born in Duffel, Belgium
1969 Degree from architecture at Hoger Architectuurinstituut Sint-Lukas, Brussels
1970 Foundation of T.O.P. Office

Teaching positions
Theory of Architecture, Section Interior Design of Sint-Lukas Hoger Instituut voor Binnenhuisarchitectuur en Bouw, Brussels, Belgium
Theory of Architecture, Section Architecture at Hoger Architectuurinstituut Sint-Lukas Ghent-Brussels, Belgium
Tutor 4th year architecture studio at Hoger Architectuurinstituut Sint-Lukas Ghent-Brussels, Belgium
Guest teaching in Mâcon, Bourges, Lyon, Montpellier, France
Tilburg, Delft, Rotterdam, Groningen, Amsterdam, NL
Berkley, USA

Selection of work
1969 Europe Crossing, urban project for Brussels, Belgium
1979 Les halles, urban project for Paris, France
1985 Consolidation Project for the Ponte dell'Accademia, Venice, Italy
1986 Europe Central Station project for an elevated railway for the T.G.V. over Brussels, Belgium
1988–90 Rearrangement Hoog-Catharijne + T.G.V. station, Utrecht, The Netherlands
1990 Bridge over the Venidse, Hoorn, The Netherlands
1992 Hotel Stok, private house, Albrandswaard, The Netherlands
1993 Project for the artistic design of the Rheinuferstraße, Düsseldorf, Germany
1993 Social housing project Heerlijkheid de Hollein, Ghent, Belgium

Major exhibitions
1983 Galerie Media, Neuchâtel, Switzerland
1986 Galerie Claire Burrus, Paris, France
1988 Technische Universität, Berlin, Germany
1990 RAMGALERIE, Rotterdam, The Netherlands
Provinciaal Museum, Hasselt, Belgium
Galerie Montevideo, Antwerp, Belgium
Union of Architects, Moscow, Russia
1991 Storefront Gallery for Art & Architecture, New York, USA
MUHKA, Museum of Contemporary Art, Antwerp, Belgium
Städtische Galerie im Lenbachhaus, Munich, Germany
Rijksmuseum Kröller-Müller, Otterlo, The Netherlands
1993 Museum of Modern Art, Brussels, Belgium
1994 EV+A, Limerick, Ireland
Translokation, Graz, Austria

Publications among others
1983 Manifesto to the Order, Luc Deleu, Antwerp, Belgium
1987 Postfuturismus ?, Luc Deleu, Antwerp, Belgium
1989 Ethique de l'architecture, Collection Point de Vue, Saint-Benoit du Sault, France
1991 Luc Deleu & T.O.P. Office, 1967-1991, exhibition catalogue, MUHKA, Antwerp, Belgium
Luc Deleu, A Self-Power Man, Geert Bekaert in ARCHIS, 4/91
1992 Luc Deleu, Jos Vaandenbreeden in A+114, 1/92

Prizes / Awards
1989 Winning project: Project Noarderleech, Friesland, The Netherlands
1990 Award Visual Arts 1990 of the Flemish Community
1993 Laureate 1993 sculpture - three-dimensional art, Foundation E. Blanlin Evrart

Orban Planning Manifesto — Luc Deleu

1973
Starts Developing the Concept Orban Design
(Orban Manifesto and Propositions)

As long as we cannot move away from the earth in masses, or cannot import from space, the earth is a planet completely dependent upon itself, apart from the (necessary) solar energy and maybe other (not identified, but necessary) space energy.

One third of the worlds population is starving. This means that the agricultural area is already one third too small to provide for the real needs. Although (next to intensifying the production per m^2) we could try, with enormous efforts, to expand the agricultural area in deserts, steppes and bare grounds, it is a fact that we will have to use as much as possible of the "open space" in the agglomerations for food production. All the more because it would be wise to spare jungles, forests, woods and other natural environments, or even better, to extend them (spare areas), if possible.

If these priorities are accepted, theoretically the surface of urban agglomerations almost cannot be increased anymore, which could bring the inhabitation of the earth in a difficult position. If we want to grant everybody a maximal living comfort, living will have to be organized a lot more efficiently than it has been the case up to now. Urban space will have to be used much more intensively. In this critical stage, it would be better for everybody to try and organize their own living situation individually, following their own taste, means, possibilities and limitations. This is analogous to the completely decentralized organization of plant life (phytocenosis) in which every specimen takes all responsibilities within the limitations and possibilities of the habitat. On the other hand, the macro enterprises of corporate bodies (structured groups of individuals, such as associations, limited liability partnerships, unions, parties, clubs, pressure groups, etc...) should be subjected to very stringent rules, in view of bringing the macro influences and macro land consumption of those enterprises in the ecotope (the whole of environmental elements and biocenosis [1]) into balance with the micro influences and micro consumption of the individual. This is analogous to nature, where the biological balance remains steady in an environment with a great variety of species: the influences on one specific species are more varied, where, on the other hand, the balance in natural environments where only a few species are available, is more easily upset: an important growth of one specific species may occur (plagues).

All that is disturbing and unnecessary must be disposed of (shot into space). What remains should be stored in a clear and compact manner (avoiding one-dimensional use of these storage places). Because all biological communities (antropocenosis [2], zoöcenosis [3], phytocenosis, microcenosis [4], and mycocenosis [5]) are closely linked to each other, attention must be paid not to suffocate either one of them. This means that pollution should be kept to a minimum and that everything possible will have to be recycled. Especially the biological refuse will have to be recycled most efficiently and re-spread over the agricultural area. In this way, we will loose as little as possible of the bio-elements (needed for the phytocenosis).

Luckily, oceans and seas (whose biocenosis is in a critical stage) still form a spacial reserve, twice the available space on land. Thus, the complete world population could be housed on 1.000.000 passenger ships (40.000 tons). On 2.000.000 ships, they could even enjoy a fair degree of comfort. The total Belgian population could perfectly lead a mobile life on 5.000 passenger ships (40.000 tons).

I dare hope that the above world image of „momental times" makes it perfectly clear that town planning and architecture

[1] Community of all living organisms
[2] Human community
[3] Animal community
[4] Community of bacteria
[5] Community of fungi

Ich wage zu hoffen, daß das obige Weltbild der „Momentzeiten" klar vor Augen führt, daß Stadtplanung und Architektur aus einer neuen „orbanen" Perspektive betrachtet werden sollten. Während der „Momentzeiten" setzen Stadtplanung und Architektur orbane Prioritäten. Die ästhetischen Schwerpunkte und Stilrichtungen der „Nicht-Momentzeiten" gelten nicht mehr in einer Situation der „Do-it-yourself-Architektur" und in selbstgemachten Städten, in denen jeder einzelne die städtische Umwelt gestaltet.

Die Funktion des Stadtplaners und Architekten (Orbanplaner) hat sogar eine völlig neue Bedeutung angenommen. Sehr ähnlich zur (abbildenden) Funktion der Malerei (in der westlichen Kunst) nach der Erfindung der Photographie hat sich die Funktion und Bedeutung der Stadtplanung und Architektur (Orbanplanung) wesentlich gewandelt. „Information" (das Reduzieren von Ungewißheit) ist nun ein wichtiger Teil der Aktivitäten von Orbanplanern in den „Momentzeiten"; sie sind Medien, Trendsetter und/oder Dorfnarren etc. Sie entwerfen, veröffentlichen, führen auf, zeigen, realisieren oder spielen etc.

Von nun an ist der „freie Raum" ihr Ziel. Anstelle von Infrastruktur, Bestimmung des Erdraumes und dessen Umwandlung in etwas Eindimensionales, verwendet der Orbanplaner nun Ultrastrukturen, wobei der Erdraum ohne Beschränkung der Vielfalt an Möglichkeiten ausgeweitet wird.

Der Orbanplaner wurde primär zu einem Theoretiker, der in einigen wenigen Fällen seine visionären Ideen an bestimmten Plätzen des Planeten Erde verwirklicht. Der Planet Erde, auf dem die Orbanplanung unter dem Einfluß der Aktivitäten jedes Einzelnen verwirklicht wird, ist zwar dynamisch und entwickelt sich laufend weiter, doch kann die Erde zu jedem Zeitpunkt der „Momentzeiten" als abgeschlossen betrachtet werden.

1972
- Vorschlag für eine mobile Universität (in Antwerpen)

1973
- Vorschlag für die totale Dezentralisierung (von Antwerpen)
- Vorschlag für die völlige Abschaffung der Verkehrsregeln (in Antwerpen)
- Vorschlag für die vollständige Abschaltung der öffentlichen Beleuchtung

1974
- Vorschlag für einen völligen Naturismus (in Brüssel)
- Vorschlag zur Anpflanzung von Obstboulevards [1]
- Vorschlag zur Umstellung auf 12 Volt [1]
- Vorschlag über das Anlegen städtischer Misthaufen
- Vorschlag zur Einführung von Plastikgeld (in Brüssel)
- Vorschlag für langen Rasen
- Vorschlag für eine offene Kanalisation (in Brügge) [1]
- Vorschlag für mobile Denkmäler

1975
- Vorschlag für einen internationalen Misthaufen in der Sahara
- Vorschlag für nackte Olympische Spiele (in Montreal)
- Vorschlag für die städtische Holzproduktion (in Antwerpen)

1976
- Vorschlag, nuklearen Abfall zur Sonne zu schießen
- Vorschlag autofreier Mittage [1]

1977
- Vorschlag für Fernsehsendungen ohne Programmgestaltung
- Rat zur Verwendung von Gemüseschachteln anstelle von Blumenschachteln
- Rat zur Konsumverweigerung
- Vorschlag für ein Bewässerungssystem mit Regenwasser [1]
- Vorschlag für sichtbare Telefonleitungen [1]

[1] Futuristischer Vorschlag für urbane Agglomerationen

should be considered from a new "orbanic" point of view. During "momental times" town planning and architecture make use of orbanic priorities. The aesthetic priorities and the styles of the "non-momental times" no longer apply in a situation of do-it-yourself architecture and self-made cities, in which every individual determines the urban environment.

The function of the town planner architect (orban planner) has a totally different meaning. Very much the same as the (pictorial) function of a painting (in western art) after the invention of photography, town planning and architecture (orban planning) underwent an important change of function and meaning. "Information" (reduction of uncertainty) is now an important part of the "momental" orban planner's activities; he is a medium, a trendsetter and/or town fool, etc... He designs, publishes, performs, shows, realizes, or plays, etc...

From now on, "free space" is his goal. Instead of infrastructures determining earth space and making it one-dimensional, the orban planner now uses ultrastructures, enlarging earth space without limiting the variety of possibilities.

The orban planner becomes primarily a theoretician who, in rare cases, realizes his visionary views on spaces of the planet earth. The planet earth, though dynamic and evolving, on which orban planning realizes itself under the influence of the actions of all individuals, can be considered as complete at any moment in "momental times".

1972
- Proposal for a mobile university (in Antwerp)

1973
- Proposal for decentralization (of Antwerp)
- Proposal for complete abolishment of traffic rules (in Antwerp)
- Proposal for complete disuse of public lighting

1974
- Proposal for complete naturism (in Brussels)
- Proposal to plant fruit avenues [1]
- Proposal to switch to 12 Volts [1]
- Proposal for the implantation of urban dunghill(s)
- Proposal to introduce plastic money (in Brussels)
- Proposal for a long lawn
- Proposal for open sewerage (in Bruges) [1]
- Proposal for mobile monuments

1975
- Proposal for an international dunghill in the Sahara
- Proposal for naked olympic games (in Montreal)
- Proposal for urban wood production (in Antwerp)

1976
- Proposal to shoot nuclear waste into the sun
- Proposal for car-free noons [1]

1977
- Proposal for non-programmed TV broadcasts
- Advice for vegetable-boxes instead of flower-boxes
- Advice for consumption strikes
- Proposal for an irrigation system using rainwater [1]
- Proposal for visible telephone wiring [1]
- Proposal for visible electricity cables [1]
- Proposal to classify the ('77) car models as monuments [1]
- Proposal to classify the public transport as monument [1]
- Proposal to classify city ruins as monuments [1]
- Proposal to declassify monuments and recycle them into social housing
- Proposal for free masonry [1]

[1] Futurustic proposal for urban agglomerations.

Barcelona Towers, 1989

- Vorschlag für sichtbare Stromkabel [1]
- Vorschlag, die Automodelle (des Jahres '77) zu Monumenten zu erklären [1]
- Vorschlag, das öffentliche Verkehrssystem zum Monument zu erklären [1]
- Vorschlag, städtische Ruinen zu Monumenten zu erklären [1]
- Vorschlag, Monumente freizugeben und in Sozialwohnungen umzuwandeln
- Vorschlag für die Freimaurerei [1]
- Vorschlag für öffentliches Geflügel [1]
- Vorschlag zum Schutze des Unkrauts [1]
- Vorschlag für städtische Landwirtschaft [1]
- Vorschlag für städtische Bienenstöcke (plus Blumen)
- Rat zum Schließen des Zoos (in Antwerpen)

1978
- Vorschlag für ein gemischtrassiges Begegnungszentrum (in Antwerpen)
- Vorschlag zur Abschaffung des Gesetzes vom 20. 2. 1939 [2]
- Vorschlag zum Gemüseanbau auf Dachgärten
- Vorschlag zur Umstellung der Landwirtschaft auf Bioenergie
- Vorschlag zur Reduzierung des Landverbrauchs
- Vorschlag zur Einstellung von Freizeitaktivitäten

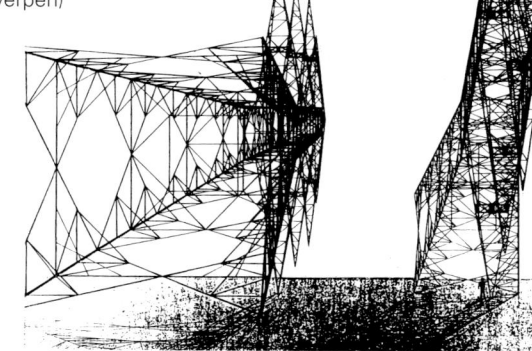

Hochspannungsmasten / High Tension Pylons

- Proposal for public poultry [1]
- Proposal for protection of weeds [1]
- Proposal for urban agriculture [1]
- Proposal for city beehives (plus flowers)
- Advice to close the Zoo (in Antwerp)

1978
- Proposal for a center for interracial (in Antwerp) intercourse
- Proposal for abolition of the law of 20.2.1939 [2]
- Proposal for roof horticulture
- Proposal to switch to biological power in agriculture
- Proposal to diminish land consumption
- Proposal to stop leisure activities
- Proposal to stop defence
- Proposal for the restoration of the public transport
- Proposal for road softening

1979
- Proposal for revaluation of gypsies and barges
- Proposal (project) for recycling of Belgium into agrarian country. [3]

[1] Futuristischer Vorschlag für urbane Agglomerationen
[2] Gesetz über den Berufs- und Titelschutz für Architekten

[1] Futurustic proposal for urban agglomerations.
[2] Law on the protection of title and profession of architect.
[3] see "Last stone of Belgium"

- Vorschlag zur Abschaffung der Landesverteidigung
- Vorschlag zur Wiederherstellung des öffentlichen Verkehrs
- Vorschlag zur Straßenenthärtung

1979
- Vorschlag zur Neubewertung von Zigeunern und Hausbootbewohnern (als moderne Nomaden)
- Vorschlag (Projekt) zur Umwandlung Belgiens in ein Agrarland [3]
- Vorschlag (Projekt) zur Neubewertung von Ackerland (in Belgien) [3]
- Vorschlag für eine städtische Forstwirtschaft
- Vorschlag für städtische Viehhaltung
- Vorschlag für städtischen Gemüsebau
- Vorschlag für städtische Obstgärten
- Vorschlag für städtische Fischteiche
- Vorschlag für städtische Weiden

1980
- Vorschlag für Bürgersteige auf den Dächern
- Vorschlag für die Legalisierung von Graffiti
- Vorschlag für städtisches Wild

1988
Beginn der Entwicklung des Konzepts „Maßstab und Perspektive"
Beginn einer Reihe von Plänen für Infrastruktureinrichtungen

1991
Beginn einer Studie für eine Reise um die Welt in 80 Tagen

1995
Studie für die „Unangepaßte Stadt"

[3] Siehe „Last stone of Belgium"

- Proposal (project) for the revaluation of farmland (in Belgium) [4]
- Proposal for urban forestry.
- Proposal for urban cattle
- Proposal for urban horticulture
- Proposal for city orchard
- Proposal for urban fishing ponds
- Proposal for city pastures

1980
- Proposal for roof pavements
- Proposal for the legalization of graffiti
- Proposal for urban game

1988
Starts developing the concept "Scale and Perspective"
Starts with a series of designs for infrastructures

1991
Starts study for Journey around the World in 80 days

1995
The Study unadapted City

[3] see "Last stone of Belgium"

Europe Central Station; project for an elevated railway for the T.G.V. over Brussel, Belgium, 1986-1989

Empty spaces in the city – zones of densification. Green link Stadlau, Vienna 22

On the eastern fringe of the core area of the municipal district of Stadlau we find a flat grass plot of a width of about 80 m between the two rows of buildings belonging to a housing estate built in the 1960s and the 1970s. At the time of the construction of the estate, the area had been earmarked for the planned construction of a motorway, which, however, was then actually built somewhere else. The area is part of a green link in a north-south direction, continuing to the Lobau foreland, the Lobau waters, and to the recreational area of the New Danube in the south.

The grass plot with a size of approximately 2 hectores to a limited extent is used by the inhabitants for recreational activities and in its present form requires but little care. Still, it is quite obvious that the area does not live up to the creative, functional, and ecological requirements and expectations of an urban green zone.

The task of the new definition of the area is connected with an architectural densification of the estate aimed at, in connection with the urban development policy goal of, an "internal expansion".

Grünverbindung Stadlau, Wien 22

A strange attractor in Vienna

1. Approach
Connecting the islands/project Stadlau

The first reflection was that our site Stadlau as "Open Space" cannot be considered separate from a bigger unity, a wider context and a larger area. That is why before setting to work on the smaller site a vision for a larger area should be presupposed.
This general vision for the larger whole we found present in the report of the council for zones of urban development:

"Vienna to the year 2000 and beyond" [1]

A. Tokens of development

Together with new appearing lifestyles, innovative and experimental residential and office buildings should be created.
They form tokens of development along new lines.
The various lifestyles, leisure-time habits, special interests and personally cherished values should be considered as a basis for projects.
Hereby several themes can be used to develop certain (new) models:

---

[1] Summary of the recommendations of the Council for Zones of Urban Development
New Urban Development
Matters of principle concerning attitudes towards planning (recommendation)

autofreies Leben; multikulturelles Leben; Leben als Alleinerzieher; Nähe zur Natur (landwirtschaftliche Freizeitbeschäftigung), ökologisches Wohnen; Berufsgruppen mit neuen Kombinationen von Arbeit und Freizeitaktivitäten (Verquickung von Arbeitsstätten und Wohnungen); in Großfamilien lebende Zuwanderer, Integration älterer Menschen/Behinderter, dezentrale soziale Infrastruktur (Kontainerbüros), multifunktionale Zentren (Jugendzentrum, Bibliothek, Werkstätten ...); Projekte für Frauen.

B. Landschaft und offener Raum
(„Stadplanung durch Grünraumplanung")

Grüne/offene/leere Räume sind zentrale Komponenten der Infrastruktur und wichtige Planungselemente. Deshalb sollten sie nicht mehr länger als „Überbleibsel" betrachtet werden. Durch eine differenzierte Behandlung der offenen Räume (allmählicher Übergang vom Privaten, zum Halböffentlichen und wieder zum Privaten) kann ein neues urbanes Verhalten, urbaner Charakter bewirkt werden. Ein „robustes" System von geschützten Grünräumen (die durch Grünverbindungen miteinander verknüpft sind) sollte aufgebaut werden:

- Ausweisung oder praktische Tabuisierung: Einsatz (traditioneller) Landschaftselemente wie Alleen, Wälder, ...
- Erhaltung landschaftlicher Orientierungspunkte und Aufbau einer landschaftlichen Identität, z.B.: Dorfzentren, Gärten, Feldwege, Gassen, Natur- und Kulturdenkmäler;
- Einführung ökologischer Landwirtschaft, biologischen Ackerbaus, städtische Landwirtschaft;
- Implementierung von „Superzeichen" als Blickfang: parkartige Gebiete als Kulturprojekt (Kunst in öffentlichen Räumen).

C. Verkehr

Öffentliche Verkehrsmittel, Fußgänger und Radfahrer müssen gegenüber dem motorisierten Individualverkehr begünstigt werden. Neuen Siedlungsformen wie dem „Wohnen ohne Autos" muß Vorrang gegeben werden, wobei auf folgendes geachtet werden muß:

- Schaffung eines kleinteiligen Systems von Wegen und Plätzen
- Akzeptanz der örtlich typischen Anordnung von Wegen und Straßen
- Identifikationspunkte des öffentlichen Verkehrs
- Schaffung eines flächendeckenden Systems ununterbrochener Netze von Fußgänger- und Fahrradwegen

Der öffentliche Raum sollte frei von parkenden Autos sein. In Hinblick auf Quantität und Qualität sollte den Straßen in ihrer Funktion als wichtigster öffentlicher Raum besondere Aufmerksamkeit geschenkt werden.

D. Mitbestimmung

Die Öffentlichkeit muß die Pläne, die erstellt werden, verstehen und erfassen können. Aber neben der Planung sollten auch die Phasen der Umsetzung und Nutzung von der Mitbestimmung erfaßt werden. Deshalb sind Möglichkeiten zur Selbstverwaltung zu schaffen, z.B.:

- Bereitstellung von Grundstücken für Wohnexperimente
- Bereitstellung von Räumen und Gebäudeteilen, für die die Bewohner selbst Nutzungsformen entwickeln können, z.B.:

ein zusätzlicher, nutzungsneutraler Raum (pro Wohnung)
eine geräumige Loggia als Außenraum (pro Wohnung)
zusätzlich mietbare Räume (für Beratung, Hobbyräume, privates Kindertagesheim)
eine geräumige Eingangshalle pro Wohnhaus

- Nutzungsrechte und -pflichten für (halb-)öffentliche Räume

car-free living; multi-cultural living; living as a single parent; proximity to nature (leisure-time farming), ecological living; vocational groups with new mixes of work and recreational activities (interwinement of working places and dwellings); immigrants living in large families; integration of elderly/handicapped persons; decentralized social infrastructure (container offices); multi-functional centers (youth center, library, workshops,...); projects for women.

B. Landscape and open space
("Urban planning through green space planning")

Green/open/empty spaces are a central component of infrastructure and important elements of planning. Therefore they should no longer be considered as "left-overs". By means of discernent treatment of the open spaces (gradual transition from private, semipublic to private) a new urban behaviour, urban character can be engendered.
A "robust" system of safeguarded green spaces, interconnected by green connections should be established:

- desinging or virtual tabooization: use of (traditional) scenic elements as avenues, woods,...;
- preserving of scenic landmarks and constitution of scenic identity: village centers, gardens, field paths, lanes, natural and cultural monuments;
- introduction of ecological agriculture, biological farming, town-land agriculture;
- implementation of "supersigns" as visual landmarks: park-like areas as a cultural project (art in public spaces).

C. Traffic

Public transport, traffic on foot or bicycle must be favoured above motorized individual traffic. Priority must be given to new forms of settlement such as "living without cars", thereby paying attention to:

- the creation of a system of paths and plazas consisting of small parts
- acceptance of locally typical layouts of paths and roads
- identification points of public transport
- the creation of an area-wide system of uninterrupted networks of footpaths and bicycle paths

The public space should be free of parked cars.
Special attention should be paid to the street as a most important public space in terms both of quantity and quality.

D. Participation

The public must understand the plans that are being made and be able to grasp them. But besides planning, the participation should also include the phases of realization and utilization. Therefore, opportunities for self-management must be created:

- providing plots of land for living experiments
- providing rooms, parts of a building that occupants themselves can develop utilization forms for, e.g.:

one additional, utilization-neutral room (per flat)
a spacious loggia as an external room (per flat)
rooms that can be rented extra (for consulting, hobbies, private day-care for children)
one spacious hall per residential building

- Utilization rights and responsibilities of (semi)-public spaces

To admit this "participation", institutional and architectural anchoring should be kept light. Demonstrative image intentions are not desirable.

Studying these recommendations of the council I was struck by the similarity of their points of view with my Orban Manifesto (1980) and Proposals (1972-1980). The vision of the council was stated verbally and has not been realized in a visible way. Although it did not give a spatial image we found that it could be considered as a usable strategy for the future. The recommendations could be made more concrete and meaning could be added to it.

Since we could state that "open space" corresponds to all parts left blank on the map of Vienna (i.e. agricultural areas, eventually in decay, green areas,...) we should create a more precise scope. We can assume that the participants should look for qualities, and starting from these qualities, add possiblilities with which a spatial image should be built up for the open space in Vienna (eventually independent from the given site Stadlau). In that way functions are grafted onto the existing city, thus building up space.

As an example for this we made a list and some sketches of workable tools, fitting in with the vision for Vienna as expressed in the recommendations of the council for zones of urban development.

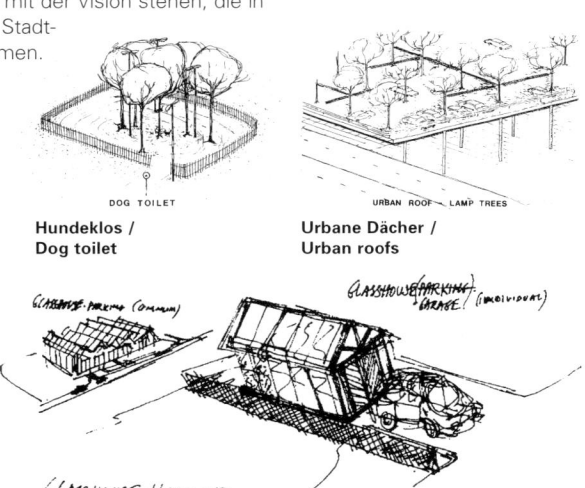

Hundeklos / Dog toilet

Urbane Dächer / Urban roofs

Glashäuser: Kulturzentrum und Parkgarage /
Glass houses: Cultural center and parking garage

Environmental development:
Urban dunghills
Beehives + flowers
Fishing ponds
Greenhouses
Fruit hedges as screens
Urban roofs
Unaccessible spaces

Infrastructure development:
Parking
Open sewerage
Visible telephone wiring
Visible electricity cables
Car traffic
Dog toilets
Moving walks

Another starting point, we thought, could be a formal spatial analysis. Here, plans are colored, urban spatial compositions are made, entities created. Both working methods can be combined (different persons do different things, depending on the person); these different working methods must finally lead to a concrete result.

We have attempted to create a frame in which the above mentioned vision of the council for zones of urban development might function along with the straightforward development of society we actually know.

Our findings are reflected in a dialectic of an urban scheme with the actual situation. This model of development for Vienna is an extension in the northeast part of Vienna, on the left bank of the Danube, following the rural model, with more freestanding buildings (name it the sector principle) developed by Le Corbusier in 1950 for Bogotá and realized in Chandigarh. In the northeast part of Vienna, there are small artificial lakes with which, using roads and canals, a first urban composition of the largest order was set up, the directions based on existing directions of roads and railroads. This model was conceived along the lines of the city´s expansion policy namely a patchwork with living enclaves.

Entwicklungsmodell Wien Nord /
Model of development Vienna north

und Kanälen eine erste Stadtkomposition der ersten Ordnung erstellt wurde, wobei die Ausrichtung auf den bestehenden Straßen und Schienenwegen basierte.

A second proposal we made was an (elevated) direct connection of Stadlau with the Prater across the Danube.

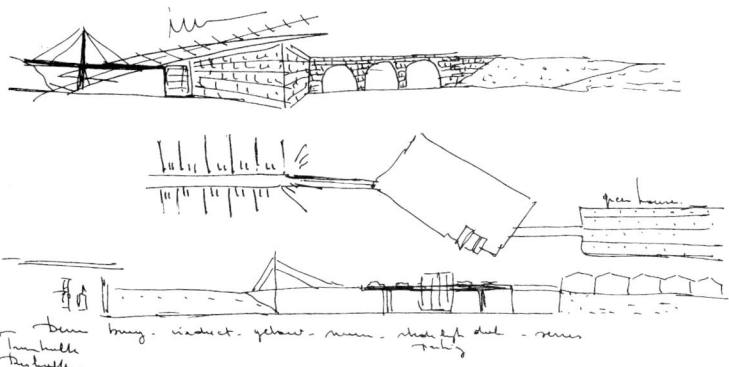

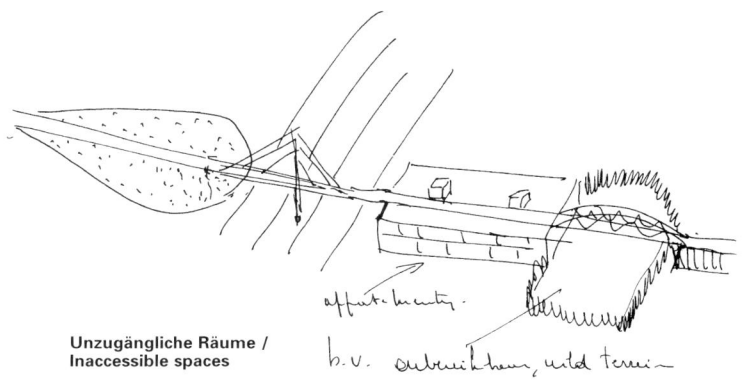

**Unzugängliche Räume /
Inaccessible spaces**

Dieses Modell wurde im Einklang mit der Wiener Stadterweiterungspolitik konzipiert, nämlich als ein „Patchwork" mit Wohnenklaven. Ein zweiter von uns gemachter Vorschlag war, eine direkte (erhöhte) Verbindung zwischen Stadlau über die Donau zum Prater zu schaffen. Dieses urbane Schema und die Skizzen – das Ergebnis primärer Reflexionen – sollten das Anlaufen der Arbeiten beschleunigen und eine Grundlage für tiefgreifende Diskussionen bilden.

This urban scheme and these sketches - the results of a preliminary reflection - were meant to generate a quick start of the work and to provide a basis for profound discussion.

Ergebnisse

Results

Der Arbeitsablauf in der Gruppe war darauf ausgerichtet, ein beinahe veröffentlichungsreifes Endergebnis zu erzielen und in einem Rahmen zu arbeiten, in dem die Gruppe über dem Einzelnen steht, um so eine konsistente Präsentation zu erreichen.

The working process of the group was based upon the aim towards a final presentation and working in a concept where the group prevailed on the individual in order to come to a consistent presentation.

Als die Gruppe erstmals den Stadtplan von Wien studierte bzw. in Wien unterwegs war, stellte sie fest, daß es in Wien viel freien Raum gibt, was zu der Einstellung führte, daß es sich dabei um Lücken handelt, die man schließen kann.
Zweitens wurde bemerkt, daß der soziale Wohnbau am linken Donauufer in der Schaffung von Inseln (mit oder ohne architektonischer Qualität) besteht, die von jeder Art von Infrastruktur völlig abgeschnitten sind. Diese Vorortgebiete sind eine Art von Wohn = Schlafghettos, wo abgesehen von den Wohnbauten so gut wie nichts vorhanden ist. Sie bilden eine endlose „Ausbreitung" von Wien, wodurch viel freier Raum verbraucht wird.
In diesem Sinne betrachten wir sie als falsche Wege in der Stadtentwicklung.
Die dritte Bemerkung war, daß das öffentliche Verkehrsnetz und insbesondere die U-Bahn- und Straßenbahnverbindungen am linken Donauufer sehr schlecht ausgebaut sind.

The first remark of the group when regarding the map of Vienna, or by being in Vienna, was that there is a lot of empty space in Vienna. This results in a lack of respect for it and in an attitude towards empty space as something that can be filled. The second remark was that social housing development on the left bank of the Danube is seen as making islands (with or without architectural quality), completely disconnected from any infrastructure. These suburban areas are a kind of living = sleeping-ghettos where besides housing almost nothing is provided. They form an infinite "spreading - out" of Vienna, thereby consuming a lot of open space. In that sense we considered them as wrong urban developments.
The third remark was that the public transport, and especially the metro and tramway system, are very poor on the left bank.

Daraus entwickelte sich das folgende Projekt:

Out of these points came the following project:

1. Um den freien/ offenen Raum in Wien wirklich zu erhalten, definierten wir neue Mindestgrenzen für bauliche Eingriffe durch die Stadt Wien. Wir erstellten eine Karte, in der wir diese Grenzen auf sehr pragmatische Weise festlegten, nämlich in einer Entfernung von 400 m zur nächsten U-Bahn- oder Straßenbahnhaltestelle. In diesen Zonen könnte eine Verdichtung vorgenommen werden. Diese Entscheidung ergab einen ersten Rahmen.

1. In order to really preserve empty / open space in Vienna we defined new minimal borders for building intervention in the city of Vienna.
A bordermap was made on which these borders were fixed in a very pragmatic way, namely at 400 m walking distance from a metro or tramway. In this zone a densification could take place. This decision created a first frame.

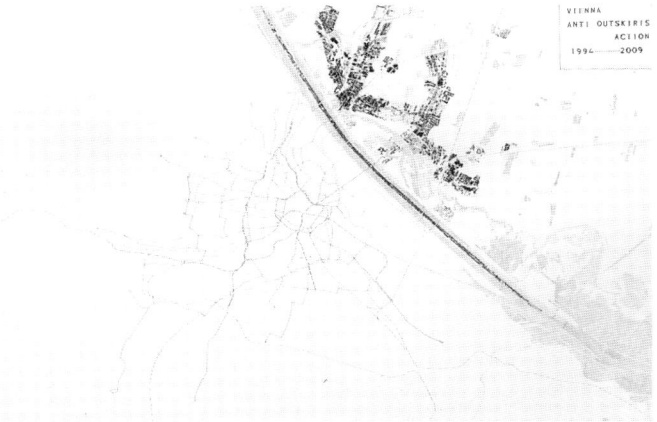

2. In the report from the council for zones of urban development, "Vienna to the year 2000 and beyond", they foresee a need for social dwellings for 10 000 inhabitants a year over the next 15 years. Looking at the bordermap, and because a city should develop the areas with the best urban potentials, it seemed very logical to us to project onto the Danube island an urban development scheme.

**Entwicklungsmodell Wien Nord /
Model of development Vienna north**

23

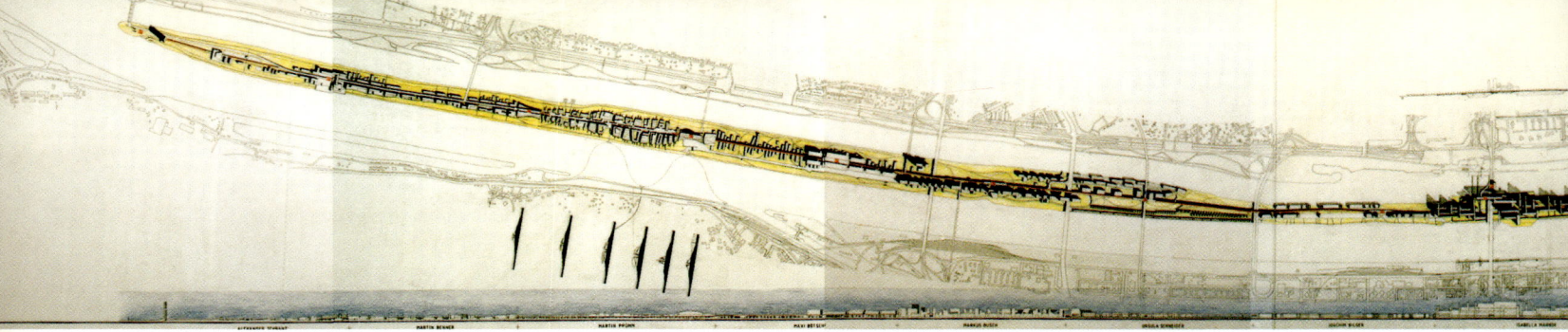

City attractor – Donauinsel / City attractor – Danube island

2. Im Bericht des Stadtentwicklungsbeirates "Wien ins 21. Jahrhundert" wird während der nächsten 15 Jahre ein jährlicher Bedarf an Sozialwohnungen für 10.000 Bewohner prognostiziert.
Betrachtet man nun diese „Grenzkarte" und berücksichtigt man, daß eine Stadt die Gebiete mit dem besten urbanen Potential erschließen sollte, erschien es uns sehr logisch, auf der Donauinsel ein Stadtentwicklungsprojekt anzusiedeln. Da ein vorherrschendes Merkmal der Insel ihre Begrenztheit ist, ist jede Stadterweiterung zu einem bestimmten Zeitpunkt abgeschlossen und kann nicht mehr fortgesetzt werden. Wir berechneten also, daß eine hochdichte Erschließung der Donauinsel für 150.000 bis 300.000 Bewohner möglich wäre und für die nächsten 15 Jahre ausreichen würde, während andernorts der doppelte oder dreifache Platz dafür benötigt würde.

Since a strong feature of the island is that it is limited, at any certain moment, any urban extension is finished and cannot be continued. So rather than using double or triple the surface of the Danube island somewhere else (ex. on the left bank), we calculated that a V.H.D development (Very High Density development) for 150 000 to 300 000 habitants on the Danube island was possible and would be sufficient for the next 15 years.
This new city district would stress on social housing developments connected by a new subway line (U7) of 22 km. This subway line offers a lot of new connections with the existing and planned public transport lines.
As we were very enthusiastic about the idea of making the expansion of Vienna for the next 15 years on the Danube

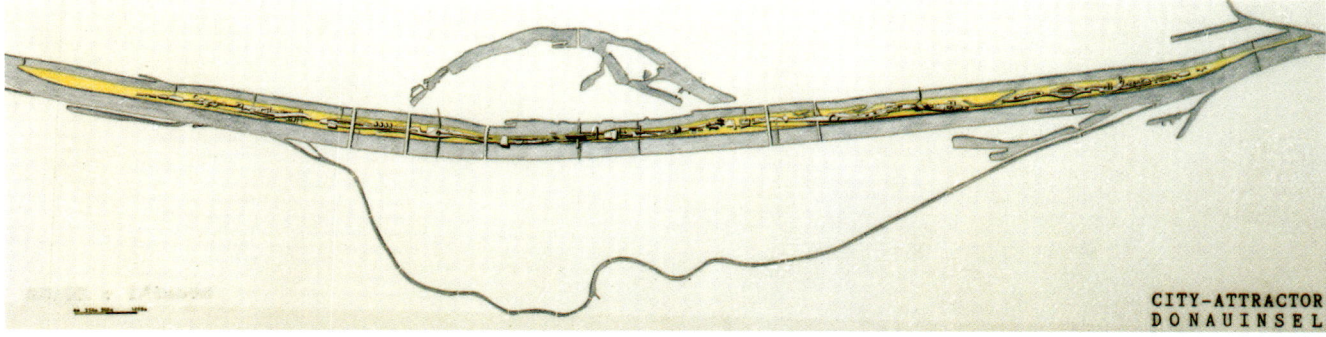

City attractor

Dieser neue Stadtteil würde im sozialen Wohnbau vorrangig behandelt werden und eine neue U-Bahnlinie (U7) von 22 km Länge erhalten, die viele neue Anschlüsse zum bestehenden und geplanten öffentlichen Verkehrsnetz bieten würde.
Da wir von der Idee sehr begeistert waren, die Erweiterung Wiens in den nächsten 15 Jahren auf der Donauinsel zu konzentrieren und dadurch die Umgebung Wiens zu erhalten, beschlossen wir, ein Bild des neuen Stadtteils zu entwerfen.
Die erste Strategie in der Gestaltung des Stadtteils war die Aufteilung der Insel in 16 Parzellen. Die Verantwortung für jede Parzelle wurde dann einem Studenten übertragen. Der einzige Faden, der sich durch alle 16 Parzellen und Entwürfe zog, waren die U-Bahn und die Autobahn. Im Zuge der Erstellung dieses Plans ergaben sich viele interessante Diskussionen: Fragen der Planungsintentionen, Dichte, Imageaufbau, Verbindungen und Grenzen, Natur, ...

Nach Fertigstellung dieses ersten Plans beschlossen einige Studenten, ihn abzuändern. Sie machten einen Vorschlag in kleinerem Maßstab, wobei sie von einem homogenen Image ausgingen und nicht von einem aus 16 verschiedenen Designs bestehenden Bild.

island and by doing that, preserving the surroundings of Vienna, we decided to design an image for the new city district.
The first design strategy was to divide the island into 16 lots. Each lot was then given to one student. The only continuous thread through the 16 different lots and designs was the subway line and motorway. By drawing this plan a lot of interesting discussions took place; questions about planning intensions, about densities, about image - building, about connections and borders, about nature,......

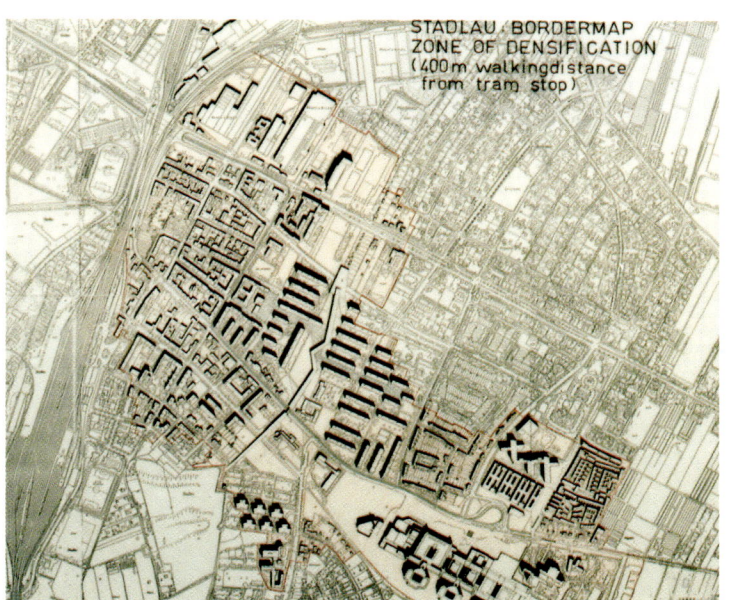

After this plan was finished some students decided to make a variation on this first plan. They made a proposal on a smaller scale, starting from one homogeneous image instead of an image built up by 16 different designs.

3. Concerning Stadlau it got situated within the new city-borders on the bordermap.

To conclude automatically that Stadlau should be densified and built up would be too simple because also in densified areas there is a need for

Verdichtungsbereiche /
Zones of densification

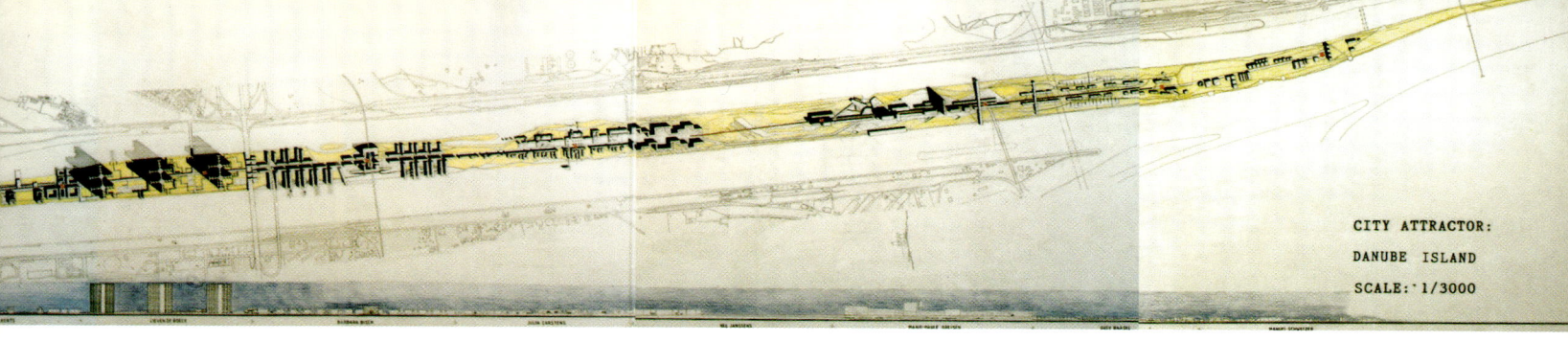

3. Was Stadlau anbelangt, so befindet sich dieses Gebiet nun innerhalb der neuen Stadtgrenzen auf der „Grenzkarte".

Daraus automatisch zu schließen, daß Stadlau verdichtet und verbaut werden sollte, wäre zu einfach, da auch in verdichteten Gebieten offene Räume benötigt werden. Deshalb wurden parallel zwei Vorschläge entwickelt.
Der erste Vorschlag konzentrierte sich auf eine Verdichtung des Geländes durch eine soziale Wohnanlage mit öffentlich zugänglichem Dach und einem Parkdeck, die sich wie eine Art Magnet durch Stadlau ziehen und mehrere Wohninseln miteinander verbinden würde, anstatt eine neue Insel ohne Verbindungen zu schaffen.

Der zweite Vorschlag bezog sich auf die Erhaltung des freien Raums in Form eines öffentlichen Parks.

open spaces. Therefore two parallel proposals were developed. One proposal was densifying the site by social housing with a public roof and a parking deck as a kind of strange attractor through Stadlau connecting more housing islands instead of creating a new island with no connections.

The other proposal was to preserve the empty space as a public park for the surroundings.

A strange Attractor – Verdichtungsvorschlag:
Wohnbau mit öffentlich zugänglichem Dach durch Stadlau /
A strange Attractor – densification proposal:
housing with public roof throughout Stadlau

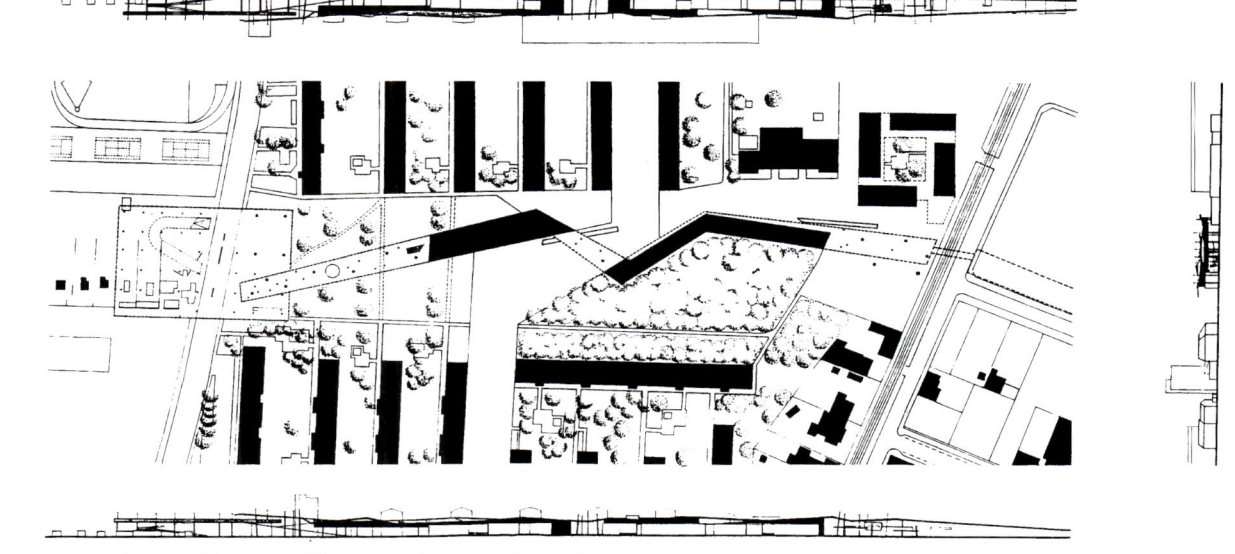

Stadlau: sozialer Wohnbau mit öffentlich zugänglichem Dach und Parkdeck /
Stadlau: Social housing with public roof and a parking deck

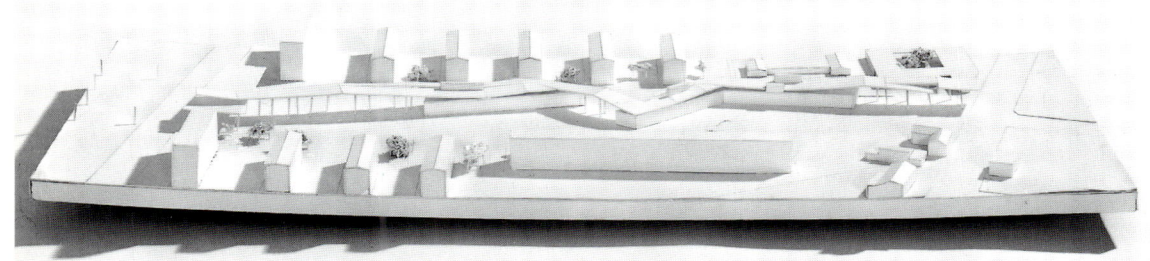

Modell Stadlau, sozialer Wohnbau /
Model Stadlau, Social Housing

**Projektgruppe / project group
Adriaan Geuze**

Assistent: Bart Goldhoorn

Stefan Bernard

Erwin Bot

Tobias Gaupp

Claudia Hüttner

Micheal Kuhn

Imel Kunz

Edda Kurz

Johannes Neher

Anja Planiscek

Lorenz Promegger

Judith Reeh

Angelika Rehe

Nigel Sampey

Dieter Spath

Ando Yoo

**Projektgruppe / project group
Adriaan Geuze**

Adriaan Geuze Rotterdam

1960 born in Dordrecht, The Netherlands
studies at the Agricultural University Wageningen
1985–87 Masters Degree in Landscape Architecture;
chairman and senior designer WEST 8 landscape architects Ltd.;
editor of Archis; secretary of SLA Foundation;
Supervisor Landscaping Schiphol, Amsterdam Airport

Teaching positions
Ecole National Supérieur de Paysage Versailles, Paris, France
Instituta Architectura Urbana, Barcelona, Spain
Polytechnical University of Delft, The Netherlands
Academy of Architecture Amsterdam / Rotterdam / Tilburg,
The Netherlands
Lectures: Kobe Institute of Architecture, Japan
Ruhr Universität Duisburg; Karlsruhe Universität, Germany
Flemish Board of Architecture Brussels, Belgium
Park Design Panorama, Rotterdam, The Netherlands

Selection of work
Schouwburgplein, Rotterdam
Market, dam area Rotterdam
Environment, gardens ABN-AMRO Bank, Amsterdam
Environment, gardens VSB-Bank, Utrecht
National Steel Industry, Hoogovers
Amsterdam Schiphol Airport landscaping, gardens, masterplan
Amsterdam Waterfront Project, public space, greenery
Teleport Amsterdam, greenery

Major exhibitions
1990	National Institute of Architecture Rotterdam, Prix de Rome, NL
1990	Rotterdam Kunsthal, urban renewal, NL
1990	Melnikov Festival, Moscow, Russia
1991	Stadt am Fluss, Kassel, Germany
1991	National Institute of Architecture Rotterdam, park design, NL
1993	Impressions from Japan, Beurs van Berlage Amsterdam, NL
1993	Sloterdijkpark, Amsterdam, NL
1993	AIR Alexander, Kunsthal Rotterdam, NL
1994	Borneo/Sporenburg, ARCAM Gallery Amsterdam, NL

Publications among others
1987	Het onderbroken leven
1987	Een forum voor de Rotterdammers
1988	Openbare Ruimte Rotterdam
1989	De Periferie als centrum
1991	Het genot van de leegte l.o.v. Grafisch Nederland
1992	Beyond Darwinism, Academie van Bouwkunst Amsterdam
1993	Stadt-Parks / Urbane Natur in Frankfurt am Main; Parks für Städter
1993	De sensade van het angeprogrammeerde, manifest voor de Maasviakt, publ. in Archis 1993 several articels in the magazines: Archis, De Architekt, Groen, Topos, Garten und Landschaft

Prizes / Awards
1989	First prize competition International Forum of Young Architectoral Institutes
1990	Prix de Rome, urban design and landscape architecture
1993	First prize PPP Stationsquare Bergen op Zoom

Sittin' on the dock of the bay Adriaan Geuze

The city of the second half of the 20th century is a vibrant, expansive rainforest harbouring the immense potential of mass culture. It is a city without boundaries; its space is dictated by motion and time, and by the media. The city-dweller is exposed to a bombardment of commercial illusions that try to trap him in dreams about a fictitious nature. He is coerced by the picturesque - shopping centers which look like medieval lanes and sour milk straight from farms with thatched roofs, safari trips and the unspoilt nature of cigarette ads. The explosion of the late 20th century city blurs the distinction once so clear between city and country, city and nature. The new city is an airy metropolis, a multi layered system of villages, woods, nature reserves and farmlands. It has been transmuted into a latterday cultivated landscape with every sort of enclave evolving at seemingly random places. In its topography, the urban layout resembles a gigantic Suprematist painting. New programmes contrast with archeological fragments. The city has recolonized the existing landscape, giving the agrarian landscape an urban demeanour.

Mass culture nurtures the possibilities offered by welfare, technology, mobility. His excellent physical condition enables the urbanite to run marathons, to ski and surf. The urbanite is self-assured and well-informed, finds his freedom and chooses his own subcultures. The city is his domain; exciting and seductive. Like a nomad he commands vast areas in this new landscape, continually changing his surroundings; when a commuter, a pleasure seeker, a traveller. He has proved himself capable of finding his way around the new landscape and of making places for his own. The urbanite spends a great deal of his time travelling. The city is the ultimate opportunity to escape, and the urbanite is an explorer, creative and inquiring.

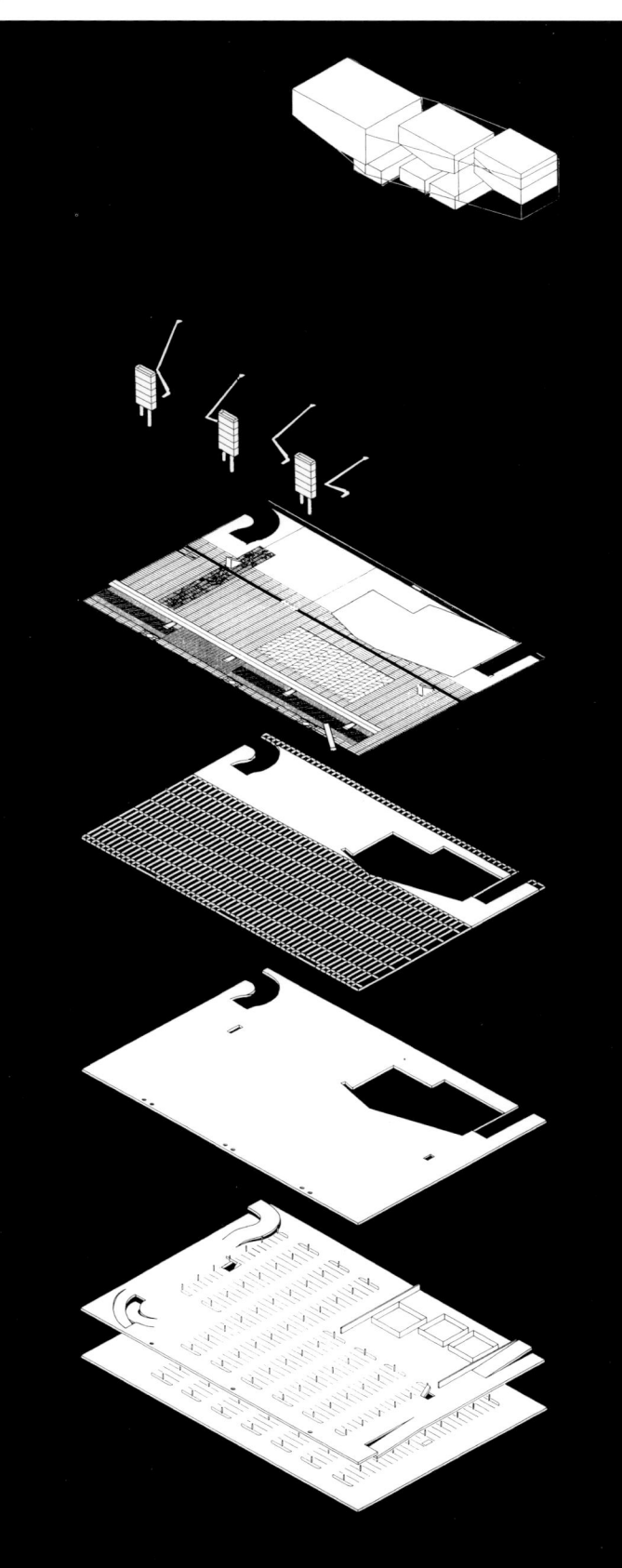

Ontwerp Schouwburgplein Rotterdam, 1994 (WEST 8)

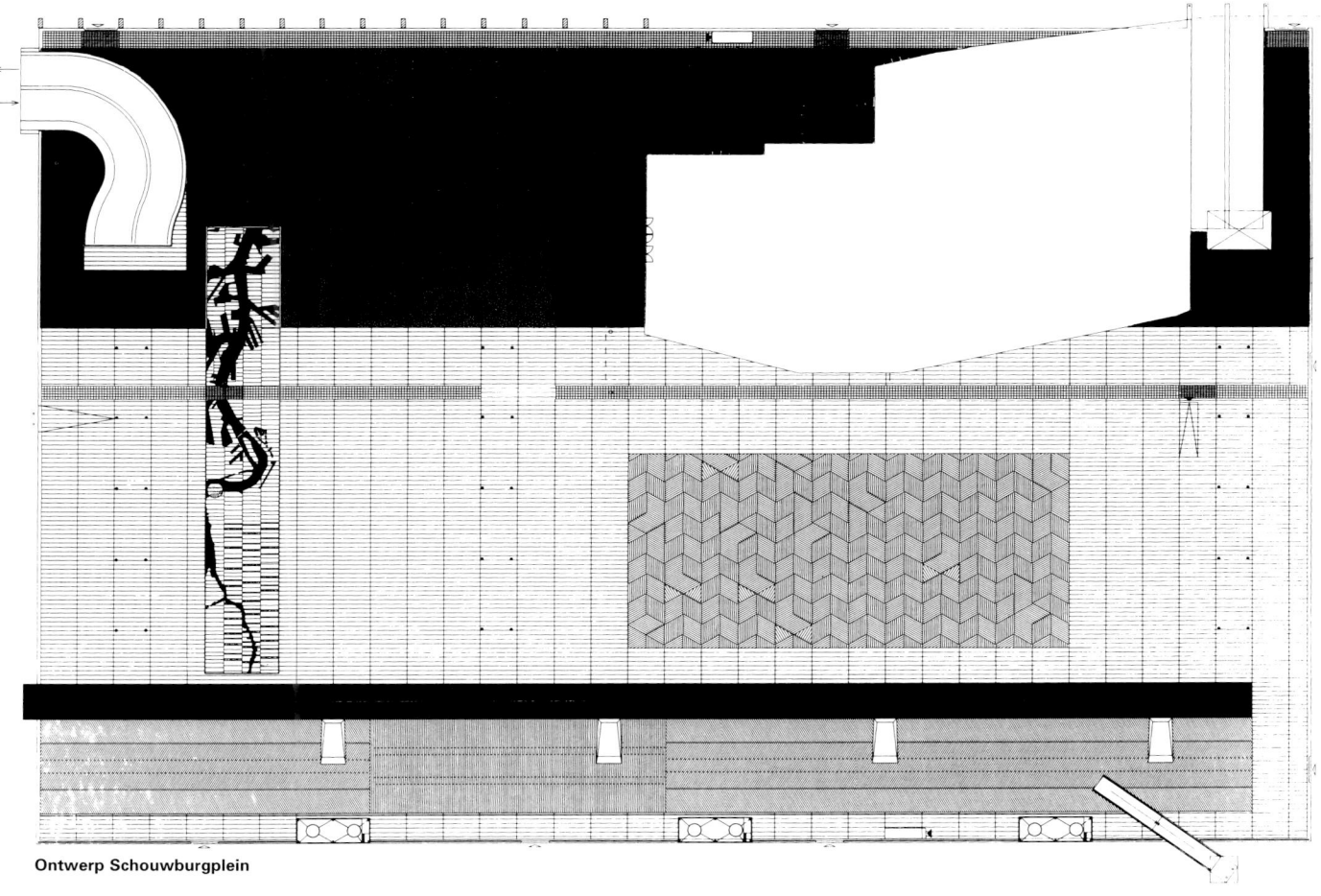

Ontwerp Schouwburgplein

Mehrere Standorte

Gerüstet mit seinen vielen Erscheinungsformen tritt der Städter einmal als Elternteil oder als Nachbar, einmal als Kollege, als Vergnügungssüchtiger oder als Tourist auf. Er gehört verschiedenen Subkulturen an und hat Zugang zu vielen Netzen.
Alter, Ausbildung und Einkommen haben gravierende Auswirkungen auf seinen Geschmack und seine Leistung.
Die Interessen des Städters und seine austauschbaren Vorlieben werden jedesmal mit neuen Orten und Umgebungen verknüpft. Es ist eine Illusion für ihn, ein ideales Haus zu finden, das jedem einzelnen seiner Wünsche entspricht. Sein individuelles Universum umspannt ein großes Gebiet. Er hat viele „Zuhause", mehrere Adressen: eine Wohnung in der Stadt, eine Datscha im Polder, einen Bunker in den Dünen, sein Auto und seinen Wohnwagen, das Büro, den Sportclub, seinen Stammtisch im Restaurant, das Hotel im Ausland, das Boot am See und das Schlafzimmer einer geheimen Geliebten. An jeder dieser Adressen ändert er entsprechend sein Auftreten.

Heimatbasis

Trotz der vielen Adressen führt der neue Städter kein ziel- und planloses Leben. Die Familie, seine Lieben, Arbeit und Hobbies geben

Several addresses

Armed with his many guises, the urbanite operates, now as parent of neighbour, then as colleague, pleasure-seeker, tourist. He belongs to various subcultures and has access to taste and performance.
The interests of the urbanite and his interchangeable preferences are each time linked to new places and surroundings. Finding an ideal house meeting his every need is for him an illusion. His individual universe spans a large area. He has many "homes", several addresses, a flat in the city, a family dacha in the polder, a bunker in the dunes, his car and caraban, the office, the sports club, his regular table at the restaurant, the hotels abroad, the boat on the lake, and the bedroom of a secret love. At each address his guise changes accordingly.

Home base

Despite his many addresses the new city-dweller doesn´t lead an aimless, drifting life. Family, loved ones, work and hobbies structure his existence. Yet one of his addresses is preeminent, the one around which all the others are organized. This is his home base, but not necessarily the

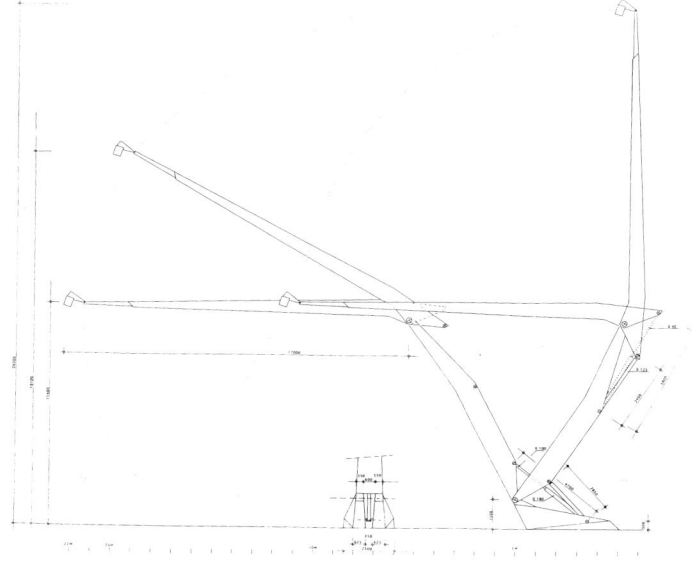

Ontwerp Schouwburgplein

seiner Existenz Struktur. Aber eine seiner Adressen ist vorrangig und zwar jene, um die herum alle anderen organisiert sind. Dies ist seine Heimatbasis, aber nicht unbedingt das „gesamte Haus", das ihm alles, was er braucht, bietet. Diese Heimatbasis verleiht seiner Individualität expliziten Status und Ausdruck. Mit einer beträchtlichen Fläche ist sie von Natur aus nach innen gerichtet und kann flexibel gestaltet werden. Der Grundriß offenbart eine ununterbrochene Reihe von Räumen, in denen funktionelle Akzente erst in zweiter Linie unterschieden werden, wie z.B. Küche, Wohnzimmer, Vorratsraum, Veranda u.ä. Ihr Bewohner ist kreativ und macht sich das Potential und die Einschränkungen ihrer Räume zunutze. Er weiß helle und auch dunkle Plätze, innen und außen, für das, was sie sind, zu schätzen. Der größte Wert der Heimatbasis besteht in der absoluten Privatsphäre, die der Städter hier genießen kann. Hier kann er meditieren und seine geheimsten Pläne hegen. Die ideale Heimatbasis hat einen Eingang, der direkt zum öffentlichen Raum führt. Dieser öffentliche Raum genügt dem ursprünglichen Begriff der „Straße" – gerade, schmal mit hohen Bordsteinen auf beiden Seiten.

Collage: Ontwerp Schouwburgplein

Die Straße bietet keine unnötige Begrünung und Variation, sie ist weder ein Labyrinth noch gibt sie vor, ein friedlicher, unschuldiger Ort zu sein. Sie entspringt der Tradition des Unprätentiösen, des Öffentlichen, wo die Anwohner nur so viel von sich preisgeben, wie erforderlich ist, um gute Beziehungen zueinander aufzubauen. Die Straße bindet die Heimatbasis an die anderen bestehenden Räume an, wobei das öffentliche Leben in bestimmten charismatischen öffentlichen Räumen seinen Höhepunkt findet. Hier wird der Städter herausgefordert und erfreut.

Authentische Gefühle

Auf dem Weg zu den anderen Adressen durchquert der Städter den Raum auf unvergleichliche Weise. Die Autobahn bietet das Äquivalent für einen Spaziergang durch die schönsten Landschaftsgärten des 18. Jahrhunderts. Wenn der Weg durch eine malerische Landschaft den Besucher an einer Reihe pittoresker Anekdoten vorbeiführt, dann treibt das Auto den Städter durch eine Stadtlandschaft mit fesselnden Objekten und unerwarteten Ausblicken voran. Die Stadt und die Landschaft dienen als Hintergrund für die begleitende Bewegung, so daß die Geschwindigkeit, die sanften Kurven der Straße und die Abfolge von Bildern viel von einem Film an sich haben.

Reisen ist eine Sucht. Der Städter, der all der imitierten Natur und der Werbesprüche überdrüssig ist, erfährt das Reisen als ein Hochgefühl mit therapeutischer Wirkung. Nicht nur die Weiten des Marschlandes, ausgedehnter Kornfelder und Buchten, sondern auch die Ikonen der zeitgenössischen Kultur: Silhouetten von Städten und Flughäfen, der nächtliche Anblick von Industrieanlagen, Spinnennetze aus Hochspannungsleitungen, athletische Brücken und Dämme. Bewegung vermittelt ein Gefühl für Maßstab und Proportionen in Relation zur Welt. Für den Städter ist sie ein Quell der Begeisterung und des Staunens. Der Heroismus der Landschaft erfüllt ihn mit neuer Energie und Inspiration: "Sittin' on the dock of the bay".

"complete house" supplying him with everything he needs. This home base gives explicit status and expression to his individuality. With a considerable surface area, it is introverted by nature and flexible by arrangement. The ground plan unfolds an unbroken sequence of spaces, in which functional accents are distinguished only in the second instance, such as kitchen, living room, storeroom, patio and so on. The inhabitant of the home base is creative and exploits the potentials and restrictions of its spaces. He is able to appreciate light as well as dark spaces, inside and outside, for what they are. The greatest value of the home base is the absolute privacy the urbanite can enjoy there. In it he can meditate and hatch his secret plans. The ideal home base has an entrance directly onto the public space. This public space satisfies the original notion of - "street" - straight, narrow and with high curbs on either side. The street has no unnecessary greenery and variation, it isn't a labyrinth, nor does it pretend to be a peaceful, innocent setting as in the suburbs. It springs from the tradition of the unpretentious, the public, where those living on it divulge only what is necessary to build up a good relationship with each other. The street binds the home base with the other spaces along it, with public life culminating in certain public spaces with charisma. Here is where the urbanite is provoked and delighted.

Authentic sensations

On the way to other addresses the urbanite makes a journey through space that is quite without equal. The motorway offers the equivalent of making one's way through the most beautiful 18th century landscape gardens. If the scenic path conveys the visitor along a sequence of picturesque anecdotes, the car propels the city-dweller through an urban landscape of arresting objects and unexpected vistas. City and landscape serve as stage scenery for accompanying movement, so that the speed, the gentle bend in the road, and the succession of images have everything of a film.

Travelling is an addictive affair. Tired of all the imitation nature and the rhetoric of commercials, the urbanite experiences travel as a "high" with a therapeutic effect. Not only stretches of marshland, expansive cornfields and bays, but also the icons of contemporary culture: silhouettes of cities and airports, the nighttime decor of industrial sites, spider's webs of high tension cables, athletic bridges and dams. Movement generates a sense of scale and proportion with regards to the world. To the urbanite it is a source of rapture and wonder. The heroics of the landscape invest him with renewed energy and inspiration: "Sittin' on the dock of the bay".

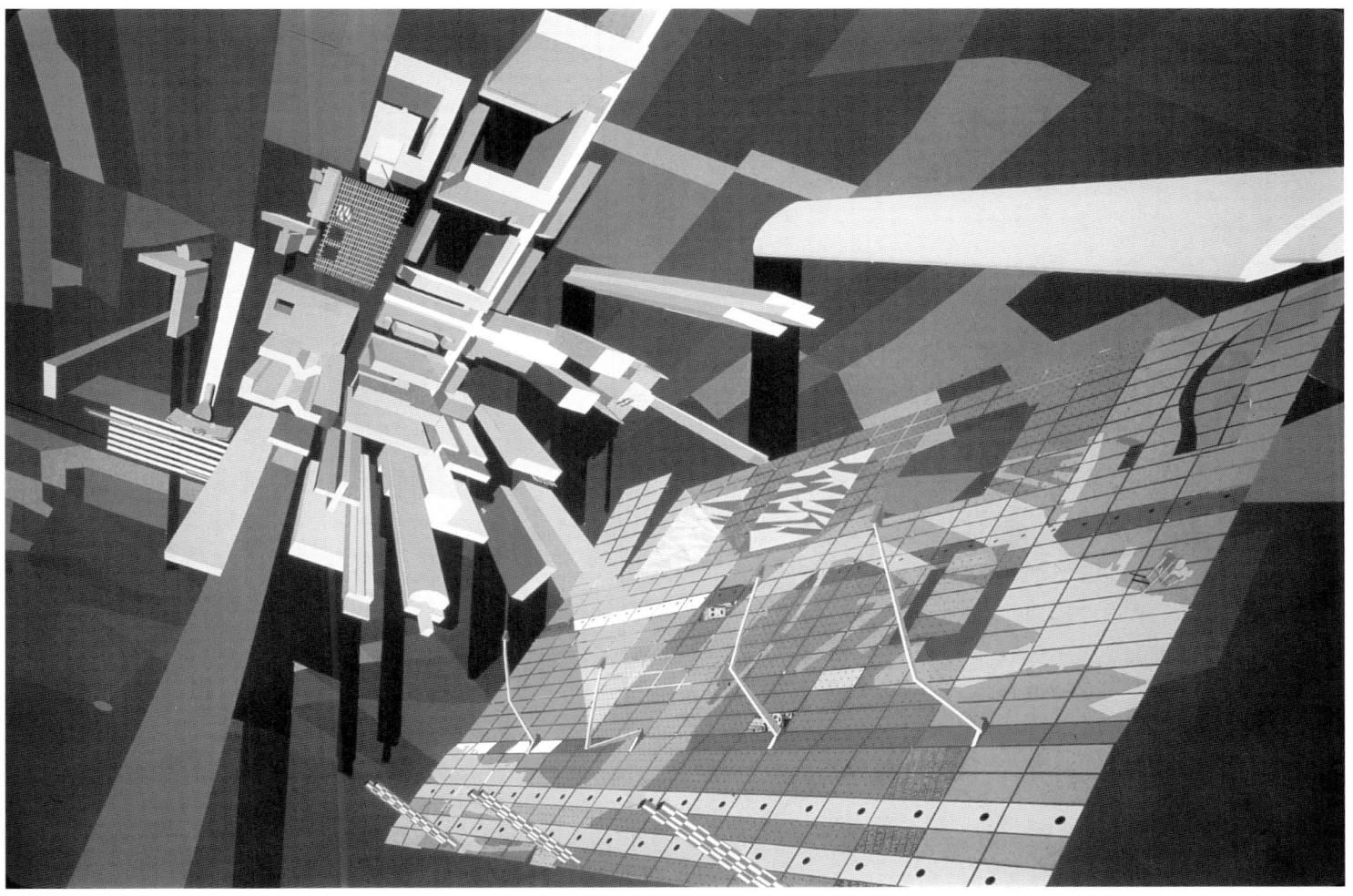

Collage: Ontwerp Schouwburgplein

Infrastructure and landscape connections – open spaces for new settlement areas. Tramway-terminal Leopoldau, Vienna 21

The terminal of a new tramway line (featuring a news agent loop, etc.) is to be located on an area scheduled for use as a green zone at the intersection of two thoroughfares at the western end of the old village center of Leopoldau. The coincidence of the spatial traffic elements, industry, agriculture, village structures, etc. This case characterizes an exemplary urban situation. The planned new tramway line will constitute the link of new settlement areas with the puplic transport system.

The area bordered by Siemensstraße and Leopoldauerstraße shall be designed as an open space. The area is part of a green stretch reaching from the city's Northern outskirts via zones of predominantly agricultural use along the housing estate of Großfeldsiedlung via the Donaufeld to the Old Danube. A watercourse with ecological functions leading from the Marchfeld Canal in the north of the city to the Old Danube might be created in this green stretch.
A planned new main thoroughfare cuts through the green stretch in the north of the planning area, thus also creating a demand for adequate crossings and passages. A total of approximately 750 flats are planned to be constructed on two longitudinal plots south of the adjacent Leopoldauerstraße.

Leopoldau, Wien 21

A yearning for authenticity

Public Space on North Bank of the Danube, Vienna

Design Study 1994

The brief called for a design for a small area surrounding a projected tram stop at the village of Leopoldau in the northeast of Vienna. An analysis of the site made clear that a "funky" design for the public space would only serve to camouflage the complex set of problems dogging northeast Vienna. This part of the city has persistently been neglected by planners in favour of the museum-like center. The upshot of this neglect is a fascinating patchwork of billboards, hypermarkets, industries, ancient village centers, new residential developments, geraniums, excavations, gardens and ghettos. Now that Vienna´s population is growing for the first time in decades under the migration from the former Iron Curtain countries, this area has the potential of expanding into the 21st century as a counterpart to the historic city center. Cheap farmland is being made free for private enterprises, putting the lower middle class dream of a personal paradise within its grasp. The gardens belonging to individual houses provide the foundation for a new and varied ecology. It is however for its essence that the area receives a structural identity of its own. Instead of a complicated urban planning mode, it is imperative that this new garden city unfolds a strategy that invests in preserving large tracts of open space. A strategy that replaces the dogmatic polarity of green and built land

Eine Strategie, die die dogmatische Polarität zwischen grünen und verbauten Gebieten durch die subtile, ausgewogene Anwendung von Maßnahmen, die von der Flächenwidmung bis zu einfühlsam gestalteten Objekten reichen, überwindet. Eine Analyse der bestehenden, dominierenden, parallelen Linien in der Landschaft diente als Basis für die Erstellung eines Straßenmusters, das auf alle neuen Siedlungen angewandt werden kann. Große Grüngebiete wurden als Verkettung von öffentlichen Parks angelegt und bringen Ruhe und kühle Luft. Die bestehenden und künftigen Schottergruben sind in einer einzigen Zone konzentriert, wo sie große Wasserflächen für Erholungszwecke schaffen. Die Großmärkte befinden sich alle in einem Industriegürtel entlang der neuen Autobahn. Ein Netz von Fahrradwegen sorgt dafür, daß Haltestellen und nahe gelegene Dörfer innerhalb von maximal zehn Minuten zu erreichen sind. Die alten Dorfkerne, wie z.B. Leopoldau, die gemeinsam das Rückgrat des Gebiets bilden, werden alle in Bausch und Bogen auf die Denkmalliste gesetzt. Als Denkmäler werden sie jene Punkte bilden, um die sich Geschäfte, Cafés, Restaurants usw. in den nächsten Jahren konzentrieren werden.

with a subtle and well-balanced deployment of measures extending from zoning regulations to sensitively designed objects. An analysis of the existing dominant parallel lines in the landscape was the springboard from which to produce a street pattern applicable to all new settlements. Large green zones configured as a concentration of public gardens bring both peace and cool air. The existing and continuing gravel pits are clustered in a single zone, generating large water features for recreation. Hypermarkets are concentrated in a commercial belt along the new motorway. A network of bicycle paths sees to it that stations and nearby villages centers, such as Leopoldau, which together form the spine of the area, are placed en masse on the monuments list; as such they will form the points were shops, cafés, restaurants and such like will be concentrated in the years to come.

Analysen / Analyses:

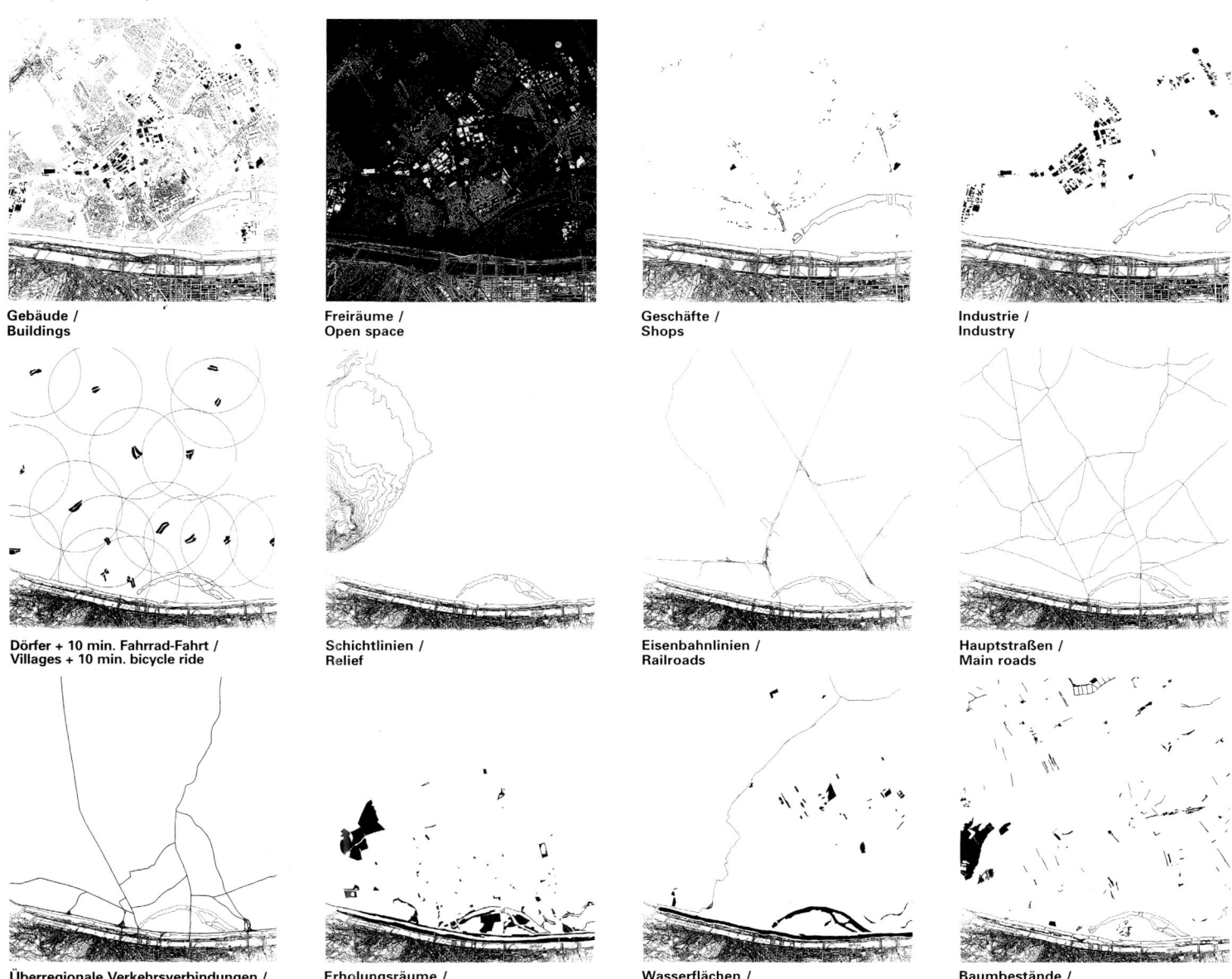

Gebäude / Buildings

Freiräume / Open space

Geschäfte / Shops

Industrie / Industry

Dörfer + 10 min. Fahrrad-Fahrt / Villages + 10 min. bicycle ride

Schichtlinien / Relief

Eisenbahnlinien / Railroads

Hauptstraßen / Main roads

Überregionale Verkehrsverbindungen / International road connections

Erholungsräume / Recreation areas

Wasserflächen / Water

Baumbestände / Woodland

Strategie / Strategy:

Collage, Leitplan Wien Nord: Grünplanung /
Collage, masterplan Vienna north: green framework

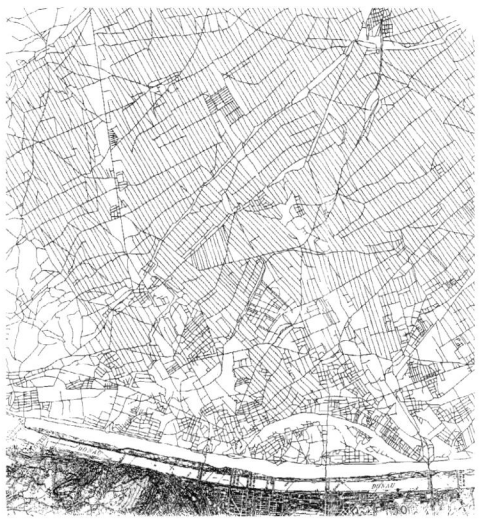
Szenario Parallele Struktur /
Parallel line scenario

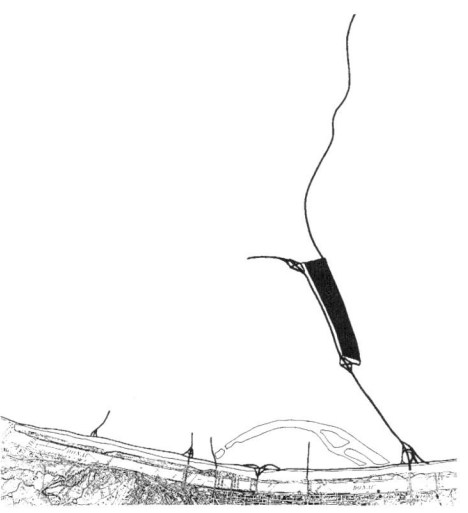
Autobahn und Einkaufszone /
Highway and shopping strip

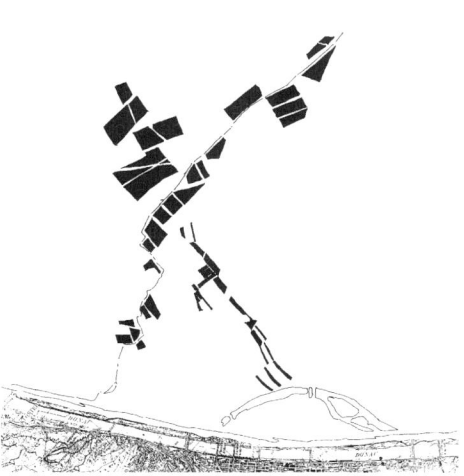
Baumpflanzungen /
Plantations

Wasserflächen /
Water

Waldgebiet /
Woodlands

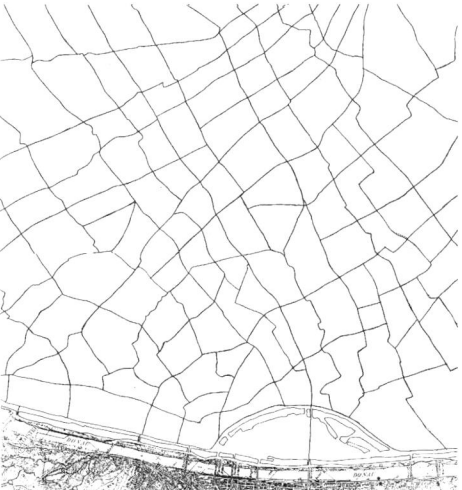
Radweg-Netz /
Bicycle network

Strategie Grünland /
Green strategy

Strategie Wohnbau /
Housing strategy

Leopoldau:

Parzellierung /
Parcellation

Parallele Parzellierung /
Parallel parcellation

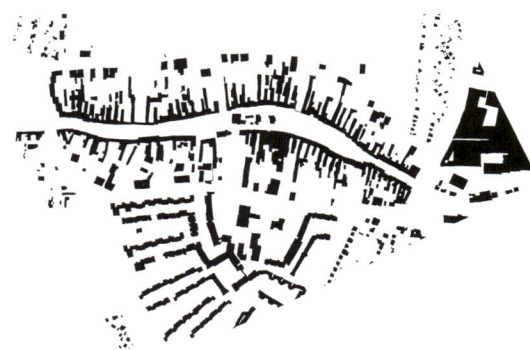
Leopoldau Bestandsaufnahme /
Leopoldau existing situation

Parzellierung /
Parcellation

Modell /
Model

Anatomische Verletzung /
Anatomical lesion

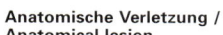

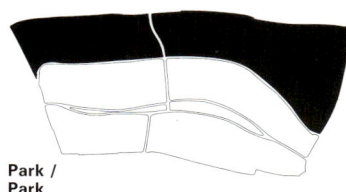
Park /
Park

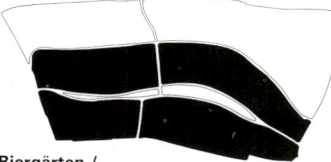
Biergärten /
Beer gardens

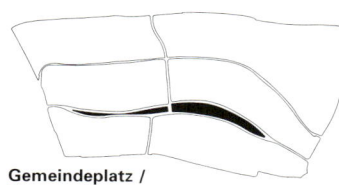
Gemeindeplatz /
Community square

Vorschlag für Leopoldau /
Leopoldau proposal

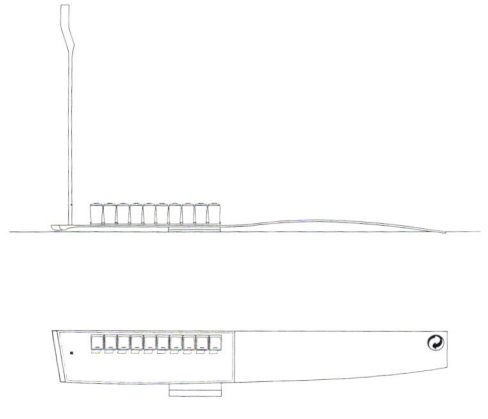
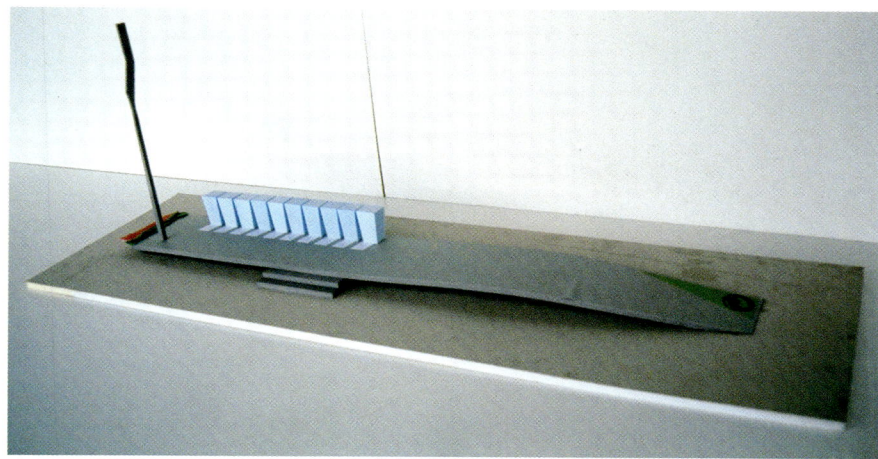

Wiederverwertungsstelle /
Recycling point

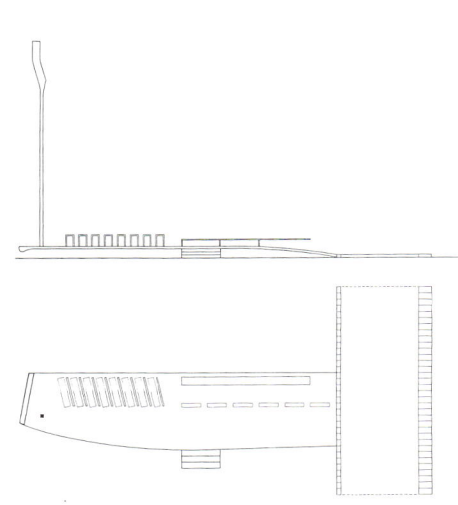
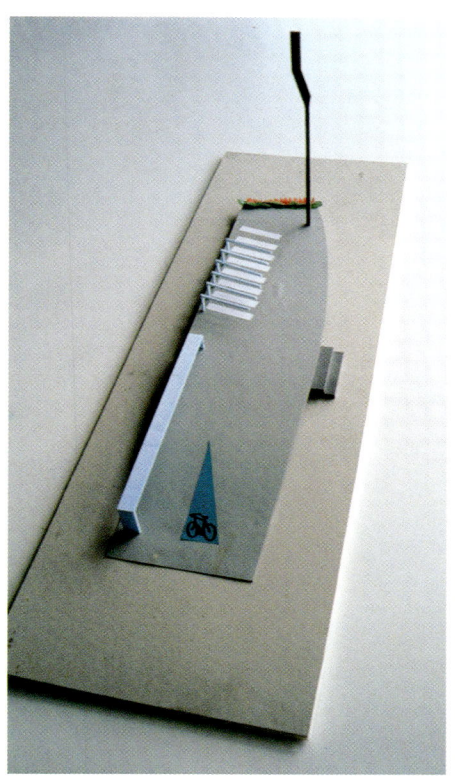

Wiederverwertungsstelle /
Recycling point

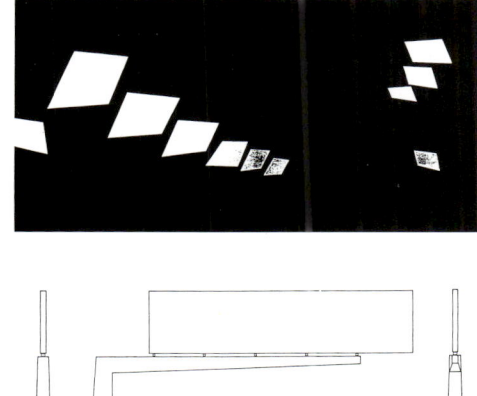

Plakatwand /
Billboard

**Projektgruppe / project group
José Llinás Carmona**

Assistent: Joan Vera

Konstantin Biek

Marco Camplani

Fabrizio Gallanti

Gianpaolo Gritti

Silvia Contreras Lopez

José Adriao da Costa Martins

Ana Isabel Ferreira e Costa

Arturo Frediani

Katja Heimanns

Piero Luconi

Claudia Möller

Raffaella Panico

Pedro Pacheco

Armando Oliver Suinaga

Christiane Tinkhausen

Reinhold Zolnierz

José Llinàs Carmona Barcelona

1945 born in Castellón de la Plana, Spain
1969 Degree of architecture from the Architecture School of Barcelona

Teaching positions
1970–89 Teacher at the Higher School of Architecture of
 Barcelona, Project Department
1983–84 and
1987–88 Tutor in the Project V Department of the Higher
 Technical School of Architecture of Vallés
 Teacher invited in seminars and courses in Santander,
 Baeza, Almería, Lisboa, Barcelona, Lausanne, Graz, Vienna, Paris

Project
1991 Commissioner of the exhibition „Josep Maria Jujol"
 organized by the School of Architects, Cataluña

Publications among others
 Articles published in different national and international
 reviews, for example, about the buildings of Mies van der Rohe,
 Josep Maria Jujol, Alejandro de la Sota and José Antonio Coderch

 Monograph of Josep Maria Jujol, published by Taschen Verlag,
 Germany.

Über das ungewohnte Umgehen mit freiem Gelände Llinás Carmona

Bevor ich zum 5. Wiener Architekturseminar eingeladen wurde, hatte ich noch nie in einem Kontext gearbeitet, der so wenige urbane Bezüge hatte (ich glaube, die Vorgangsweise ist generell in Spanien unüblich). Normalerweise steht man in Spanien vor einem ganz anderen Problem: es geht darum, Platz zu schaffen und damit aufzuhören, in dicht besiedelten städtischen Bereichen, die das Ergebnis komplexer historischer Entwicklungen sind, bebaubare Quadratmeter erzeugen zu wollen.

Die Problemstellung des Workshops ging genau vom Gegenteil aus: Auf einer weitläufigen, ebenen Fläche mit vage definierten Grenzen sollte ein Erholungsraum geschaffen werden, der mit der Natur in Verbindung steht und in Hinblick auf Nutzen und Baufläche ebenfalls unklar definiert war.

Bei der ersten Besichtigung kamen mir nur wenige Ideen, da ich ja, wie bereits eingangs erwähnt, daran gewöhnt bin, umgekehrt zu arbeiten, d.h. vergleichbar mit jemandem, der in einen vollen Autobus steigt und einen Sitzplatz sucht, sich durch das Gedränge kämpft, um sich einen Platz zu erobern, auf dem er sich dann schließlich niederläßt und von dem aus er Kontakt und Dialog mit den Nachbarn sucht.

Bei Projektbeginn wurden die Studenten zunächst in Gruppen aufgeteilt. Jede Gruppe untersuchte den Ort nach spezifischen Grundsätzen. Das ergab verschiedene Schlußfolgerungen: z.B., daß man grundsätzlich die vom Marchfeldkanal vorgegebene Längsbewegung, oder umgekehrt, die transversale Richtung der Straßen des Stadtteils im Norden unseres Arbeitsgebiets betonen wollte. Die Auswertung war nur sinnvoll, wenn man die Kräfte, die das größere Umfeld regieren, zu erfassen versuchte; oder wenn man im Gegenteil, von den physischen Merkmalen des Gebiets – wie geographischen und topographischen Charakteristika, Sonnenbestrahlung oder Besonderheiten der Grenzen – ausging.

Schließlich wurde ein zusammenfassendes Dokument erarbeitet, das das Gebiet als im wesentlichen von zwei Merkmalen dominiert beschreibt: vom Marchfeldkanal und den „strips" (Streifen) – seiner ursprünglichen Einteilung, die auch in seiner heutigen Morphologie noch vorhanden ist.

About the unusual treatment of empty spaces Llinás Carmona

Before I was invited to participate in the 5th Vienna Architecture Seminar, I never worked in a context with so little urban references (I think that this approach is generally uncommon in Spain). Usually, we face a completely different problem in Spain: we have to create space and refrain from trying to create built-up square meters in densely populated urban areas which resulted from complex historical developments.

The task of the workshop was just the opposite: a recreation area which is connected to nature and little defined as regards its utilisation. Building space was to be created on an extensive, flat area with vaguely defined boundaries.

**Wohnhaus mit 28 Wohnungen, Barcelona, 1992–95 /
Residential building with 28 apartments, Barcelona, 1992–95**

During the first visit to the site, I had only a few ideas because, as I said before, I am used to working the other way round, i.e. comparable to somebody who enters a crowded bus looking for a free seat and pushes through the crowd to secure a seat where he finally sits down and tries to get into contact with his neighbours and to establish a dialogue with them.

First of all, at the start of the project, we divided the students into groups. Each group investigated the site based on their own principles which yielded different conclusions: they suggested, for example, that, on principle, the longitudinal orientation defined by the Marchfeld canal or, on the contrary, the transversal orientation of the streets in the neighbourhood to the north of our site was to be emphasised. The analysis, which included our site, only made sense if we tried to cover the forces governing the wider environment; or, on the contrary, if we started from the physical characteristics of the site – such as geographic and topographic features, sunlight or special features of the boundaries.

Finally, a synthesis was prepared which described the site as being defined essentially by two characteristics: by the Marchfeld canal and the "strips" – the site's original division which is still reflected by today's morphology.

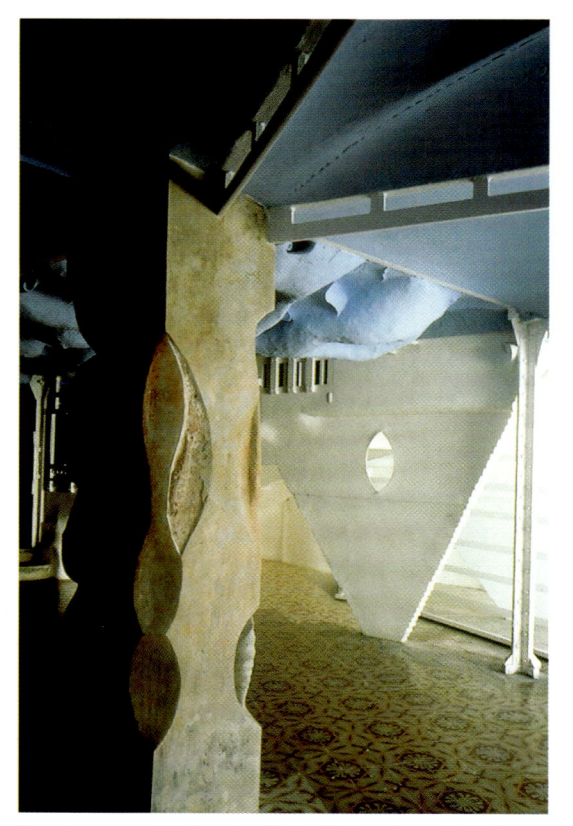

**Renovierung und Umbau des Teatro Metropol von Architekt Josep M. Jujol, Tarragona, 1992–95 /
Renovation and re-construction of the Teatro Metropol by the architect Josep M. Jujol, Tarragona, 1992–95**

Von diesem Einvernehmen ausgehend, wurden von den Studentengruppen in den unterschiedlichsten Ansätzen verschiedene Planungsvorschläge erneut vorgebracht, welche in den Graphiken im Anhang zusammengefaßt sind.

Dazu ergab sich dann im Workshop eine Diskussion darüber, ob man abschließend verschiedene Vorschläge (die Ausführung der vorher erwähnten) oder einen einzigen, als Zusammenfassung der interessantesten Ideen aller Gruppen vorstellen sollte.

Die Idee, einen einzigen Vorschlag zu präsentieren, wurde schließlich bevorzugt, und für mich begann damit der interessanteste Teil des Workshops.

Gemeinsam wurde ein Gesamtplan erstellt, und erneut teilte man die Ausführung auf mehrere Gruppen auf. Eine Gruppe behandelte die Grünflächen und das Ufer des Marchfeldkanals, eine andere die Gebäude, wieder eine andere die künstliche Beleuchtung, die Verkehrswege etc.

**Mittelschule in Torredembarra /
Middle school in Torredembarra**

Das Ergebnis wird in den Graphiken der Studentenprojekte veranschaulicht. Meiner Meinung nach handelt es sich dabei weniger um einen Entwurf für die Bebauung des Raums, als vielmehr um eine Vorbereitung für eine hypothetische Verwendung. Es gibt keine abbildbaren Vorschläge, sondern es handelt sich um die Aufarbeitung der Spezifika des Ortes. Ich glaube, daß das eine Folge des vorher erklärten Arbeitsprozesses ist. Ich persönlich war mit dem Ergebnis sehr zufrieden; vor allem aber freute ich mich über die Hingabe, die Ernsthaftigkeit und die Kenntnisse der beim Workshop anwesenden Studenten und Architekten.

Based on this agreement, various planning proposals were prepared again by the student groups following diverse approaches which were summarized in the drawings included in the annex.

In this context we discussed in the workshop whether we should present several final proposals (elaborating on the ones' mentioned above) or only one proposal comprising the most interesting ideas developed by all the groups.

The idea of making only one proposal was eventually adopted and then, for me, the most interesting part of the workshop began.

Together we prepared a master plan and, once more, this task was split up among several groups. One group dealt with green space or the banks of the Marchfeld canal, another one worked on the buildings and still another one discussed artificial lighting, traffic paths, etc. The results are illustrated by the drawings of the student-projects. In my opinion this is less a plan for occupying this site but rather prepares it for hypothetical utilization. There are no image proposals, but only plans elaborating on the specific features of the site – I think that they are a consequence of the working process described above. Personally, I was very satisfied with the result and, I particularly, enjoyed the devoted and serious work as well as the knowledge of the students and architects participating in the workshop.

**Mittelschule in Torredembarra, Provinz Tarragona), 1993–96 /
Middle school in Torredembarra, province of Tarragona, 1993–96**

Neue Freizeiträume – Landschaftselemente im Entwicklungsgebiet. Jugendfreizeitanlage, Wien 22

Das für die Bearbeitung vorgesehene Gebiet liegt an einer nach Norden führenden Ausfallstraße. Die Bedeutung und damit auch die Verkehrsbelastung dieser Straßenverbindung ist durch die Öffnung der Grenze zur heutigen Tschechischen Republik, aber auch durch die Siedlungsentwicklung außerhalb Wiens, gestiegen. Mit den neuen baulichen Verdichtungen südlich von Stammersdorf zählt die Brünnerstraße zu den wichtigsten Entwicklungsachsen der Stadt. Angestrebt wird zudem die Ansiedlung von Betrieben um Arbeitsplätze vor Ort zu schaffen. Ein besonderer stadträumlicher Vorzug dieses Entwicklungsgebietes sind die vorhandenen Freiflächen, die durch den neuerrichteten Marchfeldkanal zu einem ausgedehnten Grünraumsystem verbunden wurden. Entlang der Brünnerstraße ist auf dem Planungsgebiet eine Randbebauung vorgesehen. Ein maßgeblicher Teil des Areals soll unbebaut bleiben und in Verbindung mit dem Grünzug Marchfeldkanal als Freifläche zur Verfügung stehen.

Auf einem als Sonderfläche gewidmeten Teil des Areals, zwischen einer geplanten Sporthalle und einer geplanten Kindertagesheimstätte, soll eine Freizeitanlage für Jugendliche geschaffen werden. Das Angebot soll sich dabei, zusätzlich zu den Erfordernissen der neuen Siedlungsgebiete, auch an einem gesamtstädtischen Bedarf orientieren. Das Projekt könnte damit einen Ansatz zur Ausbildung von Image und Identität für den neuen Siedlungsraum bieten.

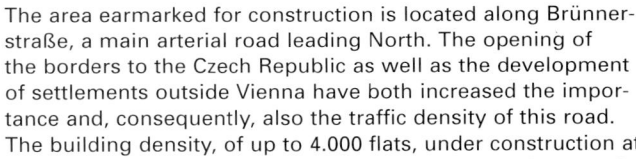

Jugendfreizeitanlage Anton-Schall-Gasse, Wien 21

New Leisure Centers – scenic elements in development areas. Leisure center for young people, Vienna 21

The area earmarked for construction is located along Brünnerstraße, a main arterial road leading North. The opening of the borders to the Czech Republic as well as the development of settlements outside Vienna have both increased the importance and, consequently, also the traffic density of this road. The building density, of up to 4.000 flats, under construction at present, South of Stammersdorf, make Brünnerstraße one of the city´s most important development areas.

The available empty spaces are a particular, urban advantage of this development area and are linked up to an extensive green area system by the newly built Marchfeld Canal. Road side buildings shall be constructed on the planning area along Brünnerstraße. An important part of the area shall be left vacant and shall constitute an open space together with the green belt of the Marchfeld Canal.

Recreational facilities for children and young adults shall be constructed in one part of the area dedicated for special pupases and located between the planned gymnasium and the planned day care centre. The offer shall not only satisfy the demands of the new residential areas, but shall also orient itself by the necessities of the city as a whole. Thus the project might constitute a basis for the creation of an authentic image and identity for the entire settlement area.

Strips

Wiener Architekturseminar
Architektur des leeren Raumes – Landschaft Wien

Den ersten Teil des Seminars widmeten wir dem Verständnis des Standortes. Das Gelände wird im wesentlichen durch folgende Elemente bestimmt:

1. Marchfeldkanal

- Der Kanal wirkt wie ein Einschnitt in der Ebene

2. Die geometrische Einteilung der Felder

- Die Einteilung ist vorwiegend auf die Eigentumsverhältnisse, aber auch auf den Einfluß des Nordwest-Windes zurückzuführen.

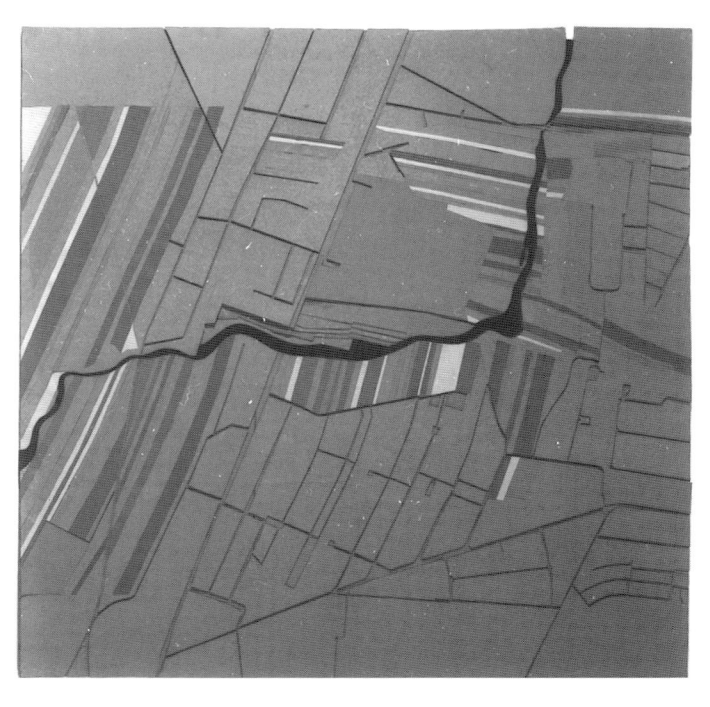

Strips

Viennese Seminar on Architecture
Architecture of the empty space – Landscape Vienna

We dedicated the first part of the seminar to an understanding of the site. Basically, the form of the territory is defined by:

1. The Marchfeldcanal

- the canal appears like a cut in the flat

2. The geometric division of the fields

- the division is mainly related with the property, but also with the wind from the northwest.

3. Verstärkung der Geometrie durch die vorhandene Vegetation.

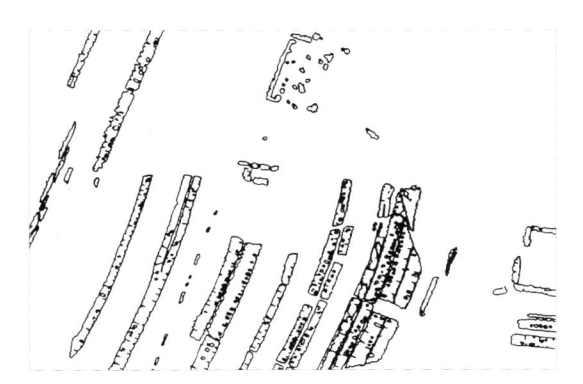

3. Reinforcement of the geometry by the existing vegetation.

4. Vorhandene Gebäude, die den Projektstandort begrenzen:

- Kaserne
- 4000 neue Gebäude
- Gartensiedlung

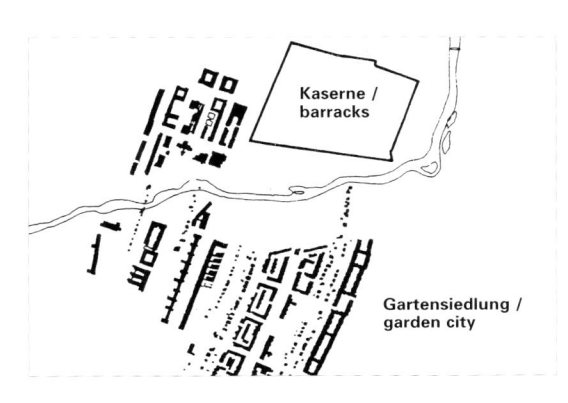

4. The presence of buildings that limit the site of the project.

- barracks
- 4000 new buildings
- garden city

5. Die Anordnung der Wege und Kommunikationsleitungen wurde aus der Organisation des Gebiets abgeleitet.

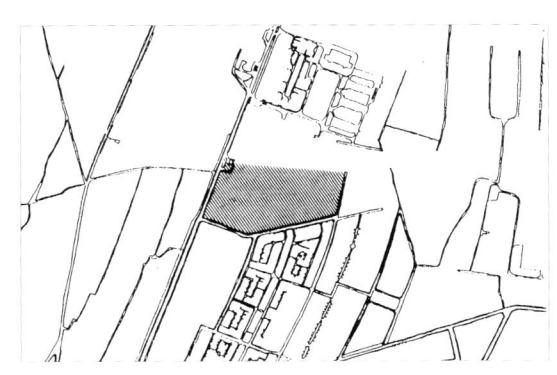

5. The lay-out of the tracks and communication lines derived from the organization of the territory.

6. Beziehung des Standorts zur Einteilung der vorhandenen Grundstücke.

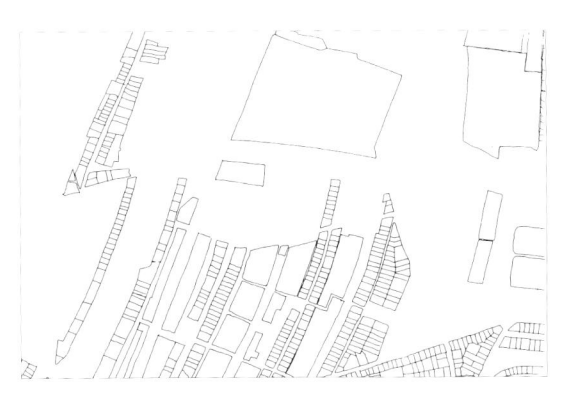

6. Relation of the site with the division of the existing plots

Der zweite Teil der Arbeit definiert die Bedingungen, die wir für das Projekt als wichtig erachten:

A. Verwendung der Streifen zur Organisation, Unterteilung und Strukturierung des Geländes.

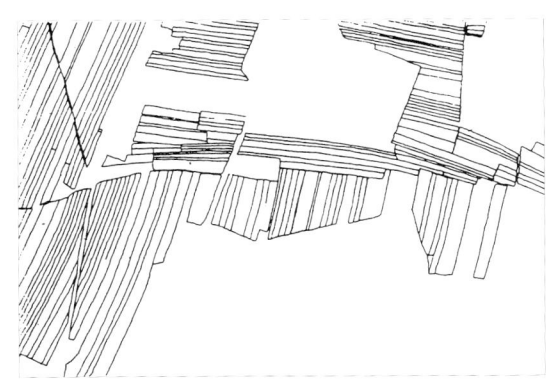

The second part of the work defines the conditions that we consider important for the project:

A. Using the strips to organize, to divide, and to structure the site.

B. Vermeidung einer Definition der Grenzen des Geländes, indem:

- die vorhandene Geometrie der Gartensiedlung, die einen starken Einfluß auf den Standort ausübt, genutzt wird;
- der östliche und der westliche Teil des Geländes entlang des Kanals verbunden werden.

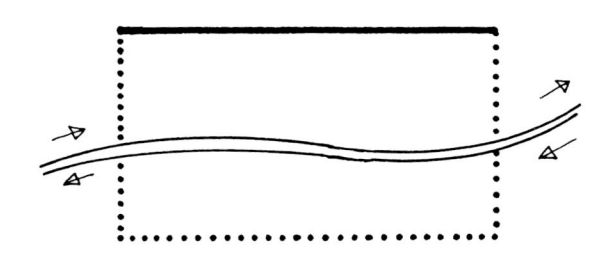

C. Verstärkung der Beziehung zum Westen, wo sich eine bedeutende Wohnanlage und ein öffentliches Zentrum befinden, indem:

- wir versuchen, unseren Standort wie einen offenen Erholungsraum, der mit der westlichen Seite verbunden ist, zu gestalten;
- eine Beziehung zwischen dem Projekt und der westlichen Seite hergestellt wird;
- diese Beziehung durch eine Änderung des Querschnitts des Kanals unter der Brücke unterstützt wird.

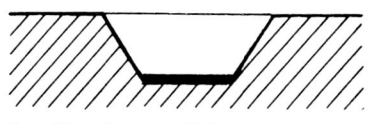

D. Der Kanal als eine Achse des Standorts:

- Nutzung der beiden unterschiedlichen Seiten des Kanals.
- die Streifen auf den beiden Seiten des Kanals sind unterschiedlich ausgerichtet.

Wir erachten dies aufgrund der unterschiedlichen Sonneneinstrahlung als wichtig.

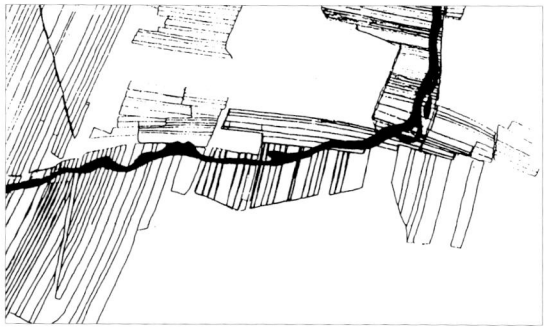

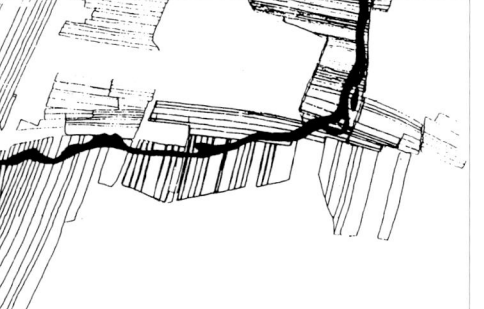

E. Wir plazieren die Gebäude (oder vielmehr die verbauten Flächen) unter Verwendung:

- der Streifen im Hinblick auf ihre Dimensionen.
- des Kanals im Hinblick auf ihre Position.

Wir sorgen dafür, daß sich die Menschen hauptsächlich auf der Südseite des Kanals bewegen müssen.

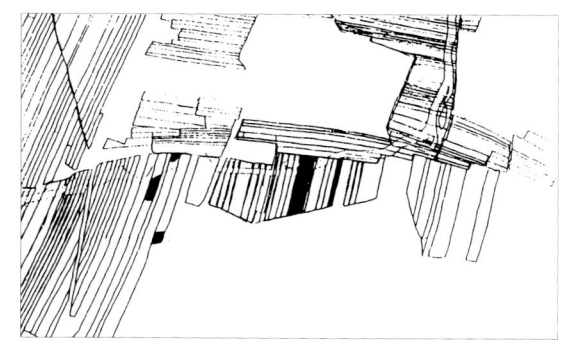

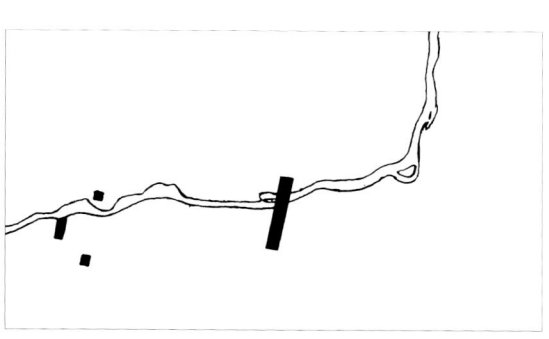

derzeitiger Querschnitt / existing section

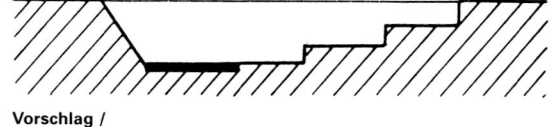

Vorschlag / proposal

Die beste Seite zum Verweilen, kein Verkehr / The best side to stay, no circulation

Die beste Seite zum Gehen, bestehende Grenze des Kanals / The best side to walk, existing border of the canal

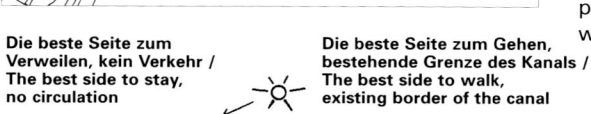

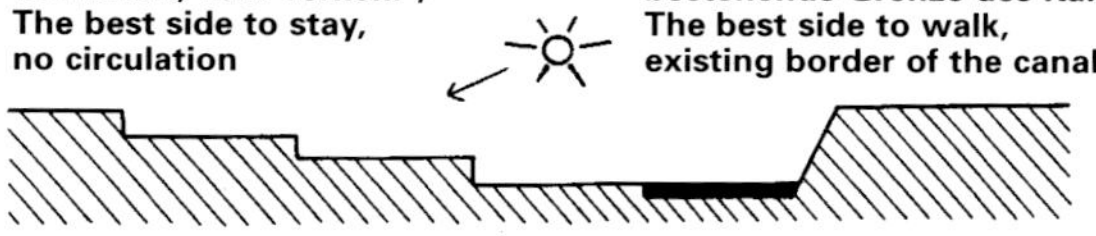

B. Leaving undefined the limits of the site:

- by using the existing geometry of the garden city, which has a strong influence upon the site.
- by connecting the east and west part of the site along the canal.

C. Increasing the relation with the west, where an important residential and public center is located by:

- trying to develop our site like an open space for recreational use connected to the west side
- establishing a relation between the project and the west side.
- facilitating the relation by changing the section of the canal, beneath the bridge.

D. The canal as an axis of the site,

- using the two distinct sides of the canal.
- the direction of the strips is different on the two sides of the canal.

This we understood as being important, considering the relation with the sun.

E. We located the buildings (constructed surfaces),

- using the strips, with regard to their dimensions
- using the canal, with regard to their positions

We assure that the main movement of the people must be on the south side of the canal.

F. Ausweitung der Fußgänger- und Fahrradwege entlang des Kanals, sodaß sie sich wie ein Spinnennetz auf unserer Seite erstrecken.

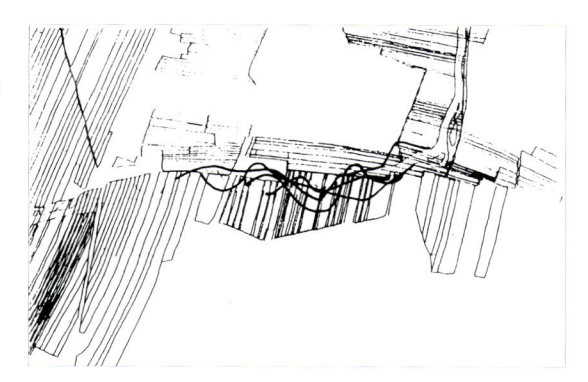

F. Extension of the pedestrian and bicycle paths along the canal, to create a kind of spider net towards our side.

G. Wir wollen künstliche Beleuchtung so einsetzen, daß unterschiedliche Funktionen zum Ausdruck gebracht werden. Hiezu muß diese mit dem Ortstyp (Kanal, Zugang, Sport usw.) und der Zeit (Jahreszeiten, Schnee, usw.) in Beziehung gesetzt werden.

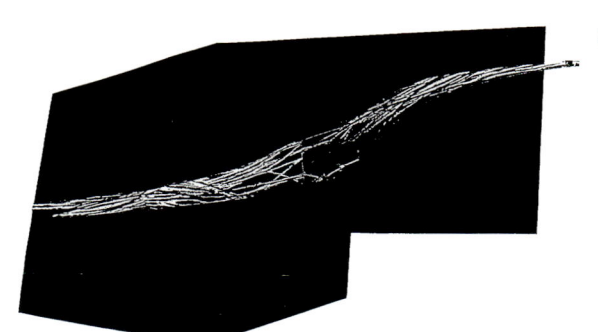

G. We wanted to use artificial light to express the different functions. It had to be related with the type of location (canal, access, sport...) and with time (seasons, snow...).

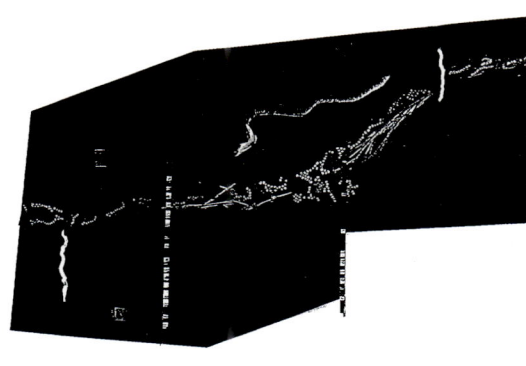

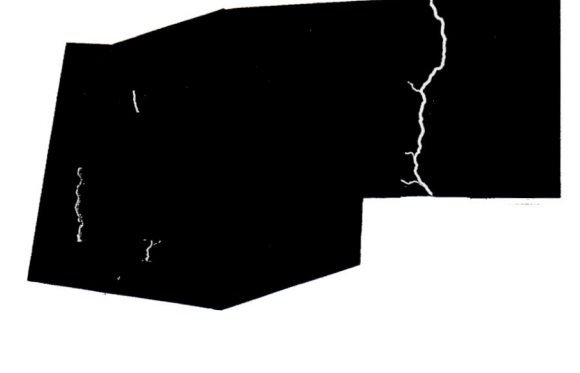

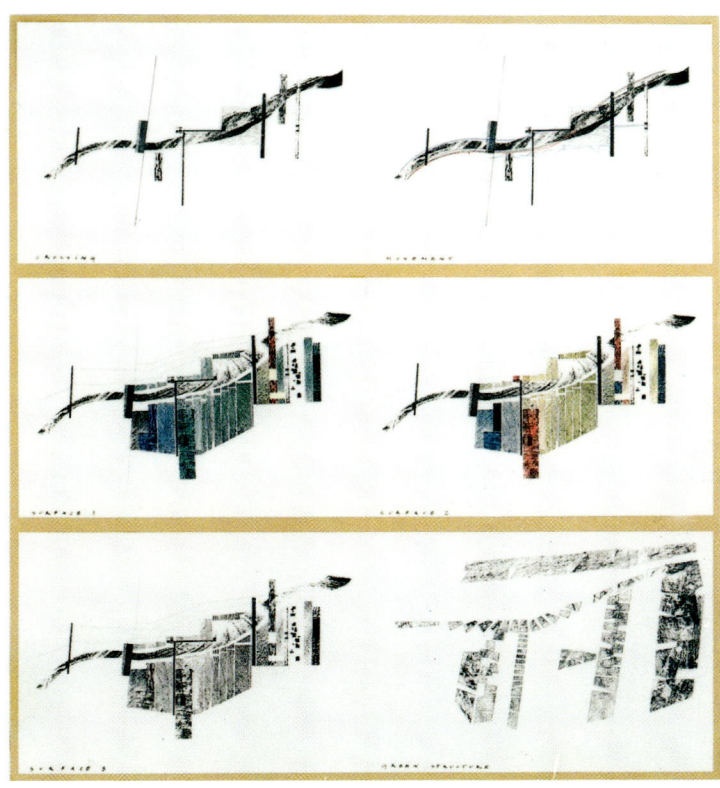

**Gesamtprojekt/
Final project**

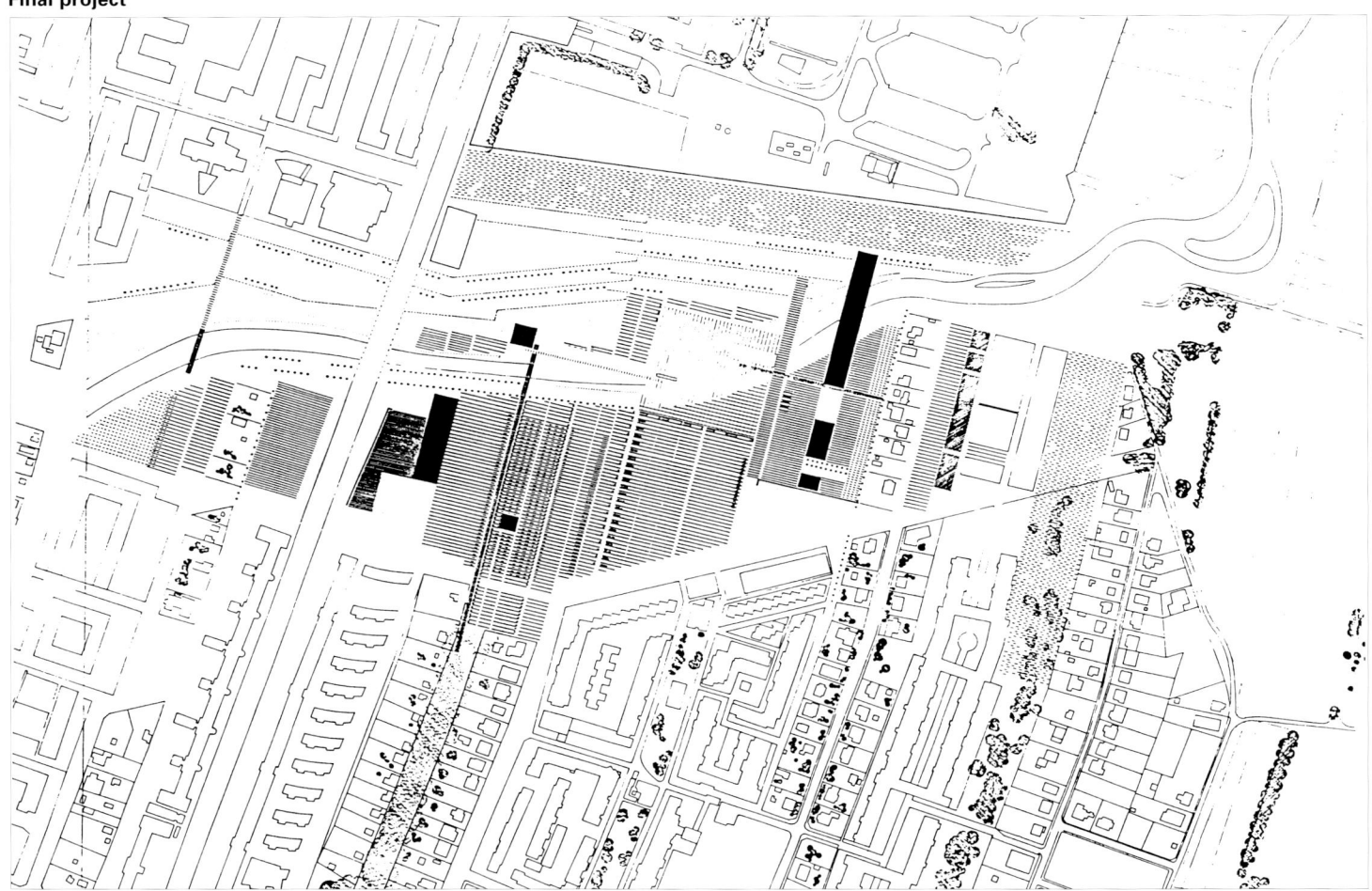

**Gesamtplan des endgültigen Projekts /
Masterplan of the final project**

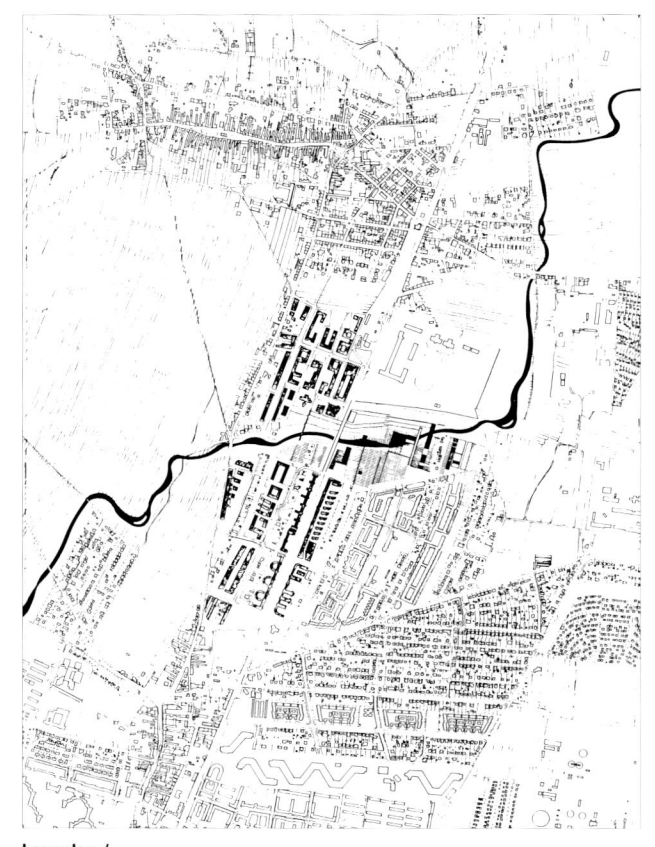

**Lageplan /
Siteplan**

Beispiele für die von den Studenten erstellten Projekte /
Examples of the projects realized by the students

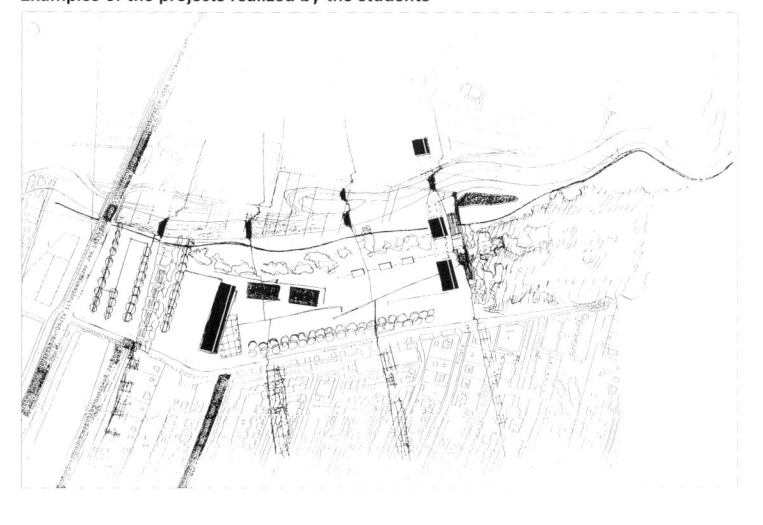

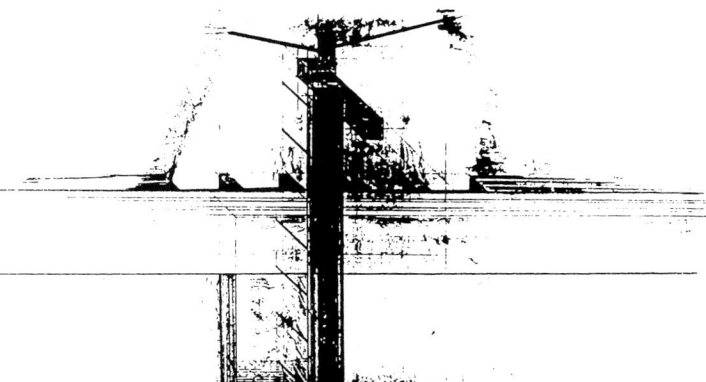

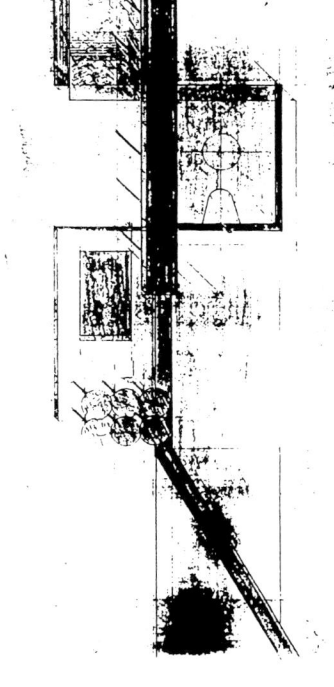

**Projektgruppe / project group
Mark Mack**

Assistent: Francie Moore

Maria Benesch

Cord Bertko

Illaria Brocchini

Susanne Fritzer

Marco Gillio Tos

Yvonne Glowatzki

Susan Hippen

Ursula Kose

Lars Krückeberg

César Henriques Matos e Silva

Chris Peck

Anne-Maria Pichler

Michael Prytula

Roland Tusch

Ulrich von Ey

Chris Wallace

Mark Mack Los Angeles

1949	born in Judenburg, Austria
1963–68	Technical High School, Graz, Austria
1973	Degree of Architecture at the Academy of Fine Arts, Vienna, Austria
1973–76	Collaboration with Hausrucker and Emilio Ambasz, New York
1976	Foundation of "Western Addition", organization devoted to fine architecture
1978	Partnership with Andrew Batey (Batey & Mack)
1980	Co-founder and editor of Archetype Magazine
1984	Foundation of his own firm MACK

Teaching positions

1977–96	Lectures at the Universities of California, Southern California, Miami, Colorado, Oregon, Washington, Arkansas, Princeton University, J.P. Getty Center Santa Monica, SCI ARC, L. A., USA: Graz Technical University, Austria; Academy of Fine Arts Munich, Germany; Architectural Association, Great Britain; (amongst others)
1992	Professor of Architecture at the University of California, Berkley, USA

Selection of work

1980	Bellevue Townhouses, Pasadena, USA
1984	Greentree Commons, Sacramento, USA
1985	J.P. Getty Center for the History of Art and the Humanities, Santa Monica, USA
1986	Bogner Showroom, New York, USA
1987	Bogner Store, Munich, Germany
1988	Boise Museum of Art (Expansion and Remodel), Boise, USA
1989	Headlands Center for the Arts, Sausalito, USA
1991	Kashii District Housing, Fukuoka, Japan
1991	Candlestick Park, San Francisco, USA

Major exhibitions

1974	Carnegie Mellon University, Pittsburgh, USA
1980	Yale University, New Haven, USA
1988	Berlin Kunsthalle, Berlin, D
1989	Centre Pompidou, Paris, F
1992	Leo Castelli / Larry Gagosian Gallery, New York, USA
1993	Santa Monica Contemporary Museum, Santa Monica, USA
1993	The Royal Institute of British Architects Heinz Gallery, London, GB
1993	San Francisco Museum of Modern Art, San Francisco, USA
	UCLA Graduate School of Architecture and Urban Planning, Los Angeles, USA

Publications

1979	New Americans, Catalogue, Rome, I
1980	Young Architects, Catalogue, Yale University, USA
1980	Biennale, Catalogue, Venice, I
1985	Art, Architecture & Landscape, Catalogue, San Francisco Museum of Modern Art, USA
1987	The Emerging Generation in the USA, Catalogue, GA Gallery, Tokyo, J
1988	Berlin: Denkmal oder Denkmodell?, Catalogue, Kunsthalle, Berlin
1989	14 x Amerika - Gedenkbibliothek: Architects From the U.S. Planning For Berlin, Berlin, D

Prizes / Awards

1984	Architectural Record, Award for Excellence in Planning and Design: Villa in Corpus Christi (with Batey & Mack)
1986	Sonoma League for Historic Preservation, Award of Excellence: Knipschild Residence (with Batey & Mack)
1989	Architectural Record, Award for Excellence in Planning and Design: Whitney Residence, Santa Monica
1990	Progressive Architecture Design Citation Award, Kashii District Housing, Fukuoka

Corporal architecture Mark Mack

Back in Vienna

I am glad that I can come back to Austria in such a nice way as to be invited to lectures and exhibitions. I feel like a drop out who left Austria in the early 70's after a lot of turbulence in the academy and architectural culture of that time. It was really a kind of non physical time for most of us. We did not generate buildings or forms, we generated ideas and programs, and everybody else as well as architects were involved in the form giving of our environment. And in this kind of climate of the 1970`s, Vienna seemed very programmed to me, very grey, very distant. Not only did I come from the province and had to set foot into this imperial city but I also felt that the sophistication and internal academic rigor was a little bit over my head. So I gladly accepted the invitation to work for an architecture group which didn't quite have there act together but nevertheless worked on the roof tops in New York. So just one day after graduation from the Academy I landed in New York and was thrown into a whole different environment. Not only physically but also mentally. While Vienna was a city of excuses, New York at that time was really a city with no excuses. Everything was seemingly happening, there were events of leisure, events of culture which were too many to count. In New York it seemed that nothing was set. New York was an exciting place for me. Still I felt that the kind of exposure the city and the complexity the city offered was still a little bit too strong for my kind of useful, and fairly simple head at that particular time. So I went to California which was and still is, a very primitive area. Not primitive in a sense that there is no culture or that there is no structure, but the stucture itself is very loose and very unorganized. The unbound wildness of the countryside, and the unstructured city life is in contrast to the sophisticated urban patterns and urban articulation which we know from Europe or even from the East coast of America. In order to do architecture again, I had to relearn architecture because the kind of architecture I was exposed to in school and the kind of architecture which I did in New York, was of highly conceptual nature and did not really lend itself to a kind of physicalness. So at that time in California there was an architectural vacuum in which one had to articulate oneself in order to gain physical form. It was also a place were physicalness, bodyness and the relationship to the elements was of high priority. So in this kind of physical climate I was very much attracted to go towards a more physical interpretation of architecture and away from a conceptual level.

Duality

The area where I grew up, Styria, the architectural iconography was very tight, produced by the climatic condition. When we went on vacation we went to places which were a physical and mental excitement. It was always a very simple place full of a different kinds of climatic conditions, Greek Islands and the Dalmatian coast and the architecture in itself stood out as an element which was much more in contrast with the strong elements of nature. The same kind of attitude I recaptured in San Francisco. I was less interested in the complexity of the city itself but rather in the very strong and robust nature around San Francisco. And this kind of duality also prompted my first real investigations into architecture. This was a conceptual project which was called "10 Californian houses", and it was a substitute for real architectural work, investigations and manipulation of architctural programs.

Vienna Housing

Forefathers

The architectural precidence and forefathers was very much in the back of my head – the kind of education I got in Vienna under Roland Rainer and the overpowering and conceptual yet physical work of Adolf Loos became a guide in terms of relating sociological and cultural ideas to architecture. The houses which interested me were the kind of houses that came not only out of the "Raum-Plan", but which also dealt with an exterior manipulation of space. And even earlier work of Irving Gill in California, around 1906, was experimenting with similar ideas, not so much in space but in terms of articulation and connection of interior and exterior space, and came away with a very clear and open language of architecture. Or Rudolph Schindler – his kind of 20's and experimental attitude about architecture, his open spaces which he created to sleep outside, to see architecture as a kind of promoter of health. Exterior living was and is an influence when you live in California, especially Southern California.

Stremmel house

First houses

So my first houses were really a kind of combination of all these forefathers and influences, and grew out of the previous occupation with the landscape and the idea of the house being transformed, or the architecture transforming the landscape. The first house, which I call the "Anti-Villa" was a semi underground house, rooms in front built into a hill. The rooms are just really lined up one by one, looking south, and a struggling vine is growing over the front, hopefully shading the structure.

Generic rooms

The next projects continued to work with the landscape which mainly generate a typology of sort. When I started working in the Napa valley, which is quite different from San Francisco, in fact, it has almost a North African or Southern Spanish climate. It is vulcanic and very dry, that is why good wine can be made there. I looked for a similar house typology to do houses, which in this case is not only a house but also a small winery for a wine-maker. I looked at these southern typologies, the atrium houses, the house with big walls around it to create an internal shade structure through walls, with two workshops in front of it, with the house starting properly in the back. This created a strong architecture working against the nature, not in a kind of destructive way, in a way that nature can be complimentary in terms of color.
A kind of autonomous state of architecture, against nature, or in relationship to nature. Another principle for these houses was the idea of privacy, or of the notion of a publicness, as well as a privateness.

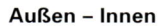

Privateness

When I lived in Vienna you were never invited into somebodys house because you always met in cafes, you met in public places, you never really penetrated into the sort of innermost portions of the house, you maybe waited in the hall or maybe in the living room but you never went into the kitchen or the bedroom. When I came to America the moment you enter a house, you are shown the bedroom because there is no closet to put the coats. So everybody is invited into the bedroom to put their coat onto the bed. Then you know the most private part of the house. It generates a kind of attitude about how guarded and how one lives with a certain sense of privacy which is very different from the European example. Similarly the picture window which looks out over the kind of useless front lawn is also an invitation to look inside the house. When you draw the curtains, neighbours might think something bad is going on. So you always leave it open, and the lamp, in this sort of suburban stillife, is very present. I tried with some of these house types to counteract this element of transparent privacy. So some of the next houses are really a kind of a variation on this theme. I tried to develope, through this a series of experiments, a language - a kind of Californian language, which I more and more refined and then used in larger projects.

Exterior – interior

The idea of creating an exterior space goes back to the ideas of Schindler and the early health movement in California. The idea that you can sleep outside, that you actually can live outside. In California you only need a garden with a roof to sleep under. This makes a house. Another idea of these houses is the idea of inner compactness, almost in a Loosian sense, to create a "Raum-plan", the sectional plan, idea of small rooms, high rooms stacked on top of each other. Inside rooms make it to outside rooms, elements in which a trellis interweaves the exterior with the interior, and creates not a facade but rather a permeable structure in which you can go in and out. The most Californian house for me is in Reno, Nevada.

Larger projects

The larger projects are really dealing very much with the experience from these smaller elements, houses, and furniture. In an urban park near San Francisco, Candlestick Point, which was a collaboration between a landscape architect, an artist, and myself. We tried not only to create a park landscape, but we also had to provide a theater space, an outdoor perfomance space, and in addition, programmatically we tried to make the connection to the water more immediate, more pleasant. There was a lot of wind coming from one direction, which created this kind of dune-like earth mounts behind which there is no wind, and where you can have picnics. Also the artist made a wind gate, which is a kind of wind organ. When wind arrives it blows through various holes and creates a sound. But the building itself is very simple, it had one body which is the body of the theater, the backstage, one part which was the auditorium, and then one part which sticks out, and becomes again a trellice, a pergola which makes the links to the landscapes and containing the functions which are to service the whole park. For a project in Berlin, which was a competition, an extension to an existing "American library" because it was funded by America.

I wanted to make a kind of non-monumental sort of library, something which reaches out onto a plaza, creates a covered space, a pergola, an entry approach to the library. This wing was going to be the childrens' library. So to create a kind of open space, a free space which serves the city and also serves the library. Not a kind of monument because there were already so many in Berlin. Another project, Arts Park in Los Angeles, was an artistic Childrens Center in an area which is a retention basin for the Los Angeles' floods, all this area is artificially created on a very low point and can store a lot of water. There is already one lake inside here so all of the structure had to be lifted up from the ground a certain height in order to keep safe from the water. So we tried to create again a kind of very open structure, a sort of tree-like roof which both serves as a tree-house building environment, but also a blanket fort which will be essentially an outdoor corridor under which all these buildings are connected the theater, the restaurant, the mediatheque, the exhibition space, the administration, and the class rooms. All of them are separated and articulated by colored and different materials, and strung along this corridor.

The trellis as mediator

For a competition for a museum in Napa Valley, I tried to make the center of the museum, the lobby if you will, or the distribution center for all the kind of activities of an outdoor space. The entry and the portico become one, in a climate which is very outdoor oriented, a continuation of the outdoor space going through the meeting room, the administration, and the museum all coming off this central pergola. Many ideas which were really important for me, in terms of learning from the houses, I could employ in a large kind of demonstration project in Japan. We were invited by Arata Isozaki who collected Steven Holl, Rem Koolhaas, myself, Ishiyama, Portzamparc from Paris, and Tusquets from Spain to do a kind of perimeter city. All the housing developments in Japan are pretty much linear, slab buildings because they face south and easily get the requirements for sunlight and ventilation and all the circulation is on the north side. I got a kind of corner site, and early on tried to formulate some ideas about this particular site. There was a residential street with a three story height limit and a commercial street which had a six story height limit. So going up to this kind of boundary I created two sides with one a residential side, and then a commercial side. The next idea I wanted to fulfill was a variety of living, different units, and different opportunities of living in one building. Walk up apartments and stores, two story maisonettes or duplexes, and then atrium houses on top. And the third idea was to create public space, semi-private space and then private space, gradually separating these spaces from each other.

Californian lessons

In a way coming back to Europe, I tried to introduce lessons of the Californian Home and the ideas which were developed in a climate of openess, and ease of life, with a confused sense of privacy and public realm. And I hope to explore this sense of open, loose, undogmatic and colorful design attitude for the Seminar and the Area of the Erdberg district. In Vienna.

Fukuoka Wohnbau / Fukuoka housing

Integration und Aufwertung – Landschaftsplan für suburbane Stadtgebiete. Erdberger Mais, Wien 3

Das „Erdberger Mais", vormals Teil der Aulandschaft der Donau, später erwerbsgärtnerisch genutzt, bezeichnet heute ein Industrie- und Gewerbegebiet – Standort historischer städtischer Versorgungsbetriebe ebenso wie öffentlicher Einrichtungen (Staatsarchiv, Zollamt, u.a.), die aus zentralen Lagen abgesiedelt wurden. Eine mit Vollanschluß angebundene, stark belastete Stadtautobahn durchquert in Hochlage das Gebiet. An der Endstelle der U-Bahn im Nordosten des Gebietes existiert eine Park & Ride - Anlage mit Büros und Geschäften. Östlich der Autobahn, auf einem ehemaligen großen Schlachthofareal, haben sich Unternehmen des Textilgroßhandels, Speditionen, u.a. etabliert. Ein kleiner erhaltener Teil dieses Areals an der Baumgasse beherbergt ein wichtiges Veranstaltungszentrum der jungen Musikszene („Arena"). In etwas weiterer Gehentfernung befinden sich vier historische Gasometergebäude, für die neue, hochwertige Nutzungen angestrebt werden.

Im Zuge von Strukturanpassungen und Modernisierungen werden Flächen für neue Nutzungen disponibel. Damit ergibt sich eine Chance, die Kontinuität einer problematischen städebaulichen Entwicklung, die das Erscheinungsbild einer zerteilten, suburbanen Zone mit z.T. prekären Nutzungen, räumlichen Barrieren, etc. über lange Jahre geprägt hat, zu unterbrechen und eine Aufwertung und Urbanisierung des Gebietes zu ermöglichen.

Einen wichtigen Beitrag dazu könnte eine zusammenhängende Landschaftsplanung aus bestehenden und noch zu schaffenden Grünräumen, landwirtschaftlichen Flächen, Landschaftselementen (Terrassenkante) und Bezügen zu nahen Landschaftsräumen (Donaukanal, Prater) leisten. Eine anspruchsvolle Grün- und Freiraumplanung sollte dazu beitragen, die räumliche Isoliertheit von Nutzungen (Nutzungsinseln) zu verringern, Barrieren zu überwinden und Leerräume zu integrieren.

Erdberger Mais, Wien 3

Integration and upgrading – landscape plan for suburban city areas. Erdberger Mais, Vienna 3

The "Erdberger Mais", once part of the Danube meadows, then later used for commercial gardening, today is mainly used for industrial and commercial purposes - the site of historical Viennese utilities as well as public institutions (State's official archive, customs office, etc.) were relocated from central locations. An elevated city highway with a local exit and high traffic density crosses the area. We find large park & ride facilities featuring an integrated office - and shopping center, at the terminal of the underground line in the North-East of the area. East of the highway, textile wholesalers, carriers, etc. have set up shop on the premises of a former slaughterhouse. A small, preserved part of this historical area on Baumgasse houses an important venue for the young music scene ("Arena"). Four historic gasometer buildings, for which new, high-quality uses are being aimed at, are located at a somewhat greater walking distance.

Areas become available for new uses as part of structural adaptations and modernizations, providing an opportunity for interrupting the continuity of a problematic urban development, characterized for many years by the appearance of a split, suburban zone of partly precarious uses, spatial barriers, etc. and enabling an upgrading and an urbanization of the area.

A continuous landscape planning, consisting of already existing and still to be created green zones, agricultural areas, landscape elements (terrace edge), and references to nearby landscapes (Danube Canal, Prater, etc.) might constitute an important contribution.

A high-quality planning of the green and undeveloped areas might help to reduce the spatial isolation of uses, overcome barriers, and integrate undeveloped zones.

Manifest für das kontrollierte Chaos

Annäherung

Der Erdberger Mais fungierte bisher als Abstellraum der Stadt. Das Durcheinander und die Verschiedenartigkeit seines Inhalts machen diesen Ort, an dem Industrie, Wohnen, Kultur und Freizeit wahrhaftig miteinander vermischt werden, lebendig. Das Gebiet ist durch seine Offenheit, Nutzungskombinationen und seine ungeplante Entwicklung ein ungewöhnlicher Stadtteil, der somit auch auf unkonventionelle Weise erschlossen werden kann. Die alte Stadt baute auf alten Konzepten auf, wohingegen die neue Stadt in Hinblick auf die derzeitigen und künftigen Anforderungen an Verkehr, Kommunikation, Interaktion, Wohnen und die Interessen der Einwohner geplant werden sollte. Den neuen Entwicklungsgebieten kann man nicht die Muster der Vergangenheit aufoktroyieren. Neue Strukturen und Organisationsformen müssen diesem neuen Geist der Toleranz und den vielseitigen Funktionen des Ortes Ausdruck geben. Dank der Vielschichtigkeit und der Komplexität der Planungsideen können Gruppen von unterschiedlicher Herkunft, verschiedenen Alters und von mannigfaltigen kulturellen Werten hier zusammenleben. Die neue Stadt muß Platz für alle bieten. Der weltweite Trend zu sozialem und beruflichem Aufstieg führt zu einer homogenen Stadt. Randgruppen, wie Jugendliche, Obdachlose, Senioren und

Manifesto for controlled chaos

Approach

Erdberger Mais has functioned as an neglected space by the city. The jumble and diversity of its contents create a vitality for the place. Industry, housing, culture and leisure are truly mixed together. The area is an abnormal part of the city in its openness, mixture of uses, and unplanned development. It, therefore, can be developed in a non-traditional way. The old city was built based on old parameters, and the new city should be planned according to the current and future requirements of traffic, communication, interaction, housing, and people's interests. Patterns of the past cannot be duplicated over the new areas of development. New structure and new organization need to express this new spirit of tolerance and flexible functions of the place. Through layered and intermixed planning, groups of different ages, origins, and cultural values can live together. The new city must give room to everybody. The global trend of gentrification and upward mobility is producing a homogenous city. The people on the fringe of these patterns, like the youth, homeless, elderly and foreigners are less and less tolerated. Open layers of the city development where people can have free choice in their decisions about living and

Ausländer, werden immer weniger toleriert. Offene Gegenden, in denen Menschen frei über ihre Lebensweise und ihr Umfeld entscheiden können, sind in der Stadtentwicklung notwendig. Die neuen Stadtbewohner finden ein neues Arbeits- und Freizeitumfeld vor. Intensivere Arbeitsbedingungen verlangen immer mehr Möglichkeiten zum Streßabbau. Der Trend zu kürzeren, aber häufigeren Urlauben bedeutet, daß die neue Stadt Freizeit- und Erholungsgebiete, sowohl innerhalb, als auch außerhalb der Stadt, braucht. Durch die niedrigeren Kosten und die bessere Organisation der weltweiten Mobilität kann der Städter leicht in exotische Gefilde entfliehen, wobei unsere neue Stadt allerdings auch nahe, kurzfristige Zuflucht- und Regenerationsmöglichkeiten braucht. Wohnhäuser müssen neuen Anforderungen einer sich verändernden Bevölkerung und sich wandelnder Lebensformen gerecht werden. Die Straßenmuster entstanden zur Zeit der Pferdekutschen und Eisenbahnen. Neue Fortbewegungsmittel werden die Straßen und die Entwicklung der neuen Stadt prägen. Fahrräder, Rollerblades, windbetriebene Experimentalfahrzeuge, elektrische Schnellzüge, effizientere Autos, Flugzeuge und kleine Boote werden neue Pfade und Verbindungen schaffen. Der Erdberger Mais bietet die Möglichkeit, der neuen offenen Stadt, die in einem kontrollierten Chaos auf mehreren Ebenen organisiert ist, Gestalt zu verleihen.

their environments are needed. The new city dwellers are facing a new environment of work and leisure. More intense working conditions demand more and more stress relief, and the trend towards shorter but more frequent vacations means the city needs leisure and recreation areas both inside and outside the city. Cheaper and more organized global mobility gives the city dweller exotic escapes, yet the demand for nearby and short term escape and regeneration is also necessary for our new city. Housing will conform to new demands of changing demographics and changing lifestyles. Street patterns were formed at a time of horse drawn carriages and railroads. New forms of transportation will shape the streets and urban development of the new city. Bikes, rollerblades, wind driven experiments, electric fast trains, more efficient cars, airplanes and small crafts will create new paths and connections. The Erdberger Mais offers a possibility to give form to the new open city, which is organized by layers of controlled chaos. In concepts for controlled chaos, the Erdberger Mais was able to absorb the abnormalities of the city which makes it a vital place. Some organization is needed to pull this area together and make it part of the city, connecting the site with other parts of the city and creating new spaces for the city.

Monumente
Der Erdberger Mais wurde zu einer Art Lagerraum für alles, was die Homogenität der Altstadt störte. Alle sperrigen, unangenehmen oder merkwürdigen Funktionen wurden völlig ungeordnet hierher abgeschoben. Diese Eigenschaft sollte dadurch betont werden, daß man freien Raum für spezielle Aktivitäten vorsieht. Dies kann nicht mit einem traditionellen Stadtplan, sondern nur mit einer Vision für eine neue Stadtlandschaft erreicht werden. Wir schlagen mehrere große, autonome Gebäude vor, deren Maßstab ein Magnetfeld erzeugt, das das Gebiet definiert und strukturiert. Gemeinsam mit den Gasometern und anderen bestehenden Gebäuden, wie dem Schlachthof und der Arena, verleihen sie dem Ort Orientierung und Identität. Die neu ausgerichteten Monumente können verschiedene Funktionen haben, da es sich ja um multifunktionale und mehrzonige Gebäude handelt. Sie ermöglichen nicht nur ein künftiges Wachsen dieses Gebiets durch die Bereitstellung von Raum, sondern auch eine Konzentration von offenem Raum. Wie große Steine oder Ameisenhaufen definieren die Monumente den Raum, sodaß er relativ „leer" bleiben kann.

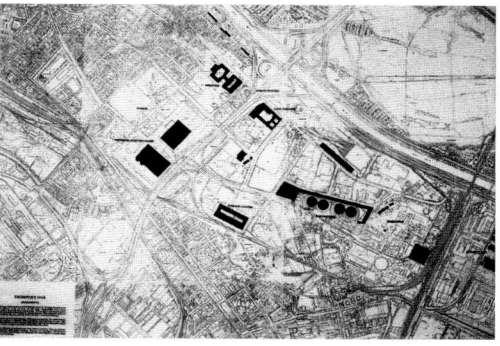

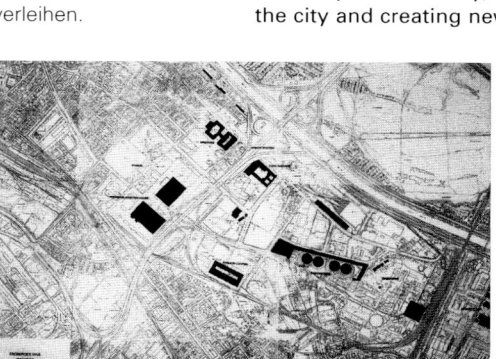

Monumente / Monuments

Monuments
The Erdberger Mais has become a kind of storage space for all things that disturbed the homogeneity of the old town. All the bulky, disagreeable and curious functions were deposited there without order. This quality of disorder should be enhanced to provide a free space for special activities. This cannot be achieved with a traditional city plan, but only with a vision for a new city landscape. We propose several large buildings which are autonomous. The scale of these buildings produces a magnetic field that defines and organizes the area. With the Gasometers and other existing monuments such as the slaughter house and the Arena, they give orientation and identity to the place. The new monuments can have several functions. They are all multifunctional and multi-zoned buildings. These monuments allow, not only for the future growth of this area through the provision of space, but also for a concentration of open space. Like large stones or anthills the monuments define the space so it can stay relatively "empty".

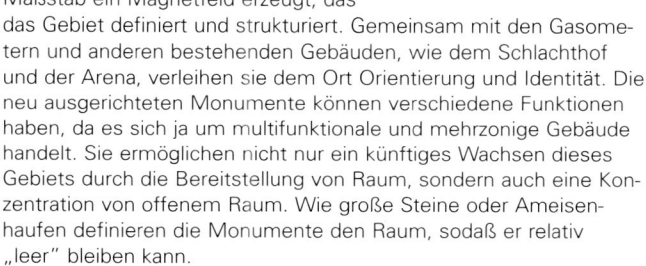

Wohnbau
Das Zentrum des Geländes wird durch das Fehlen von Wohnbauten bestimmt. Zur Belebung jedes Stadtgebietes benötigt man Wohnungen, doch die Anforderungen des lebenswerten und erstrebenswerten Wohnens, wie Licht, frische Luft, Infrastruktur und Grünraum werden am Erdberger Mais nicht überall erfüllt. Wir schlagen mehrere Wohnlösungen für dieses Gelände vor. Im offenen Gebiet wird eine niedrige Wohnanlage mit hoher Dichte in die kleinen landwirtschaftlich genutzten Grundstücke und Häuser integriert. Sowohl im Agrar- als auch im Industriegebiet werden Wohntypen vorgeschlagen, bei denen eine leichte Wohnstruktur Arbeitsbereiche überlagert. Wohn- und Arbeitseinheiten werden in die Struktur des Schlachthofes eingefügt. In den eher industriellen Gebieten werden kleine Appartementhochhäuser in den verschiedenen, übrig gebliebenen offenen Räumen verteilt, während im Westen traditionellere Wiener Wohnblöcke die Verbindung über die Schlachthausgasse verstärken. Größere Wohnanlagen, wie z.B. für Studenten und

Housing
The center of the site is characterized by the absence of housing. To vitalize any area of the city, housing is needed. Yet the requirements for liveable and desirable housing: light, fresh air, infrastructure and greenspace, are not widely available in Erdberger Mais. We propose several housing solutions for the site. In the open area, a low rise high density development is integrated with the small agricultural plots and houses. In both the areas of agriculture and industry, types of housing are proposed in which a light structure for living is superimposed over working zones. Live/work units are inserted into the slaughter house structure. In the more industrial areas, small apartment highrises are interspersed into the various left over open spaces. To the west more traditional Viennese block housing will reinforce the connection across Schlachthausstraße. Larger housing compounds like student housing, a senior home and transient housing complex will be combined with the large buildings (the monuments) on the site.

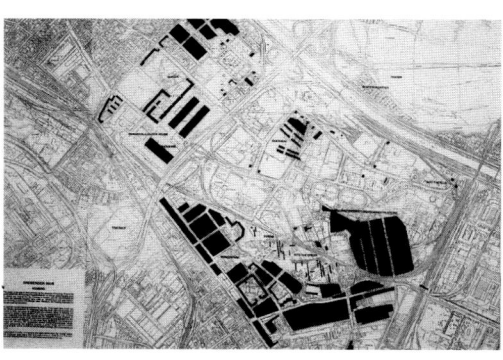

Wohnbau / Housing

Pensionisten sowie Durchgangswohnungen, werden mit den großen Gebäuden (Monumenten) auf dem Gelände verknüpft. Durch die Umstrukturierung des Verkehrs, der Verbindungen und des offenen Raums wird der „leere" Raum im Erdberger Mais zu einem vitalen und nutzbaren Lebensraum.

Industrie

Im wesentlichen werden die Industrie- und Bürogebiete im Erdberger Mais so bleiben, wie sie jetzt sind. Wir werden sie mit verschiedenen anderen Ebenen überlagern, sodaß dieser Ort einen vitaleren Charakter erhält. Dieses Schichtprinzip ermöglicht die Koexistenz von Funktionen, die sich ansonsten wohl nicht vermischen. „Schlechte" Branchen (Geruchsbelästigung und Emissionen) werden abgesiedelt, wodurch der Raum für andere Zwecke frei wird. Die Gaswerke werden eingeschränkt und die Anlage/der Technopark der Technischen Universität wird mit den Industriekomplexen im Erdberger Mais verbunden. Die Ebenen der Monumente und Verbindungen bieten Raum, in dem sich Branchen verschiedener Gestalt und Form ausdehnen können. Im Erdberger Mais steht die Industrie, die Form und Charakter des Gebietes prägte, für die Geschichte des Geländes. Dieser ungeordnete und freie Geist sollte erhalten bleiben. Die „Aufwertung" oder Verbesserung des Geländes muß so vonstatten gehen, daß der „freie" und „leere" Raum des alten Erdberger Mais bewahrt werden kann.

Verbindungen

Trotz seiner Nähe zum Zentrum Wiens hat sich der Erdberger Mais auf unkonventionelle Weise entwickelt. Wir versuchen, ihn in das Gefüge der ihn umgebenden Stadt zu integrieren und gleichzeitig den abwechslungsreichen, offenen Charakter des Standortes zu wahren, der sich aufgrund seiner Barrieren (Schienen, Donaukanal, Autobahn) und der ungewöhnlichen, hier angesiedelten Funktionen (Gaswerke, Schlachthof, Staatsarchiv und kleine Landwirtschaftsbetriebe) entwickelte. Die Einführung einer höheren Dichte, zusätzlicher Wohnanlagen, öffentlichen Raums, von Kulturzentren und mehr öffentlichen Verkehrsmitteln erfordert es, neue Prototypen für die Verbindung der ungleichartigen Gebiete des Erdberger Mais zu finden. Wege für alternative Fortbewegungsmittel, wie Fahrräder, Rollerbladers, für Fußgänger und öffentliche Verkehrsmittel müsen geschaffen werden. Verschiedene Verbindungsstrategien werden eingesetzt, um das Schicksal dieses „leeren Raums" zu formen. Überbrücken und Durchdringen der Grenzen und Barrieren des Geländes: Plattformen zum Prater und neue Funktionen und Aktivitäten unter der Autobahn – Kirche, Stadion, Markt, Erholung am Kanalufer, Sporteinrichtungen und Kurbad. Umwandlung der bestehenden Infrastruktur für neue Zwecke: Bahnsteige und Autobahnrampen für Erholungszwecke. Verwendung von Wohnelementen zur Verbindung: Wohnanlagen mischen sich mit Industrie- und Agrargebieten. Die Konzentration auf die Verbindungen verschiebt den räumlichen Schwerpunkt des Geländes vom Objekt in einer Landschaft zum Raum dazwischen und macht somit den ehemals „leeren" Raum zu einem bedeutungsvollen, positiven Raum. Der „leere" Raum heilt die Risse und Barrieren des Geländes.

Offener Raum

Der neue offene Raum verbindet das bestehende Wohngebiet visuell und programmatisch mit dem Industriegebiet, den Schlachthof mit den Gasometern. Der offene Raum wird entlang der Sichtachsen der bestehenden und neuen Monumente geschaffen.

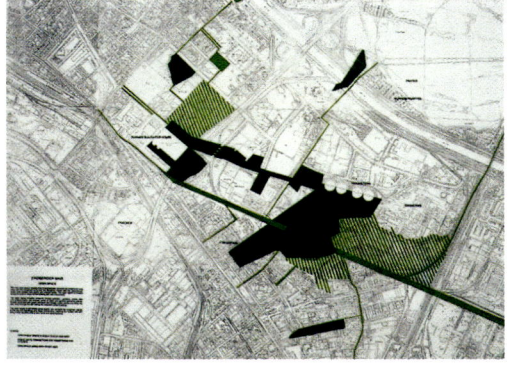

Verbindungen / Connections

Offener Raum / Open space

Reorganization of traffic, connections, and open space make the "empty" space of the Erdberger Mais into a vital and useable area in which to live.

Industry

Basically, the industrial and office areas in Erdberger Mais will remain as they exist now. We will overlay several other zones with these to create a more vital character for the place. This layering principle allows for the coexistance of functions that otherwise may not mingle. Bad (odors and emissions) industries will be removed from the area, thus freeing the space for other uses. The Gas Works will be reduced and the development/techno park on the Technical University will be linked with the Erdberger Mais industrial complexes. The layers of monuments and connections provide expansion space for industries of different shapes and forms. In the Erdberger Mais the industry represents the history of the site and has shaped the form and character of the site. This unordered and free spirit should remain. The "gentrification" or improvement of the site must progress in a manner that the "free" and "empty" space of the old Erdberger Mais can be preserved.

Connections

Despite its proximity to the center of Vienna, the Erdberger Mais has developed in an untraditional way. We seek to integrate it into the fabric of the surrounding city, while retaining the varied, open nature of the site. This character has developed due to the barriers on the site (rail lines, Danube Canal, the freeway) and the unusual functions located there (gasworks, slaughter house, city archives and small scale agriculture). The infusion of higher density, additional housing, public space, cultural centers and more public transportation into the site makes it necessary to find new prototypes of connections for the disparate areas of the Erdberger Mais. New forms of transportation, such as bicycles, rollerskates, pedestrian paths and busses need to be accomodated on the site. Not only new paths and bustops are necessary, but new forms of connections as well. Several strategies of connecting are used to shape the destiny of this "empty space". Bridging and penetrating the borders and barriers of the site: Platforms to the Prater and new functions and activities under the freeway - church, stadium, market, hardscape recreation, sport facilities, and spa. Converting existing infrastructure to serve new purposes: Railroad platform walkways and ramps of the freeway for recreation. Using housing elements to connect: housing mixes with industrial and agricultural areas. The concentration on the connections shifts the spatial emphasis of the site from the object in a landscape to a focus on the space in-between and, therefore, makes the former "empty" space into a meaningful and positive space. The "empty" space repairs the rifts and barriers of the site.

Open space

The new open space visually and programatically connects the existing housing area with the industrial zone and the slaughter house with the Gasometers. The open space is created along the lines of vision of the existing and new monuments.

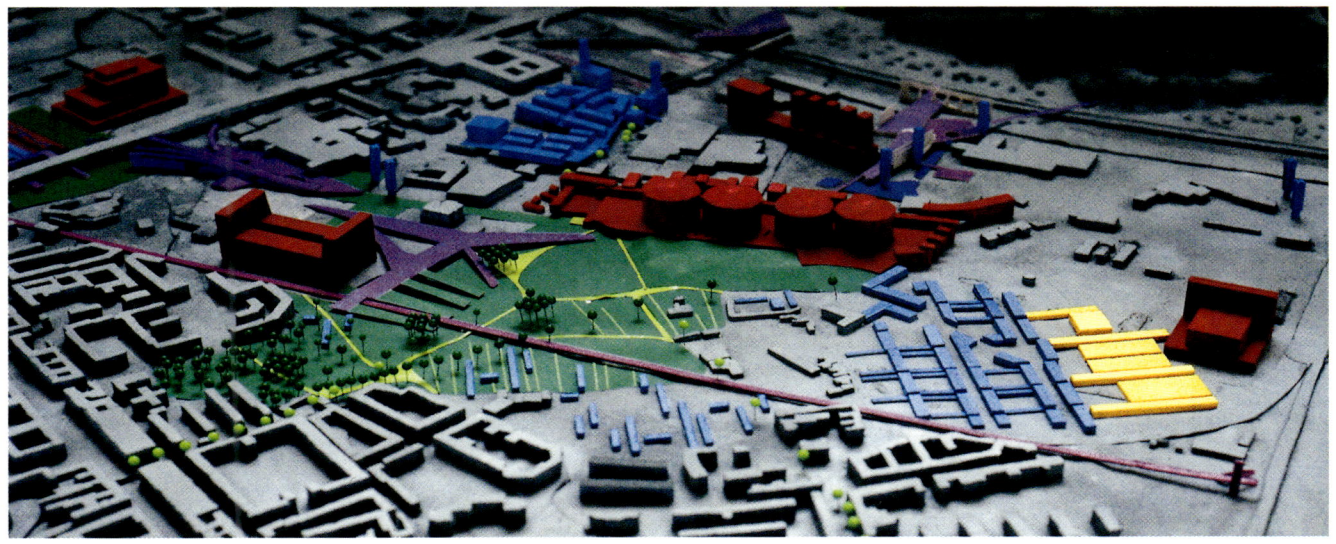

Präsentationsmodell / Presentation model

Einzelprojekte

Ulrich von Ey

Auf dem ganzen Gelände wirken große Bauten als Orientierungspunkte und strukturieren es für den Besucher. Diese großen Gebäude bieten Raumreserven für das wachsende Gebiet, wobei eines ein Sport- und Schwimmzentrum sowie Studentenwohnungen enthält. Die bestehende Verwaltung der Gaswerke wird gemeinsam mit einer Angestelltenschule und einer Reparaturwerkstätte für industrielle Ausrüstung und Autos in einem anderen Gebäude untergebracht werden. Das Modezentrum umfaßt Einzelhandelsgeschäfte, Büros, einen Präsentationsraum und einen Großhandelsmarkt.

Ulrich von Ey

Lars Krückeberg und Marco Gillio Tos

Die bestehenden Wahrzeichen (die Gasometer und die Arena) geben dem Gebiet derzeit seine Identität. Ihre Kraft wird durch das Einbringen neuer Funktionen verstärkt: U-Bahnstation, Einkaufszentrum, Hotel und Büroraum. Die Erinnerung an das Vergangene und das Potential des künftigen Charakters wird weiterentwickelt, sodaß besondere Plätze geschaffen und neue Lebensformen ermöglicht werden.

Lars Krückeberg and Marco Gillio Tos

Roland Tusch

Die alte Schlachthofhalle liegt zwischen dem neuen Studentenwohnheim im Nordosten und der Technischen Universität im Westen. Durch das Einfügen von Werkstätten für Studenten und junge Künstler wird das Gebiet für die Bewohner bereichert. Die Werkstätten der Künstler und Handwerker werden in Containern untergebracht: Tischler, Schneider, Töpfer, Glaser, Maler, Bildhauer usw. Offene und geschlossene öffentliche Bereiche können für kulturelle Ereignisse genutzt werden: Kino, Performances, Ausstellungen, Vorträge, Feste etc.

Lars Krückeberg and Marco Gillio Tos

Roland Tusch

Individual projects

Ulrich von Ey

Big Buildings, placed throughout the site, act as landmarks and organize the site for the visitor. These large buildings provide resevoirs of space for the growing area. One houses a Sport and Swimming Center, and Student Apartments. The existing Gas Works Administration is housed in another along with an Employee School and a workshop for industrial equipment and cars. The Fashion Center includes Retail Space, Offices, a Showroom, and a Wholesale Market.

Lars Krückeberg and Marco Gillio Tos

The existing landmarks (the Gasometers and the Arena) currently provide an identitiy for the area. The power of the landmarks is enhanced with the infusion of new functions: U-Bahn station, a Retail Mall, and Hotel and Office Space. The memory of what was, and the potential of future character is developed to produce special places and new lifestyle possibilities.

Roland Tusch

The old slaughterhouse shed lies between new student housing to the Northeast and the Technical University to the West. The insertion of workshops for students and amateur artists enriches the area for its inhabitants. Artists and craftsmen´s workshops are housed in containers: carpenters, tailors, potters, glazers, painters, sculpters, etc.. Open and enclosed public areas can be used for cultural events: Cinema, performances, exhibitions, lectures, parties, etc.

Cesar Henriques Matos e Silva
Durch die Einbindung von Wohnraum in ein bestehendes Industriegebiet wird ein multifunktionaler Raum geschaffen. Diese neuen Wohnprojekte verbinden Wohnen mit Arbeiten. Eine neue Stadt und eine neue Lebensweise überlagern die bestehende Stadt.

Susanne Fritzer
Paare von Apartmenthochhäusern, die über das gesamte Gelände verteilt werden, dienen als Markierung und als Tore – sowohl von innen, als auch von außen. Die Gebäude sind schon von weitem sichtbar, sodaß man den Erdberger Mais erkennt. Der Blick aus den Wohnungen auf die Stadt erlaubt es den Bewohnern, ihren Platz innerhalb des größeren Ganzen der Stadt zu finden, wodurch ihr Heim ein Gefühl für den Ort vermittelt. Leichte Wohnstrukturen überlagern Arbeitszonen (landwirtschaftliche Grundstücke) und sorgen so für eine neue Art des Wohnens.

Cord Bertko
Neue Wohnanlagen, die alte Stadttypen anklingen lassen, setzen die Dichte der traditionellen Stadt in das öde Gebiet der Gaswerke hinein fort, sodaß die Lücke, die sich aufgrund der Schienentrasse durch das Gelände zieht, geschlossen wird. Auch neue Industriebauten tragen zu dieser neuen Dichte bei.

Clint Wallace
Die Verbindung über den Donaukanal führt den Fußgänger- und Fahrradverkehr gemeinsam über die ungleichen Gebiete von Schiene und Straße. Straßenverkäufer und Parknutzung erstrecken sich vom Prater nach Erdberg. Geneigte Ebenen steigen zwischen den einzelnen Teilen an, grüne und bepflanzte Gebiete reichen in das städtische Ödland hinein und ermöglichen leichte Verbindungen, kontrollierten Zugang und ein Überschneiden mit bestehenden Verkehrsknoten.

Chris Peck
Schon die Anfänge des ausufernden Autoverkehrs werden durch die Schaffung eines zentralen Parkplatzes, der mit einer grünen Hülle versehen wird und die verschiedenen angrenzenden Gebiete des Standortes anbindet, bekämpft. Wohngebäude werden an den Rändern der neuen öffentlichen Hauptverkehrsstraße angesiedelt, Monumente ragen durch sie hindurch und Fuß- und Fahrradwege überqueren sie.

Cesar Henriques Matose e Silva

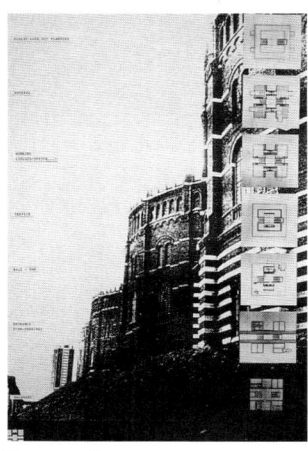

Susanne Fritzer

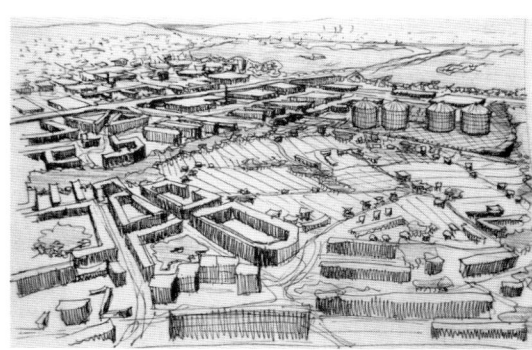

Cord Bertko

Clint Wallace

Chris Peck

Cesar Henriques Matose e Silva
The insertion of housing into an existing industrial area creates a multifunctional space. This new housing combines living and working. A new city and way of living is superimposed over the existing city.

Susanne Fritzer
Pairs of highrise apartment towers placed throughout the site serve as markers and gateways for both the person inside the building and outside,. From the outside, the buildings can be seen from far away and can be a landmark of the Erdberger Mais. The views of the city from inside the apartments allow the dweller to place himself within the greater whole of the city, giving a sense of place to the home. Light structures for living are superimposed over working zones (agricultural plots), providing a new way to live.

Cord Bertko
New housing that replicates old city types continues the density of the traditional city into the barren area of the old Gas Works, mending the gap through the site created by the railroad tracks. New industrial buildings also contribute to the new density.

Clint Wallace
Connection over the Danube canal brings pedestrian and bicycle traffic together over the disperate areas of the train and streets. Street vendors and park usage extend from the Prater to the Erdberg. Tilted planes ramp between the various parts, green and planted parts reach into the urban wasteland creating an ease of connection, controlled access, and over-lap with existing transportation points.

Chris Peck
The beginnings of automobile related sprawl are combatted by providing a large central parking area covered with a green skin which connects the various adjacent areas of the site. Housing is tucked under the edges of the new public thoroughfare, monuments project through it, and pedestrian and bike paths pass over is.

Susan Hippen
Die bestehenden Autobahnanlagen werden aufgelassen, abgetrennt und mit verschiedenen städtischen Funktionen neu besiedelt. BMX-Radfahrer und Rollerblader vergnügen sich auf den oberen Flächen, während darunter Platz für eine neue Kirche ist. Die Autobahn, die bisher eine Barriere war, wird nun durch einen neuen Markt überspannt.

Maria Benesch
Eine Reihe von Plätzen erstrecken sich am Donaukanal und verbinden die neuen Wohntürme mit dem Prater. Boote können hier anlegen und den neuen Wasserkanal hinauf zu den Gasometern und in das Gelände hinein fahren. Diese neuen Wasserwege lassen das alte Bett des Kanals anklingen und erinnern den Besucher an den Platz des Erdberger Mais in der Geschichte

Michael Prytula
Die Umwandlung der alten Schlachthofbahnstrecke in ein Erholungsgebiet heilt den Riß im Gelände. Die Eisenbahn trennt nicht mehr, sondern verbindet vielmehr das Gelände. Durch die Schaffung von Plattformen, eines Fahrradweges und eines Aussichtsturms kann der Besucher von vormals unbrauchbaren Gebieten voll profitieren.

Yvonne Glowatzki
Durch das Aufstellen von Stadtmöbeln auf dem ganzen Gelände wird die Nachbarschaft vereint. Die Schirme bieten eine Substruktur für das Gelände, die kulturelle und öffentliche Räume organisiert. Diese Schirme sind vielseitig, sie erfüllen je nach Jahreszeit und Veranstaltung unterschiedliche Funktionen: Bushaltestellen, Zeitungsstände, Telefonzellen, Kartenverkäufer, Bänke etc.

Ursula Kose und Anne-Marie Pichler
Das große, neue offene Grüngebiet erstreckt sich zwischen den Gasometern und den neuen und alten Wohngebieten des Geländes im Süden. Plätze sind wie Räume in einem Haus: man braucht verschiedene Bereiche für verschiedene Aktivitäten: Essen, Baden, Schlafen, Spielen usw. Die Nutzung des Grünraumes ändert sich in Abhängigkeit von der Zeit: Tag/Nacht, Wochentag/Wochenende, Winter/Sommer.
Dieser offene Raum ist ein Platz, wo die Bewohner dieser Gegend neue Formen des Zusammenlebens finden können. Der offene Grünraum ist ein Experimentierfeld für neue Lebensformen.

Susan Hippen

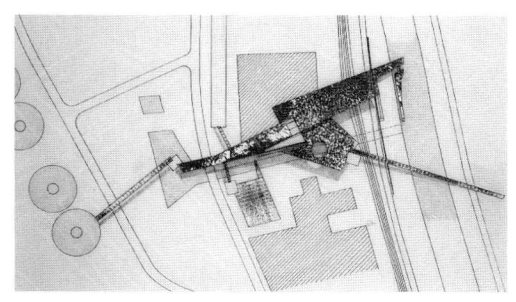

Maria Bensch

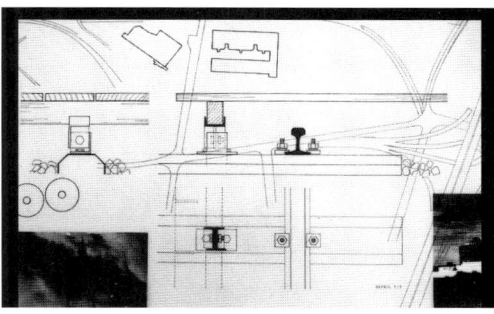

Michael Prytula

Yvonne Glowatzki

Ursula Kose und Anne-Marie Pichler

Susan Hippen
The existing freeway infrastructure is abandoned, severed and newly inhabited by various urban functions. BMX bikers and roller bladers enjoy the upper surfaces, and a new church fits underneath. What was previously the barrier of the freeway is spanned by a new market.

Maria Benesch
A series of plazas span the Danube Canal and connect the new housing towers with the Prater. Boats can dock at these plazas and float up the new water canal to the Gasometers and into the site. These new water connections are memories of the old path of the canal and remind the visitor of the Erdberger Mais' place in history.

Michael Prytula
The transformation of the old slaughterhouse railroad into an area of recreation mends the rift in the site. The railroad no longer divides, but connects the site. The creation of a plattform and bike path and observation tower allows visitors to take full advantage of previously unusable areas of the site.

Yvonne Glowatzki
Scattering urban furniture throughout the site unifies the neighborhood. The umbrellas provide a substructure for the site that organizes cultural and public spaces. These umbreallas are flexible, offering functions that change with the seasons and current events. Bus stops, news stands, phone booths, ticket vendors, benches, etc.

Ursula Kose and Anne-Marie Pichler
The new large open green area runs between the Gasometers and the new and existing residential areas of the site to the South. Spaces are like rooms in a house; different areas are for different activities. Eating, bathing, sleeping, playing, etc. The uses of the green space changes with time: day/night, weekday/weekend, winter/summer.
This open space is a place where the inhabitants of this neighborhood can find new ways to live together. The open green space is a playground for experiments in living.

**Projektgruppe / project group
Ippolito Pizzetti**

Assistent: Daniela Moderini

Philipp Althammer

Kirsten Bauer

Ales Bizjak

Giuliana Bosco

Maria Cristiana Costanzo

Alessandra Criconia

Luca M.F. Fabris

Alessandra Manzoni

Silvia Pericu

Illaria Presezzi

Antonella Salerno

Erika Skabar

Paola Tenaglia

Silvia Vignoli

**Projektgruppe / project group
Ippolito Pizzetti**

Ippolito Pizzetti Rom

1926 born in Milan
1959 degree in Italian Literature from the University of Rome

Teaching positions
14 years as visiting professor at the Faculty of Architecture at the University of Rome, Palermo, Venice, Ferrara

Selection of work
Participation on national and international competitions as landscape architect

Publications
1968 "Libro dei fiori in 3 volumes", Garzanti, Milano
1975 "Flowers - A Guide for your Garden", in 2 volumes, Harry N. Abrams, New York
1986 "Piccoli Giardini", Rizzoli, Milano
1974–85 "Pollice Verde", (Green Thumb), various articels for the magazine "Espresso" and the italian papers "Corriere della Sera", "La Stampa", "Abitare" etc. directed "L'Ornitorinco", a series of books for Rizzoli and "Il corvo e la colomba" for Franco Muzzio editore.

Kommt der Genius Loci geflogen
Ippolito Pizzetti

Ich besitze nie Bilder von den Gärten, die ich geplant, oder besser gesagt, die ich realisiert habe. Nicht, weil ich nicht gerne photographiere. Tatsächlich habe ich viele Menschen photographiert, Gesichter, Katzen, Mädchen, aber niemals Gärten; ich zeichne auch gerne, aber ich würde nie von einem Garten, den ich geplant habe, eine Zeichnung anfertigen.
Ich gestalte die Gärten an Ort und Stelle, vom ersten Moment an, an dem ich den Platz sehe, wo ich einen Garten entwerfen soll, und dann entsteht ein Garten in meinem Kopf – aber mit seinem eigenen Rhythmus.
Dann muß ich sehen, wie dieser Garten in meinem Kopf mit der Realität des Ortes zusammenpaßt. Ich meine, mit allen Dingen, die schon dort sind. Ich gebe zu, ich muß Licht und Schatten sehen und fühlen, die Gegenwart der Dinge an diesem Ort, die ich einbeziehen und ausschließen werde. Ich muß die Dimensionen sehen, und alles muß offen sein, um plötzliche Einfälle zuzulassen, die niemals alle zusammen kommen, sondern im Lauf des Prozesses. Meiner Ansicht nach muß ein Garten oder Park gefühlt, begangen werden, und das kann ich mit einer Zeichnung nicht tun.
Das passiert mir auch mit Gebäuden: Sie sprechen erst dann zu mir, wenn ich sie an Ort und Stelle sehe, an ihrem Ort. Ausstellungen überzeugen mich nie. Um mir einen Eindruck von den Dingen zu machen, brauche ich die Gegenwart der Dimensionen.
Genauso empfinde ich bei Musik. Seit meiner Kindheit ist Musik sehr wichtig für mein Leben, aber ich kann nicht Noten lesen.
Ich brauche die Aufführung.
Und damit ein Garten für mich eine Bedeutung erlangt, muß er sich selbst aufführen.

Es ist nicht wahr (so wie viele Leute glauben), daß der Genius Loci mit dem Ort entsteht, zu dem er gehört, den er bewohnt und den wir als sein Reich ansehen.
Es gibt keinen einzigen Ort auf der Welt, der schon von Anfang an seine eigene Identität gehabt hätte: Auch Götter müssen geboren werden, um Opazität zu gewinnen, d.h. eine Form anzunehmen, gesehen und gefühlt zu werden. Und der Genius Loci ist auch ein Gott, wenn auch ein kleiner, und er enthüllt sich plötzlich in einem bestimmten Moment der Geschichte.
Ich bin geneigt anzunehmen, daß es – ebenso wie in der menschlichen Geschichte – auch so etwas wie einen Nachfolger des Genius Loci geben kann. Als die Donau vor langer Zeit ein Gebiet wie die Leopoldau einnahm, in viele Arme und Wasserläufe unterteilt, da war – so glaube ich – der Genius Loci sicher ein anderer als der heutige. Es gab ihn schon (die Bäume waren hauptsächlich Pappeln und Weiden), aber er muß anders gewesen sein als der gegenwärtige, der (ich weiß nicht, in welchem Teil des Himmels) nun darauf wartet, herabzusteigen in die ungeheure Leere und Plattheit des Ortes, der einmal eine Au war.

Mit diesen Göttern geschieht das, was in der Natur geschieht, wenn eine Art aufgrund verschiedener Zufälle und Ursachen seltener wird oder ausstirbt und verschwindet, eine andere Art ihre Stelle einnimmt und sie mit ihrer eigenen Kennung und Physiognomie erfüllt.
Und wie das in der Geschichte so ist, kann viel Zeit vergehen zwischen dem Verschwinden oder dem Tod eines Genius Loci (denn schließlich können ja die kleinen Götter wie Dryaden, Hamadryaden, Baum- oder Quellnymphen sterben, wie wir wissen) und dem Erscheinen des nächsten – wofür es im übrigen keine Garantie gibt.

Der Genius Loci erscheint an einem Ort im Flug, wie ein Vogel, der einen Platz zum Landen und Nestbauen sucht; oder er kann mit einem Schiff kommen, mit Menschen oder Ratten. Er ergreift Besitz von dem Ort und bleibt nur, wenn er ein Gleichgewicht zwischen Zivilisation und Proportionen finden kann, einen Maßstab des Ortes, der ihm angemessen ist und es ihm ermöglicht, sich zu enthüllen und zu bleiben (vielleicht mit unserer Hilfe).

The genius Loci comes flying
Ippolito Pizzetti

I never have pictures of the gardens I have planned, or rather, of those I have created. It is not that I don't like to take photographs. Actually I have photographed a lot of people, faces, cats, girls, but never gardens. I also like to draw, but I would never draw the gardens I plan.
I do the gardens on-site from the very first moment I see the place where I have to design, and then a garden starts to design itself in my mind, but with a rhythm of its own.
I have to see how this garden I have in mind fits with the reality of the place. I mean, with all the things which are already there. I confess I must see and feel the lights and the shadows, the presence of things which are in the place and which I will include or exclude. I have to see the dimensions, and everything must be open to allow for sudden suggestions which never come all at once, but rather in the course of the process. In my opinion, a garden or park has to be felt, walked in, and one cannot walk in a drawing.

The same happens to me with buildings: they don't talk to me until the moment I see them in a place, in their place. Exhibitions never convince me. To get an impression of things, I need the presence of dimensions.
It is the same for me with music; since my childhood, music is very important to me but I cannot read even one single note. I need to have it performed.
And to have a meaning for me, a garden must perform itself.

It is not true, as many people believe, that the Genius Loci is born with the place it belongs to and inhabits, or which we consider its realm.
There is not a place in the world which from the very beginning, has had an identity of its own: even gods have to be born to acquire opacity, which means to take form, to be seen and felt. And the Genius Loci is a god too, even if one of the minor ones, and it reveals itself suddenly at a certain moment in history.
I tend to think that - just as it happens in the history of mankind - there can also be a succession for the Genius Loci. I think that when the Danube once occupied a territory like that of the Leopoldau, dividing into many streams and branches, its Genius Loci differed from the one it has now. Of course, it already existed (the trees were mostly poplars and willows) but it must have been different from the current one that is now – in what part of heaven I don't know – waiting to descend onto the vast nothingness and banality of the place that once had been "eine Au" (a river wetland).
The same thing happens to those gods, as in nature, when, because of different accidents and reasons, a species is becoming rare or dying out and disappearing, while another one is taking its place and endowing it with its own imprint and physiognomy.
There can be long gaps (just as in history) between the disappearance or extinction of one Genius Loci (because also the minor gods like dryads, hamadryads or the nymphs of trees or springs can die, as we know) and the arrival of the next, which in any case cannot be taken for granted.
The Genius Loci comes to a place on the wing, like a bird looking for a place to land and to nest; or it can also come with a ship, with human beings or rats. It takes possession of the place and stays only if it can find a balance between civilization and the proportions, the scale of a place which suits it, and gives it the possibility to reveal itself and to endure (maybe with our help).

LUEGER FICHTE
gepflanzt von der Gemeinde Wien
im Jahre 1906

Grünraumvernetzung – Neue Freiraumqualitäten für bestehende Stadterweiterung. Großfeldsiedlung, Wien 21

Die Wohnanlage „Großfeldsiedlung" im Norden der Stadt mit ca. 6.000 Wohnungen wurde in den Jahren 1967–74 errichtet. Der Charakter der Anlage wird geprägt durch einen hohen Grün- und Freiflächenanteil und durch eine gemischte Bebauung, die neben 11-geschoßigen Wohnbauten z.B. auch Reihenhausanlagen innerhalb der Siedlung aufweist. Einfamilienhäuser, Kleingärten, Freizeitanlagen sowie Betriebs- und Gewerbeflächen kennzeichnen die Randzonen.

Fußwegverbindungen bieten Abfolgen differenzierter Grün- und Freiräume, die hinsichtlich Gestaltung und auch Funktionalität z.T. jedoch nicht mehr den heutigen Anforderungen und Erwartungen entsprechen bzw. vorhandene Möglichkeiten und Qualitäten ungenutzt lassen.

Eine für die Bearbeitung vorgeschlagene Wegachse durchquert den westlichen Teil der Großfeldsiedlung in Ost-West Richtung. Sie verbindet den im Westen der Siedlung verlaufenden Grünzug entlang verschiedener öffentlicher Einrichtungen mit dem neuen Stadtteilzentrum. Ein erst zu schaffender Zugang wird die Anbindung an den Grünzug Nordrand-Donaufeld herstellen. Die derzeit noch großteils landwirtschaftlich genutzten Flächen sollen im Rahmen einer zusammenhängenden Landschaftsplanung, evtl. unter Einbeziehung eines möglichen Wasserlaufes (Dotierungsbach), gestaltet werden.

Connecting green spaces – new qualities of open space for existing extension areas. Großfeldsiedlung, Vienna 21

The housing complex of "Großfeldsiedlung" in the Northern part of the city consists of approximately 6000 flats and was built between 1967 and 1974. A high percentage of vacant areas with generous greening, and a mixed building structure featuring both 11-storey residential buildings as well as terraced houses are characteristic of the complex. Detached houses, small gardens, recreational facilities, as well as areas of commercial and industrial uses are all typical on the fringe zones.

The foot paths within the complex offer a sequence of green and vacant areas, differentiated with regard to both space and function. These spaces, however, no longer fulfill today´s requirements with regard to design and functionality and/or existing possibilities, and qualities remain unused.

An axis suggested for study crosses the Western part of Großfeldsiedlung in an East-West direction, linking the green stretch in the West of the complex along various public institutions (school, church, etc.) to the new district centre. An access which still remains to be created will provide the link to the green stretch from the northern outskirts to the Donaufeld. The areas still predominantly used for agricultural purposes at the moment shall be designed as part of a continuous landscape planning, possibly also integrating a watercourse.

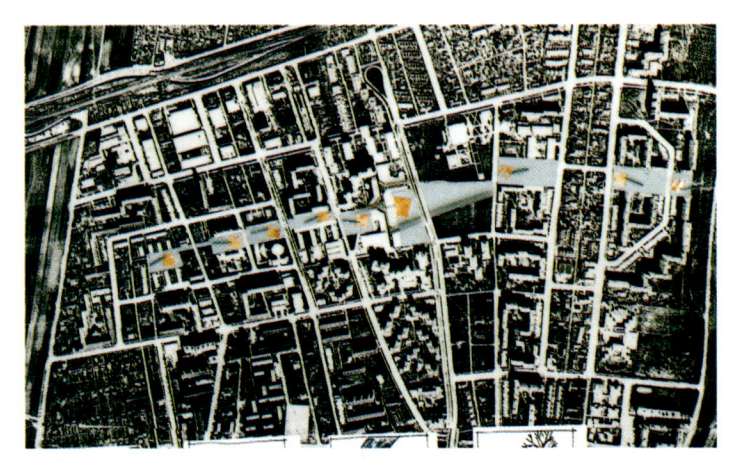

Großfeldsiedlung, Wien 21

Zwiegespräch zwischen Mann und Baum

Die schwebende Siedlung

Als wir zum ersten Mal das Gelände am anderen Donauufer besichtigten (die Leopoldau und ihre Umgebung), wo wir unser Projekt durchführen sollten, waren wir schockiert – das ist der richtige Ausdruck – wie wenig wienerisch, ja wie unwienerisch es dort aussah. Nicht nur fehlten „Dinge", für Wien typische Merkmale, sondern vor allem die Zwischenräume, die diese „Dinge" erzeugen.

Das eine muß klar sein, es ging nicht um bloße Nostalgie – wir erwarteten überhaupt nicht, etwas zu finden, Grinzing oder kein Grinzing, das in der Vergangenheit, im Biedermeier und später, ein Merkmal der Stadt geworden ist wie „die Linde und die Laube" – aber es sind die Balance und die Harmonie zwischen diesen Elementen und dem offenen Gelände rundherum, ihr Negativ, ihr Schatten, die aus Grinzing und anderen Orten in der Stadt diese „offenen Schutzorte" machen, wie F. L. Wright das humane Heim nannte, das die Architektur für den „freien" Menschen errichten sollte – nicht diese Schachteln ohne Türen und Fenster, in denen – wie ein

Dialogue between man and tree

The floating "Siedlung"

When for the first time we visited the area on the other bank of the Danube - the Leopoldau and its surroundings - where we were to execute our project, we were shocked - that's the right word - by how little Viennese, or even worse, how "un-Viennese" it looked. Not only did it lack "things", features typical of Vienna; what was more, it lacked the spaces in-between which those "things" produce.

We did not think at all - and this must be made clear, it is nothing to do with naked nostalgia for the past - that we would find anything, Grinzing or no Grinzing, which over the past, beginning in the Biedermeier era and going on and on, has become a feature of the city, as "the lime tree and the pergola" - but it is the balance and harmony between those elements and the open space around them, their negative, their shadow, which transforms places like Grinzing and others in Vienna into those "open shelters" which Frank Lloyd Wright meant to be the human home which architecture must build for the "free"

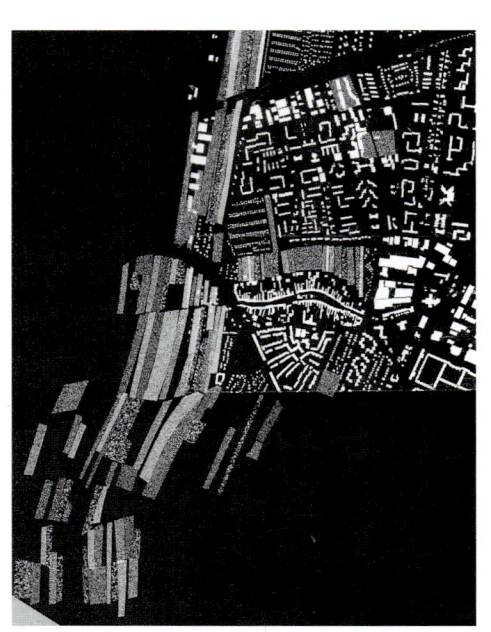

Strukturen: Großfeldsiedlung – Leopoldau – Grünzug /
Structure: Großfeldsiedlung – Leopoldau – breen link

humanity, and not the boxes without doors and windows - as the philosopher has it - into which an adjusted humanity locks itself, where the "logos" is excluded and left to oblivion. It is just that: this neurotic use of space we found in the "Siedlung" - gardens which are not really gardens because they lack the soul of a garden, and boxes into which a disturbed humanity locks itself, unwilling to be seen or to see beyond the immediate boundaries; layers and layers of hedges and fences, and "vacant", not "open", spaces inbetween. An architecture which has either a front or a back, either head or tail, either yin or yang, either lights or shadows: an unisex achitecture.
So when coming out of the "Siedlung" we entered the "Grünzug" or "Grünkeil" ("green axis" or "green wedge") opposite, we felt like stepping into the Promised Land: open to the sky and to all things in it, clouds, birds, sun, moon and wind; the only place there that was able to re-establish a balance, a dialogue between ourselves and the open space and the trees in it, just like in Klee's "Zwiegespräch zwischen Mann und Baum"

Philosoph das ausdrückt – eine angepaßte Menschheit sich einsperrt, wo der „logos" ausgeschlossen ist und dem Vergessen anheimfällt.
Eben das ist es - die neurotische Raumnutzung, die wir in der Siedlung fanden: Gärten, die gar keine richtigen Gärten sind, weil ihnen die Seele des Gartens fehlt, und Schachteln, in denen sich eine gestörte Menschheit einsperrt die nicht gesehen werden und auch nicht über ihre unmittelbaren Grenzen hinausblicken will, Schicht um Schicht von Hecken und Zäunen und „leere", nicht „offene" Räume dazwischen. Eine Architektur, die entweder eine Vorder- oder eine Rückseite hat, entweder Kopf oder Zahl, Yin oder Yang, Licht oder Schatten ist eine Unisex-Architektur.
Als wir aus der Siedlung heraustraten und im Grünzug oder Grünkeil gegenüber landeten, fühlten wir uns wie im Gelobten Land: eine Öffnung zum Himmel und zu allem, was es da gibt: Wolken, Vögel, Sonne, Mond und Wind; der einzige Ort, der die Möglichkeit hatte, wieder ein Gleichgewicht zu schaffen, einen Dialog zwischen uns und dem offenen Raum und den Bäumen darin, so wie das in Klees „Zwiegespräch zwischen Mann und Baum" gemeint ist.

Nomaden / Nomads

Eine Öffnung zum Himmel

Wir wollen betonen, daß wir mit dem Grünzug nicht nur eine Grenze erzeugen wollen, ein Bollwerk gegen den Baudruck, der droht, das ganze Land jenseits der Donau zu einem Schmelztiegel, einem Potpourri aus Schrebergärten (die keine Schrebergärten mehr sind), kleinen Fabriken, überall verstreuten Gebäuden ohne Sinn und Gestalt zu machen, sondern im Gegenteil, etwas schaffen wollen, das schon heute eine Bedeutung hat und in Zukunft immer mehr an Bedeutung gewinnen wird, über zwei, drei, vielleicht noch mehr Jahrhunderte; und wir wollten nicht, daß ein Wald oder Park im klassischen Sinn entsteht und natürlich auch keine Allee, sondern eine echte

An opening to the sky

What we want to stress is that with the "Grünzug" we do not merely want to create a boundary, a stronghold against the pressure to build, which threatens to change the entire zone across the Danube into a melting-pot, a medley of "Schrebergärten" (allotment gardens) which no longer are allotment gardens, of small factories, of buildings scattered about without purpose or design - but rather something that is of significance now, but will attain even more significance in the future, for two, three, perhaps even more centuries. We didn't want it to be either

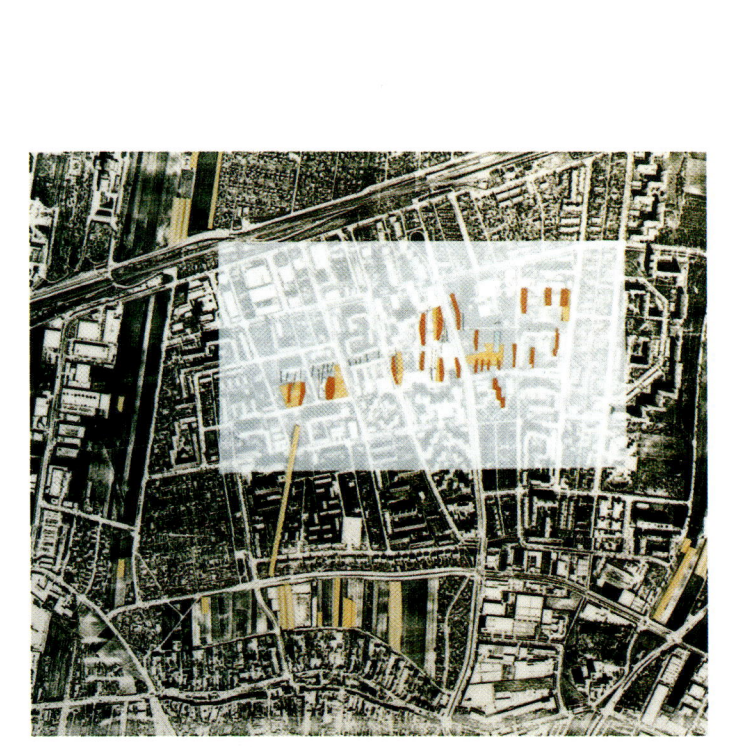

Die Großfeldsiedlung im Zustand „entstehender" Architektur / The Großfeldsiedlung at the condition of an architecture coming into existence

Arterie dieses Raums, wie das der Fluß ist, beherrscht von – oder besser, bestehend aus – Eichen und Buchen; die Eichen werden riesige Bäume werden (damit meinen wir, daß sie hier im Grünzug den Platz haben werden, den sie brauchen, um im Laufe der Zeit die Riesen zu werden, die sie im ausgewachsenen Zustand nun einmal sind). Ein Ort soll entstehen, an dem die Bäume, die Eichen (in der Vergangenheit der Hauptbestandteil der Wälder im germanischen Raum, wie Mythen und Gedichte zeigen) „wieder" – wie F. L. Wright es ausdrückt – „ein Raumgefühl schaffen, eine Öffnung, nicht ein Einschliessen", ein Ort wo diese Bäume Licht und Schatten, Nuancierungen, Schwere und Leichtigkeit erzeugen und sich voll entwickeln können. Und unter den Bäumen, auf Bodenniveau, wird es eine lange Reihe verstreuter steinerner Rechtecke geben, die den Verlauf des Grünzugs nachvollziehen und auf einer anderen Ebene betonen.
Die Eichen und Buchen des Grünzugs entwickeln sich in natürlicher Weise nach ihrem eigenen Rhythmus, den wir leicht vorhersehen können: Jedes Jahr wachsen sie an Umfang und Bedeutung ihrer „Endform" entgegen; im Gegensatz dazu ist die Siedlung – und das ist offensichtlich und nicht abzuleugnen – heute in einem Zustand der „entstehenden Architektur", und wir können sicher sein, daß die Siedlung in der gegenwärtigen Form keinen Bestand haben wird. Glücklicherweise.

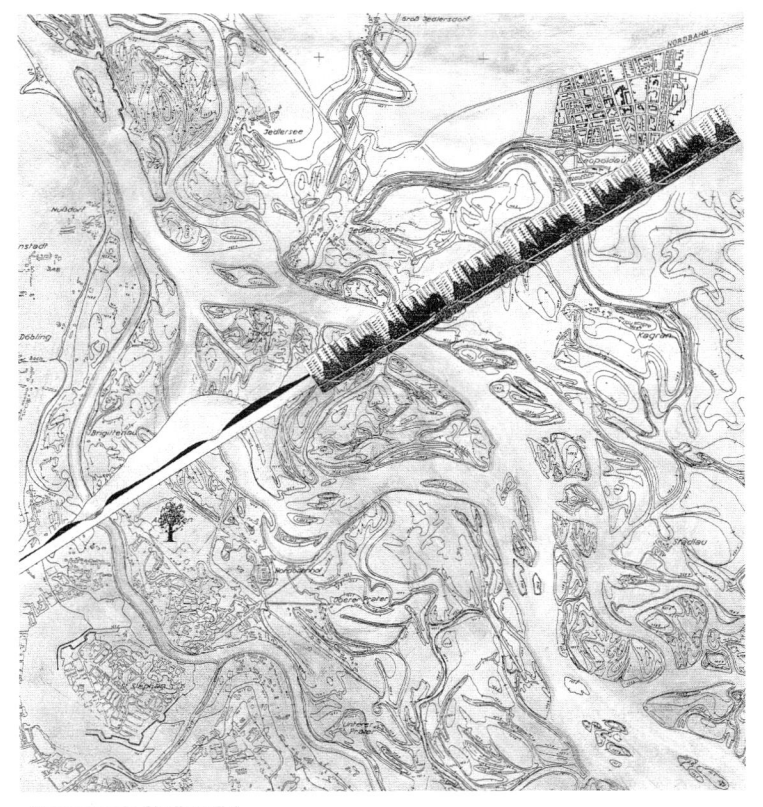

„Schwebende Siedlung" / "Floating Siedlung"

a wood or a park in the traditional sense, and of course not an avenue, but a real artery of that space (such as the river), dominated by, or rather, consisting of, oaks and beeches. The oaks will grow into giant trees (by giants, we mean that here in the "Grünzug" they will have all the space they need to become, in time, the very giants they are in their maturity) - a place in which the trees, the oaks - in the past the main element of the forests in the Germanic lands (as in myth and poetry) - again can create, as F. L. Wright puts it, a feeling of space as "an opening and not a closing-up"; where those trees, in a way, will give birth to lights and shadows and nuances, to heaviness and lightness, and develop into their full-blown shape. And beneath the trees, and at the level of the ground, there will be a long series of scattered rectangles of stone, which will follow the progression of the "Grünzug" and emphasize it at another level.
The oaks and beeches of the "Grünzug" develop naturally with their own, easily foreseeable rhythms: with every year of their life, they will grow in size and significance towards their final shape; on the contrary, the "Siedlung" - and this is obvious and cannot be denied - is now in a condition of "architecture in the making"; thus we can be sure that it will not last in its present form. Fortunately.

Die grüne Kathedrale

In allen Projekten, die wir für die Siedlung entworfen haben existiert eine Konstante: Der zentrale Platz, den wir auf eine niedrige Ebene gelegt haben (wie im dreidimensionalen Modell erkennbar), die Ebene der Felder, ein Herd, ein Kern, dem gegenüber der Rest der Siedlung sich wie eine Art schwebende Kruste verhält, die morgen oder übermorgen entfernt und durch eine – wie wir hoffen – sinnvollere und dauerhaftere Architektur ersetzt werden kann. So haben wir schließlich und endlich ein Paradoxon, – das keines ist – insofern, als die Siedlung ein „work in progress" darstellt, das nach der einen oder anderen Richtung hin unvorhersehbaren Veränderungen unterliegen wird.

Die Großfeldsiedlung im Zustand „entstehender" Architektur /
The Großfeldsiedlung at the condition of an architecture coming into existence

The green cathedral

In all our projects that we developed for the "Siedlung" there is one constant: the central square which we positioned at a lower level (as one can see in the three-dimensional model), the layer of the fields, a hearth, a core around which the rest of the "Siedlung" appears like a sort of floating crust that tomorrow, or the day after, may be taken down and substituted by (hopefully) a more meaningful and lasting architecture.
So in the end, we have a sort of paradox – which really isn't a paradox at all – in that the "Siedlung" is a "work in progress" that will be subjected to unforeseeable changes in one way or the other.

"Die Kunst gibt uns nicht das Sichtbare zurück, aber sie macht es sichtbar."
(Paul Klee)

"Art doesn't give the visible back, but it makes it visible."
(Paul Klee)

Wir sahen in einem Buch eine Zeichnung von Klee: Ein Mann liegt im Gras, unter der Krone eines Baumes, der sich über die gesamte Körperlänge des Mannes neigt, wobei nur der Kopf hervorschaut und den Himmel, die Wolken oder auch die Vögel darin anblickt; und da dachte ich an die Gefangenen am Ende des ersten Aktes von „Fidelio", wenn sie in den Hof des Schlosses hinausdürfen und singen:

We saw in a book a design by Klee. a man lying on the grass under the crown of foliage of a tree bent on his body as much as it is long and only with his head protruding, looking into the sky, to the clouds and whatever birds are in the air; and also it came to me think of the prisoners at the end of the first act of "Fidelio", when they are allowed in the courtyard of the castle, and sing:

„O welche Lust, in freier Luft den Atem leicht zu heben! Nur hier, nur hier ist Leben, der Kerker eine Gruft."

"Oh welche Lust, in feier Luft den Atem leicht zu heben! Nur hier, nur hier ist Leben, der Kerker eine Gruft."

Nach Wright hat die Architektur die Kraft, die Möglichkeit zu prüfen, ob die Menschen eines Volkes frei sein werden oder nicht, ob sie sich in dem riesigen, offenen Schutzort heimisch fühlen, oder aber in Schachteln angeordnet sein werden, die den „logos" ausschliessen und dem Vergessen überantworten. Die Menschen sind nur dann frei, wenn ihr Heim sie aufschließt anstatt einschließt.

According to Wright, architecture has the power to access the possibility whether the people of a nation will or, will not be, free, if they will be at home in the vast open shelter or aligned in boxes which exclude the logos to give it away to oblivion. People are free only when their home is declosing instead of closing.

„Das Austrocknen ist das Schlimmste, ist beunruhigender als die Zerstörung. Die Zerstörung schiebt nur beiseite, was bis zu diesem Moment gewachsen ist oder gebaut wurde; das Austrocknen gestattet kein zukünftiges Wachsen oder Bauen."
(Martin Heidegger)

"The drying up is worst, is more worrying, than the destruction. Destruction sets aside only what up to that moment has grown or been built: the drying up doesn't allow any future growth or building."
(Martin Heidegger)

„Der Wald ist der Ort der Nuancen."
(Robert Pogue Harrison)

"The forest is the place of nuances."
(Robert Pogue Harrison)

Eiche / oak

Schatten /
Shadows

Schatten /
Shadows

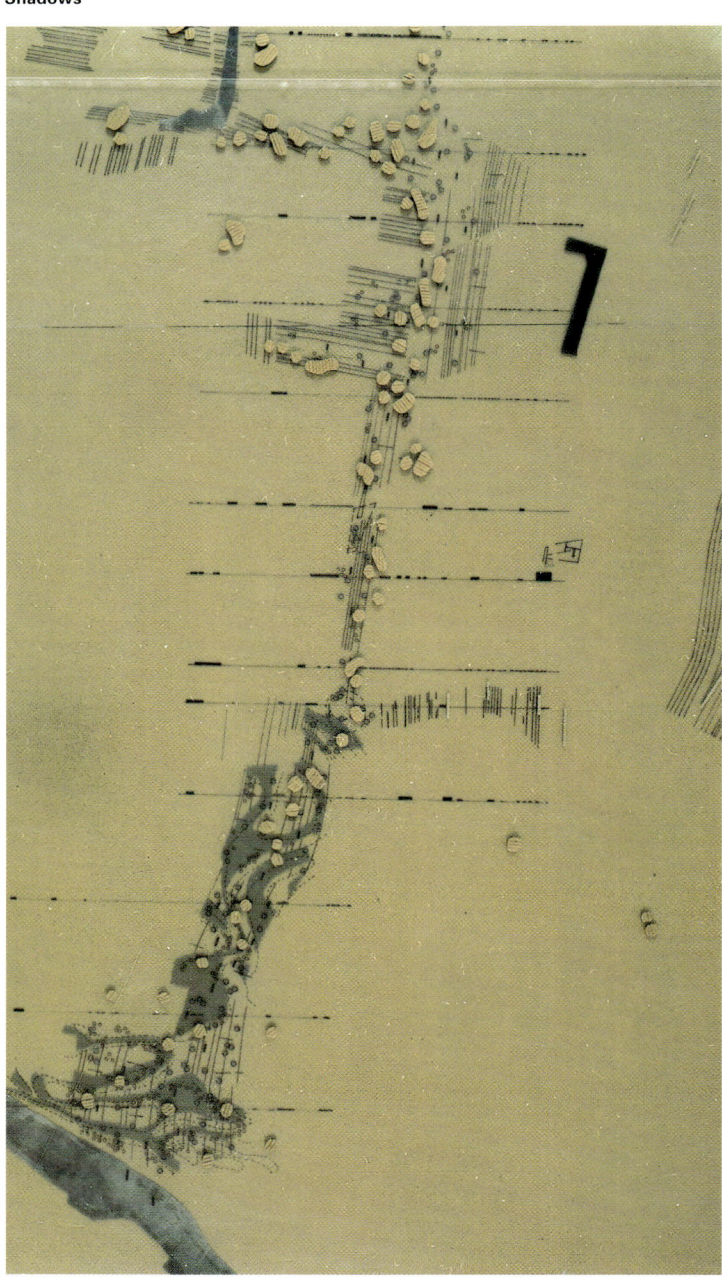

Grünzug, Wien Nord /
Green link, Vienna North

Grünzug, Wien Nord /
Green link, Vienna North

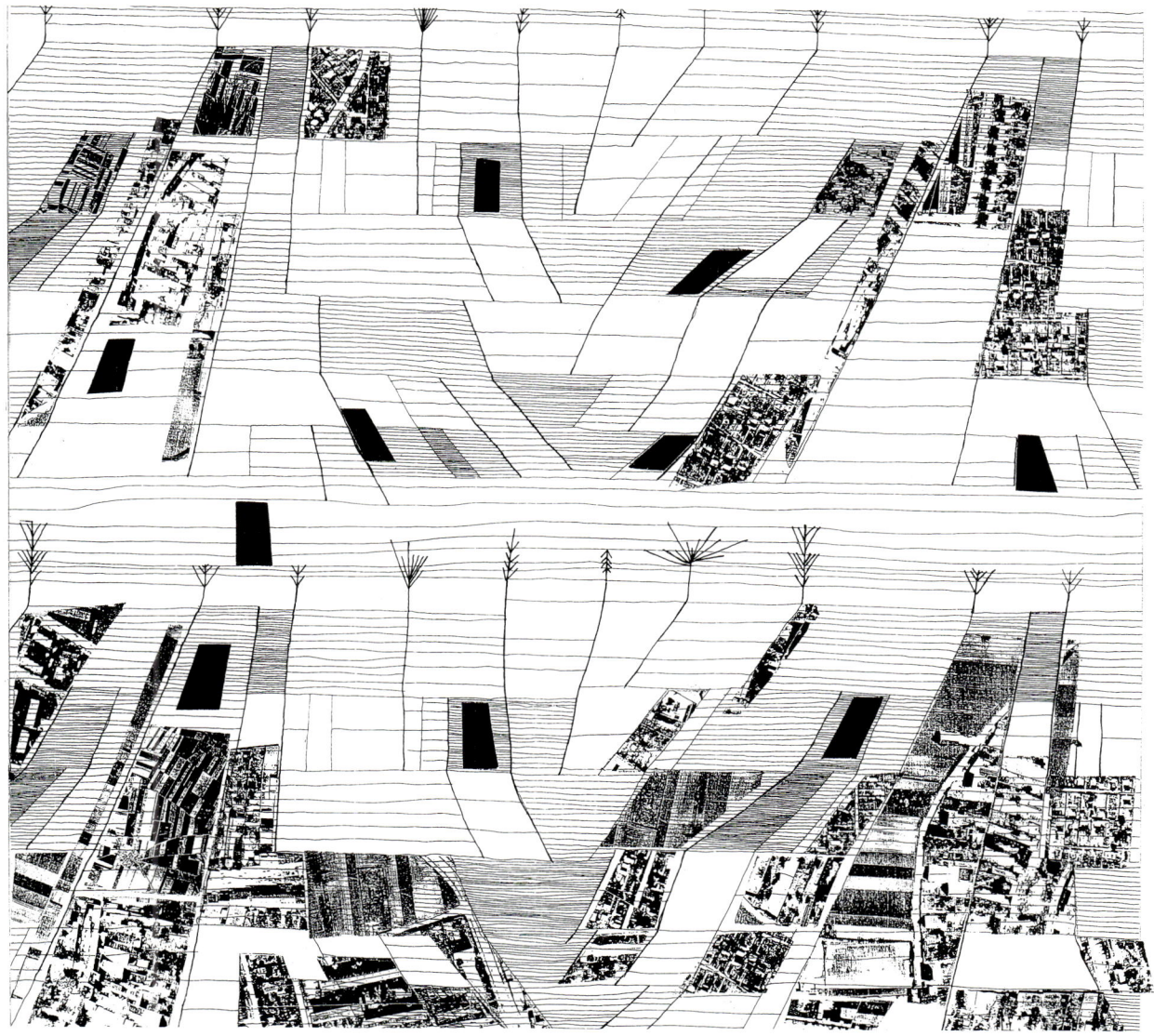

Grünzug – Steinzeichen /
Green link – stone marks

„Markierungen" Grünzug /
"Marks" green link

**Projektgruppe / project group
Martha Schwartz**

in collaboration with Jennifer Ann Luce

Roland Bonzio

Renny Booth

Silvia Braun

Carsten Fulland

Annette Hammer

Andreas Holzapfel

Heidelinde Holzinger

Markus Jatsch

Guntram Lill

Wolf Opitsch

Ingrid Seelos Bauer

Mathias Staubach

Volker Stengele

Joanna Van Oppen

Harald Vavrovsky

Renée Wagner

Johannes Wolgast

Martha Schwartz Boston

1950	born in Philadelphia, USA
1976–77	Harvard University Graduate School of Design; Landscape Architecture Program
1973	University of Michigan, Ann Arbor, Bachelor of Fine Arts Degree
1977	University of Michigan, Ann Arbor, Master of Landscape Architecture
1990	Foundation of Martha Schwartz, Inc. for landscape design

Teaching positions

Adjunct Professor of Landscape Arcitecture: Harvard University Graduate School of Design
Visiting Critic: Harvard University Graduate School of Design, Rhode Island School of Design, University of California
Lectures: Berlin Technical University; University of Michigan; Melbourne University; Power Plant, Toronto; Urban Developement Forum, Hamburg; Academie of Applied Arts, Vienna; Technical University, Munich amongst others.

Selection of work

1982	NECCO Garden, Hayden Gallery, M.I.T.
1983	Winner of the Competition for King County Jail Plaza, Seattle
1984	Artist for Candlestick Park Recreation Area, San Francisco
1987	Artist for Austin Airport, Austin
1987	Winning Entry, Artist for Todos Santos Plaza Competition, Concord
1988	"Turf Parterre", for "The New Urban Landscape" Exhibition, World Financial Center, New York
1989	Los Angeles Center, Los Angeles
1994	Central Artery and Tunnel Project, Boston
1994	Metro-Dade County, Miami Sound Wall, Miami Beach

Major exhibitions

1982	Chicago Institute of Contemporary Art, Ohio Foundation of Arts
1986	Main Art Gallery, California State University, Fullerton
1986	Urban Design Center, New York
1987	Vanguard Gallery, Philadelphia
1988	Olympia & York, New York
1991	Henry Art Gallery, University of Washington
1991	Max Protetch Gallery, New York
1995	Cultural Center, Pfäffikon, Schweiz
1995	Harvard Graduate Design, Cambridge

Publications among others

1985	Insight / On Site, Perspectives on Art in Public Spaces, edited by Stacy Paleologos Harris, Washington
1988	American Landscape Architecture: Martha Schwartz, by Toru Mitani, SD Magazine, Japan
1989	P/A Profile, Peter Walker und Martha Schwartz, Progressive Architecture
1989	The Innovators, Newsweek, October 2
1991	Environmental Design, by Margaret Cottom-Winslow, PBC International
1991	Perspectives: Landscape Architecture, by Anne Whiston Spirn, Diana Balmori, Martha Schwartz, Progressive Architecture
1992	Piscines, by Sophie Roche-Soulie, Sophie Roulet, Publications du Moniteur
1992	Parc de la Citadelle, by Martha Schwartz, Pages Paysages # 4
1992	Landscape & Common culture Since Modernism, by Martha Schwartz, Architecture California, vol. 14, # 2
1994	A Crab for Baltimore?, by Andy Brown, Landscape Architecture

Prizes / Awards

1983	Visiting Artist in Residence, Villa Romana, Florence, Italy
1987	Urban Design Award, Atlanta
1989	ASLA Design Award Urbanology Show: Turf Parterre
1989	ASLA Merit Award, Rio Shopping Center, Atlanta
1991	Resident, American Academy in Rome
1991	ASLA Merit Award, Becton Dickinson Atrium
1991	ASLA Honor Award, The Citadel Grand Allée
1994	Landscape Architecture Residential Design, Second Place, Dickenson Residence

The landscape of neglect Martha Schwartz

As a culture we care little about the visual quality of the environment in which we live. Our cities, and to an even greater degree, our suburbs, are not only environmentally degraded, they are also visually and spiritually degraded. It is most apparent in our public open spaces: our streets, vast parking lots, fringes of "landscape" around suburban homes and office buildings, rooftops, shopping centers, and commercial strips. These neglected landscapes add up, piece by piece, to the ubiquitous ugly environment so identifiably "American."

I have witnessed the attitudes that continue our enviroment´s devaluation. The allocation of funds clearly reflects priorities. While a lot of lip service is given to "landscape" and "environment," when push comes to shove, they are never as important as interior (or exterior) decoration. The landscape budget consistently serves as the slush fund for building overruns. As a result, the landscape is almost always left impoverished, if not eviscerated.

Our society believes that nature is a God given commodity, like fresh air, and resents having to pay for it. As we must commit money and effort to cleaning our air, we must commit money and effort to forming a new attitude about the built landscape that embraces development, and recognizes that "landscape" is not interchangeable with "nature", which in turn is not synonymous with "wilderness". However much we romantisize the wilderness, the urban/suburban landscape cannot evolve "naturally" as a field might evolve into a forest. Its evolution must be designed.

In my experience, I have found that Modernist dogma continues to dominate landscape architecture in the minds of architects, even though most architects have moved beyond it in their own realm. Consistent with Modernist design tenets, the acceptable role of "landscapers" is to provide the passive, sylvan setting for the building - a pleasant background that "doesn´t compete" sculpturally with the architecture. In this view, the landscape must provide environmental "white noise", subliminally read at best, shorn of visibility, narrative, and, God forbid, any physical or intellectual hard edges. The picturesque landscape paintings of Nicholas Poussin and Claude Lorrain illustrate the ideals of a "proper" landscape where the natural landscape and the man made object inform each other but never touch. In Modernist terms this becomes Corbusier´s vision of high-rise buildings nestled into unmanipulated landscapes.

Fortunately for our firm, not many architects call us for this kind of servicing. Those who insist on this vision as the only model for landscape tend to stay away (hence we have a very small practice). On the bright side, we´ve had the great pleasure of working with many forward thinking architects such as Bernardo Fort-Brescia, Stanley Saitowitz, Mark Mack, Arata Isozaki, and Philip Johnson, who are curious about the landscape as a related

Jacob Javits Plaza, Federal Plaza, New York

narrativen oder – Gott bewahre – physisch oder intellektuell harte Kanten aufweist. Die pittoresken Landschaftsbilder von Nicholas Poussin und Claude Lorrain veranschaulichen das Ideal einer „richtigen" Landschaft, wo die natürliche Landschaft und das vom Menschen erzeugte Objekt einander durchdringen, aber nie berühren. In bezug auf die Moderne entspricht da Corbusiers Vision von Hochhäusern inmitten von unmanipulierten Landschaften.

Glücklicherweise wenden sich nicht viele Architekten für diese Art von Aufträgen an unsere Firma. Wer auf diese Vision als das einzige Landschaftsmodell besteht, bleibt in der Regel fern (deshalb sind wir ein sehr kleines Unternehmen). Zu den angenehmen Seiten dieser Situation gehört, daß wir das große Vergnügen hatten, mit vielen vorausblickenden Architekten wie Bernardo Fort-Brescia, Stanley Saitowitz, Mark Mack, Arata Isozaki und Philip Johnson zu arbeiten, die der Landschaftsgestaltung als verwandter Kunstform neugierig gegenüber stehen. Ich glaube, daß die Postmoderne dazu beigetragen hat, das Interesse der Architekten am Garten als Artefakt und der ihm eigenen Fähigkeit, Architektur zu erweitern und zu verstärken, neu zu wecken.

In dieser Hinsicht sehe ich den Status unseres Berufs gegenüber den Architekten positiv. Da die Architekten darauf geschult sind, den Bezug der Architektur zur Kunst zu verstehen, sind sie eher als Landschaftsarchitekten geneigt, das künstlerische Potential zu sehen, das der Landschaft innewohnt. Viele können erkennen, wie nützlich die Definition eines neuen Vokabulars ist, mit dem man auf ehrliche und unromantische Weise mit unserer verbauten Umwelt umgehen kann. Solche Architekten sehen ganz klar, daß ihr Projekt durch eine interessante Standortgestaltung wirklich aufgewertet wird, und sind bereit, die Kontrolle über diesen Bereich, mit dem sie weniger vertraut sind, abzugeben.

Planer sind sich immer mehr der Landschaft bewußt geworden, insbesondere da sie zu einem weiteren Aspekt auffälligen Konsums und Prestiges wurde. In jedem Fall gibt es Risse in den versteinerten Vorstellungen unserer Kultur darüber, was eine Landschaft ausmacht. Vorstellungen, in denen noch immer die romantische englische Landschaft des 19. Jahrhunderts herumgeistert.

Trotz all dieser Fortschritte hat die städtische/vorstädtische Landschaft in unserer Kultur fast keinen Status. Sie ist ein ungeliebtes Ödland, das von Architekten weitgehend ignoriert, von den meisten Landschaftsarchitekten geschmäht wird und für die Erschließungsfirmen unsichtbar ist. Zur Entwicklung einer visuellen Sprache, die unser Wachstum formen und Ordnung und Schönheit in unsere Städte und Vororte bringen kann, müssen wir uns der kollektiven Mißachtung der von Menschenhand gestalteten Umwelt stellen.

**HUD Plaza Verbesserung, Washington, D.C. /
HUD Plaza improvements, Washington, D.C.**

art form. I believe the Post-Modern movement helped to revive architects´ interest in the garden as artifact, and in its intrinsic ability to extend and amplify architecture.

In this regard I view the status of our profession vis-á-vis architects positively. Because architects are trained to understand architecture's relationship to art, they are more disposed than many landscape architects to see the artistic potential inherent in the landscape. Many can see the utility in defining a new vocabulary that can deal with our built environment in an honest, non-romantic way. Such architects have a clear understanding that their project will be truly enhanced by interesting site design and are willing to relinquish control over this area with which they are less familiar.

Developers have become increasingly aware of the landscape, especially as it has become another item of conspicuous consumption and prestige. For whatever reasons, there are indeed cracks in our culture´s glaciated ideas of what constitutes a landscape, ideas which still roam around in the romantic English countryside of the 1800s.

Sadly, these advances notwithstanding, the status of the urban/suburban landscape in our culture is almost non-existent. It is an unloved wasteland, largely ignored by architects, reviled by most landscape architects, and invisible to the development industry. In order to develop a visual language that can shape our growth and bring order and beauty to our cities and suburbs we must face our collective neglect of our manmade environments.

Stadtraumlandschaft – Identität und Erinnerung. Landschaftspark Eßling, Wien 22

Eßling, eines der historischen Wiener Dörfer nördlich der Donau, umfaßt heute ein weitläufiges Gartensiedlungsgebiet im Osten der Stadt, nahe der Stadtgrenze. Das Siedlungsgebiet wird im Süden vom Vorland des Augebietes Lobau begrenzt und im Norden und Osten von ausgedehnten Agrarflächen, die dem Landschaftsraum Marchfeld zugehören. Weiter im Nordwesten des Gebietes erstreckt sich das große Areal eines ehemaligen Flughafens. Das Flugfeld Aspern ist in der langfristigen Planung als Standort für eines der größten Stadtentwicklungsprojekte Wiens vorgesehen. Auf einer begrenzten Fläche nördlich des Ortskernes ist die Gestaltung eines Grünraumes geplant, der auch einen Übergang in die offene Landschaft bezeichnen soll. Bestimmendes Element dieses geplanten Grünraumes ist ein historisches Speichergebäude aus dem 18. Jahrhundert, einst Napoleons Hauptquartier während der Schlacht von Aspern 1809.

Die Erwartung an den zu gestaltenden Grünraum geht über eine örtliche Erholungs- und Freizeitfunktion hinaus. Mit der Schaffung eines attraktiven landschaftlichen Rahmens für ein interessantes Baudenkmal, könnte eines der für den Raum Wien Nord gewünschten, identitätsstiftenden Raumelemente entstehen.

Eßling, Wien 22

Landscape of periphery areas – identity and memory scenic parkland of Eßling, Vienna 22

Eßling, one of the historical Viennese villages north of the Danube, today is comprised of an extensive garden housing estate in the east of the city near the city boundaries. The development area borders the foreland of the Lobau meadows in the south, and extensive agricultural areas belonging to the Marchfeld region in the north and east. Further to the north west of the area lie the extensive premises of the largest urban development projects in Vienna.

Plans exist for a grass-covered open space adjacent to the village centre in the north also intended as a transitional zone to the open landscape. A historical warehouse dating from the 18th century, once used by Napoleon as headquarters, during the battle of Aspern in 1809, is the determining element of this planned parkland area.

The expectations for the green area to be designed go beyond local recreational and leisure purposes. The creation of an attractive and scenic frame for an interesting architectural monument might also produce one of the identity giving elements so much desired for the part of Vienna situated north of the Danube.

Napoleon hat hier nicht geschlafen

Landschaft an der Peripherie

Annäherung

Unser Gelände befindet sich in Eßling, das 30 km vom Zentrum Wiens entfernt liegt und in 30 Minuten mit öffentlichen Verkehrsmitteln, in 60 Minuten mit dem Fahrrad bzw. in 180 Minuten zu Fuß erreicht werden kann. Von den Arealen, die beim Workshop untersucht wurden, liegt es am weitesten vom Wiener Zentrum entfernt und ist am stärksten als Vorort geprägt.

Unsere Aufgabe war es insbesondere festzulegen, was in dem 7,6 ha großen Gebiet direkt um einen alten Getreidespeicher geschehen solle. Dieses Gebäude hat angeblich eine enge historische Verbindung zu Napoleon. Während des Feldzugs von 1809 soll er hier sein Hauptquartier aufgeschlagen haben. In diesem Gebäude, dem sogenannten „Schüttkasten", befindet sich ein kleines Museum, das uns darauf schließen läßt, daß Napoleon hier einige Zeit verbrachte. Unser Gelände würde daher logischerweise eine Erweiterung oder einen Zusatz zu diesem „Napoleonmuseum" bilden.

Schlacht von Aspern am 21 Mai 1809 / Battle of Aspern Mai 21, 1809

Napoleon did not sleep here

Landscape on the periphery

Approach

Our site is located in the town of Eßling which is situated 30 km from central Vienna, 30 minutes away by public transportation, 60 minutes by bike, or 180 minutes by foot. Of all the sites to be examined at the workshop, it is farthest from Vienna and most suburban in character.

Our specific task was to define what should happen in the 7,6 hectare area which immediately surrounds an old granary building. This building is purposed to have a close historical connection to Napoleon. It was inferred to us initially that Napoleon located his battle headquarters in this building during the War of 1809, where he was successfully repulsed by the Austrians. The building, called the "Schüttkasten" contains a small museum which leads us to conclude that Napoleon spent some time in this structure. Our site therefore, would logically become an extension or adjunct to this "Napoleon Museum".

Schüttkasten, Eßling Wien 22

Ort: Wiens Landwirtschafts- und Technikgeschichte läßt sich ausgezeichnet an diesem Ort zeigen; Agrarland, der Fluß, Schiffe, Kanalisierung, Ölgewinnung, Steinbrüche und Stadterweiterung /
Place: Vienna's agrarian and technological history is eloquently described in this place; natural marshland, farmland, the river, shipping, canalizing, oil refining, quarrying and urban expansion.

Bei der Begehung des Geländes wurde unsere Aufgabe immer unklarer. Der Standort des Schüttkastens selbst hat eine problematische Lage an der Rückseite von Eßling, wie es bei solchen Dörfern üblich ist, an einer Straße mit Bauernhäusern, die die Aufmerksamkeit auf die zur landwirtschaftlich genutzte Landschaft lenken. Private Raumkorridore mit Hausparzellen, Scheunenhöfen und Privatgärten führen zu ihm. Der Schüttkasten liegt am Übergang zwischen den hinteren Grenzen der linearen Bauernhöfe und den offenen Weizenfeldern.

Darüber hinaus sollen die direkt im Osten angrenzenden Grundstücke für eine Schule und eine neue Wohnanlage erschlossen werden.

Dieser neue und scheinbar zufällige Entwicklungsbeginn macht die Verbindungen zwischen dem Schüttkasten und seinem Standort noch unklarer. Nach dem Bekanntwerden der Entwicklungspläne für die Zukunft, die die Schaffung von 10.000 bis 20.000 Wohneinheiten in der unmittelbaren Umgebung beinhalten, scheinen die Verbindungen dieses Monuments zur historischen Agrarlandschaft kaum mehr zu existieren. Und wirklich wird die Identität und die Gestalt von Eßling als Straßendorf inmitten eines riesigen offenen Raums umgeben von Weizen mit ziemlicher Sicherheit nicht mehr lange erhalten bleiben. An diesem Punkt hatten wir nicht nur keine Antworten für unser eigentliches Gelände mit Hinblick auf seine Nutzung und seine Umgebung gefunden, sondern schienen auch die Identität des Dorfes Eßling selbst verloren zu haben. Alles war völlig offen. Wir wußten, daß wir Distanz zu unserem Projektgelände gewinnen mußten, um ein klares Bild der zukünftigen Entwicklung gewinnen zu können. Die einzige Möglichkeit, wie wir wieder zum Areal zurückfinden konnten, war, es zu verlassen, um weitere Informationen zu beschaffen.

Wir gingen von unserem Projektareal, dem Schüttkasten, aus und begannen mit der Entdeckung der Elemente der „freien Räume": es gab Bäume, Felder, Wohnhäuser, Kirchen, Öltanks, einen Fluß, Straßen, Autos sowie Menschen.
Durch eine Analyse entdeckten wir schließlich Muster im offenen Raum mit unterschiedlichen Merkmalen. Abgestimmt auf die Art und Weise, in der Menschen in diesen Räumen leben und sich durch sie bewegen, sowie auf die zukünftige Entwicklung Wiens in Richtung auf unser Gelände versuchten wir Beziehungen zwischen diesen Räumen herzustellen, um den derzeitigen und künftigen Bewohnern des Eßlinger Gebiets ein Gefühl der Nähe zur Stadt und zur Natur zu geben.

Upon our site visit, our mission became increasingly unclear. The "Schüttkasten" itself was ambiguously situated at the rem of the town of Eßling which, as is traditional of such villages, hugs the road with farm houses, which lead one's attention back to the agricultural landscape. Private corridors of space including house plots, barnyards und private gardens. The "Schüttkasten" sits at the border between the rear limits of the linear farm lots and open fields of wheat.

In addition to this, the lots to the immediate east are to be developed into a school and new housing project.

This new and seemingly random beginning of development further obscures the connections between "Schüttkasten" and its site. It seems, that after discovery of future development plans, which includes the creation of 10,000 - 20,000 units of housing into the immediate landscape, that connections of this monument to its historical agricultural landscape, is doomed to be lost. In fact, the identity and form of Eßling, as a small town clustered along a road, in a vast open space filled with wheat, is most certainly doomed at this point. Not only had we not found the answers of our immediate site in terms of use and adjancies, it seems that we had lost the identity of the small, town of Eßling itself. All bets were off. We knew we had to pull way back from our project site in order to get a clear picture of the future. The only way we could possibly find our way back to our site, was to leave it in a search of information.

We started from our project site, the Schüttkasten, and began our discovery of what existed in the "empty spaces": there existed trees, agricultural fields, homes, churches, oil tanks, a river, roads, cars as well as people.

Through analysis, we came to discover patterns of open spaces of differing characteristics. Combined with how people live in and travel through these spaces, and what the future development of Vienna will be in our site's direction, we attempted to make relationships between these spaces so that there was a greater sense of connections to both the city and to nature for people who now live and will come to live in the Eßling area.

We have suggested a landscape infrastructure which will provide corridors of connections between Eßling and Aspern, Eßling and the airfield development, Eßling and New Eßling, all of these communities to Vienna, and ultimately all to the Greenbelt.

Bauplatz: Die Proportion von 1:8 hebt unseren Bauplatz von der Landschaft ab, ein 12km langer, von Süd nach Nord verlaufender Streifen. Der Schüttkasten ist das Zentrum. Anbauflächen bilden die äußeren Grenzen. /
Site: The proportion of 1:8 distinguishes our site in the landscape; a strip 12 km long running from south to north. The Schüttkasten is the centre. Agrarian fields defines its outer limits.

Wir schlugen eine landschaftliche Infrastruktur vor, um die herum die 10.000 bis 20.000 neuen Wohneinheiten, die in diesem Gebiet gebaut werden, angesiedelt werden können. Diese Landschaften werden für das Leben der Bewohner dieser neuen Stadt Identität, Brennpunkt und örtliche Bestimmung bieten.

Die vorgeschlagene landschaftliche Infrastruktur schafft Verbindungskorridore zwischen Eßling und Aspern, Eßling und dem Flugfeldgelände, Eßling und Neu-Eßling, zwischen all diesen Gemeinschaften und Wien sowie dem Grüngürtel.

Wir sehen die Landschaft nicht als leeren Raum. Sie muß manipuliert und für bestimmte praktische und geistige Nutzungszwecke gestaltet werden. Wir wollen eine Reihe von Landschaften vorschlagen, die die formale Struktur und die von Maschinen geprägten Muster von Agrarlandschaften anklingen lassen, die durch künftige Entwicklungen sicherlich verloren gehen werden.

Diese neue Agrarlandschaft ist so angelegt, daß sie für soziale und kulturelle Zwecke in Besitz genommen werden kann. Doch die Erinnerung an diesen Ort landwirtschaftlichen Ursprungs wird bewahrt und als ein Schatten innerhalb der neuen Eßlinger Landschaften und schließlich innerhalb unseres ursprünglichen Geländes, des Schüttkastens, zum Ausdruck gebracht.

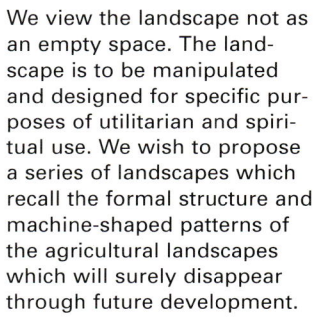

We view the landscape not as an empty space. The landscape is to be manipulated and designed for specific purposes of utilitarian and spiritual use. We wish to propose a series of landscapes which recall the formal structure and machine-shaped patterns of the agricultural landscapes which will surely disappear through future development.

This new agricultural landscape is designed to be inhabited for social and cultural purposes. But the memory of this place of agricultural origin, will be preserved and expressed as a shadow within the new landscapes of Eßling and ultimately within our original site, the Schüttkasten.

Studentenarbeiten, Beispiele:

Silvia Braun

Die Stadt ist keine hermetische Struktur, die Stadtentwicklung keine hermetische Disziplin, beide sind offene Gebiete, in denen sich verschiedene Einflüsse manifestieren und einander überlagern.

Stadt- und Freiraumbilder erfordern heutzutage mehr und mehr Sensibilität und Interesse, ebenso wie absolute Lebensanschauungen mit einem Ja-Nein-Denken von relativen Lebensanschauungen mit den Möglichkeiten von ja, nein und vielleicht abgelöst werden. Unsere Gesellschaft wird immer heterogener, differenzierter und gleichzeitig immer konfrontationsreicher.

Für unterschiedliche Gesellschafts- und Interessensstrukturen benötigen wir verschiedene Lebensformen und eine Infrastruktur, in der sich Teile dieser Gesellschaftsstruktur begegnen können. Diese Bereiche müßten frei von jeder Gesellschaftsordnung sein und uneingeschränkte Bewegungsfreiheit und Kommunikationsmöglichkeiten bieten. Dies kann nur durch eine Unterscheidung von geregelten und wirklich offenen öffentlichen Bereichen erreicht werden.

Randlagen einer Stadt sind so weit vom Zentrum entfernt, daß sie den Inhalt des Zentrums nicht widerspiegeln können und keine Identifikation mehr möglich ist. Randgebiete, die noch nicht als privater, geregelter öffentlicher („halböffentlicher") bzw. ungeregelter öffentlicher Raum definiert wurden, könnten eventuell das Potential haben, als neue Magneten für die Identifikation, den Austausch, die Konfrontation und Annäherung der Menschen an der Peripherie zu dienen.

Wolf Opitsch

Landschaft und Stadtbild einer europäischen Stadt wie Wien müssen in einem anderen Kontext als bisher gesehen werden.

Einige Ereignisse der jüngsten Vergangenheit und einige, die sich für die Zukunft abzeichnen, postulieren einen neuen Zugang zur Erfahrung, zum Lesen und damit zur Planung.

Zitate wie „Die Stadt kann nicht geplant, sondern nur antizipiert werden", sind nur die logische Konsequenz daraus. Der völlig verschwommene Begriff der Stadtgrenzen wird zu einem wichtigen Punkt für die wachsende Stadt.

Dieses Gebiet wird durch seine einzigartigen Elemente, wie Landwirtschaft, Industrieanlagen, Wohngebiete innerhalb der enormen Landressourcen gekennzeichnet.

Die Beziehungen sind weder städtisch noch ländlich.

Die Gesamtheit wird nicht in die Entwicklung einbezogen, ja sie wird sogar übergangen.

Obwohl das Nebeneinander der einzelnen Elemente bestimmte Qualitäten hat, erhalten einige Attribute erst in anderen Schichten Bedeutung, wenn sie zueinander in Beziehung gesetzt werden.

Entfernungen, Maßstäbe können in einer menschlichen Relation nicht erfaßt werden, da die bekannten Elemente fehlen. Raum erscheint oft nicht wie erwartet oder ist stärker präsent als angenommen. Innerhalb der Entwicklung wird es wichtig sein, die ausgeprägten Qualitäten der Elemente zu bewahren und ihre bereits vorhandenen Attribute zu nutzen.

Examples of student projects:

Silvia Braun

The city is no heretic structure, urban development no hermetic discipline, both are opened fields in with different influences superpose and manifest one another.

Town and free space-images of this day call for more and more sensibility and interest, in the same measure as the absolute view of life of Yes- or No-thinking is changed to relative views of life of Yes-No-Perhaps.

Our society becomes more and more heterogenous and differentiated and at the same time more and more confronted together. For different social and interest-structures we need different types for living and infrastructure, where parts of these social structures come together. At the same time we need areas for the meeting of all social structures. These areas had to be free of any social order, with the freedom of movement and communication. Only by distinguished regulated public areas and really opened public areas this can be achieved. Peripheral areas of a city are so far away from the city-center, they can't reflect the content of the center.

At this distance there is no identification possible. Peripheral areas which are not yet defined as private, regulated public ("semi-public") and unregulated public perhaps could be the potential for attractors for new identification, interchange, confrontation and approach of the various people in the periphery.

Wolf Opitsch

Landscape and cityscape of a european city like Vienna must be read in a different context than it used to be. Some events of the recent past and some to be expected in the future postulate a new approach towards the experience, reading and therefore planning.

Quotations like "city can not be planned only anticipated" are just a logical consequence. The totally blurred notion of the city borders becomes an important issue for the growing city. This area is characterized by its unique elements like agriculture, industries, housing within the vast resource of land.

The relationships are neither urban nor rural. The collectivity is not involved with the development bit even passed. Although single elements being next to each other has certain qualities. Some attributes gain meaning in other layers when they are set in connections to each other. Distances, scales can not be grasped in a human relation because the known elements are missing. Space does often not appears as expected or is stronger present as thought to be. Within the development it will be important to conserve the distinct qualities of the elements, to use their attributes they already offer.

Stadt Gärten / Town gardens

Andreas Holzapfel
Die von uns vorgefundenen Städte und die sie umgebenden Landschaften sind das Ergebnis verschiedener Gesellschaften, die sie zu dem gemacht haben, was sie heute sind. Mehr denn je steht die Stadt für die Koexistenz und die Abfolge von zahllosen Ideologien, Gesellschaften, Traditionen, Lebensweisen und -rhythmen ... Das Resultat ist ebenso heterogen und interessant wie seine Nutzer. Deshalb kann es heute nicht Aufgabe eines Stadt- oder Landschaftsplaners sein, Gemeinschaftsmodelle zu erstellen. Vielmehr müssen Strategien gefunden werden, wie alte Ideen aufgenommen und in neue Konzepte integriert werden können, ohne die Morphologie aus den Augen zu verlieren.

Und es muß zahllose, verschiedene Arten von Freiräumen geben, mit einer faszinierenden Vielfalt der Charaktere, Funktionen, Definitionen, Formen ...

Harald Vavrovsky
Der Schwerpunkt liegt auf dem Leben, z.B. Familie, Bildung, Arbeit, Egoismus, Ziele

Der Schwerpunkt liegt auf der Umgebung, z.B. Wohnung, Haus, Bezirk, Stadt, Land, Staat, Nation, Kontinent, Welt, Kosmos

Der Schwerpunkt liegt auf der Phantasie, z.B. Gefühle, Emotionen, Gedanken, Erfahrungen, Schmerz, Erwartungen

Ein Schwerpunkt ist somit etwas Öffentliches und etwas Privates, je nach Ansicht, Position und Erfahrung.

Was ist öffentlich? Alles, was man zeigt, was man äußert, was für andere und das Umfeld erfahrbar ist.
Ohne das eine gibt es das andere nicht, somit ist die Privatsphäre ein Teil des Öffentlichen.
Die Grenze der Interaktion zwischen Öffentlichem und Privatem ist das Interessensgebiet, seine Durchdringung ist das Zensurieren, die erkennbare Linie der Veränderung.
Die Elemente dieser Grenze sind: eine Schwelle, eine Barriere, ein Tor, ein sich verengender Pfad usw.
Das Vokabular ist: Zugang, Verwendung von Material – Nutzungsänderung, Weite und Intimität, Orientierung, Verbindung zu einem größeren Element oder Raster, hinein & hinaus, innen & außen, im Mittelpunkt und außerhalb des Mittelpunkts.

Andreas Holzapfel
The city, and the landscape as we find them, are results of different societies which made them. Today, city means more than ever the coexistence and succession of countless ideologies, societies, traditions, ways and rhythms of life... The result is as heterogenous as it´s users, and as interesting. So the job of an urban or landscape planner today cannot be to form real models, but to find strategies which accept the old ideas and integrate all the new ones and always looking on a morphology.

And there have to be countless different kinds of free spaces with their fascinating diversity of characters, functions, definitions, forms...

Harald Vavrosky
The focus is in the middle of someones life, a focus might be:

family, education, work, egoism, goals.
The focus is in the middle of someone`s surroundings, a focus might be: apartment, house, district, city, country, state, nation, continent, world, cosmos.

The focus is in the middle of someone´s imagination, a focus might be: feelings, emotions, thoughts, experiences, pain, expectations

So a focus is a public as well as a private thing, depending on the view, position and experiences.

What is public? Anything one shows, what he utters, which is experienceable by others, by the surrounding.
A line drawn straight divides two areas without any connotation about which is public which is private, if you draw a curved line it will start to enclose an area which implies privacy and public. Without the one there is not the other, so privacy is an enclosure in public.
The border of interaction of public and privacy is the area of interest, the penetration is the censoring, the noticeable line of change.
The elements of this border are: a threshold, a barrier, a gate, a narrowing of the path, etc.
The vocabulary is: access, use of material - the change of use, vastness and intimacy, orientation, the connection to a greater element or grid, in & out, inside & outside, focus & out of focus.

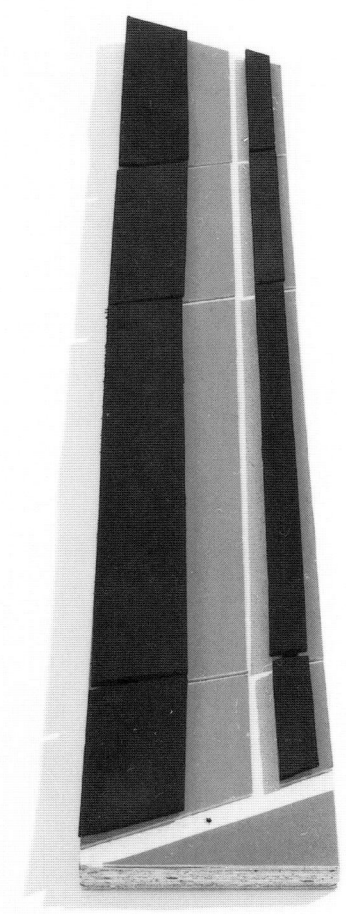

Luftstreifen Park / Airstrip park

Schüttkasten Park – Gedenken – Weizen / Schüttkasten park – memory – wheat

**Pflege unserer Landschaft – Proportion 1:8 / 70 x 500cm; ein 3,5m² großes leeres Grundstück wird jedem Bewohner Wiens zugeteilt /
Nurturing our landscape – a proportion 1:8 / 70 x 500 cm a plot of 3,5m² open space allotted to each citizen of Vienna**

Der Landschaftsplan als Infrastruktur: Das Dorf Eßling hat sich stark in die Umgebung ausgeweitet. Baumstreifen haben sich von der Lobau im Süden Richtung Norden ausgedehnt und verbinden bereits einen der „natürlichsten" Bauplätze Wiens.

1. Ein Erholungsraum reicht bis an einen der städtischen Gebiete, das seinen Weg durch die Ost-West Achse der Stadt hindurch „wackelt".

2. Ein zentraler Streifen folgt der historischen Allee, welche unter Maria Theresia gepflanzt wurde.

3. Ein dritter Streifen erlaubt einen geraden Landschaftszug durch welchen möglicher Wohnbau im Osten definiert wird; Landschaft ist von hier an ein Katalysator.

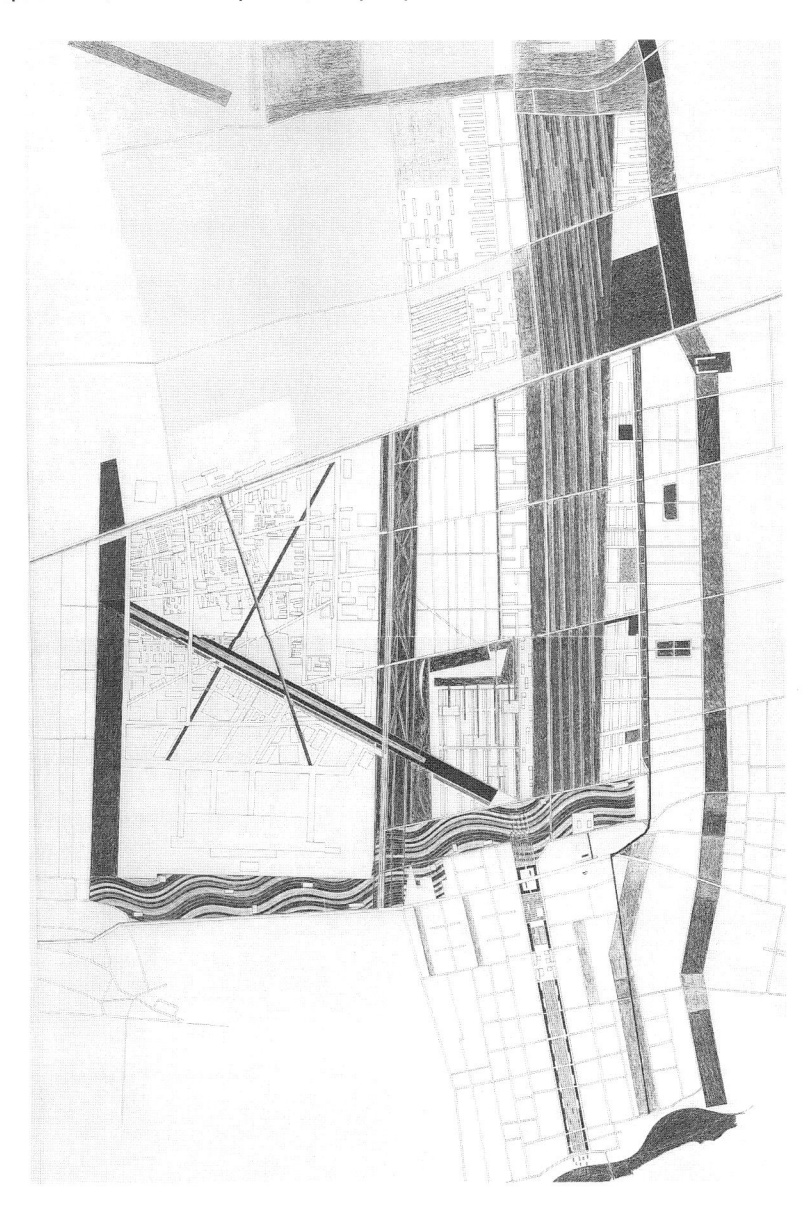

The Landscape plan as infrastructure: The town of Eßling has now expanded reaching its fingers of landscape out towards much of its rich surroundings area. From the Lobau to the south, tree strips move northward connecting one of Viennas most "natural" sites to the town.

1. A recreational strip reaches to the main civic grounds that "wiggle" their way throught the east-west axis of the town.

2. A centre strip follows the historic allee planted by the royal huntsmen of Maria Theresia.

3. A third strip allows a linear landscape path to define new housing on the eastern edge, landscape is now catalyst.

Räume, räume Boris Podrecca

Der öffentliche Raum hat in den 60er und 70er Jahren durch die Fußgängerzonen eine Schematisierung durchlebt. Es wurden aber zumindest gewisse konsensuelle Prämissen und interdisziplinäre Ansätze für eine gemeinsame Plattform entwickelt.

Heute, in der Zeit der unbegrenzten Möglichkeiten, ist der öffentliche Raum beinahe zum Freiwild geworden. Von Avantgardeapotheosen bloßer Gestualität bis zu restaurativen Piktogrammen und Mimikris mutierte der öffentliche Raum zu einem Ring einzelner Aktionen merkantiler oder kunstnaher Art. In diesem saftarmen Szenario erschien vielen die Flucht in die integrative Askese des virtuellen Raumes als einzige Ist-Zeit-Alternative.

Bei unserem 6. Wiener Architekturseminar liegt die Betonung auf „DER öffentliche Raum", was nicht auf das Diktat neuer Regeln, das Gerede vom genius loci oder auf irgendwelche Homogenisierungsversuche der Straßen und Plätze hinzielt. Vielmehr wird nach einer neuen Stadtethik (statt Ästhetik) gefragt, nach einer Langzeitverantwortung des Gestalters und nicht nach beschränkter Haftung.

In einer Zeit, die zugleich durch Überschuß und Armut an Gestalt charakterisiert ist und sich gerade im Übergang von der mechanischen in die elektronische Ära befindet, ist es Aufgabe unseres Architekturseminars, neue referentielle Ideogramme abzurufen, um sie schon im Entstehen hinterfragen zu können. Auf einem solchen Übungsfeld kann vor allem der Gefahr einer Eurotisierung des öffentlichen Raumes zumindest partiell entgegengesteuert werden. Die rettende Norm gebärdet sich nur anfangs als Samariter, um einmal exekutiert zum Kraus'schen „Es lebe das gleiche Unrecht für alle" zu führen.

Angehende und konsakrierte Bau-Künstler, bekannte Nordlichter und mediterrane Maestri, Exoten und Lutheraner treffen sich in Wien, um Studenten und jungen Architekten die freie Poetik ihrer Erfahrungen zu lehren und sie am weitläufigen Territorium dieser Stadt anzuwenden. Eine Stadt, in der in Zukunft, wie es scheint, der große sinfonische Klang Transdanubiens langsam, aber sicher zum kammermusikalischen Timbre eines adretten Trios aus Stadt, Developer und Architekten mutiert. Diesem Szenario wird auch das Wiener Architekturseminar in Zukunft Rechnung tragen müssen, um der Gefahr, den vorgelebten Elan einer bloßen Veranstaltungskultur zu opfern, zu entgehen.

Spaces, spaces Boris Podrecca

In the 60's and 70's, public space was schematized in an urban environment, revolving around pedestrian areas. Nevertheless, certain consensual premises and interdisciplinary approaches for a common platform were developed.

Today, in these times of unlimited opportunities, public space has almost become something of a common prey. Ranging from avant-garde excesses of sheer gesticulation to restorative pictographs and mimicry, public space evolved into an arena of commercial or art-like acts of expression. Against the background of this lifeless scenario, many saw an escape into the integrative asceticism of virtual space as being the only real-time alternative.

At our 6th Viennese Seminar on Architecture, we focus on "The public space", not meaning that we intend to prescribe new rules, debate upon the genius loci, or strive to bring about a homogenization of streets and squares. We rather embark on the quest for new ethics (not aesthetics), for a long-term responsibility instead of limited liability for the designer.

Today, in a period of transition from the mechanical to the electronic age, where abundance and scarcity of form are closely intertwined, it is the duty of our architecture seminar to evoke new referential ideograms, only to challenge them as soon as they begin to evolve. In particular, a test field of this kind is likely to - at least partially - protect us against the hazards of eurotization. Because the standard that comes to the rescue only behaves like a good Samaritan at the beginning, but when implemented once, it leads us to Karl Kraus' "Long live the same injustice for all".

Established architectural artists and those in the making, famous northern stars and Mediterranean maestri, architecture philosophers and writers gathered in Vienna to teach students and young architects the free poetry of their experience and apply it on the spacious territory of this city. A city in which the great symphonic sounds of Transdanubia slowly but steadily mutate into the timbre of a smart chamber music trio made up of city, developers, and architects. The Vienna Architecture Seminar must also consider this scenario in the future so as to avoid seeing its initial élan turning to a mere cultural event.

Architektur Zentrum Wien

Projektgruppen

6. Wiener Architekturseminar
DER öffentliche Raum

Project groups

6th Viennese Seminar on Architecture
THE Public Space

26 | 08 – 17 | 09 | 1995

Veranstalter / Organizer
Architektur Zentrum Wien
Museumsquartier
Burggasse 1, A-1070 Wien
Telefon: (43)-1-522 31 15
Fax: (43)-1-522 31 17

Das Seminar erfolgt
werkstattartig in intensiver
Betreuung und Diskussion;
Gastvorträge.

The seminar will consist
of workshops, with ample
opportunity for guided
work and discussion;
Guest Lectures.

Seminarleitung / Seminar Coordinators

Boris Podrecca
Dietmar Steiner
Wien

Projektgruppen mit / Project groups with

Mariano Bayón
Madrid
Ben van Berkel
Amsterdam
Michelangelo Pistoletto
Turin
Fabio Reinhart
Lugano
Dagmar Richter
Los Angeles

23 von 80 Tage Wien

**Projektgruppe / project group
Mariano Bayón**

Assistent: Stephan Zehl

Sönke Anderson

Boris Bezan

Heike Buchmann

Aljuse Dekleva

Maria Eugenia del Rio Villar

Michael Gaisser

Thilo Gumbsch

Britta Christine Klingebiel

Vlatka Ljubanovic

Xavier Ros Majó

Christiane Schmitz

Mima Suhedoic

Schorsch Michael Tschürtz

Jonathan Tugores Kirtley

Carlos Asensio Wandoseii Garcia

Henner Winkelmüller

Mariano Bayon Madrid

1942 born in Madrid
1967 graduated at the Escuela Tecnica Superior de Arquitectura, Madrid

Teaching positions
1976 to now: teacher at the Higher Technical School of Architecture, Madrid

Selection of work
1987 Corrala dwellings, Madrid
1989 Exhibition Center Madrid
1990 Collective dwellings with patio, Palomeras, Madrid
1990 Office building and passage, Santander
1991 Restoration and enlargement Avilés Theatre, Asturias
1992 Spanish electricity network company building, Sevilla
1994 Villaverde library, Madrid
1994 Spanish Museum of Architecture, Madrid
1995 Tower and complex of social dwellings, Fuencarral A, Madrid
1995 ABC comercial center, Madrid
1995 Avilés Market, Asturias
1995 Pedestrianisation of the historic Center of Avilés

Major exhibitions
1990–93 Bienal de Arquitectura española.
1991 Weissenhof Galerie, Stuttgart
1992 Haus der Architektur, Graz
1993 Dansk Arkitekturcenter, Copenhagen
1993 Colegio de Arquitectos, Alicante
1993 Colegio de Arquitectos, Madrid
1996 Biennale di Venezia

Publications among others
1964–69 Critical texts about architecture in the spanish magazine „Arquitectura"
1991 Mariano Bayón, 1991, Monographie, Architektur Galerie am Weissenhof, Stuttgart
1992 Mariano Bayón, Catalogue, Haus der Architektur, Graz
1993 Mariano Bayón, Catalogue, Dansk Arkitektur Center, Copenhagen
1993 Mariano Bayón, Catalogue, College of Architects, Alicante, Madrid

Prizes / Awards
1980 National architectural prize, Spain
1981 National urbanism prize, Spain
1987 College of Architects Prize, Madrid
1988&91 City Council Architectural prize, Madrid
1980, 1986, 1987, 1991 Europa Nostra prize

Vom Prinzip des minimalen Aufwands Mariano Bayón

Meine langjährige Erfahrung hat mir gezeigt, wie sich gebaute Objekte und Leerräume ineinanderfügen – im Außenraum wie im Innenraum.
Häufig kommt es zu einer Neudefinition der Begriffe „außen" und „innen", wobei die Grenzen nicht mehr eindeutig erkennbar sind: innenliegende Plätze, einem größeren Volumen abgerungene, ambivalente Räume, raumteilende Straßen, ein Freiraum, der sich im Innersten einer dichten Verbauung öffnet – außen liegendes Inneres – ins Innere verlagerte städtebauliche Elemente. Im Mittelmeerraum und in den orientalischen Ländern ist man mit diesem architektonischen Vokabular bestens vertraut.

Das sind natürlich Aspekte, die erst a posteriori beobachtet werden können. Sie verbinden sich aber mit dem Verständnis von Stadt als Einheit in der Vielfalt und mit der Strategie der Demontage des Gebauten, die mit der Ausdehnung des freien Raumes einhergeht, wenn man die Stadt als offenen Raum versteht.

Ich vermute, daß das Werk eines Künstlers seinem Wesen entspricht, und daß er arbeitet, um die innere Ordnung seiner selbst und der Dinge zu erfühlen und zu erforschen.

Meiner Meinung nach ist es die Aufgabe der Architektur, ein System zu schaffen, das intuitiv Ordnungen erfaßt und repräsentiert, die unsere Betrachtung, unser Verständnis und unserer Wahrnehmung der Welt strukturieren.

Es geht um die Schaffung eines Kräftediagramms oder besser einer dreidimensionalen Struktur von Kräften, die es vermag, ein Bild des kollektiven Bewußtseins hervorzubringen, archetypische Formen unseres Bewußtseins (nicht notwendigerweise nur Bilder, aber auch Bilder), die uns kollektiv verbinden.

On the principle of minimal effort Mariano Bayón

Many years of experience have shown me how built objects and vacant spaces join together - both in exterior and in interior spaces.
Very often the concepts "exterior" and "interior" are newly defined, and the distinctions become blurred: spaces of the interior are ambivalent spaces wrested from a larger whole, roads that divide spaces, an empty space that opens up at the heart of a densely built area - inside turned out - elements of urban development transferred into the interior. In the Mediterranean and oriental countries, one is well familiar with this type of architectural vocabulary.

Naturally, these are all aspects that can only be observed with hindsight. However, they connect with the notion of cities as a homogeneous entity in diversity as well as with the strategy of dismantling built things, that goes hand in hand with the expansion of free space, if the city is considered free space.

I presume that the work of an artist reflects his being, and that an artist works to feel and investigate things and the order within himself.

In my opinion it is architecture's task to create a system that grasps and represents the orders which intuitively structure our observation, understanding, and perception of the world.

The aim is to create a power diagram or, better still, a three-dimensional structure of powers, that can bring forth an image of collective consciousness, archetypal forms of our consciousness (not necessarily only images but also images) that make us a group.

In architecture I am committed to exploring the nature of beauty to its very depths. In this context beauty stands as the generic term and encompasses all harmony: of use, of yearning, of sharing, of invention, of planning. Beauty unsought. Beauty unspoken.

As the likeness of the positive spirit of our times, with the means of our times and the willingness to be open-minded toward them.

This search without system, generation without tension, trial without program – concrete regarding the necessity and ambiguous regarding the artistic aspect – solve at the outset the pending conflict with the superfluous and the arbitrary

But what is the substance rescued?

Possibly reduction and unity are the two artistic instincts of today, the two fields of power, that are unambiguous in themselves and the likeliest able to ease and guide our tensions and to

Design Center, Madrid, 1986–1989

Mein Anliegen in der Architektur ist es, das Wesen der Schönheit in seiner ganzen Tiefe zu ergründen. Die Schönheit steht hier als Oberbegriff und umfaßt jegliche Harmonie: die der Nutzung, der Sehnsucht, des Teilens, des Erfindens, des Planens.
Schönheit, die nicht gesucht wird. Schönheit, von der man nicht spricht.
Als Abbild des positiven Geistes unserer Zeit, mit den Mitteln unserer Zeit und der Bereitschaft, sich ihnen zu öffnen.

Diese Suche ohne Systematik, dieses Entstehen ohne Spannung, dieser Versuch ohne Programm - konkret hinsichtlich der Notwendigkeit und mehrdeutig hinsichtlich des künstlerischen Aspekts – lösen von vornherein den anstehenden Konflikt mit dem Überflüssigen und Willkürlichen.

Woraus besteht aber die gerettete Substanz?

Vielleicht sind Reduktion und Einheit heute jene beiden künstlerischen Instinkte, jene beiden Kraftfelder, die in sich eindeutig sind, und am ehesten unsere Spannungen zu klären und zu leiten vermögen und uns zur Ausgeglichenheit zu führen scheinen. Vielleicht waren sie die Grundlage künstlerischen Schaffens in jeder Epoche.

Die Einheit des Ganzen und der Teilaspekt in den Handlungen der einzelnen Menschen.

Die Reduktion, die das Aufgesetzte und Unnötige ablehnt, auf der Suche nach Substanz, nach dem Gesetz des minimalen Aufwands. Das gleiche Prinzip von Aufwand und Ökonomie hat der Physiker Maupertius im 18. Jahrhundert an der Natur beobachtet. Es ließ ihn jenes allgemeine Prinzip formulieren, wonach in der Natur jede Veränderung mit dem geringstmöglichen Aufwand zu erfolgen habe. Die Natur hält den Aufwand stets gering.

Darüber hinaus gehen Reduktion und Einheit Hand in Hand, sind ihrerseits eindeutig und sind identisch.

Reduktion bedeutet die eingehende Suche nach dem Wesen der Zweckmäßigkeit, der Zurückhaltung, schließlich der Schönheit unter Mißachtung des Falschen, des Aufgesetzten.

Hinter dem Dickicht von Sachzwängen, die das Bauen jedes Mal wieder bestimmen, verbirgt sich eine geeignete Form, die endgültige Form, der starke Kern, der alle anstehenden Fragen auf einen Schlag löst. Dort ist die Schönheit zu finden, die nicht erst gesucht werden muß, dort ist der Punkt, wo alle Spannungen, Unsicherheiten, Sehnsüchte, Widersprüche, die Wirtschaftlichkeit, die Funktion und das Denken zusammenkommen. Erst durch eine Destillation all dieser Faktoren kommt der darunter verborgene Kristall in komprimierter Form zum Vorschein.

Entkleidet vom Falschen, Aufgesetzten, Unklaren.

Immer wieder muß man dem Zuviel widerstehen, Strich für Strich, Detail um Detail, bis zur Fertigstellung des Werkes.

appear to lead us to an inner balance. Perhaps they formed the foundation for artistic work in all epochs.

The unity of the whole, and the partial aspect in the deeds of the individual.

The reduction that rejects the superimposed and the superfluous on the quest for substance and the law of minimal effort. The same principle of effort and economy was observed by the physicist Maupertius in nature in the 18th century. As a consequence he formulated the general principle according to which all changes in nature must occur involving the least possible effort. Nature always minimizes effort.
Furthermore reduction and unity go hand in hand, are unambiguous and identical.

Offices in Santander, 1987–1990

Reduction means the thorough search for the nature of functionality, of restraint, and finally of beauty that rejects the false and the superimposed.

Behind the thicket of constraints that time and time again determines building, an appropriate form lies hidden, the final form, the strong core that answers all questions at once. Here beauty can be found that doesn't require searching, here is the spot where all tension, insecurity, yearning, contradiction, efficiency, function, and thinking converge. At this point all these factors are distilled to bring to light in condensed form. The gem hidden beneath.

Divested of all that is false, superimposed, confused.

Time after time the superfluous must be resisted, line for line, detail for detail, until the work has been accomplished.

The more thorough, precise, condensed, clear, and distilled this painstaking work is done, the more authentic it will appear; it will attract attention, enter into multifarious relations and finally suspend time and space.

The aim of reducing the authentic draft is the search for unity and this unity draws nearer as realization progresses.

Je gründlicher, reduzierter, komprimierter, klarer und destillierter diese minuziöse Arbeit ist, desto authentischer wird sie erscheinen; sie wird Aufmerksamkeit erregen, vielfältige Beziehungen eingehen und letztlich Zeit und Raum aufheben.

Die Reduktion des authentischen Entwurfes hat die Suche nach Einheit zum Ziel und diese Einheit rückt mit der Realisierung immer näher.

Nur mit einer Erweiterung der Vorstellung von Stadt als Makulatur neuer dynamischer Sektoren, denen die alte Ordnung der Stadt fremd ist, nur in der Ausweitung der Idee der Stadt auf die neuen Kräfte können wir das Gefühl der Einheit wiedererlangen, die es schafft, neue, verständliche, gebaute Organismen hervorzubringen, um, wie immer, durch das Positive, das in dieser Einheit zu finden ist, herrschende Gegensätze zu versöhnen.

Bei Infrastrukturmaßnahmen, Straßen, Kanälen, Autobahnen oder Eisenbahntrassen bedarf es einer reduzierten und einheitlichen Architektur, einer einfachen und beredten, aber nicht plappernden und belehrenden Architektur, einer Bauweise, die nach Anonymität trachtet, einer Architektur, die dadurch Bedeutung erlangt, was sie sagt, und nicht wer es sagt, in der jedoch der ganze Erfindungs- und Schöpfergeist ihres Autors kondensiert ist, mit Lösungen, die der Logik der Umstände entsprechen, in Verwirklichung der herrschenden Geisteshaltung – ohne viel nachzudenken.

Only by expanding the concept of cities as draft paper for new dynamic sectors that are not unfamiliar with the old order of the city, only by enlarging our notion of the city to include the new powers, will we regain the feeling of unity that can successfully produce new, lucid organisms, built, as always, in order to reconcile existing contradictions with the help of the positive elements found in this unity.

What is needed for infrastructure measures such as streets, channels, highways, or train lines is a necessary, reduced, and uniform architecture, simple and eloquent, not chattering and preaching, a style that aspires to be anonymous, an architecture that acquires meaning by what it says and not by who says it. It should, however, condense its author's entire ingenuity and creative spirit with solutions that correspond to the logic of the circumstances, in realization of the reigning mentality - without too much reflection.

Red Electrica España, Sevilla, 1989

Housing in Gran via San Francisco el Grande, Madrid, 1989–1990

Transformation der Vorstadt –
Zentrumsbildung im Entwicklungsraum. Stadlau, Wien 22

Der Ort Stadlau entwickelte sich im 19. Jahrhundert nach der Donauregulierung und dem Bau der Ost-Bahn zu einem wichtigen Industriestandort. Stadlau liegt am Schnittpunkt wichtiger Verkehrsträger und ist heute ein dicht besiedelter Bezirksteil, dessen ursprünglich ländlicher Charakter nur noch in wenigen Bereichen erkennbar ist.

In einer angestrebten polyzentralen Struktur ist für Stadlau die Funktion eines dritten Zentrums nordöstlich der Donau vorgesehen. Der Zentrumsbereich mit Ansätzen einer lokalen Einkaufsstraße soll eine Nutzungsintensivierung und maßvolle Verdichtung erfahren. Durch Verbesserungsmaßnahmen soll eine Aufwertung erreicht werden.

Auf einem ehemaligen Fabriksareal ist die Errichtung einer Wohnanlage mit Geschäftszentrum und Büros geplant. Die Giebelwände der alten Fabrikshallen an der Erzherzog-Karl-Straße sollen als signifikantes Element in den Neubau integriert werden. Die freibleibende Fläche zur Straße stellt mit der Möglichkeit einer späteren Überbauung eine Erwartungsfläche für einen künftigen Bedarf dar.

Der vorgesehene Ausbau der Schnellbahnlinie S80 soll in Form einer neuen, in Hochlage östlich entlang des bestehenden Bahngeländes geführten Trasse erfolgen.

Für die Querung der stark befahrenen Erzherzog Karl Straße, ist die Errichtung einer Fußgängerbrücke vorgesehen. Der Markt am Genochplatz soll funktionell erhalten bleiben. Überlegt wird jedoch die Möglichkeit, den Markt auf die freie Fläche vor dem neuen Geschäftszentrum zu übersiedeln und das derzeitige Marktareal für eine neue öffentliche Nutzung zu widmen.

Transformation of the suburbs –
formation of a center in the development area. Stadlau, Vienna 22

In the 19th century after the control of the Danube and the construction of the eastern Railway, Stadlau developed from a small village into an important industrial site. Stadlau is situated at the juction of important traffic routes and constitutes the access to the eastern part of the 22nd district. Today it is a densely populated district, whose originally rural character has survived only in a few fragmental parts.

Stadlau is intended as a third centre northeast of the Danube as part of an intended polycentral structure.

The center with its rudimentary, local shopping mall shall be subjected both to a more intense use, and a rational densification. The area shall be upgraded in its structure through improvement measures.

The construction of a residental estate with a business centre and offices is planned on former factory premises. The gable walls of old factory buildings on Erzherzog Karl Straße shall be integrated into the new building as a significant element. The remaining area towards Erzherzog Karl Straße may be used for construction activities in the future.

It is planned to further develop the suburban railway line S 80 in the form of a new route running above ground east of the existing railway premises.

A pedestrian bridge shall be built for crossing the very busy Erzherzog Karl Straße. The market on Genochplatz shall be preserved in its function. However, there are certain deliberations to move the market to the free area in front of the new shopping centre and to dedicate the present market premises for new, public uses.

Stadlau, Wien 22

Der Maßstab als Maßstab

Annäherung

Die Arbeit in und um den Stadtteil Stadlau, eine Art Stadt in der Stadt, bot ein komplexes Arbeitsfeld, das all die sehr konkreten Aspekte umfaßt, die in der Entwicklung großer Städte gegenwärtig zu beobachten sind:

- Anlage umfassender urbaner Strukturen und Überlegungen zum Ausgleich auf Stadtteilebene
- einschneidende Infrastrukturmaßnahmen und kleinere Projekte
- Umsteigemöglichkeiten beim Aufeinandertreffen hochrangiger und nachrangiger Strukturen
- revitalisierte Stadtviertel einerseits, heruntergekommene andererseits
- exzessive Nutzungen und die Notwendigkeit einer Anpassung der Maßstäbe...

Das gesamte Umfeld mit all seinen Problemen, Chancen und Lösungen ist als komplexer Organismus zu sehen, manchmal deformiert und spannungsgeladen, manchmal prächtig und vielfältig, an einigen Stellen abgestorben, was die Notwendigkeit einer phantasiebetonten Bestandsaufnahme und Aufwertung unterstreicht.

The scale as scale

Approach

The work in and around the Stadlau area, a kind of city within the city, represented a very complex field of activity comprising all the very concrete aspects currently observed in the development of larger cities:

- Construction of comprehensive structures and thoughts on leveling out the Stadlau city area
- Far-reaching infrastructure measures and smaller projects
- Transfer possibilities when high-level and low-level structures meet
- Revitalized parts of the city on the one hand, run-down on the other
- Excessive use and the necessity of adapting scales...

The whole environment must be regarded as a complex organism with all its problems, opportunities, and solutions, sometimes deformed and full of tension, then splendid and multifarious, whithered and dead in some places, underscoring how necessary an inventory and revitalization performed with imagination is.

Ein Entwurf für Stadlau

Über drei Wochen hinweg wurden die Probleme Stadlaus und seine Beziehung zum Zentrum Wiens auf der Grundlage zweier fundamentaler Kriterien untersucht.

A. Wiederbelebung des städtischen und öffentlichen Lebens von Stadlau als kleiner Stadt mit selbständigem Charakter. Verbesserung von Struktur und Image, Analyse der charakteristischen Merkmale und Vorschläge zu deren Optimierung.

B. Analyse und Bewertung der Auswirkungen der alten und neuen gesamtstädtischen Infrastruktursysteme Wiens auf Stadlau, wie:

- Eisenbahnnetz;
- Straßenbahn und Autobahn, Individualverkehr;
- bestehende und künftige U-Bahnlinien;
- künftiges Kulturzentrum;
- altes Waagner-Biro-Gelände, neue Nutzung;

Systematik der Arbeit:
1. Analyse, Diskussion und Bewertung der Probleme und Chancen Stadlaus und seiner Umgebung in der Gruppe.
2. Festsetzung von Prioritäten und Vorgehensweise durch Mariano Bayón und seinen Assistenten Stephan Zehl.
3. Aufteilung der Arbeit auf drei Gruppen, die in Verbindung stehen, und zwei Alternativgruppen.
4. Abschließende Ausarbeitung eines einheitlichen Entwurfs durch die ganze Gruppe, mit alternativen Teillösungen.
5. Architektonische Annäherung an die verschiedenen Lösungen in Einzel- und Gruppenarbeit.

Der Entwurf enthielt folgende Vorgangsweisen:

Ortskern Stadlau

- Wirtschaftliche Aufwertung der Stadlauer Straße;
- Anlegung zweier neuer Plätze mit verschiedenen offenen Räumen zur Aufwertung des öffentlichen Lebens;
- Neuer Hauptplatz mit verschiedenen Elementen wie Mehrzweckhalle, Glocken- und Uhrturm;
- Öffnung und Fortsetzung der Baumbestände hin zu den am weitesten von der Ostbahn entfernten Grünzonen;
- Übergänge zu den Stadlau-Sportanlagen (Brücken);
- Optimierung des geschlossenen Ortskerns, punktuelle Öffnungen der begrünten Hinterhöfe;
- Schaffung eines großen offenen Raumes in Form eines Platzes an der Schnittstelle zwischen dem neuen Kultur- und Ortszentrum, der Bahn und Straßenbahn;
- Neugestaltung des Marktes;
- Neue Verkehrsplanung;
- Entwurf eines Grüngürtels zur Abschottung Stadlaus;

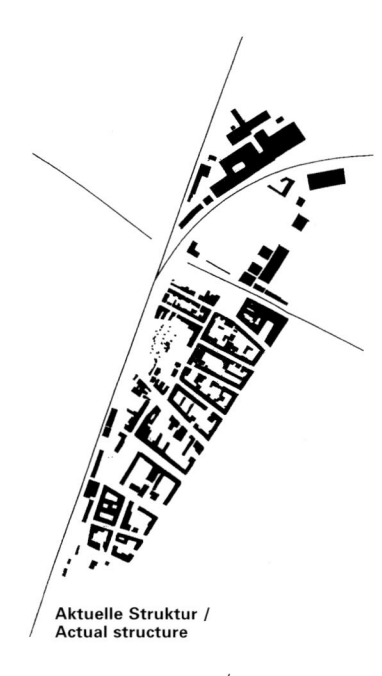

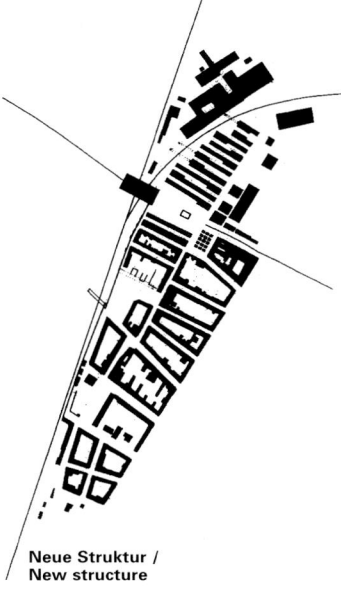

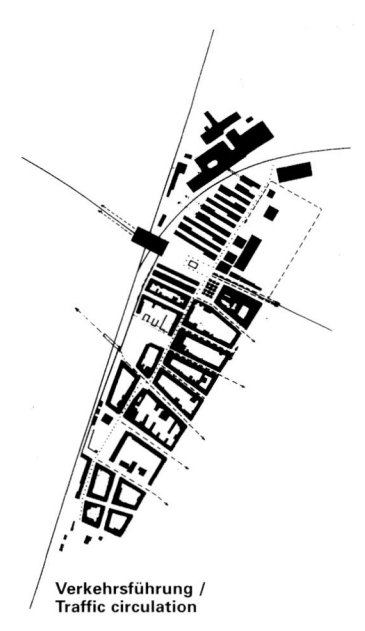

Aktuelle Struktur / Actual structure

Neue Struktur / New structure

Verkehrsführung / Traffic circulation

A draft for Stadlau

The problems of Stadlau and its relation to the center of Vienna were observed over a period of three weeks and investigated on the basis of two fundamental criteria.

A. Revitalization of Stadlau's urban and public life, Stadlau as a small town with an independent character. Improvement of structure and image, analysis of characteristic features and proposals for optimizing them.

B. Analysis and evaluation of the effects of the old and new urban infrastructure systems of Vienna on Stadlau, such as:

- railroad system;
- streetcar and highway, individual car traffic;
- existing and future subway lines;
- future culture center;
- old Waagner-Biro site, new use;

How the work was carried out:
1. Group analysis, debate, and evaluation of Stadlau's problems and opportunities and its surroundings.
2. Determination of priorities and procedure by Mariano Bayon and his assistant Stephan Zehl.
3. Splitting the work among the three groups that are linked to each other and two alternative groups.
4. Final elaboration of a uniform draft by consensus in the whole group and alternative partial solutions.
5. Approaching the different architectural solutions individually and in the group.

The draft contained the following procedures:

Stadlau center

- Increasing the economic value of the Stadlauer Strasse.
- Constructing two new public squares with different open spaces for the improvement of public life.
- New main square with different elements such as multi-purpose hall, bells, and clock tower.
- Making green zones accessible and extending tree growth to the green zones furthest away from the Eastern train line.
- Constructing a footbridge to Stadlau sports facilities
- Optimizing the self-contained center of town. Various openings. Opening the green backyard courts.
- Creating a large open space, a square at the intersection of the new cultural center and center of Stadlau that incorporates the train and streetcar lines.
- Redesigning the market.
- New traffic planning.
- Drafting a green belt to protect Stadlau.

Verkehrs- und Beförderungsinfrastruktur

Errichtung eines neuen Bahnhofs Stadlau mit folgenden Anschlüssen:
- Bahn
- U-Bahn
- Verbindung Genochplatz-Kulturzentrum (Neubau), neuer Gewerbekomplex Schulzentrum, Sportanlagen

- Neuer Platz, neuer Busbahnhof und neue Straßenbahnhaltestelle
- Errichtung von Geschäfts- und Büroflächen; offener Raum
- Neugestaltung des Marktes
- Verlängerung der Fußgängerunterführung

Neuer Gewerbe- und Wohnkomplex

- Anbindung an die Erzherzog-Karl-Straße; Verlängerung Stadlauer Straße; Schnellbahn und Kulturzentrum
- Anbindung an das Kulturzentrum; neues Bauelement (Hotel, Mehrzweckbau, fußgängerfreundliche Verbindung, etc.)

Übergang Stadlau-Ostbahn

- Verbindungsmauer über den Zweckbau hinaus
- Optische Durchbrüche und Abschlüsse

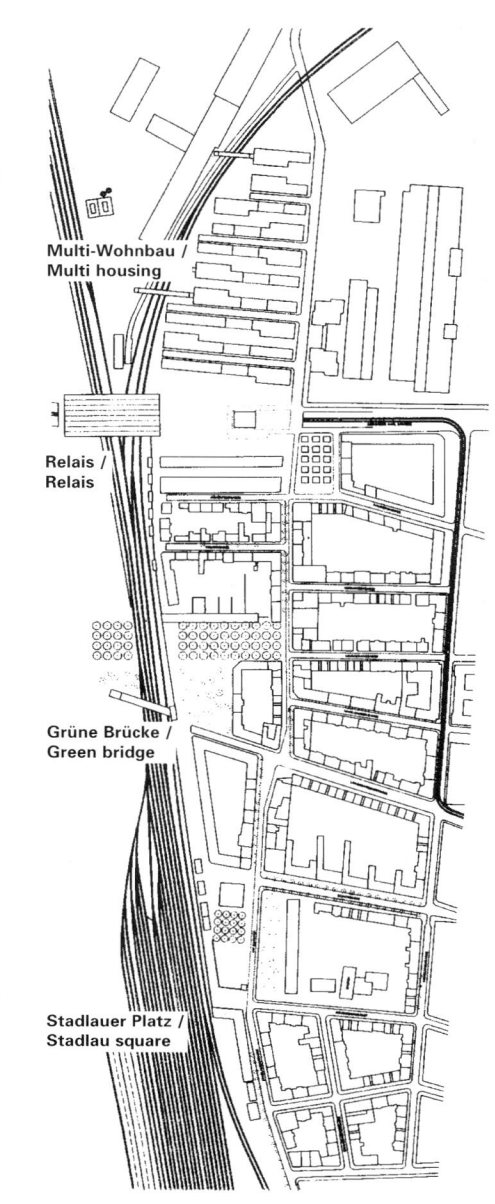

Multi-Wohnbau / Multi housing

Relais / Relais

Grüne Brücke / Green bridge

Stadlauer Platz / Stadlau square

Traffic and transport infrastructure

Constructing a new train station in Stadlau with the following connections
- railroad
- subway
- link Genochplatz cultural center (new building) new commercial center - school center - sports facilities

- New square: new bus station and new streetcar stop
- Creating new commercial and business centers. Open space
- Redesigning the market
- Extending the underpass

New commercial and housing center

- Link to the Erzherzog Karl-Strasse Extending the Stadlauer Strasse Commuter train and culture center
- Link to the culture center. New construction element hotel, multi-purpose building, pedestrian-friendly links, etc.)

Crossing Stadlau- eastern train line

- Defining the railroad as an element typical of Vienna.
- Structuring the railroad substructure using visual, rhythmical composition of closed and open elements.

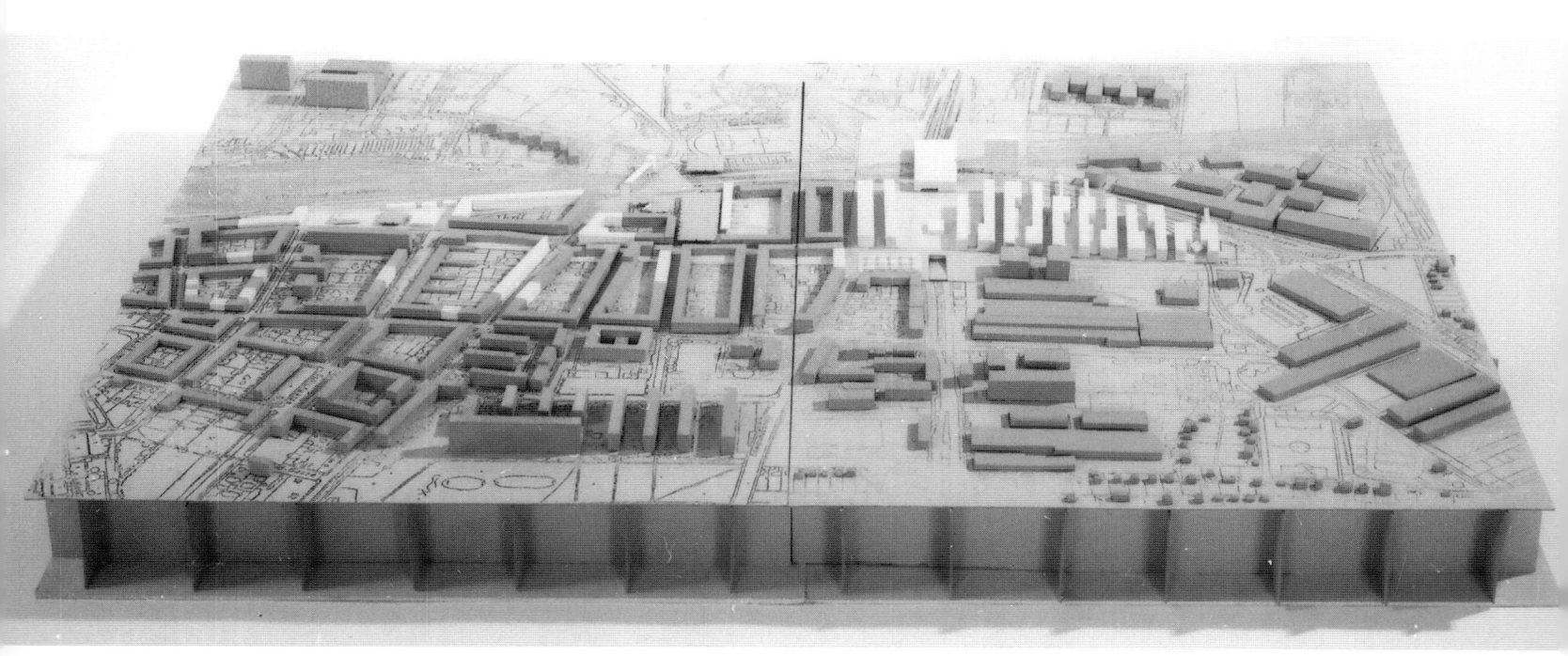

**Präsentationsmodell /
Presentation model**

Project: Multi housing

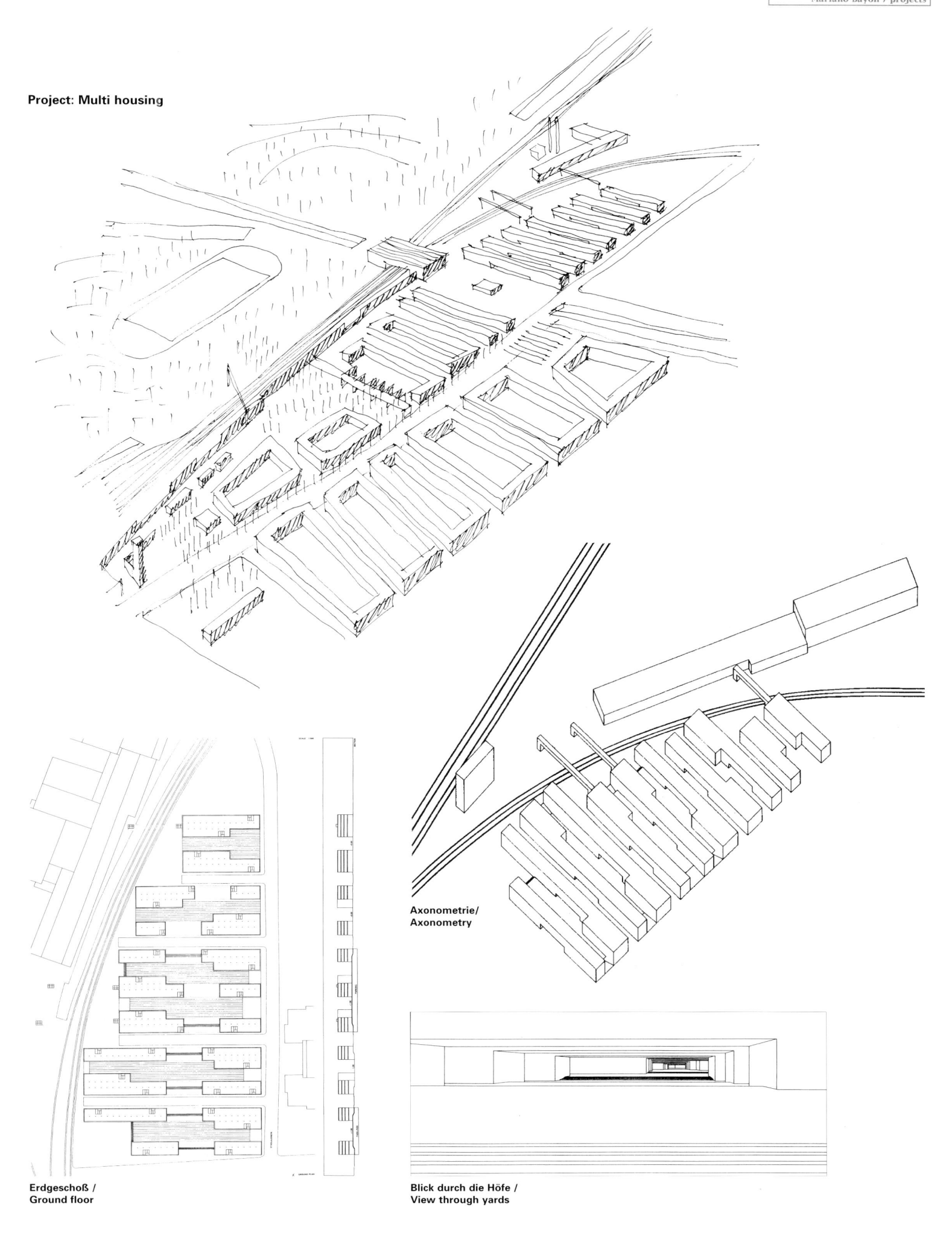

**Erdgeschoß /
Ground floor**

**Axonometrie/
Axonometry**

**Blick durch die Höfe /
View through yards**

91

Project: Relais

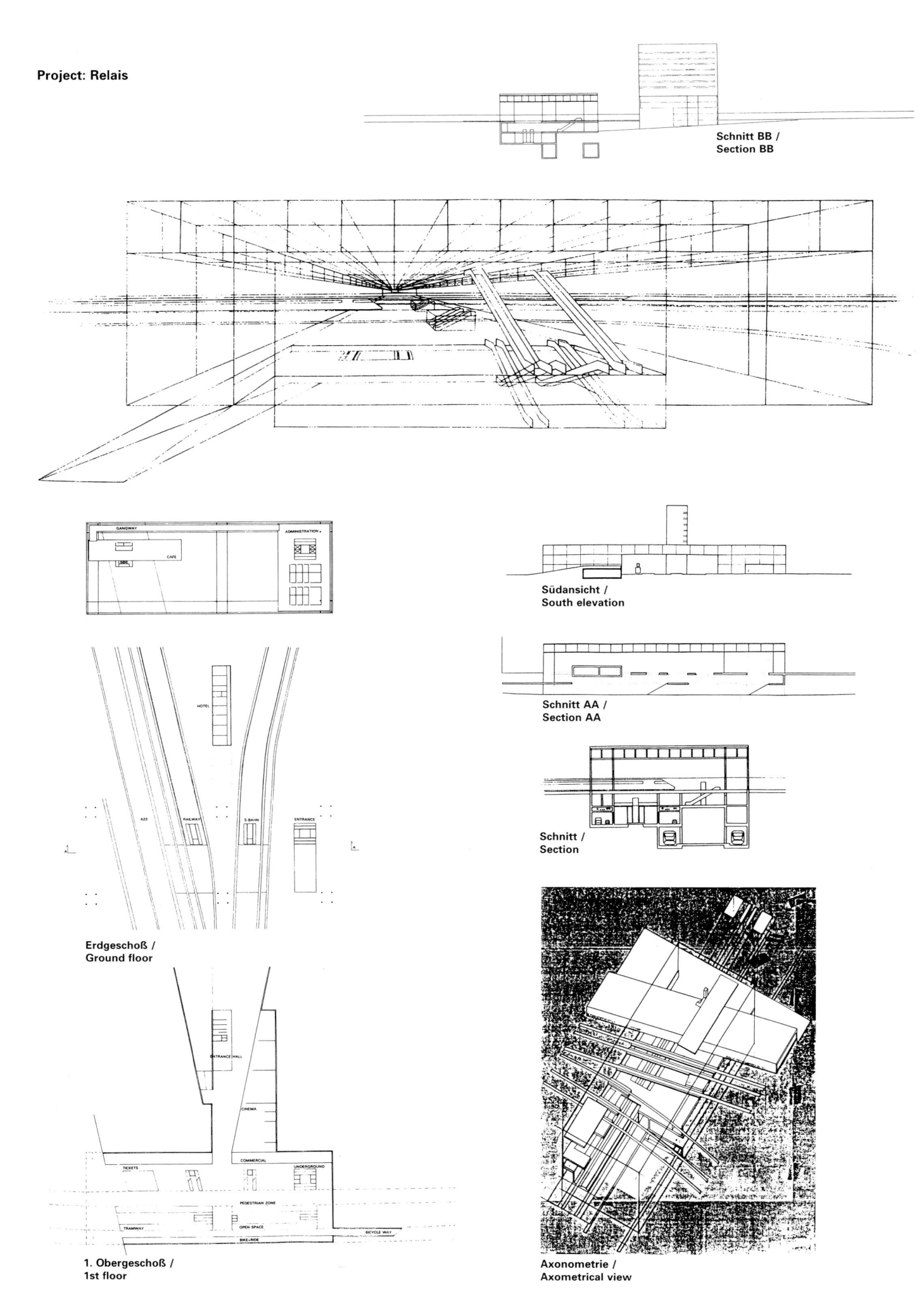

Schnitt BB /
Section BB

Erdgeschoß /
Ground floor

1. Obergeschoß /
1st floor

Südansicht /
South elevation

Schnitt AA /
Section AA

Schnitt /
Section

Axonometrie /
Axometrical view

Project: Stadlau square

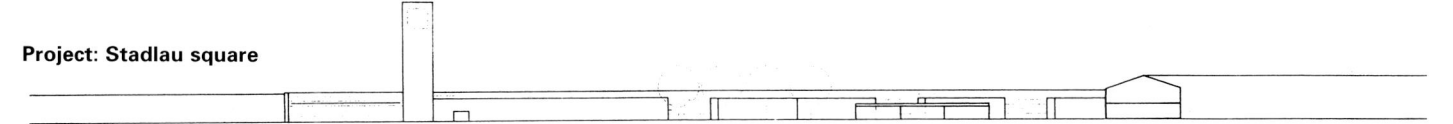

Schnitt West /
West section

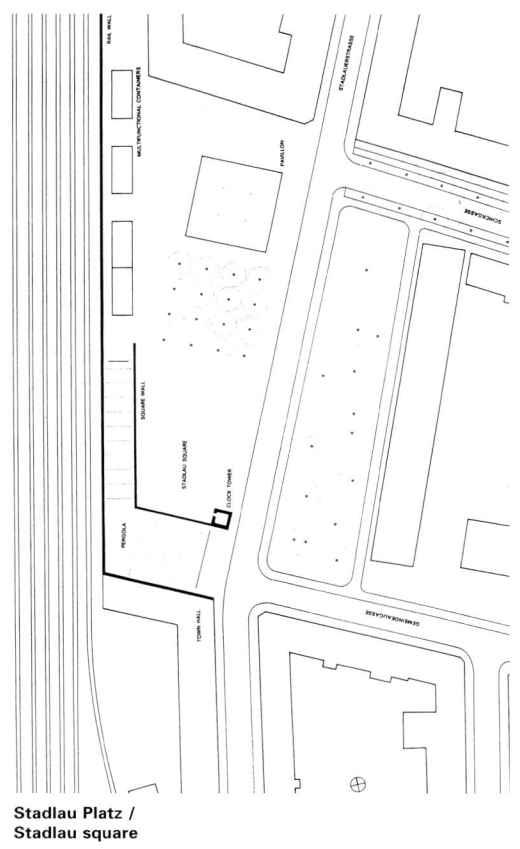

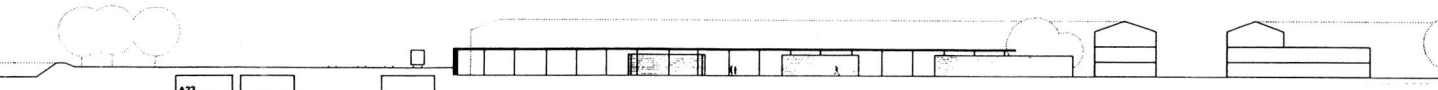

Stadlau Platz /
Stadlau square

Project: Green bridge

Grüne Brücke /
Green bridge

Grüne Brücke: Schnitt Dach /
Green bridge: section roof

**Projektgruppe / project group
Ben van Berkel**

Assistent: Hugo Beschoor Plug

Anne-Julchen Bernhardt

Henri Borduin

Laura Buran

Loris Dal Pos

Antje Ergezinger

Torsten J. Fiedler

Robert Gassner

Bettina Kraus

Marta Malé Alemany

José Manuel Magno Lopes da Silva

Andrea Perli

Klaus Poxleitner

Christian Roth

Volker Stengele

Uros Trauner

Katja Zlajpah

Ben van Berkel Amsterdam

1957	born in Utrecht
	studies architecture at the Rietveld Academie in Amsterdam
1987	Diploma from the Architectural Association in London
1988	founds the Van Berkel & Bos Architectural Bureau

Teaching positions
1994	visiting professor at Columbia University, New York
1994	visiting critic at Harvard
1994–95	Diploma Unit Master at the Architectural Association, London

Selection of work
Karboouw and ACOM office buildings
REMU electricity station
Housing projects
Aedes Gallery for Kristin Feireiss, Berlin
Museum extension; Enschede, The Netherlands
Erasmus Bridge, Rotterdam

Publications among others
1992	Ben van Berkel, monograph by 010 Publishers, Rotterdam
1993	Delinquent visionaries, a collection of essays written in cooperation with Caroline Bos, 010 Publishers, Rotterdam
1994	Mobile Forces, monograph by Ernst & Sohn, Berlin
1995	Ben van Berkel and Caroline Bos, monograph issue by A+U, No.296
1995	Ben van Berkel, monograph issue by El Croquis 72.I., Madrid

Körperliche Kompaktheit Ben van Berkel

Unbebaute Freiflächen und die solche Lückenareale füllenden Neubauten, stellen nach allgemein übereinstimmender Auffassung die größte Herausforderung an die Achitektur unserer Zeit. Zusammen allerdings bieten sie weltweit ein Bild des Bankrotts. Beharrlich weigern sich die zufällig unerschlossenen Flächen, ihre Geheimnisse preiszugeben, sie antworten nicht auf die ihnen zugewiesene Architektur, die wie ein ungebetener Gast Abdrücke auf ihrer Kehrseite hinterläßt. Dieses Dilemma liegt darin begründet, daß die Art, in der Baufläche und Architektur zusammentreffen, einer Tradition folgt, die keine Berührungspunkte zur grundlegend verschiedenen Beschaffenheit heutiger Bauareale aufweist. Allzu leicht läßt sich neues Baugelände verfügbar machen und somit anbinden an die lange Tradition der Architektur als Verkettung von Kollisionen und Konfrontationen zwischen Horizontalem und Vertikalem, zwischen physiologisch-natürlichen Kräften und menschlichem Schwindel-

KV distributing substation Amersfoort, 1993

gefühl, zwischen gläubiger Anbetung des Objekts und dem Prozeß des Verfalls. Es ist eine Tradition, in der Architektur, hervorgegangen aus primitiver Auseinandersetzung des Menschen mit seiner Umwelt, überwiegend als Ergebnis eines irrationalen Optimismus und der übermächtigen Neigung erscheint, sich mit Bauten zu identifizieren. Die naturgemäß ausweichende Beschaffenheit von Leerflächen inmitten bebauter Areale aber reagiert nur schwach auf alles, was Konflikt bedeutet. Die Flächen entziehen sich weiterhin jeder Bestimmbarkeit und lassen Gebäude, die auf ihnen errichtet werden, isoliert und ausgegrenzt erscheinen. Tatsächlich sollte man sich solchen Plätzen nur mit allergrößter Vorsicht nähern: Sich mit unbeteiligter Miene heranschleichen und, sobald man sich angenommen sieht, eingraben, erst dann sich den Eindrücken öffnen. Nur so läßt sich, in kleinerem Maß, der Zusammenstoß der Architektur mit ihrem Umfeld nachvollziehen.

Diese Art des Vorgehens, eine Abfolge verschiedener baulicher Schritte, scheint der einzig angemessene Weg zu sein, um zu den Ursprüngen von Projekten wie dem Karbouw-Bürohaus zu gelangen. Dessen Genealogie spiegelt sich, auch wenn dies gelegentlich anders gesehen wird, nicht im Räumlichen, in Form oder Grundriß, sondern einzig und allein im Prozeß der Entscheidungsfindung.

In jedem Einzelfall besteht der erste radikale Schritt darin, ein Volumen zu konzipieren, das jedwede Assoziation an gebaute Architektur ausschließt. So bezeichnen - jenseits aller Vorstellungen von Autonomie - die unakzentuiert glatten Außenwände von Karbouw, das Nijkerk-Projekt, der Piet-Hein-Tunnel, die Berliner Boxhalle und die Villa Wilbrink eine Planungsstrategie, die sich vielleicht mit den ortsbezogenen Raumkonzepten von Künstlern der Land Art wie Robert Smithson vergleichen läßt. Ihre zum Objekt gewordenen

Corporal compactness Ben van Berkel

The new inbetween areas and the new inbetween buildings are acknowledged as the greatest challenge to architecture in our time. In combination, however, they produce a universal spectacle of insolvency. The unallocated leftover spaces stubbornly refuse to reveal their secret and do not respond to the architecture entrusted to them, which is left glinting in the backyard like an unwelcome guest. The reason for this failure is that the way in which site and architecture clash belongs to a tradition that has no connections with the essentially different nature of the new locations. The new areas yield too easily to fit into the long tradition of architecture as conflict, as struggle – architecture as a linking of collisions and confrontations between the horizontal and the vertical, between physiological forces of nature and human vertigo, between the fetish of the object and the process of decay. It is a tradition in which architecture, as a product of the primitive conflict between man and environment, is largely the result of an irrational optimism and the irrepressible tendency to identify with objects. But the naturally evasive inbetween locations respond badly to conflict; they withdraw further, exposing the architecture there as isolated and restricted. Such areas should in fact be approached with the strictest caution. Steal up on them with a neutral countenance, and once accepted dig yourself in before unfurling. Only then the opportunity arises to act out the conflict of architecture at a smaller scale.

This procedure, a sequence of unlikely architectural choices, seems the only adequate account of the origins of projects like the Karbouw office; its genealogy is, in contrast to how it has on occasion been interpreted, not found in space, form or plan, but only and absolutely in the process of determining.

The first radical step in each case is to project a volume denying every architectural association. Going beyond an idea of autonomy, the smooth, nonreferential exteriors of Karbouw, the Nijkerk project, the Oudenrijn electricity station, the Piet Heintunnel, the Berlin boxhall and Villa Wilbrink signify a design strategy comparable to the site defining strategies of land artists like Robert Smithson. These objectified outer forms constitute a response to the quality of absence, or "nonspace", which is considered the main aspect of the location. This quality of nonspace which comes out of the artifice of the landscape is closely related to experiences of modernity centering on vicariousness.

Acknowledging this condition, the compact architecture of the inbetween locations subscribes to the idea of being substitutional when it deliberately excludes known architectural values. Remote and aloof, these unapproachable husks can perhaps only be described as "machine-like", although in reality they are closer to an architectural version of Nonsites; non-architectures, perhaps.

The second step in the process is that the objectified form clamps firmly onto an aspect of the location, so that the machine-like exterior is transformed. For the mixed-use building in Nijkerk the initial impression of a machine is based on its armour-plated skin; an enigmatic, introverted envelope for several companies who are concealed in its very heart without their presence being readable on the outside. Like a steel mollusc the object takes cover in the elbow of the motorway. Only later does it become clear where the location has exercised a mutative influence. Then we see that the "twist" in the building is a reversed reflection of the bend in the motorway. Likewise it then transpires that the lower level of the site in relation to the motorway has played a part in developing the roof. A fifth facade, it is at once elevation, agent of light and provider of views out.

äußeren Formen stellen Reaktionen dar auf die Qualität der Leere, der Abwesenheit von Raum, eine Qualität, die als wichtigster Aspekt der jeweiligen örtlichen Situation begriffen wird. Dieser sich aus dem Kunstcharakter der Landschaft ergebende Wert des Raumlosen steht in enger Beziehung mit Erfahrungen der Moderne, die auf die Frage der stellvertretenden Austauschbarkeit hinauslaufen.

Die sich auf Freigeländen erhebende „kompakte" Architektur steht mit dieser Kondition durchaus im Einklang. Auch zu ihr paßt das Prinzip der Austauschbarkeit, soweit in ihr als solche erkannte architektonische Werte mit Vorbedacht ausgeschlossen sind. Abgelegen und ganz sich selbst überlassen, könnte man derartige Bauhüllen in ihrer Unnahbarkeit „maschinenähnlich" nennen, obgleich sie in Wirklichkeit eher eine architektonische Standortlosigkeit verdecken. Es sind wenn man so will, Nicht-Architekturen.

Die zweite Stufe in diesem Prozeß besteht darin, daß konkretisierte Form sich an einem Aspekt der örtlichen Gegebenheit so fest verdichtet, daß sich darunter das maschinenähnliche Äußere verwandelt. Was den für verschiedene Zwecke genutzten Bau in Nijkerk angeht, so ist es dessen glatte Metallverkleidung, die als erstes den Eindruck einer Maschine hervorruft, eine unbestimmbare, nach innen gekehrte Umhüllung für mehrere hier untergebrachte Firmen, die ohne jeden äußeren Hinweis auf ihre Präsenz ihr Innerstes verbergen. Längs der Biegung einer Verkehrsstraße erstreckt sich der Bau wie eine stählerne Molluske. Erst beim zweiten Blick nimmt man den verändernden Einfluß wahr, den der Standort ausgeübt hat. Man erkennt nämlich, daß die Drehung im Gebäude leicht dem Verlauf der Straßenkrümmung folgt. Auch ahnt man, welche Rolle das Bodenniveau des Platzes und dessen Verhältnis zur Straße für die Gestaltung des Daches spielte. Einer fünften Fassade gleich, markiert es sowohl die Höhe wie es Lichtzufuhr und Ausblicke ermöglicht.

Die Anwendung gleicher Gestaltungsregeln charakterisiert die Villa Wilbrink. Zunächst taucht das Haus als undeutliches Gebilde in einer scheinbar der Wirklichkeit entrückten Landschaft auf, ein ebenso maßstab- wie räumlich beziehungsloser „special effect". Geradezu unbarmherzig ist die aufstrebende Form der Erde abgezwungen, eine unnahbar wirkende, wehrhafte Brüstung, die den auf diese Weise geschlossenen Innenhof abschirmt. Später erst stellt sich heraus, daß die ungewöhnliche Hauptform in überraschenden Richtungsbezügen zu ihrer Umgebung steht. So scheint es, als wurzelten die langen natürlichen Wasser- und Landstreifen – I-Profile andeutend – in der longitudinalen Anlage des Hauses. Gleichzeitig mit der Hinwendung zum Ursprünglichen der Umgebung wird das Motiv der Maschine aufgenommen. Dieser Moment in dem auf körperliche Kompaktheit zielenden Entstehungsprozeß solcher Projekte ist wohl derjenige, der das stärkste Potential in sich birgt.

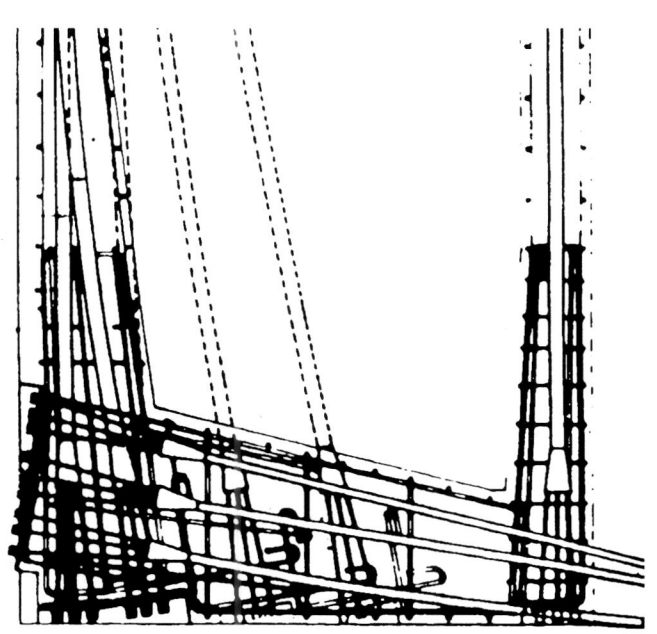

Morandi, section of framework

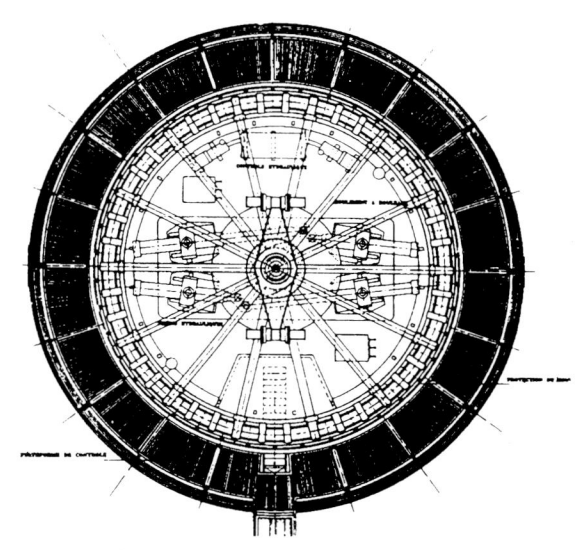

Calatrava, Médoc Swing Bridge, plan of motor room

The same order of development characterizes Villa Wilbrink. First the house looms up as an alienating shape in a nonexistent landscape; a special effect with neither scale nor context. Ruthlessly the rising form is forced up out of the earth, putting up an inaccessible and defensive parapet to safeguard the secluded character of the inner court. Subsequently this extreme principal shape turns out to relate unexpectedly to the directions of the location. The elongated strips of land and water of the original landscape have taken root in the longitudinal composition of the house like concealed I-sections. At the same time this bringing back of the original gesture to the environment transforms the machine theme. This episode in the process underlying the corporal compactness of these projects is probably most charged with hidden potential. Reverting the emblemetically nonreferential, irrelated machine surface back to the site has the effect of a slow fuse.

In the Berlin Schloß this process leads to a discrepancy in the perception of the Building; from a distance it appears as one volume. In reality, however, the complex consists of three separate volumes with curvilinear edifications which are stretched out in quasi-elastic obliviousness of architectural solidity. In berlin, like a film projected at double speed, mutations that should take a lifetime have been accelerated beyond comprehension. Instead of being subjected to a gradual change which involuntarily leaves its mark on the material surroundings, the city has been struck by the effects of multiple encroachment without delay or remission, resulting in a profound fissure at the level of the concept. Responding to this, the project's complex identity relies on the duality of external solidity and internal cuts through a massive void.

In essence this combination of aloof, unnatural skin and deep engagement with the site is one of conflict and denial, both choices being diametrically and principally opposed to each other. Their being combined in such a tight package, such compact architectural bodies, emphasizes the radical nature of the procedure underlying these projects.

The compactness of this architecture is probably its most defining characteristic, as well as being a confirmation of the machine analogy. As distinct from a building composed of mathematically finite figures, a project like the Nijkerk or Karbouw building obviously presents a single compact volume, built up nonetheless from dissimilar interlocking elements. The fact that these buildings are not defined by lines and angles, but by sections of spheres and circles, makes them turn inward and be volumetrically self-referential. That volumetric compactness provides a counterweight to the loose and universal nature of the locations.

Die Entscheidung für die emblematisch unbestimmte, beziehungslose Außenhaut der Maschine bei deren gleichzeitiger Bindung an einen Standort stellt gleichsam den Effekt einer verlangsamten Zündung her.

Zu einer Diskrepanz der Wahrnehmung kommt es beim Projekt für das Berliner Stadtschloß. Aus der Ferne erscheint der Bau als ein einziges Volumen, in Wirklichkeit aber besteht der Komplex aus drei Einzelbauten mit einem verbindenden öffentlichen Raum, deren vermeintliche Elastizität jede Vorstellung von architektonischer Gediegenheit vergessen läßt. Gleich einem mit doppelter Geschwindigkeit ablaufenden Film ist in Berlin, jenseits des normalen Fassungsvermögens, ein auf Lebenszeit angelegter Wandel beschleunigt worden. Hier liegt keine schrittweise erfolgte Veränderung vor, die der Umgebung unmerklich ihre Spuren aufgedrückt hätte; vielmehr ist die Stadt unmittelbar und in ganzem Ausmaß von den Folgen natürlicher Einwirkungen betroffen, mit dem Ergebnis, daß sich durch das Konzept ein tiefer Riß zieht. Die komplexe Identität des Projekts basiert auf der Dualität äußerer Solidität und interner Schnitte durch eine große Leere. Ihrem Wesen nach entspricht die Kombination von abweisend unwirklicher Außenhaut und weitreichend verpflichtendem Bekenntnis zum Standort der Spannung zwischen Konflikt und Verweigerung; beides steht sich diametral und grundverschieden gegenüber. Ihre derart feste Bündelung, ihre zu so kompakten Baukörpern zusammengefaßte Präsenz unterstreicht das Radikale, das in der Gestaltung solcher Projekte liegt.

Die Kompaktheit dieser Architektur ist ihr wohl am häufigsten erörtertes Merkmal, womit sich die Analogie zur Maschine bestätigt. Deutlich abgesetzt von einem Bau aus endlichen mathematischen Figuren, bilden Projekte wie das Nijkerk- und das Karbouw-Gebäude jeweils ein kompaktes, wenn auch aus ungleichartig verschachtelten Elementen errichtetes Einzelvolumen.

Die Tatsache, daß die Bauten nicht durch Linien und Winkel, sondern durch Kugel- und Kreissegmente bestimmt werden, läßt sie nach innen gerichtet und - im Hinblick auf ihre Masse – auf sich selbst verweisend erscheinen. Diese an ihrer Ausdehnung gemessene Ballung stellt zur locker-unbestimmten Beschaffenheit des Ortes das Gegengewicht dar.

Die Kompaktheit trägt auch zur Betonung des Gegenständlichen dieser Architektur bei, wenngleich die vom Objekt ausgehende Faszination sich vor allem in dessen veränderlichen und instabilen Teilen zeigt. Wie Jeff Koons Staubsauger aus ihrem Alltagsbereich herausgelöst und in einen künstlerischen Kontext gebracht hat, so treten unvermutet auch hier spezifische Qualitäten des Objekts in den Vordergrund. Mit der Konzeptuellen Kunst hat das Ergebnis allerdings nichts gemein. Bei diesen einzelnen Objekten geht es nicht um das Demonstrieren dessen, was Yves Klein „immaterielle malerische Sensibilität" genannt hat, auch nicht um den Nachweis, daß jedes und alles sich in Kunst oder Architektur ummünzen läßt. Ihre Bedeutung resultiert vielmehr aus dem Aufeinandertreffen von Objekten im Sinne der Freudschen Erweiterung des Selbst, des menschlichen Tuns und Verlangens.

Gleichzeitig finden sich alle den Menschen leitenden Prozesse eliminiert, die hinter diesen Objekten stehen. Voraussetzung ist, daß man sie so leidenschaftslos betrachtet, als seien sie ins Licht des Magischen Realismus getaucht und mit all ihren gegenläufigen Möglichkeiten in klinischer Kälte ausgebreitet, ohne jeden Anflug von Symbolik. Der Gedanke, Objekte verfügten zur Bestimmung ihrer Identität über irgendein Maß an Freiheit, scheint abwegig und gänzlich unvereinbar mit der Realität, in der Objekten jeweils nur die Identität zugestanden wird, die sich mit allgemein anerkannten Gebrauchszwecken deckt. Löst man sich indessen von dieser sicheren Denkgewohnheit, dann wird das Objekt sofort weniger akzeptabel. Ebenso läßt es sich nicht mehr unter einem Gesichtspunkt mühelos manipulieren.

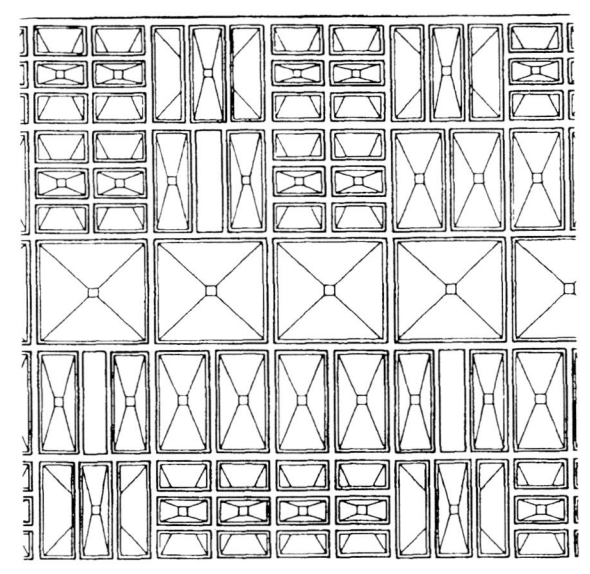

Grain elevator, distribution floor

The compactness further serves to emphasize the objectivity of this architecture, yet the fascination with the object is centred in particular around its mutability and instability. Comparable to the manner in which Jeff Koons has isolated vacuum cleaners and placed them in an art context, this brings specific qualities of the object into focus. The issue here is not that of conceptual art; demonstrating "immaterial pictorial sensitivity" in the words of Yves Klein, or seeking to demonstrate that everything and anything can be labeled art or architecture, is not the intention behind these isolated objects. Their significance centres on the impact of objects as Freudian extensions of the self, of human acts and desires.

At the same time all human guiding processes behind objects are eliminated when looked at in this dispassionate way, placed in a Magic Realistic light, with all their perverse possibilities coldly and clinically on display without a trace of symbolism. The idea that objects themselves possess any amount of freedom as regards the identities they may adopt seems absurd; it clashes totally with our familiar reality, where objects are only allocated the identity that coincides with our accepted use of them. By abandoning this secure thought, objects at once become less acceptable and less easy to manipulate from the one vantage point.

Considering certain qualities of the projects in this light destabilizes the notion of purposeful design. As more and more factors come into play the process detaches itself from its beginnings and proceeds to live a life of its own. While starting out as a nonreferential, machine-like envelope, the compact architectural body which, in the second phase of the design process was abruptly connected to its roots in the location after all, in this third stage suddenly changes again as it becomes an independent object with unforeseen implications. In this way it could be said that the characteristic details, which emerge one by one as the process unfolds and the building comes into focus, have questionable origins. The glass eye of Karbouw, the overhang of the Oudenrijn electricity station, and the ventilation grates of the service buildings of the Piet Hein Tunnel are like secondary objective mutations. These transformations of component parts go beyond cosmetic or prothetic concerns; in the same way that an extreme personality such as Yukio Mishima transformed himself from existentialist writer to bodybuilder to samurai imperialist, with each transformation bringing with it a radically new identity, these details encompass a fundamental re-thinking of the identity of the project.

Thus the three-tier process of achieving architecture on those widespread, unallocated inbetween locations whose only characteristic is that of fleeting, elusive "modernity", concludes with letting go once more. Corporal compactness

In solchem Licht besehen, erschüttern gewisse Eigenheiten eines Projekts die landläufige Vorstellung von zielgerichtetem Planen. Weil zunehmend mehr Faktoren ins Spiel kommen, löst sich der Prozeß von seinen Anfängen und nimmt ein Eigenleben an. Als nicht klar bestimmbar maschinenähnliche Hülle begonnen und dann - in der zweiten Planungsphase - fest mit seinem Platz verwurzelt, verändert der massige Baukörper sich im dritten Stadium plötzlich ein weiteres Mal zu einem selbständigen Objekt mit nicht vorhergesehenen Implikationen. Insofern könnte man von einem fragwürdigen Ursprung jener charakteristischen Details sprechen, die sich parallel zum Entstehen des Baus bilden und ihn ins Blickfeld rücken. So muten denn auch das gläserne Auge von Karbouw und die Ventilationsgitter an den Versorgungsbauten des Piet-Hein-Tunnels wie kleinere Objektmutationen an.

Mit nochmaligem Neuansatz endet so der sich dreifach gliedernde Prozeß, in dem Architektur auf jenem nach allen Seiten offenen, unbestimmbaren Gelände entsteht, das sich zwischen bebauten Arealen erstreckt, in Zonen, deren einziges Merkmal ihre schwer definierbare, vage „Modernität" ist.

Körperliche Kompaktheit läßt auf eine auf Abstand bedachte Haltung schließen, die sich auf völliges Selbstvertrauen gründet. Da ist nichts, was sich dem Bauplatz hinzufügen ließe; einzig und allein besteht das Vorgehen im ständigen Verwerfen, im Rückgriff auf Früheres sowie darin, daß man sich auf das Projekt einläßt, indem man Vorgefundenes verwandelt. Es kann deshalb nie ein einfaches Unterfangen sein, ein derartiges Projekt aufzurollen; statt eines einzigen thematischen Fadens gibt es ein ganzes Gewirr von Anfängen und unvollendet aufgegebenen Teilstücken. Kompakt nicht nur in ihrer physischen Erscheinung, sondern auch der Begriffsstruktur nach, beziehen solche Projekte sich auf jeder Ebene ihres Entstehens allein auf sich selbst, einer Schneckenhausspirale gleichend, nur nach innen gerichtet und das Objekt selbst unablässig verwandelnd.

V. Vasarely, „Two lovers embracing"

signifies a distancing tactic that aims to be utterly self-reliant. There is nothing to attach to on site; the answer is to relinquish endlessly, revert and retreat into the project, and transform what is found there. Unraveling these projects will therefore never be a straightforward procedure; instead of a single smooth thematic strand, there is a tangle of beginnings and abandonings. These projects are compact bodies not just physically, but also conceptually as on each level they belong only to themselves, like a snail's shell spiralling inwards, but transforming its own object all the while.

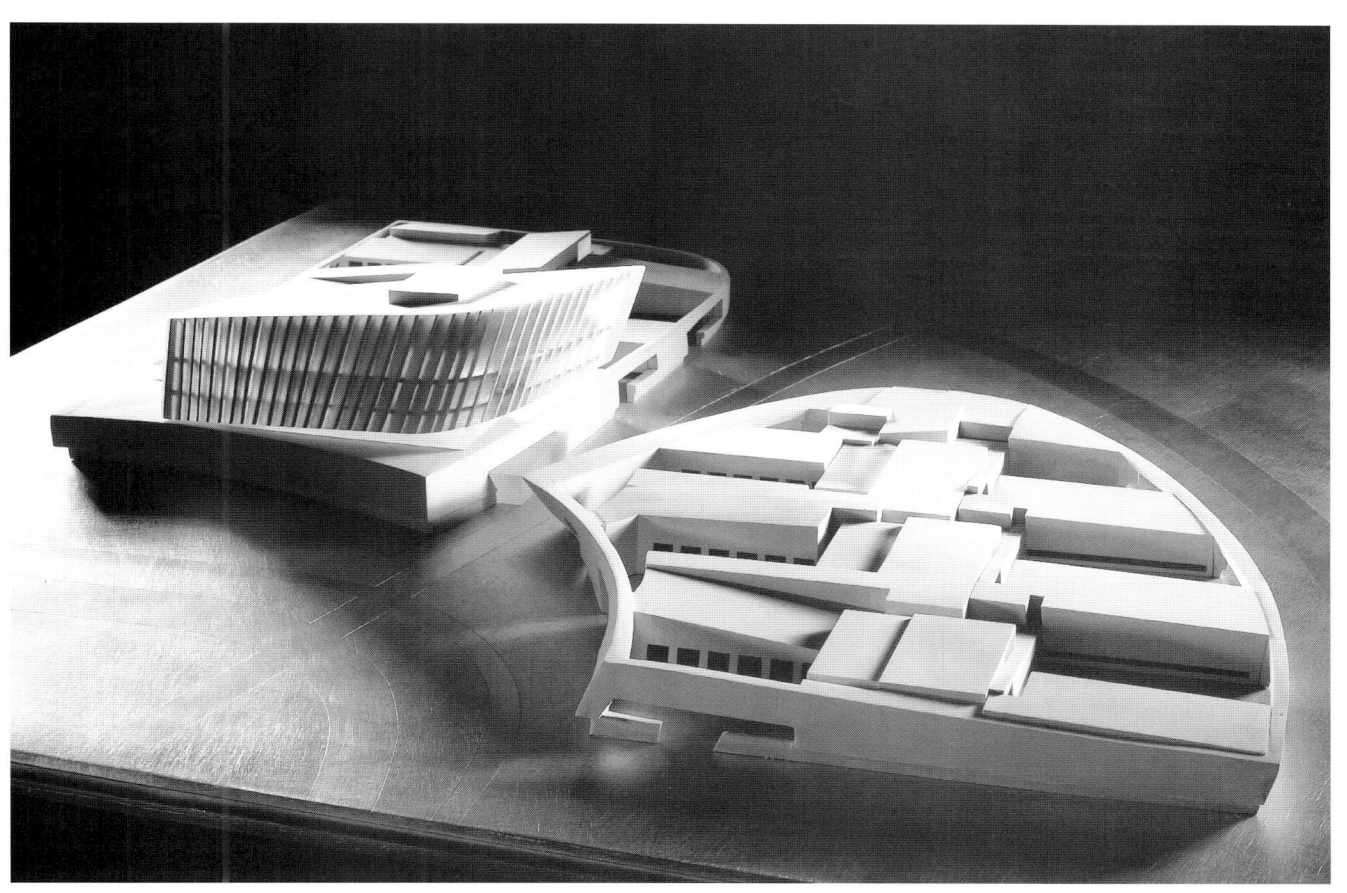

International center for the mentally handicapped, SWUZ II, Amsterdam, 1994–1997

Impuls Zentrumserweiterung – Akzentuierung und Aufwertung. Fußgängerzone Favoritenstraße, Wien 10

Die Fußgängerzone Favoriten auf dem, im 10. Bezirk gelegenen Teil der Favoritenstraße, ist eine der am stärksten frequentierten Wiener Geschäftsstraßen. Die Fußgängerzone verläuft über der U-Bahnlinie 1 bis zum Reumannplatz, der einen eindeutigen räumlichen Abschluß bildet. Der stadteinwärts an die Fußgängerzone anschließende Abschnitt der Favoritenstraße endet am Südtirolerplatz, einem stark belasteten Verkehrsraum beiderseits des Gürtels, welcher als einer der verkehrsreichsten Wiener Straßenzüge eine starke Barriere zu den inneren Stadtbezirken bildet.
Östlich des Südtirolerplatzes erstrecken sich ausgedehnte Anlagen der Post bzw. des Wiener Südbahnhofes. Auf einem Teilbereich im Süden des Bahngeländes ist längerfristig die Schaffung eines neuen Bahnhofes als Durchgangsbahnhof für internationale Züge in Richtung Süd/Ost bzw. als Station für künftig auszubauende Schnellbahnverbindungen vorgesehen.
Die Verlängerung der Fußgängerzone, die Gestaltung der Straßen- und Platzräume, insbesondere des Südtirolerplatzes, die Verbesserung bzw. Schaffung von Wegebeziehungen sowie evtl. die Situierung von Nutzungen mit Magnetwirkung sind mögliche Elemente einer städtebaulichen Aktivierung und Aufwertung des Gebietes.

Impulse of a centre's expansion – activation and revaluation. pedestrian precinct Favoritenstraße, Vienna 10

The pedestrian precinct of Favoriten along the 10th district section of Favoritenstraße is one of Vienna´s most important shopping districts. The pedestrian precinct streches above underground line 1 to Reumannplatz, which constitutes a clear, spatial endpoint. The section of Favoritenstraße running from the pedestrian precinct in the direction of the city centre ends at Südtiroler Platz, a very busy junction on both sides of the Gürtel, one of the busiest Viennese streets constituting a strong barrier towards the innercity districts.
East of Südtiroler Platz we find the vast premises of the post office and of Vienna´s Southern train station. One of the part south of the station has been earmarked for the future construction of a new, multi-level station for international south/east bound trains as well as for suburban railway links to be established in the future.
The prologation of the pedestrian precinct, the development of the streets and squares, in particular of Südtirolerplatz, the improvement and/or creation of new path-connections as well any possible location of usages of magnetic attraction are possible elements of city architectural activation and revaluation of the area.

Favoritenstraße, Wien 10

Organisation der Struktur

Computer und Architektur

Der Computer bietet dem Architekten einen Einblick in ein Gebiet, welches einst völlig unerreichbar für ihn war. Dies verschafft ihm heute viel mehr Mitsprachemöglichkeit bei Ziviltechniker-Projekten. Gleichzeitig jedoch kann dieses Argument nicht getrennt von anderen Interessen gesehen werden; der öffentliche Raum einer Computersimulation einer Stadt, ergänzt diese durch ein neu kalkuliertes Imagebild eines neuen Stadtphänomens.

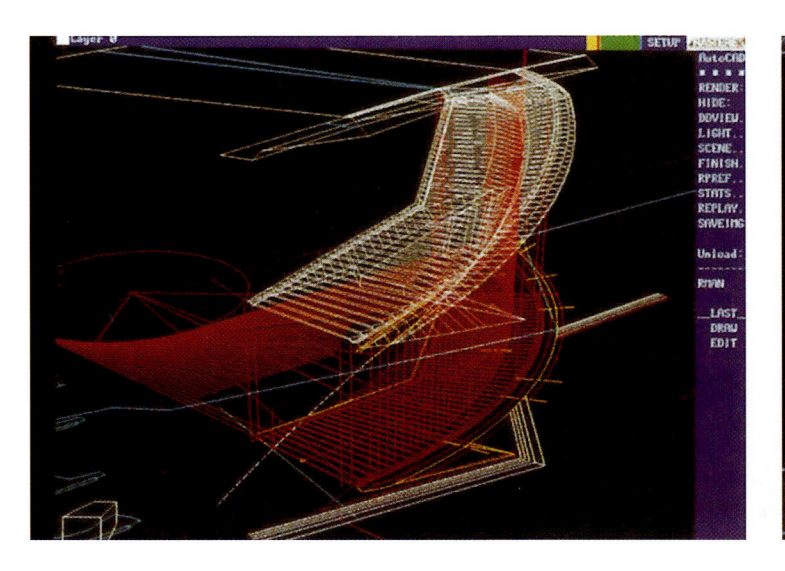

Organization of structure

Computer and architecture

The computer offers the architect so much insight into a field once largely beyond his grasp, that he now has a much greater say in engineering projects. At the same time this argument cannot be seen distinct from other interests; the shared, public space of the computer simulations that of the city, supplementing it with a new calculated image of urban phenomena.

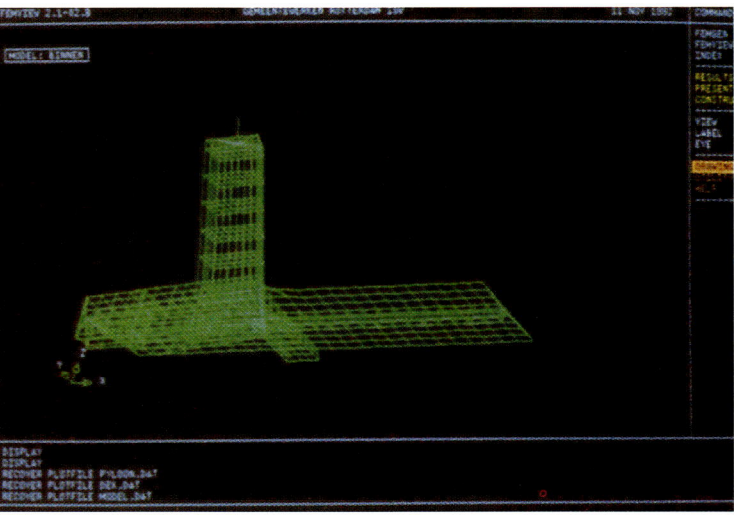

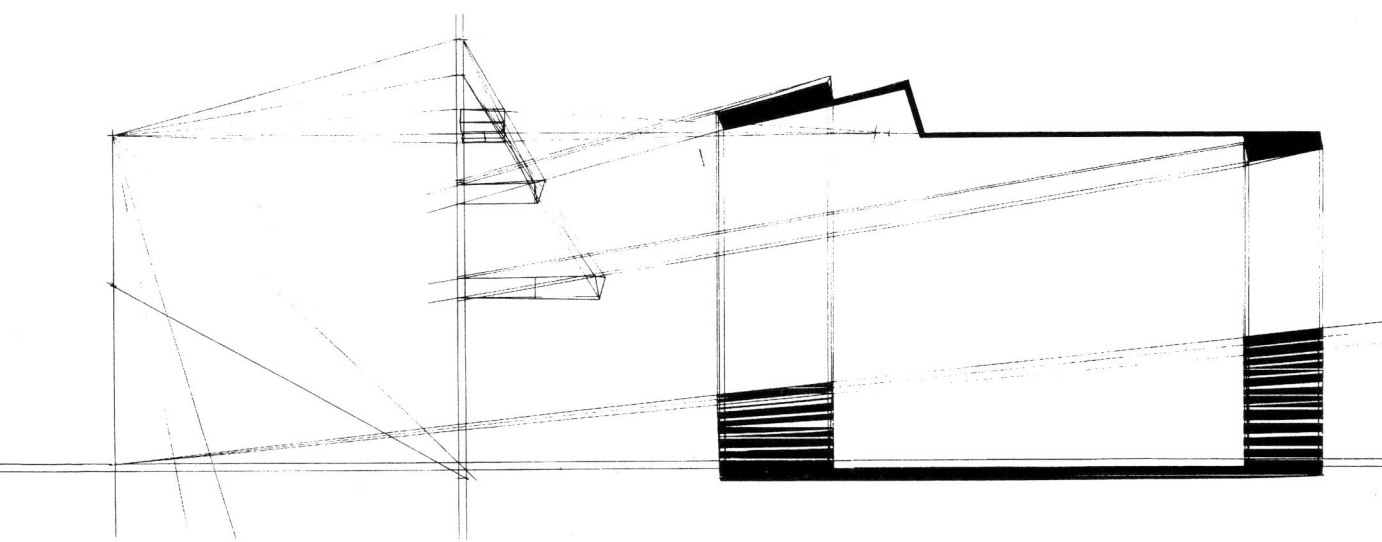

Bettina Kraus: „so far so close"

Konstruktion zweier Gebäude aus einer Ebene /
Construction of two buildings out of one plane

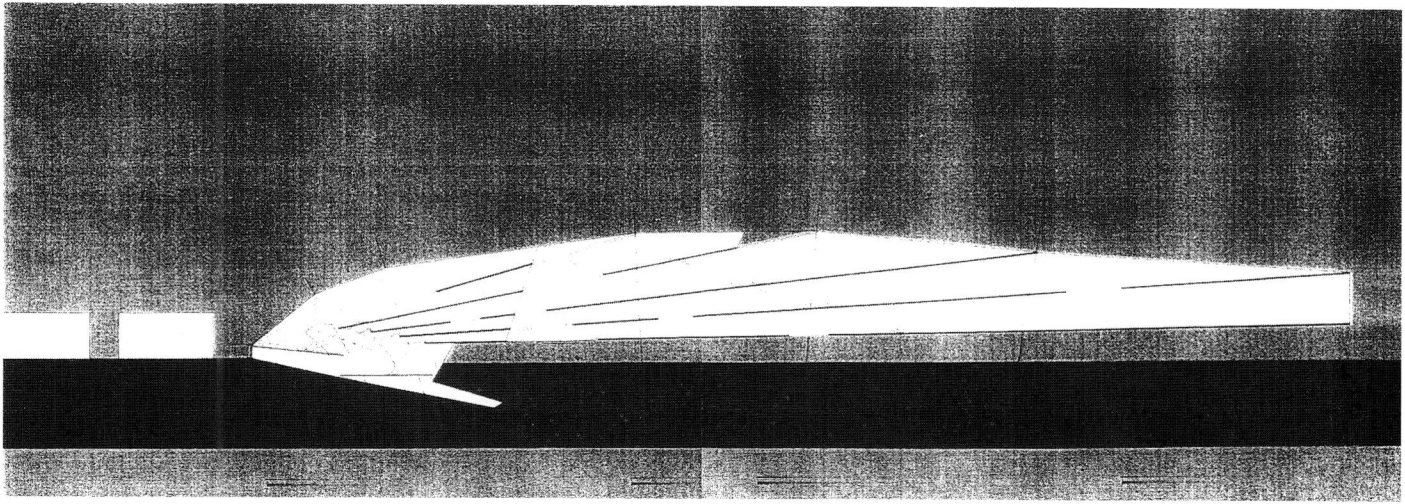

Torsten Fiedler: „Kaleidoscopic garden"

Eine Organisations-Struktur hinter der Wand kann durch eine „Obersicht", eine „Untersicht" und durch ein Inneres, welches Raum für öffentliche Veranstaltungen bietet, beschrieben werden. Die Haut dieser Struktur wird durch die vorhandenen Sichtlinien („Untersicht") geformt. /
An organizational structure behind the wall can be described by an "oversight", an "undersight" and an inside, which gives space for a number of public events. The skin of the structure is formed by the existing sightlines ("undersight").

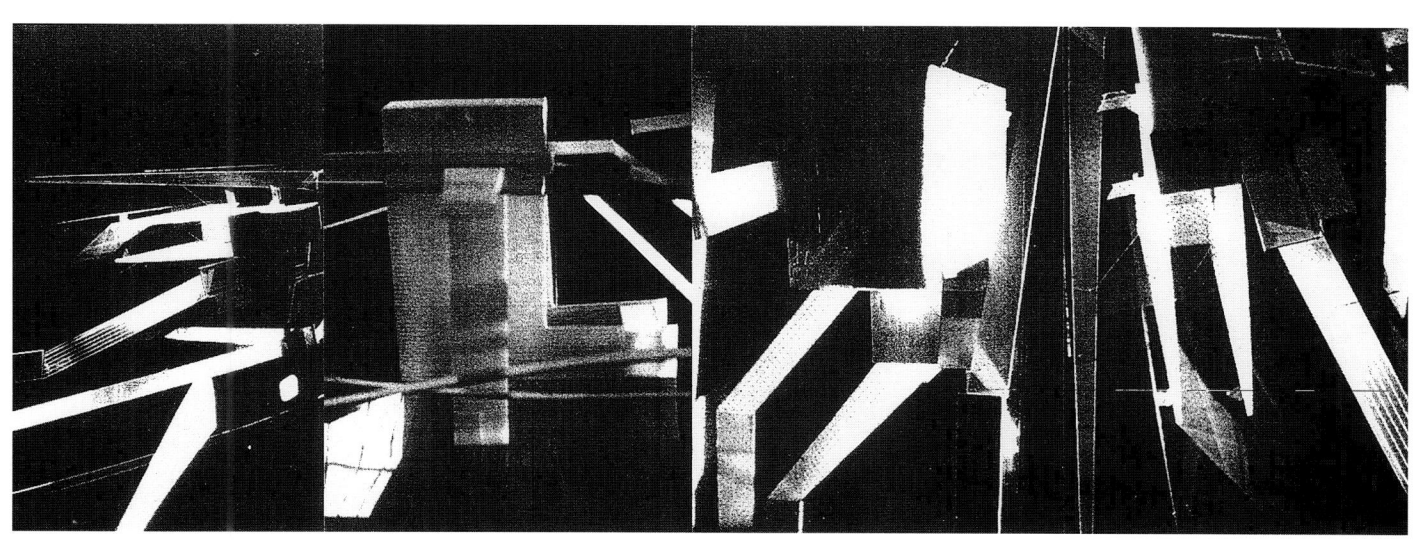

Robert Gassner: "Infrastructure Balcony"

Abstraktes Modell, 5 verschiedene Arten von Bewegung über den Infrastrukturbalkon. Dargestellt entsprechend der Geschwindigkeit und der Art des Reisens oder Ruhens. /
Abstract model, relating 5 different means of movement travelling across the infrastructural balcony. These are shown according to their speed and nature of travel and resting.

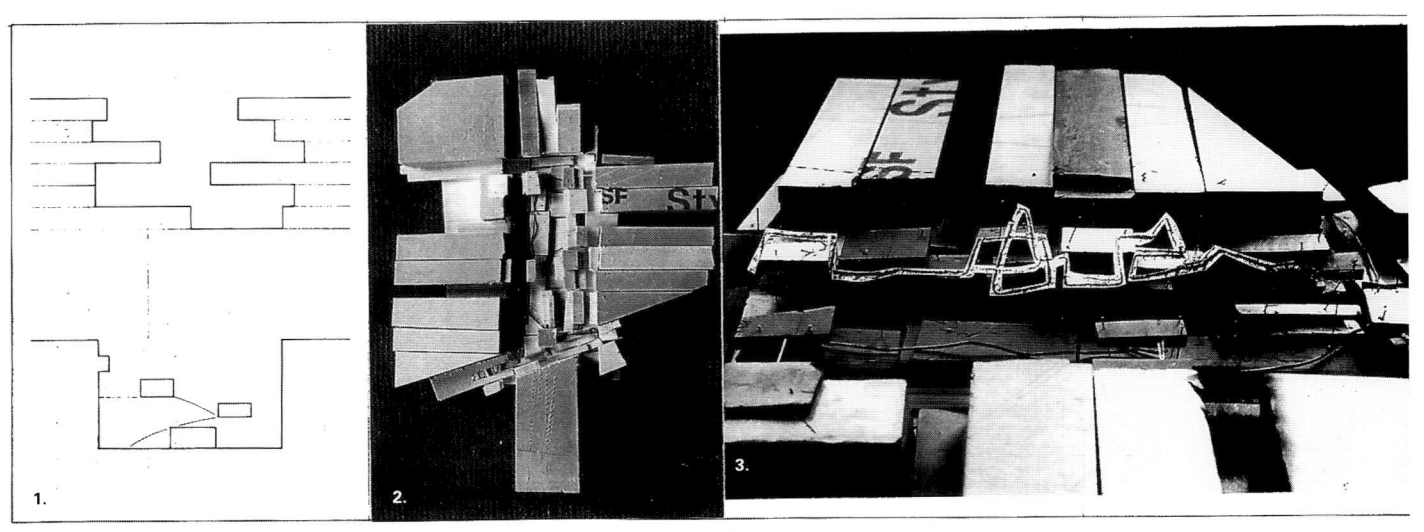

Volker Stengele: "Pushing and pulling the limits"

1. „Stoßen und Drängen" organisiert den Raum zwischen den bestehenden Gebäuden
2. Viktor-Adler-Platz durch „Stoßen und Drängen"
3. Bewegungen der Passanten durch das Hauptgebäude – Infrastrukturelement

1. Pushing and pulling organizes the space between the existing buildings
2. Viktor-Adler-Platz by pushing and pulling
3. Movement of people throught the main building – infrastructural element

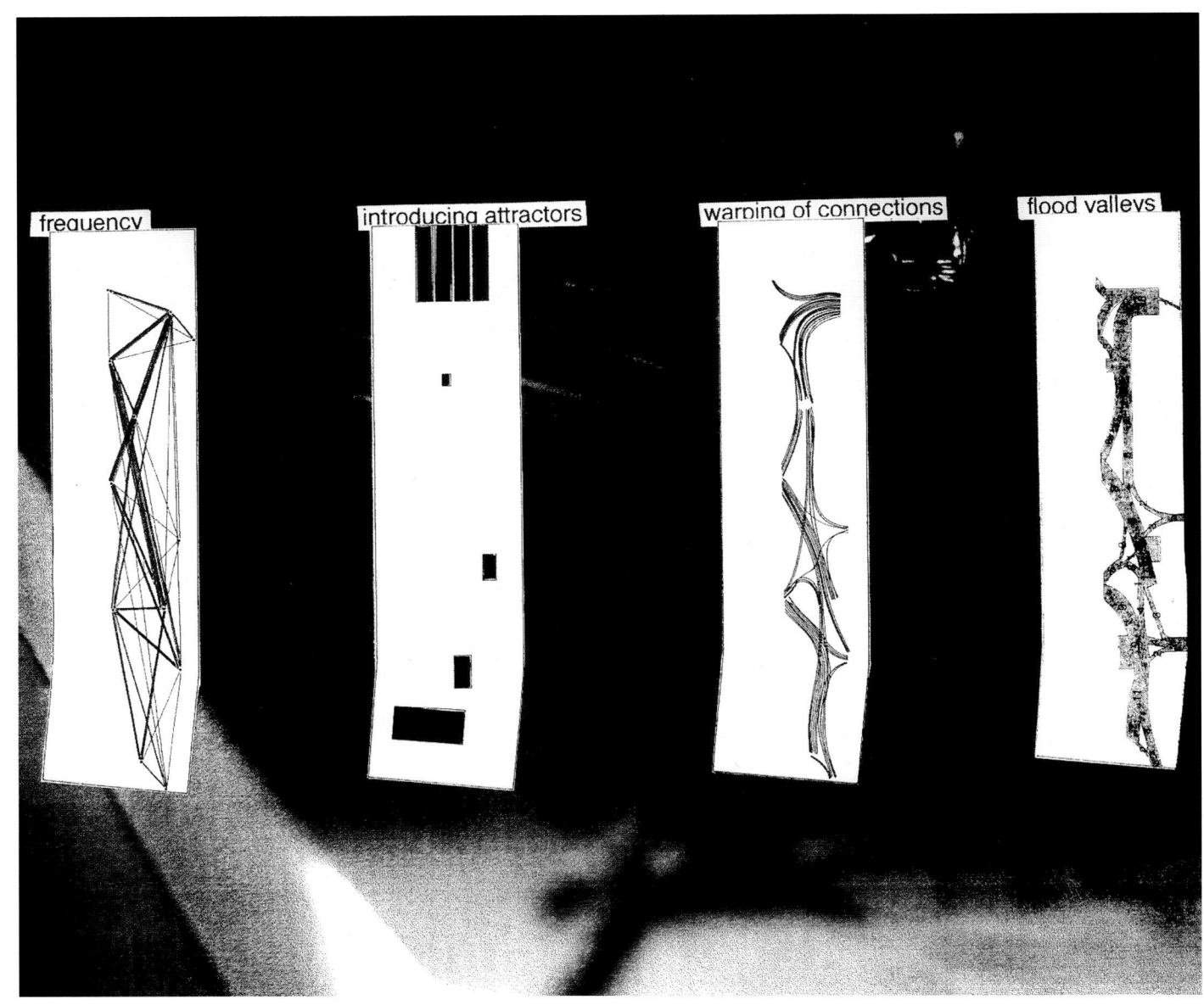

Anne-Julchen Bernhard, Christian Roth: „Punkt und"

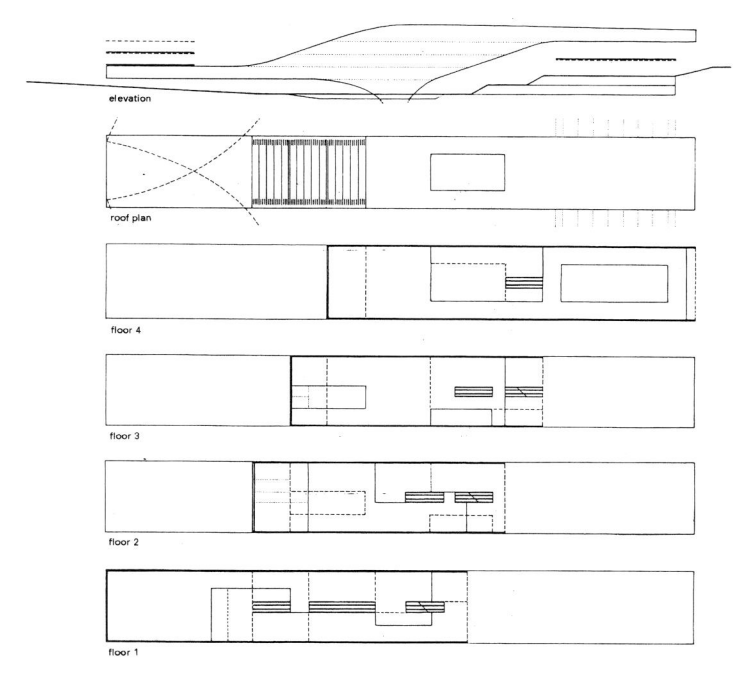

Marta Malé Alemany

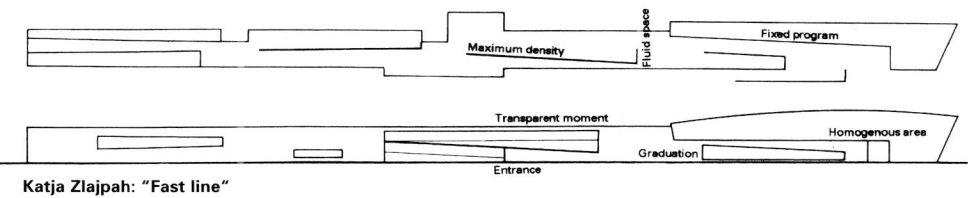

Katja Zlajpah: "Fast line"

**Organisation der Struktur /
Organization of structure**

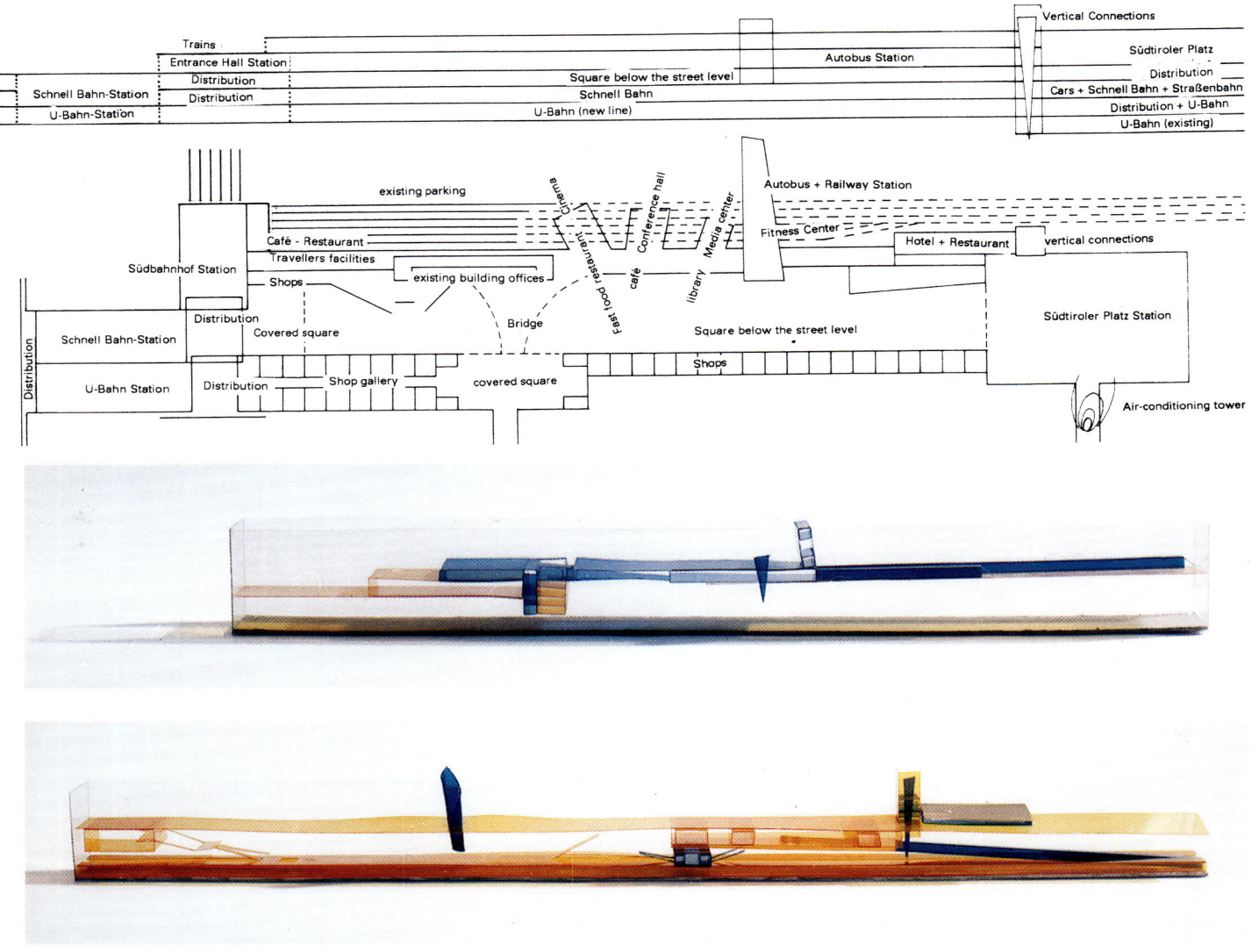

Laura Buran, Doris Dal Pos: "Organization of structure"

Schema – Plan und Schnitt durch das Projekt /
Schematic plan and section of the project

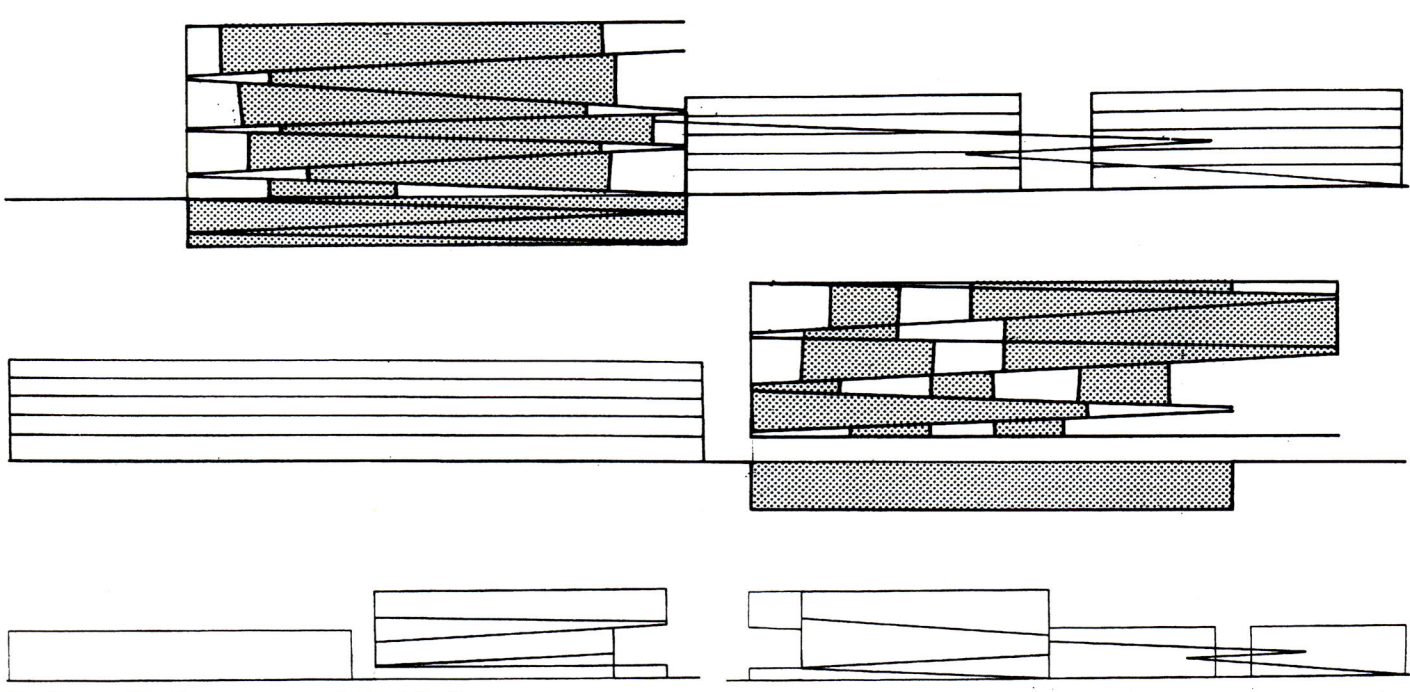

Uros Trauner: "New interwoven space; fluid and fixed"

Präsentationsmodell mit auswechselbaren Teilvarianten /
Presentation model with exchangeable parts

**Projektgruppe / project group
Michelangelo Pistoletto**

in collaboration with Christos Papoulias
Assistent: Alexej Dallas

Marko Appollonio

Nelo Auer

Jens Boymann

Anna Claramunt Ciuró

Barbara Crevatin

Lorenz Dexler

Astrid Hübner

Joao dos Santos Simoes

Brigitte Keller

Tomaz Krusec

Rok Oman

Antonio Paolin

Armona Pistoletto

Duarte Soares Iema

Ales Znidarsic

Michelangelo Pistoletto Turin

1933 born in Biella, Italy

Teaching positions
1992 Professor at the Academy of Fine Arts, Vienna

Selection of work
1967 theatre and performances called "The Zoo"
1973 one person show at Kästner Gesellschaft, Hannover
1974 one person show at Matildenhöhe, Darmstadt
1977 realizes the opera „Neither" with Samuel Becket and Morton Feldmann for the Opera house in Rome and for the Metamusik Festival of Berlin
1979–81 solo exhibitions and perfomances in the USA at Rice Demenil Museum, Houston; Georgia Museum of Art, Athens; Museum and City of Atlanta; San Francisco Museum of Contemporary Art; L.A.I.C.A., Los Angeles; Clock Tower, New York

Major exhibitions
1959 first one-person exhibition at galleria Galatea, Torino
1964 participation at the international exhibition of "Nouveau Realism" and "Pop-Art", Museums of Berlin, Bruxelles, Wien, Paris
1966 first retrospective at Walker Art Center, Minneapolis USA
1969 retrospective at Boymans van Beuningen Museum, Rotterdam
1976 retrospective at Palazzo Grassi Venice
1978 one year in Berlin with DAAD grant: solo exhibition at Nationalgalerie and in 14 places of the city
1983–84 solo exhibition at Palacio de Cristal, Madrid
1986 solo exhibition in Toronto, Art Gallery of Ontario and in Eindhoven, Stedelijk van Abbemuseum
1988 solo exhibition at PSI Museum New York and Baden Baden, Staatliche Kunsthalle
1989 solo exhibition Kunsthalle Bern
1990 retrospective at Galleria Nazionale d'Arte Moderna, Rome; solo exhibition at Centre de Arte Santa Monica, Barcelona and Wiener Secession, Wien
1994 retrospective at The National Museum of Contemporary Art, Seoul
1995 one-person exhibition at MMKSLW 20er Haus, Wien

participations at the Biennale in Venice in 1966, 1968, 1976, 1978, 1984, 1986, 1993, 1995 and at the Documenta Kassel in 1968, 1982, 1992

Publications among others
1969 Pistoletto, dentro fuori lo specchio, A.Boatto, Rome
1986 Pistoletto, lo spazio della riflessione nell'arte, B.Corà, Ravenna
1989 Pistoletto, G.Celant, New York
1992 Pistoletto, G.Celant, Milano
1988 A Minus Artist, Texts of M. Pistoletto, Florence

Prizes / Awards
1966 first prize at Biennale de Sao Paulo, Brasil and prize of the Belgian Critique for his one person exhibition at Palais des Beaux Arts, Bruxelles

Creative collaboration — Michelangelo Pistoletto

By way of introduction I would like to quote a motto, which to me is very important: "Per creare bisogna essere in due" (you need two to create). In my work, which I call "Creative Colaboration", this motto appears very often and in various contexts.

This is my way of escaping egocentrism, a propensity all artists usually have. A painter, for example, communicates with the outside world through the canvas. A canvas that plays the role of the "others". I, however, wish to eliminate such barriers and come into contact with others.

This also explains my interest in interacting with other disciplines, in this case architecture. Maybe I should present some of my past work since this may help elucidate the process, which has led me to this encounter.

I would like to begin with a construction that I began in the fifties and that brought me to transform painting into a "mirror image" in 1960/61. It was a life-size photography of a human being that was fixed onto the surface of a mirroring plate made of stainless steel (photo).

The static position of the person on the photograph stands in contrast to the dynamics of the figures that appear as mirror images in constant movement. This makes the person part of the dynamics at the same time. The surrounding architecture is reflected in the image, and the contemplator, who is also directly reflected in the image becomes part of this piece of art. The visitor becomes the main actor in a work of art, is part of this art and – as in live reports – becomes the dynamic subject. Contemplator and artist exchange roles.

"Spiegelbild" 1962, 220 x 120 cm /
"Mirror Image" 1962, 220 x 120 cm

The factor "time" is the decisive element in these constructions, since phenomenologically seen they develop in the dimension of time, which reflects the continuous fluctuation between maximum static and maximum dynamics.

Another construction, which stands as a milestone in my life, is the „Plexiglass" series of 1964. One part of this series was called „Il Muro" (the wall). It consisted of a plexiglass pane measuring 180 x 120 cm, leaning against the wall. It defined the conceptual principle: the part of the wall that can be seen through the square plexiglass is art, the remaining part of the wall is not. The plexiglass makes a wall a concept and subject that otherwise would be an object.

In 1966 I carried out a project closely related to architecture (a "sculpture" so to say). It consisted of a ball made of newspaper. Every day the newspaper was pressed and stacked onto the ball after having been read until the ball had become as large as the entire museum hall. A ball as large as the room surrounding it. To remove the ball either the museum or this construction would have to be destroyed.

This ball represents immobility, while another ball with a one-meter diameter rolling on the streets would represent mobility.

Between 1965 and 1966 I created a group of constructions with the title "Oggetti in meno" (less objects), representing another decisive step in my career.

Zwischen 1965 und 1966 habe ich eine Gruppe von Arbeiten mit dem Titel „Oggetti in meno" (Weniger Objekte) realisiert, die für mich eine weitere, entscheidende Etappe meiner Laufbahn darstellen.

Eines dieser Werke war „Raum unter dem Bett" (auch diesmal aus gepreßten Zeitungen): der Raum unter dem Bett (er war beleuchtet) wurde zu einem Ausstellungsraum, einer Galerie, einem Museum und so zu Architektur.

Die „Oggetti in meno" sind Ausdruck der Unterschiedlichkeit und der Diskontinuität, denn keines dieser Werke gleicht dem anderen. Es ist ein Zusammenspiel von einzelnen und unterschiedlichen Werken, die das Konzept der Eindeutigkeit des Künstlers umstürzen, denn er manifestiert sich in vielen verschiedenen Entitäten: gleich viele Entitäten wie realisierte Werke. Ebenso eine Erklärung im Sinne der Dimension „Zeit". Jedes Werk ist unterschiedlich, denn jeder Moment bietet eine neue Gelegenheit. Die „Oggetti in meno" bedeuteten auch die Zerstörung des Käfigs, welcher Uniformität und Gleichmacherei darstellt.

Ich habe einige dieser Werke ausgewählt, und zwar diejenigen, die einen direkten Bezug zu Architektur und Design haben.

„Quadro da pranzo" (Eßbild) ist ein Bild, in das sich zwei Personen setzen können. Zwischen ihnen befindet sich ein Tisch, an dem sie ihre Mahzeiten einnehmen können.... (Photo).

„Casa a misura d'uomo" (Haus nach menschlichen Maß) ist ein Haus, das die Höhe eines Menschen hat. Es präsentiert sich physisch als Architektur, dreidimensional und undurchdringlich wie eine Skulptur, illusorisch wie ein Gemälde.

„Struttura per parlare in piedi" (Struktur für Gespräche im Stehen) ist eine Konstruktion aus Eisen, die dazu dient, Arme und Beine in der richtigen Höhe abzustützen, um entspannt – aber ohne zu sitzen – mit anderen zu plaudern, die sich (vielleicht) selbst ebenso abstützen.

„Colonne di cemento" (Betonsäulen) ist eine Konstruktion aus vier Säulen, die einen Freiraum umschließen, der wegen seiner völligen Einsehbarkeit nicht nutzbar ist.

Anfang der 70er Jahre habe ich einen Spiegel in zwei Teile geteilt, um im Inneren einer geteilten Einheit die Vermehrung zu schaffen.

"Space under the Bed" was part of this group (also made of newspaper pressed together): the space under the bed (the space was lit) was turned into an exhibition room, gallery, museum and thus to architecture.

**Bild eines Essens, 1965 Holz, 200 x 200 x 50 /
Picture of a meal, 1965 wood, 200 x 200 x 50**

The "Oggetti in meno" expressed the difference and the discontiuity since none of the pieces of art were identical. The interplay of individual and different constructions usurp the concept of the artist's explicitness since he/she manifests himself/herself in many different entities: as many entities as there are pieces of art. It can also be explained with the dimension of "time". Every piece of art is different since every moment offers a new opportunity. The "Oggetti in meno" also meant the destruction of the cage of uniformity and egalitarianism.

I chose some of these constructions, I chose the constructions that stand in a direct relationship to architecture and design.

"Quadro da pranzo" (Picture of a meal) is a picture which two persons can enter and sit down in. There is a table between the two at which they can eat their meal ... (photo).

"Casa a misura d'uomo" (human-sized house) is a house measuring the height of a human being and physically presenting itself as architecture, three-dimensional and impermeable like some sculpture, illusionary like a painting.

„Spiegelobelisk" 1976, Installation Palazzo Grassi, Venedig
„Mirror obelisk" 1976, installation Palazzo Grassi, Venice

Aus einem werden zwei, und in der Spiegelung zwischen den beiden Einheiten entstehen unendlich viele virtuelle Spiegel.

Dieses Werk hat direkten Bezug zur natürlichen Vermehrung. Eine Zelle teilt sich, um zwei Zellen zu bilden, und so weiter...

Im Jahre 1980 habe ich ein Theaterstück als Gesellschaftsarchitektur geschaffen. Es heißt „Anno Uno" (Jahr Eins). Die Leute aus einem Dorf in Ligurien tragen Dächer einer ganzen Stadt auf ihren Köpfen und bilden selbst die Häuser dazu. Es handelt sich also um eine lebende Skulptur, um sprechende Architektur.

Mit „Progetto Arte" („Projekt Kunst") habe ich 1994 eine Serie von Werken begonnen, die die Kunst in ein direktes Zusammenspiel mit allen Aspekten der Gesellschaft bringen – von der Politik zur Wirtschaft, von der Wissenschaft zum Theater, von der Architektur zur Musik, vom Wohnraum zur Nahrung, von der Religion zum Verhalten, von der Forschung zur Literatur, von der Philosophie zum Sport.

Heute, am Ende eines Jahrhunderts und eines Jahrtausends, da Wissenschaft und Technologie atemberaubende Fortschritte machen, während in weiten Teilen dieses neuen Planeten immer mehr Menschen in materieller Not und menschlicher Abstumpfung versinken, will „Progetto Arte" die Verantwortung der Kunst in der globalen Vision einer Welt betonen, die durch die Geschwindigkeit der neuen Kommunikationsmittel immer kleiner wird. Früher war der Künstler auch Architekt und der Architekt auch Künstler. Ich denke, daß heute, auf der Suche nach Proportion und Gleichgewicht, die gemeinsame Arbeit ein neues Projekt unserer Gesellschaft werden kann.

"Struttura per parlare in piedi" (structure for conversations while standing) is a steel construction serving as a support for arms and legs to relax in – without sitting down – and talk to other persons (maybe) also supporting themselves in the same manner.

"Colonne di cemento" (concrete pillar) is a construction made of four pillars surrounding an empty space, which because of its complete openness cannot be used.

In the early seventies I split a mirror in two so as to proliferate within a divided unit. Out of one came two, and in the reflection between the two units an infinite number of virtual mirrors came to be.

This construction was directly linked to natural proliferation. A cell divides to create a second cell and so on...

In 1980 I created a drama as social architecture. It's title is "Anno Uno" (Year One). The inhabitants of a village in Liguria carry all the roofs of a city on their heads and are therefore themselves houses. They are living sculptures, talking architecture.

I began a series of constructions in 1994 with "Progetto Arte" (Art Project) that linked art with all aspects of society – from politics to economy, science to theater, architecture to music, living space to food, religion to behavior, research to literature, philosophy to sports.

Today, at the turn of the century and millennium, at a time when science and technology are making awesome strides forward while in many parts of this world an increasing number of people are suffering material need and human minds are being dulled, "Progetto Arte" intends to underline the responsibility art bears in the global vision of a world that because of rapidly increasing means of communication is shrinking. Yesterday an artist was also an architect and the architect was an artist. I believe that today, in our search for proportion and equilibrium, working together can become a new project for society.

Michelangelo Pistoletto

„Jahr Eins" 1981, Teatro Quirino, Rom /
„Year One" 1981, Teatro Quirino, Rome

Michelangelo Pistoletto / site

**The industrial space – image carrier of the city development
Opel Austria Aspern, Vienna 22**

As a result of the changes in the framework conditions of city development policy, city expansion has again become an important topic of planning. The issues of identification and identity of the new development areas thus also obtain increased importance. This applies in particular to the largest reserved development zone in Vienna´s northeast.
The premises of Opel Austria – one of the city´s largest industrial producers with approximately 3 000 employees catering for exports – constitute an important spacial element in this connection.
A large parking space, separated from the public road by a line of trees, is located in the south of the company´s premises along the development axis of Groß-Enzerdorfer Straße. North of the premises of Opel Austria we find the former airfield of Aspern, scheduled for a city architectural development.
The public transport system, shall be considerably upgraded by the extention of a tramway line to Eßling along Groß-Enzerdorfer Straße.

The area south of Groß-Enzerdorfer Straße is scheduled for buildings. With a view to future development density, this section is reserved for a denser, urban zone. This would also imply an upgrading of the area bordering in the north – from the integration of the company parking ground into the design of the public space to construction on the premises.

Opel Austria, Aspern, Wien 22

Progetto Arte

To assess the heritage of history has become possible, now that the end of the century and the millenium is near.

The twentieth century has witnessed an exponential acceleration of scientific and technological progress. Traditional notions of space and time have changed, and mankind has entered a new dimension laid open by imagination and inventiveness. Concurrently, a contrary development has brought significant numbers of living beings to extraordinary levels of social and existential degradation.

An immense loss of "civil" balance has taken place, and an acute contrast has become manifest in the relationship between the rapidity of communication, which has brought the inhabitants of Earth closer together, and the age-old differences that have interposed themselves between one ethnic group and another, creating insurmountable distances among individuals.

It is a terrible disfunction of which artists must become aware: they must wonder what role this world reserves for them.
The matter has troubled me deeply ever since the 1950s, and I have steered my work in the direction of individual conscience and interpersonal responsibility.

Heute, an der Schwelle zum nächsten Jahrtausend, betrachte ich die Kunst als Projekt der Annäherung und Vereinigung all dessen, was getrennt ist und auseinanderstrebt, und ich bin davon überzeugt, daß die Kunst ihre Präsenz auf universaler Ebene wiedergewinnen muß.

Das Projekt

Progetto Arte geht von der Vorstellung aus, daß die Kunst die genaueste und umfassendste Ausdrucksform des Denkens ist. Und daß es daher an der Zeit ist, daß sich der Künstler seiner Aufgabe bewußt wird, Verbindungen zwischen den verschiedenen Formen menschlicher Aktivität zu schaffen.

Geht man von der Feststellung aus, daß die Idee der Zivilisation nicht mehr in Begriffen territorialer Abgrenzung erfaßt werden kann, so ließe sich etwa eine Philosophie denken, die den Begriff einer „globalen Zivilisation" ins Spiel bringt.

Ein Motto könnte lauten: „Die Distanzen abschaffen, die Unterschiede bewahren".

Ein Labor wird mit dem Ziel gegründet, einen Energiekern zu schaffen, der aus dem begrenzten Anfangsstadium hinauswächst. Es gilt, die kreativen Impulse aufzugreifen, die die Verbindungen zwischen den unzähligen bestehenden, wenngleich noch nicht formulierten, Potentialen suchen: mit dem Ziel, neue Verknüpfungen und Schaltungen zu schaffen, die die Zukunft einer den Planeten umspannenden sphärischen Struktur bilden sollen.

Progetto Arte signalisiert als Prinzip: Annäherung der Gegensätze in jedem sozialen Bereich, in ideeller und praktischer Anwendung.

Vergangenheit und Zukunft sind zwei Pole, die in der Gegenwart aufeinandertreffen. Um die Zukunft entwerfen zu können, ist es notwendig, gleichzeitig eine Vision der Vergangenheit zu entwicklen. In diesem Zusammenhang mißt das Projekt der Begegnung von Kunst und Architektur eine Rolle von grundlegender

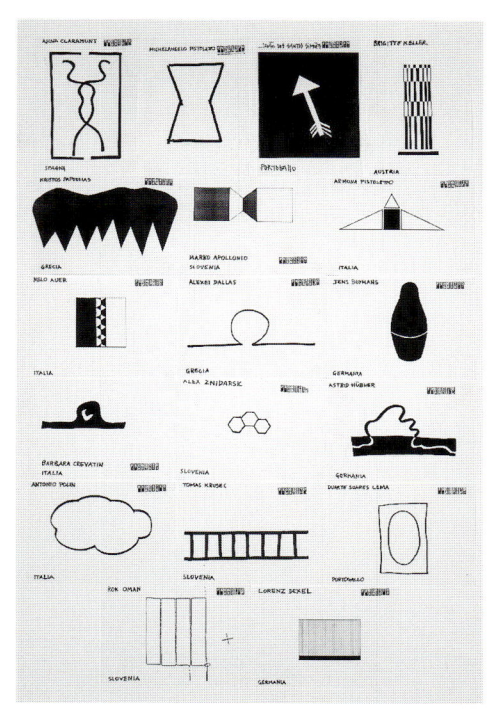

"Segno Arte" Zeichnungen der Seminarteilnehmer / "Segno Arte" drawings of the participants

„Architektur-Skulptur" zwischen den Autos des Parkplatzes vor dem Opel Austria-Werk / "Architecture-sculpture" between the cars of the parking ground in front of the Opel-Austria-plant

Now, on the treshold of the new millenium, I think of art as a potential means of gathering together and joining all that which has been excised or driven apart. I believe art must recover its universal status.

The project

Progetto Arte is based on the idea that art is the most sensitive and complete expression of human thought, and that the time has come for artists to take on the responsibility of establishing ties among all other human activities.

A basic tenet of the project is the conviction that, as civilization can no longer be understood in terms of clearly defined territories, an outlook that will stimulate the expression of a "global civilization" is necessary.

One motto, in this sense, might be, "eliminate distances while preserving differences."

On this foundation a workshop will be constructed with the intent of forming a "hot core" of energy that will radiate on a broad scale, and not just in a limited field - in other words, to gather together those creative urges that seek to unite the innumerable potentials that exist unexpressed, and to create, as a consequence, the channels of interaction that will form the spherical framework of human society on the planet.

Progetto Arte is the sign of a possible principle - that of the joining of opposites - which can be applied to all social contexts, in terms of both the ideal and the practical.

Past and future are two opposites that join in the present. Consequently, to plan the future one must look contemporaneously at the past. The project assigns a fundamental role to the encounter between art and architecture, in the

Details der Architektur-Skulptur / Details of the "Architecture-sculpture"

Pistoletto, Papoulias, Dallas und die Seminarteilnehmer vor den Modellen der „Architektur-Skulptur" / Pistoletto, Papoulias, Dallas and the participants in front of the models of the "Architecture-sculpture"

Details der „Architektur-Skulptur" / Details of the "Architecture-sculpture"

Bedeutung bei. Rückblickend sehen wir, wie Künstler und Architekt in einer Person verschmolzen, als es galt, im Einklang mit den Repräsentanten der Macht die großen Zivilisationen zu erfinden. Heute ist das sogenannte „ökonomische System" im Besitz der globalen Macht. Ein System, in dem für nicht profitorientierte Überlegungen, für den Gegenpol den Gesetzen des Profits, kein Platz ist; folglich gibt es keine Möglichkeit für eine Initiative, die eine umfassende Reorganisation der Zivilisation plant. Und doch dürfen wir nicht verkennen, daß der ökonomische Organismus, der die Verantwortung für das Fortbestehen des Ungleichgewichtes in der Welt trägt, der wichtigste Verhandlungspartner des Künstler-Arichtekten ist und daß der neue Kurs zu einer Wiederherstellung der alten Verbindung zwischen Kunst und Macht führen muß.

Ein weiteres Motto von Progetto Arte lautet: „Der Künstler als Sponsor des Denkens". Es bezeichnet ein Tauschangebot, das die konventionelle Auffassung des Zahlungsverhältnisses umkehren soll.

Wir dürfen jedoch bei all dem nicht vergessen, daß es auch und vielleicht vor allem jene Dogmen sind, die die Religionen bilden und spalten, die den Bazillus des ästhetischen und moralischen Konflikts weltweit in sich tragen. Die Strenge der dogmatischen Methodik wird den Anforderung, die heute an Interpretationen gestellt werden, nicht mehr gerecht. Die Idee eines universal gültigen Konzepts muß an die vorgegebenen Unterschiede und Partikularismen der Kulturen angepaßt werden. Daher mißtraue ich allen Positionen, die nur die eigene Meinung gelten lassen, Feindbilder suggerieren und den „Gegner" bekämpfen wollen.

In der Geschichte der Hochkulturen wurden auch Tempel und Kathedralen von den Künstler-Architekten im Einklang mit den herrschenden Mythologien und Religionen gebaut. Folglich sollte die Kunst auch heute wieder die Verantwortung für den spirituellen Bezug zwischen dem Gestern und dem Morgen übernehmen, in genauer Kenntnis des Umstands, daß auch die Kirchen – ganz unzeitgemäß – ein Grund sind für die katastrophale soziale Ungleichheit. Denn fast überall stellen diese „Kirchen" der herrschenden Wirtschaftsmaschinerie ihren Opferglauben hilfreich zur Verfügung und werden unausweichlich Komplizen der modernen Kriegsführung.

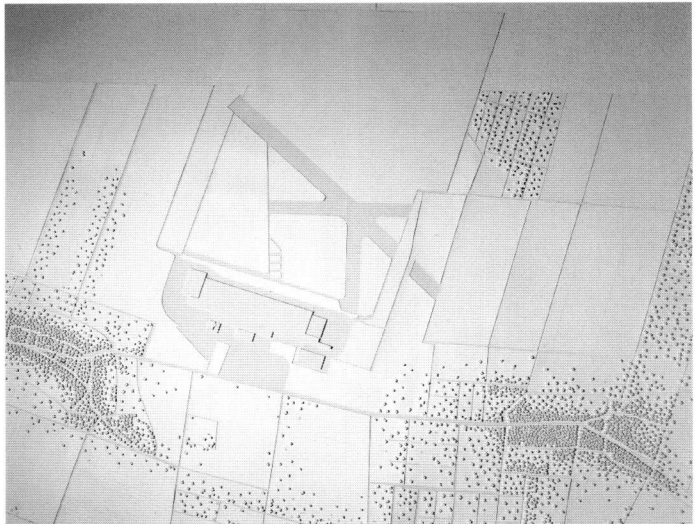

belief that artist and architect acted as one person in imagining and formulating the great civilizations of the past, and that their action was made possible by a sense of commitment on the part of those invested with public power, with whom they engaged in the pursuit of common goals. Today, global power is managed by the so-called economic system – a system in which there is no place for thought offered free of charge and hence no room for the "opposite" of the rule of profit. It follows that there cannot be an initiative that proposes to formulate a complete configuration of civilization. Nevertheless one cannot help but acknowledge that the economic system, which is responsible for creating and maintaining world imbalance, is the principal interlocutor of the artist/architect, and that the new course must lead to a restablishment of the ancient connection between art and power.

Another motto of Progetto Arte might be, "the artist as a sponsor of thought", it expresses the intention to effect an exchange of roles, as well as a reversal of the traditional conception of remuneration.

Due account must be taken also of the fact that the principles which define and divide religions probably contain the most potent seeds of aesthetic and moral conflict. The harshness of dogmatic methods no longer corresponds to today´s interpretative needs, which must reconcile the particular differences of cultures with the idea of universal concert. Hence I distrust all those positions that define their own view as the only positive one perpetrating the primitive notion by which the negative sign is assigned to a frontal enemy who must be combatted.

**Situation des Opel Austria-Werkes zwischen den Ortskernen Eßling und Aspern und dem alten Flugfeld /
Situation of the Opel-Austria plant between the villages Eßling and Aspern, and the old airfield**

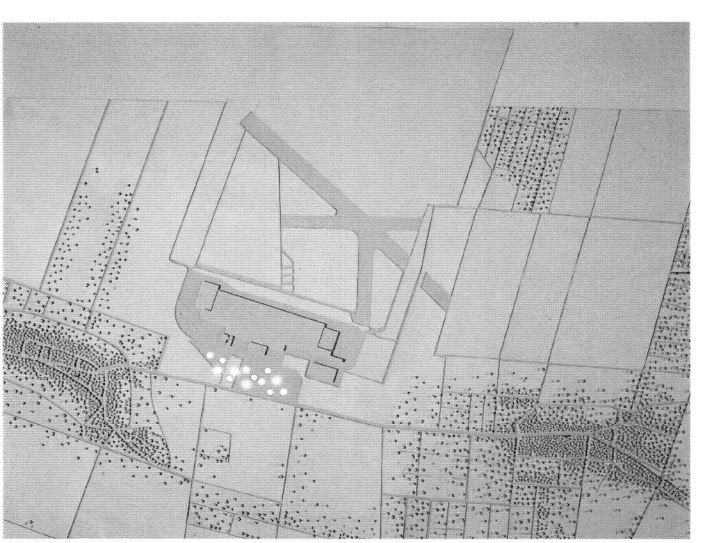

**Die leuchtenden Punkte bezeichnen die Positionen der „Architektur-Skulptur" zwischen den Autos auf dem Parkplatz vor dem Opel Austria-Werk /
The illuminating points show the position of the "Architecture-sculpture" between the cars on the parking ground in front of the Opel-Austria plant**

In the history of great civilizations, the temples, too, were designed by artist/architects acting in symphony with mythical and religious thought. Hence art must again take on the responsibility of establishing a spiritual connection between past and future – tempered by the awareness that the "churches" are also, anachronistically the cause of a disastrous social imbalance; that they continue to provide the economic system with the support of the ancient cult of sacrifice; and that this cult is an inevitable accomplice of the modern machinery of war.

„Die Unterschiede lieben" könnte ein weiteres Motto des Progetto Arte lauten. Es bedeutet nicht an feste Regeln der Vereinheitlichung und Gleichmacherei zu denken, sondern den Ausdrucksformen der Diversität, des Anderen und Fremden, freien Raum zu geben.

Für Progetto Arte gibt es daher keinen festen, vorgefertigten Rahmen, vielmehr sollen die Entwicklungslinien frei und dynamisch, fließend und flexibel sein. Sie sollen in die festgefahrenen Formen wie ein kapillares Netz eindringen, die als neues Gewebe in einer Vielfalt von Formen selbständig weiterwächst.

Another slogan of Progetto Arte might be, "love differences", which means, think not of rigid rules of uniformity and equality, but of the extensive articulation of differences.
Indeed, the project is not a preestablished and formalized design, it is a free, dynamic, fluid, supple sign that fits between the old trenches to form a capillary connection in the flesh of a new complex, self designing body.

Segno Arte

Kreative Zusammenarbeit – ein Begriff, der mich ständig beschäftigt und immer wieder in meiner Arbeit zu sehen ist, in zahlreichen Kontexten und zu verschiedenen Zeiten, in vielen Momenten.

Als ich eingeladen wurde, als Künstler unter Architekten am Internationalen Wiener Architektur Seminar teilzunehmen, bat ich meinerseits um die Zusammenarbeit mit Christos Papoulias – ich wollte die Zusammenarbeit zwischen einem Architekten und einem Künstler. Papoulias, ein griechischer Architekt, der im Rahmen des Seminars 1994 eine Gruppe leitete und sich schon immer mit Kunst beschäftigt hat, war für mich der ideale Partner, um im Rahmen eines Projekts den wahren Dialog zwischen Kunst und Architektur weiterzuführen.

Also wurde das Motto „zum Schaffen gehören zwei" für meine Arbeit wieder von grundlegender Bedeutung. Dieses Mal vor allem für das laufende Projekt „Progetto Arte", das ich als Thema und Grundlage für das Seminar auswählte.

Mit seinem Thema „Öffentlicher Raum" schien das Seminar in meinen Augen ein geeignetes Forum für die Weiterentwicklung von „Progetto Arte" wie auch für eine Partnerschaft zwischen Künstler und Architekt zu sein. Uns allen war klar, daß die Frage nach der Mischung von Kunst und Architektur gestellt werden muß. Wir machten uns jedoch auf die Suche nach einem Ort, der so weit als möglich von den runden Tischen und Diskussionen, wo der „Dialog" zwischen Kunst und Architektur üblicherweise stattfindet, entfernt sein sollte.

**Das „Segno Arte" („Kunst-Zeichen") von Pistoletto bildet eine neue Form vor dem Opel Austria-Werk, während die „Architektur-Skulpturen" in den Grünbereichen neben dem Werksgelände bzw. in das Gebiet des alten Flugfeldes gesetzt werden.
The "Segno Arte" creates a new form in front of the Opel-Austria plant, the "architecture sculptures" are being translocated to the green areas next the plant and to the area of the former airfield**

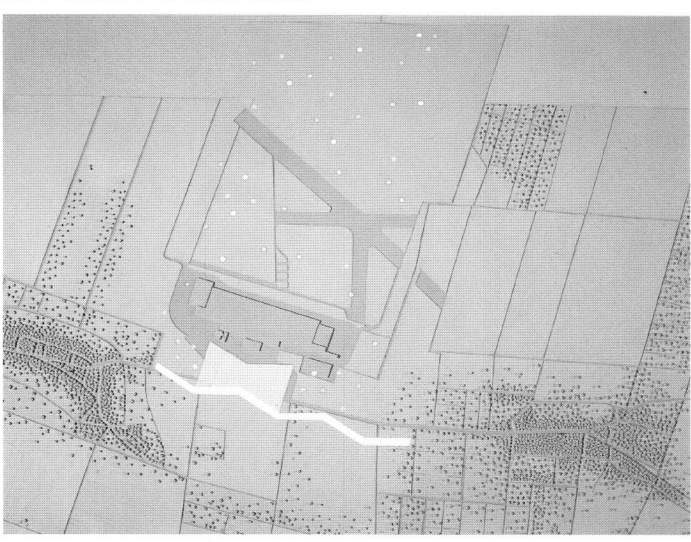

**Das „Segno Arte" vor dem Opel Austria- Werk vergrößert sich zu einem Platz mit Einrichtungen für Theateraufführungen, Musik, Kino etc. Die langgestreckte Struktur enthält Hotels, Appartments, Geschäfte und unterirdische Parkplätze, etc.
The "Segno Arte" extends to a place with facilities for theater, music, movie etc. The long structure consists of hotels, apartments, shops and parking garages, etc.**

Segno Arte

Creative Collaboration – a notion which keeps following me around, returning again in my work, in many contexts and times, in many moments.

When I was asked to participate in the Vienna International Seminar of Architecture, an artist among architects, I in turn asked for the collaboration of Christos Papoulias, an architect with an artist. Mr. Papoulias a Greek architect, who had led a group in the 1994 Seminar, and who has always been concerned with art, I saw as a partner to continue, in a project, the real dialogue between art and architecture.

Thus the motto "for creation, there has to be two" once again became essential and fundamental to my work, this time, specifically, to the "Progetto Arte", an on-going project and pursuit which I introduced as subject and basis for the Seminar.

The Seminar with its pre-established theme of "Public Space" seemed one more natural venue for the progressing of the work "Progetto Arte", as natural as the partnership of artist and architect. It was obvious to us that the whole question, the mix of art and architecture would have to be raised, but we attempted to ensure a real place of discussion as far away as we possibly could from the round tables and debates in which the dialogue between art and architecture now normally occurs.

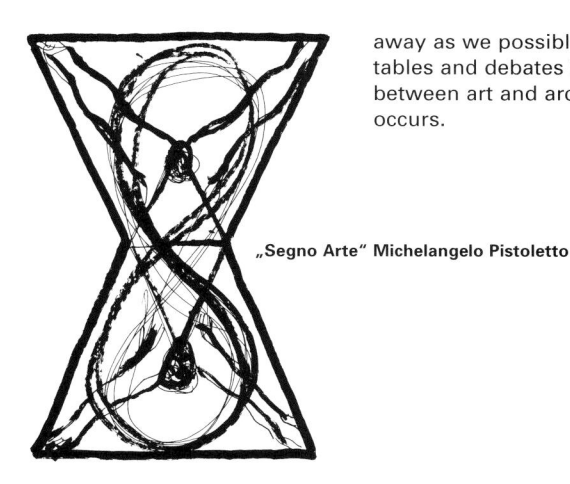

„Segno Arte" Michelangelo Pistoletto

Der von den Veranstaltern ausgesuchte Ort war ein weiter, leerer Parkplatz gegenüber dem Opel Austria - Werk in einem Außenbezirk von Wien. Hinter der Anlage bis hinauf zur Bahn befindet sich eine weitere, durch eine, lange aufgelassene Landebahn geteilte große, leere Fläche. Das Gebiet trennt die zwei Orte Eßling und Aspern.

Zur Vorbereitung für die Arbeitsgruppe stellte ich den Begriff Segno Arte in den Raum: Mein eigenes Zeichen besteht zum Beispiel aus zwei sich überschneidenden Dreiecken. Ein Winkel jedes Dreiecks ist das Zentrum des anderen. Das Zeichen stellt den ausgestreckten menschlichen Körper dar. Der Kopf und das Geschlecht sind das Zentrum jedes Dreiecks. In dieser Form können wir das Zeichen der Unendlichkeit wiedererkennen.

Ich bat die zu meiner Gruppe gehörenden Studenten, auf Grundlage meines Zeichens ihre eigenen Zeichen zu schaffen. Dann wurden die einzelnen Studenten aufgefordert, ihr Zeichen mit dem Zeichen eines anderen zu kombinieren, und somit die Möglichkeit zur Auslegung und Kommunikation zu schaffen.

Das Projekt teilte sich dann in drei Teile. Jeder Teil bestand aus drei Realisierungsphasen. Die erste Phase umfaßte den Bau von maßstäblichen Modellen, als „Architektur-Skulptur", aber auch als „Skulpturen-Architektur", Modelle, die mit dem menschlichen Körper in Verbindung standen. Sie wurden zwischen den Autos am Parkplatz aufgestellt. Das war das erste Zeichen, das auf die „attraktive" Beziehung zwischen Industrie und Stadt hinwies.

Die zweite Phase bestand in der Umwandlung des Parkplatzes in ein starkes Zeichen, wobei die Auswirkungen der Begegnung von unterschiedlichen und persönlichen Konstruktionen der ersten Phase konzentriert und diffundiert wurden. Segno Arte ist die Grundlage meiner Arbeit, die wichtige Verbindungspunkte zwischen Kultur, Geist, Schaffen und Industrie, Handel und Politik schafft. Wir stellten dieses Zeichen als Grundstein eines neuen städtischen Platzes auf den Parkplatz. Dieser wurde somit zum Ort des „Progetto Arte" und umfaßte die notwendigen Gebäude für Theater, Musik, usw. Auf der einen Seite steht das bestehende Werk, auf der anderen eine neue längliche Konstruktion mit Hotels, Wohnungen, Geschäften und einer großen unterirdischen Parkfläche. Die Verbindungsstraße zwischen den zwei Orten wird durch den neugeschaffenen Platz und durch Fußgängerwege und Straßenbahnlinien hinter das Gebiet verlegt.

The site chosen for us by the Seminar is a vast void of a parking lot facing the GM factory on the outskirts of Vienna. Behind the factory and up to the new autobahn is another huge space bi-sected by the long trace of an abandoned air strip. The territory separates the two villages of Eßling and Aspern.

I introduced, as preparation for the working group, the notion of Segno Arte: My own sign, for example, is composed of two intersecting triangles. One angle of each triangle is the centre of the other triangle. The sign is of the shape of a human body at is greatest extention. The head and the sex are the centre of each triangle. In this form we can enscribe the sign of infinity.

On this basis, I asked the students to create their own personal sign. Each student was then asked to combine his sign with that of another, thus, generating the condition for interpenetration, fecundity, communication.

The project, then, unfolds into three parts, each corresponding to three consecutive moments of realization. The first phase was the building of scale models, created as "Architecture-Sculpture", intended also as "Sculpture- Architecture", models related to the human body. They were to be placed between the cars in the parking lot. This as a first sign pointing toward the attractive conjunction between industry and city.

The second phase is based on the transformation of the parking lot into a strong sign, intending to concentrate and diffuse the effects of the encounter between the diverse and personal constructions of the first phase. A Segno Arte is a basis of my work, producing as it does crucial points of connection between culture, spirit, creation and the world of industry, commerce and politics. We placed this sign, as the beginning of a new city square, in the place of the parking lot, as a place of "Progetto Arte" including in it the necessary buildings for theater, music, cinema, etc.. On the one side is the existing factory, on the other side a new long construction including hotels, apartments, shops with extensive underground parking, a structure which connects the two existing villages. The present connecting road between the two villages is displaced by the square, and by pedestrian and tram ways, to a new road at the end of the area.

**Schaffung eines Gartens in der „Architektur–Skulptur" auf dem ehemaligen Flugfeld /
Creating a garden within the "Architecture–sculpture" on the previous airfield**

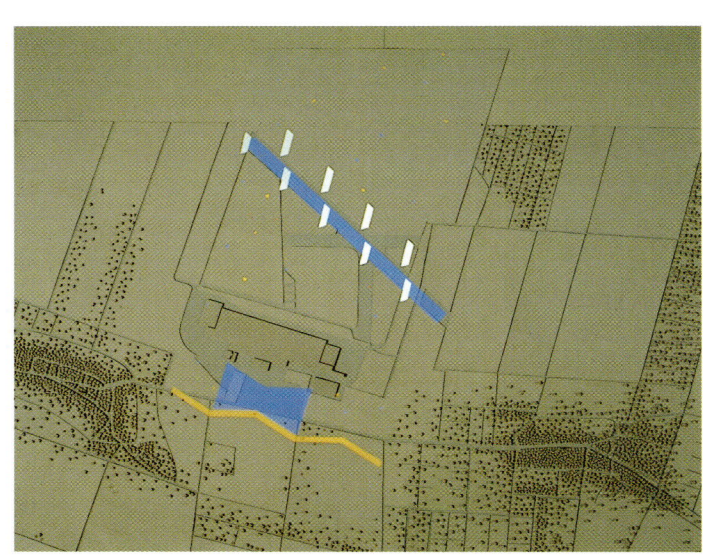

**Gestaltung einer Konstruktion für ein Geschäftszentrum entlang der alten Landebahn des Flugfeldes /
Designing of a shoping center along the previous airfield**

The square was not concieved in isolation but as central to a larger process (the third phase), that is, not just to re-create a parking lot as a social square, not just as a local solution to local concerns pertaining to a possible public space, but also as an extension of the meaning of the "urban". We found it necessary to articulate the empty land behind the factory by restoring the old airstrip as a long corridor for green areas and for a business center, which along with the existing factory would provide the basic economic justification for a new town. Thus, it is possible to arrive at that critical density of human habitation necessary to generate, maintain and attract local, national, and international participation in the activities lodged in the square.

We did not intend to plan a new town, but such planning arose naturally from our focus on the idea of centrality (the square) as an energizer of human life, the square itself energized in its relation to "Progetto Arte". A vision then in which the entire territory becomes a real urban center, the square/building as Segno Arte become a heart, an accumulator of new energy.

First "Sculpture-Architecture" spread around the parking lot. Then, in a jump of scale, they become "Architecture-Sculpture" providing the physical structure for the cultural and social activities of 30.000 new inhabitants. The "ready-made" plan of central Turin (my home city) is super-imposed on a different territory (the airstrip), an existing city-plan "ready" for any possible expansion, in which culture, spirit, commerce industry, creation, and politics are conversing, informing each other, in intimate collaboration.

Presentation of an urban structure – like the one of the city of Torino on the area of the former airfield

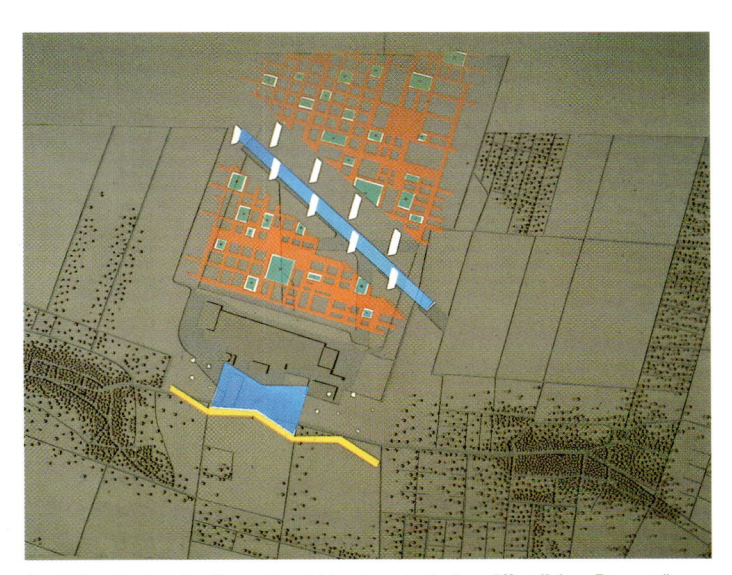

"Final version of the entire project: commercial structures are created within the "public space" and the intercultural square and the productive space of the Opel Austria plant

**Projektgruppe / Projectgroup
Fabio Reinhart**

Assistent: Urs Füssler

Branka Andric

Gabriela Bojalil Rèbora

Christoph Chlastak

Concalo Luis da Costa Louro

Heike Diehl

Björn Eisenlohr

Astrid Hillebrand

Irene Jauma Maragall

Henrike Laue

Georg Lippitsch

Gudrun Michor

Branko Miloševič Berlič

Ernst Ulrich Pfannschmidt

Francisco Manuel Pinto Rodrigues Macedo Varela

Pepe Vich Montaner

Projektgruppe / Projectgroup
Fabio Reinhart

Fabio Reinhart Lugano

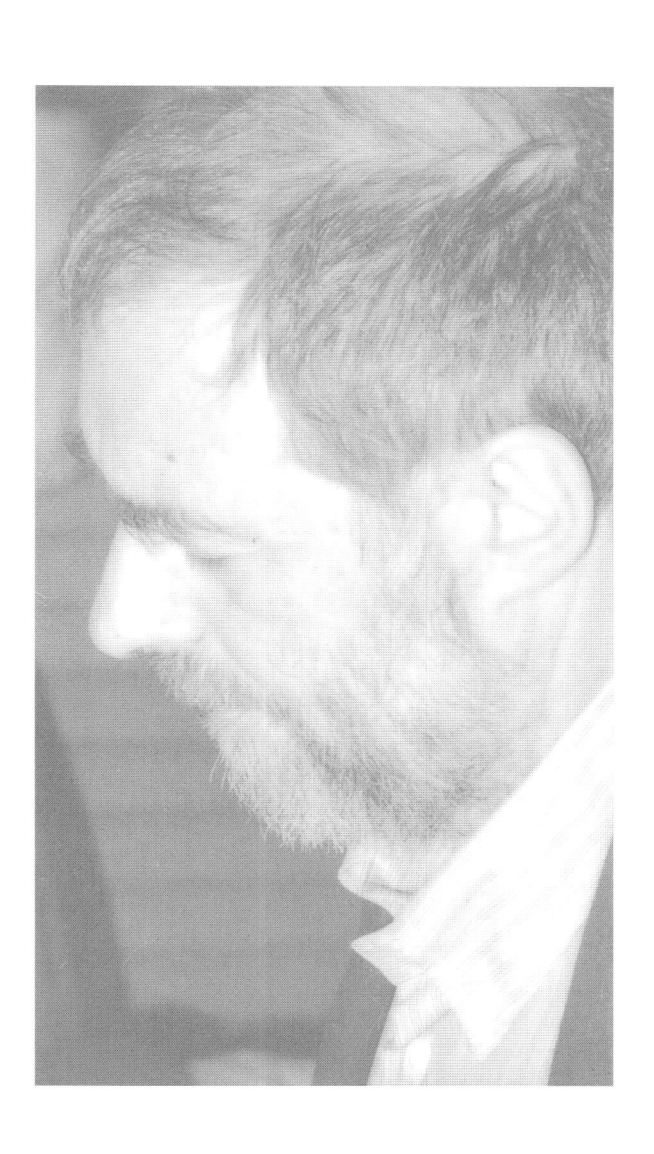

1942 born in Bellinzona, Switzerland
1968 Federla scholarship for Fine arts
1969 graduates with diploma from the Federal Polytechnics in Zurich
1970–72 Course in restoration of monuments (SPF - Z)
1970 foundation of architectural office together with Bruno Reichlin

Teaching positions
1971–72 Assistent to Dolf Schnebli at SPF-Z
1972–74 Assistent to Aldo Rossi at SPF-Z
1974–85 Lecturer at Scuola Tecnica Superiore of Lugano Trevano
1975–77 Assistent to Mario Campi at SPF-Z
1978 Visiting critic at Syracuse University, New York
1981–83 Guest Professor at Milan Politecnico
1983–85 Guest Professor at SPF-Z
1986 Guest Professor at the University of Venice
1987–93 Professor at the Gesamthochschule Kassel

Selection of work
1972–74 Casa Tonini, Torricella, with Bruno Reichlin
1974 Restauration Castel Grande, Bellinzona, with Bruno Reichlin
1976 La Cittá Analoga, Composition with Aldo Rossi, Bruno Reichlin and Eraldo Consolaccio
1983 Reconstruction of the Carlo Felice Theatre, Genova, competition, first prize with Aldo Rossi, Ignazio Gardella and Angelo Sibilla
1983–84 Compel of holiday homes, with Bruno Reichlin
1988 Moevenpick Hotel, Bellinzona, with Bruno Reichlin
1988–91 Maternity Home, Frankfurt, project
1989 Center for Art and Communication Technology, Karlsruhe, international competition for invited participants, with Bruno Reichlin
1991 Railway station Spandau, international competition amongst selected participants, second prize
1992 Casa Vatali, Viganello, with Alberto Lurati
1992 Family Home, Santo Domingo, with Alberto Lurati

Prizes / Awards
1983 first prize in the competition for the Reconstruction of the Carlo Felice Theatre, Genova, with Aldo Rossi, Ignazio Gardella and Angelo Sibilla
1983–84 first prize in the international competition for Ernsting's Miniladen, building complex, Coesfeld-Letten, with Bruno Reichlin, Santiago Calatrava
1991 second prize in the international competition for the Railway Station, Spandau, Berlin

Bedeutung schaffen Fabio Reinhart

Wenn, wie ich glaube, Architektur der Ausdruck einer kulturellen Aktivität ist, so ist es die persönliche, unausweichliche Aufgabe eines jeden, sich die geeigneten Mittel zum Handeln zu verschaffen: die kulturelle Verantwortung ist stets einzig und allein eine individuelle Verantwortung.

Die wesentlichen Implikationen sind:
Architektur heißt Kritik üben.
Die Kritik führt zu zahlreichen Formen von Architektur.

Heute wird der Architektur kein Wert mehr beigemessen; sie wird als unnütz, geradezu als Hindernis angesehen; für die Wohlgesonnensten ist sie etwas Überflüssiges: Privatsache oder Extravaganz der Architekten. Die Architektur ist zur Schmugglerware geworden. Sie wird niemals als Architektur deklariert, sondern rigoros bis zur Realisierung des Werkes totgeschwiegen, stets ohne Wissen des Käufers/Auftraggebers.

Bahnhof Spandau, Wettbewerb, 1991
Bahnhof Spandau, competition, 1991

Der Sinn eines architektonischen Werkes entsteht durch Bezüge.

Es gibt drei Arten von Bezügen:
erstens: im Werk selbst;
zweitens: unter Einbeziehung des Kontextes beziehungsweise der unmittelbaren Umgebung;
drittens: unter Ausschluß des Kontextes, beziehungsweise des Komplexes idealer Faktoren (architektonische Faktoren mit all ihren Implikationen), in die das Objekt durch Assoziation hineingestellt wird.

Ich bin nicht der Meinung vieler meiner Kollegen, die glauben, das architektonische Werk sei ein Produkt ohne Bezüge außerhalb seines eigenen Systems und seiner eigenen Poetik.

Die architektonische Qualität ist direkt proportional zu der Ebene, auf welcher die Notwendigkeit der Bezüge zum Ausdruck kommt.

So wie die Bauern aus der Wahl der Samen großen Nutzen ziehen, so können, meiner Meinung nach, die Architekten von der Fähigkeit profitieren, ihre Ideen – die mit dem Keim ihrer Arbeit vergleichbar sind – zu bewerten und auszuwählen.

Auch wenn das Gleichnis und die verwendete Metapher banal sind, so ist es sicherlich nicht das Problem, auf das sie sich beziehen: Rolle, Requisiten, Form und Größe der Planungsidee, der ich hier einige Betrachtungen widmen möchte.

Die Planungsidee ist zugleich präzise und evokativ, niemals willkürlich:
Präzise wegen ihrer historischen, kulturellen und gesellschaftlichen Bezüge.
Evokativ wegen der verschiedenen Interpretationsmöglichkeiten, die sie eröffnet, die wiederum Kritikfähigkeit für Planungsoptionen fördert und verschiedene Entwicklungen und Lösungen zuläßt.

Die verbale Form ermöglicht es einerseits über die Bezüge zu sprechen, ohne daß die konstituierenden Elemente physisch definiert sind, andererseits drückt sie präzise die erforderlichen Eigenschaften aus, die es zu erfüllen gilt und trägt so dazu bei, diese Merkmale mit größerer Präzision zu wählen.

Creating meanings Fabio Reinhart

If, as I believe, architecture is a way of expressing cultural activity, it is the personal, inevitable task of each and everyone to acquire the appropriate means: cultural responsibility is in any case merely individual responsibility.

The major implications are:
Architecture means criticizing.
Criticism leads to numerous forms of architecture.

Today, architecture is not held in high esteem; it is regarded as being useless and even an obstacle; even for well-meaning persons it is something superfluous: the architect's private affair or extravagance. Architecture has become contraband. It is never declaredly architecture, rather it is kept rigorously secret until the construction has been completed, always without the commissioning party having any knowledge.

The purpose of any architecture develops through its relationships.

There are three kinds of relationships:
firstly: in the architectural project itself;
secondly: by considering the context or the immediate surroundings;
thirdly: by excluding the context or the complexes of ideal factors (architectural factors with all their implications) into which the object is placed through associations.

I am not of the opinion many of my colleagues hold, that architecture is a product of relations outside its own system and its own poetry.

Architectural quality is directly proportional to the level at which the necessity of the relationships is expressed.

Just like farmers opt for the seed with the highest yield, architects can, in my opinion, profit from their faculty of evaluating and selecting their ideas - these are something like the core of their work.

Even if this allegory and metaphor are somewhat banal, the problem they refer to surely is not: role, requisition, form and size of the planning idea, and it is to this idea that I dedicate my observations.

The planning idea is both precise as well as evocative, however never arbitrary.
Precise because of its historical, cultural and social links.
Evocative because of the different possibilities of interpretation that arise. These also promote the faculty of criticism when planning and allow various developments and solutions.

The verbal form permits us to speak of the relationships on the one hand without physically defining the constituent elements, and on the other hand it expresses precisely the properties that are necessary. Therefore it plays a part in selecting precisely these properties.

Fabio Reinhart

Very often the use of an intermediary form, which unites word and form, is useful for ensuring precision: the form "analogous to" may harmonize precision and the faculty of evocation.

The planning idea in its original form only touches on the topic: in the complete forms we also find iconography and style, rendering the image and the motif more precisely.

The explanations of architects, those made in the construction phase, are always affirmative. During construction he/she may remain silent in ignorance or contradict, but never object. Creating knows no expressions of doubt: there is no "if" and "but".

It may however give rise to forms of doubt without contradicting the necessary fervor that goes hand in hand with commissioning of such a task. These forms of doubt may be the reaction to praise, especially in view of an excessive amount of euphoria.

If I attempted to express my personal criticism after having evaluated my work, I could only say that the best I have ever created is to be found in the ambiguity of a smile, something I have been able to achieve: happy and melancholic, bitter and beaming.

In the first architectural studio I did some practical training in, that the planning procedure was identical to that of painters whose job is to bleach the facade of a building: they proceed on a linear basis, from top to bottom; architects do the same, from 1:500 to 1:200 to 1:20 and finally to 1:5. The phases of an architect correspond to the standard fees they receive.

At the ETH in Zurich architects were less prosaic and refined in the 60s, however the planning process was more or less identical to the process of today. The procedure was characterized by the principle "form follows function"; even if not exclusively, since there was "feedback", a resounding name for the work-intensive and boring corrections that I knew of ever since I began practical work.

In my way of planning, however, only the model has changed: from painting to the confrontation with a facade. Starting from my teachers' models, I became involved with the last supper of Michelangelo, the model of my masters.

Michelangelo does not plan on a linear basis.

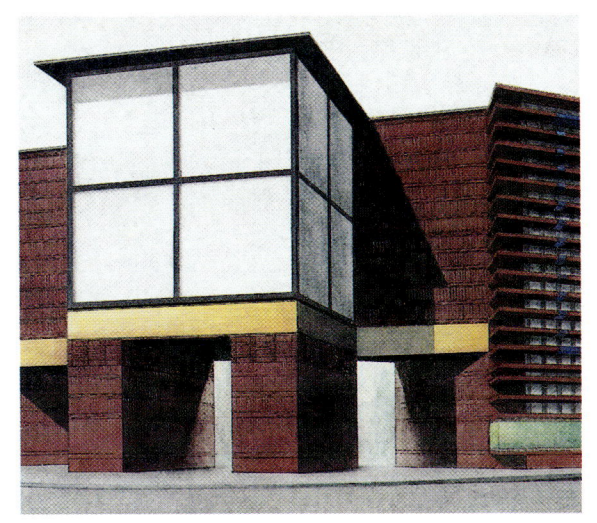

Bahnhof Spandau, Wettbewerb, 1991
Bahnhof Spandau, competition, 1991

Fabio Reinhart

dersetzung mit einer Fassade. Vom Modell meiner Lehrer ausgehend, habe ich mich mit Michelangelo eingelassen, mit dem Jüngsten Gericht, dem Modell meiner Meister.

Die Planungsweise von Michelangelo ist nicht linear.

Vergleichen wir die wenigen Linien der ersten bekannten Skizze mit dem Endergebnis – „Gedanken" wurden vielsagend die Skizzen von Michelangelo genannt – so werden wir darin bereits die allgemeinen Züge des Werks erkennen: in einem Raum ohne Rahmen, rund um den Richter und Maria drehen sich einzelne Gruppen von Seligen und Verdammten. Aber nicht nur das, in der Skizze sind bereits andere Optionen präzisiert: die Mischung der Figurengrößen, die Plastizität der Darstellung, die Bezugnahme auf vorangegangene eigene Gemälde und auf Bilder anderer.

Von Anfang an gibt es in der Vorgangsweise Michelangelos nicht nur ein Schema, sondern eine Gesamtidee des Werks, die entwickelt, präzisiert und im entsprechenden Maßstab für die kritischen Punkte kontrolliert wird.

Die Vorgangsweise bei der Durchführung der Arbeiten des Bildhauers Michelangelo bietet analog dazu ein „plastisches" Bild seiner Art zu planen. Das Endprodukt wird in seiner Gesamtheit gesehen, die Annäherung an das Ergebnis erfolgt zugleich mit verschiedenen Präzisionsgraden.

Ein heikler Punkt in der Planungsarbeit ist die Strategie – und doch ist sie für Architekten selten Gegenstand der Reflexion.

Bahnhof Spandau, Wettbewerb, 1991
Bahnhof Spandau, competition, 1991

Die Strategie ist abhängig von der Art des Problems und von den im voraus definierten Zielsetzungen.
Sie ist unter allen Optionen die ideologischste, weil sie nicht als solche erscheint. Die Gefahr besteht darin, sie als eine Naturgegebenheit zu ertragen, ohne sich ihr wirklich zu stellen.
In ähnlicher Weise kann ich, um den Begriff zu erklären, daran erinnern, daß man mich bei der ETH in Zürich in den sechziger Jahren gelehrt hat, mit Termini wie „kochen", „essen" und „schlafen" zu argumentieren, mit Termini also, die eine Funktion ausdrücken. In der Folge habe ich gelernt, als Architekt zu argumentieren, der komplexe Räume definiert und mit Substantiven wie „Küche", „Eßplatz" oder „Eßzimmer" und „Schlafzimmer" abschließt, mit Begriffen, die ihre vorhandene Räumlichkeit mit historischer Tiefe bereichern. Der Unterschied liegt auch in den Ergebnissen, er ist konkret und klar sichtbar.... und er ist nicht verbal. Es ist offensichtlich, daß es sich nicht nur um ein sprachliches Problem handelt. Es ist ein Problem der Interpretationskategorien, und die Interpretationskategorien sind kein neutrales Instrument.

Eine Strategie ist umso besser, je einfacher sie ist. Bei der Wahl der Strategie müßte man sich vor Augen halten, daß die beste und manchmal einzige Lösung eines Problems darin besteht, so zu agieren, daß sich das Problem erst gar nicht stellt.

Als ich von dem sprach, was mir am meisten am Herzen liegt, von der Frucht meiner Arbeit, sagte ich, daß ich das architektonische Werk als offenes System betrachte, das qualitativ dadurch bestimmt ist, in welchem Maße Bezüge erforderlich sind; und daß die Planungsarbeit für mich eine Form des Kritik-Übens ist.

If we compare the few lines of the first known sketches with the final results - Michelangelo's sketches were broadly described as "thoughts" – then we will already recognize the general traits of this work: in a space without frame, groups of saints and the damned are gathered around the judge and Mary. That's not all: other options have been described in the sketch as well: the different figure sizes, the plasticity of the illustration, the referral to preceding paintings of his, and to paintings of others.

From the beginning, Michelangelo did not only have a scheme but a complete idea of his work. This idea developed, became more precise, and critical points were controlled by creating it in the appropriate scale.

Michelangelo's procedure when sculpturing offers a distinct analogous "plastic" image. The final product is seen within a context. As you approach the result you enter different degrees of precision.

When planning, a critical point is strategy – and nevertheless this point is rarely contemplated by architects. The strategy depends on:
the nature of the problem and on the prospectively defined objectives.
The strategy is the most ideological of all the options since it does not appear as such. The danger lies in accepting it as something natural without actually confronting it.
By way of explaining the term, I remember how I was taught at the ETH in Zurich in the 60s to use words such as "cook", "eat", and "sleep" in my arguments, i.e. to use terms that express a certain function.
I thus learned to argue like an architect who defines complex spaces, closing with words such as "kitchen", "dining place" or "dining room" and "bedroom": terms that convey depth to the existing rooms. The difference also lies in the results, it is concrete and clearly visible... and it is no verbal difference.
It is obvious that this is no linguistic problem: it is a problem involving the categories of interpretation, and these categories are no neutral instrument.

The simpler a strategy, the better. When choosing a strategy we should keep in mind that the best and sometimes only solution to a problem is to act in a way that the problem does not even arise.

When I spoke of the things that are important to me, of the fear I have of my work, I pointed out that I regard architectural work as an open system that is qualitatively defined by the number of relationships that are necessary; and that planning, in my mind, is a form of criticizing.
Using my experience, I have pointed out the way and the planning instruments that are most appropriate for grasping the infinite complexity of all architecture. In the first, verbal phase, the strategy and planning idea are chosen: theme, picture and motif describe the project in its entirety. In the second phase, the planning hypothesis is verified and refined to perfection by examining the critical points using the appropriate instruments at an adequate scale.

Fabio Reinhart

Bezugnehmend auf meine Erfahrung, habe ich den Weg und die Planungsinstrumente aufgezeigt, die am geeignetsten sind, um der unerläßlichen Komplexität jedes architektonischen Werks auf den Grund zu gehen. In einer ersten, verbalen Phase werden die Strategie und die Planungsidee gewählt: Thema, Bild und Motive beschreiben das Projekt in seiner Gesamtheit. In einer zweiten Phase wird die Planungshypothese verifiziert und perfektioniert, indem man die kritischen Punkte unter Verwendung der geeigneten Instrumente im adäquaten Maßstab prüft.

Die konstante Bemühung, die diesem Planungsprozeß zugrundeliegt, zielt darauf ab, mit dem Werk eine Bedeutung zu schaffen, aber der rein ideelle Charakter der Bemühungen ist offenkundig. Dennoch macht erst die unausweichliche Veränderung der Kontexte die Architektur zu einem Teilhaber an Transformationen und Metamorphosen; der Verfall allein belebt sie.

Aus der Bemühung heraus, gemeinsam mit dem Werk dessen Bedeutung zu schaffen, wird man eine größere Bewußtheit, größere kulturelle Wachsamkeit schöpfen, man wird die Fähigkeit entwickeln, jene Traditionen zu wählen, in die man sich eingliedern und die man fortsetzen will. Was die Schaffung der Bedeutung betrifft, so verdanke ich es Aldo Rossi, daß ich von einer Textstelle Kenntnis habe, die in Bildern das Verhältnis zwischen dem Schaffenden, dem Werk, der Bedeutung und dem Publikum aufzeigt. Es handelt sich um einen Ausschnitt aus „Paludes" von André Gide:

„Bevor ich anderen mein Buch erkläre, warte ich, daß die anderen es mir erklären. Eine Erklärung gestatten, kommt unweigerlich einer Einschränkung des Sinnes gleich; denn, wenn wir wissen, was wir sagen wollen, so wissen wir nicht, ob wir nicht etwas anderes sagen. Man spricht immer vom anderen. – Und mich interessiert vor allem das, was ich geschrieben habe, ohne es zu wissen – jener Teil des Unterbewußten, den ich den göttlichen Teil nennen möchte. – Ein Buch ist stets eine Zusammenarbeit, und sein Wert wird umso größer sein, je geringer der Anteil desjenigen ist, der es schreibt, und je größer der Raum Gottes ist. Wir erwarten von jedem so die Enthüllung der Dinge; vom Publikum die Enthüllung unserer Werke."

Dieser Textausschnitt ist so präzise, daß es keines Kommentares bedarf.

Aber wenn es keinen Sinn hat, daß ich vom Anderen spreche, so tue ich gut daran, mit einem Wunsch zu schließen...

Da Architektur eine Ware ist, die man schmuggeln muß, wünsche ich mir, daß wir alle unser Verbrechen ausführen können: auf die Erde jenen Teil Gottes zu schmuggeln, der, wenn er Gottes ist, auch ein Teil des Paradieses sein muß. Auf Erden haben wir einen so großen Mangel an dieser göttlichen Ware, daß wir es geradezu aufgegeben haben, sie uns zu wünschen.

Mehr Paradies auf Erden zu wünschen, ist keine Utopie.

Constant efforts at the bottom of this planning process aim at creating their own meaning. The idealism of the efforts, however, is more than obvious. Nevertheless the inevitable changes of the contexts make architecture a participant in transformations and metamorphoses; decomposition alone inspires life.

From these efforts to create meaning using the architectural project comes a broader awareness, greater cultural vigilance. The architect develops the faculty to choose those traditions which he/she wishes to become part of and wishes to hold on to. As to the creation of meaning, I owe it to Aldo Rossi that I understand the use of texts that point out the relationship between the creator, the architecture, the meaning and the public with images. In this case I am refering to the words of André Gide in "Paludes":

"Before I explain my book to others, I wait for the others to explain it to me. To allow an explanation is like restricting one's own senses; we know what we want to say, but we do not know whether we are not saying something quite different than intended. We always speak of the other. - I am interested above all in what I have written, without knowing it - I wish to call this part of my subconscious the divine part. - A book is always the result of cooperation, and its value increases as the contribution of the actual author decreases and the more divinity is permitted. We expect everyone to unveil things; we expect the public to unveil our work."

This excerpt is so precise that there is no need for explanations.

If, however, there is not sense in speaking of the other, I will finish with a wish...

Since architecture is contraband that needs to be smuggled, I want all crimes to be committed: to smuggle that part of God to the world that, if it is part of God must also be part of paradise. We have such a great shortage of this divinity on earth that we have even given up wishing for it.

Wishing for more paradise on earth is no utopia.

Bahnhof Spandau, Wettbewerb, 1991
Bahnhof Spandau, competition, 1991

Das innere Wachstum der Stadt – Ergänzung und Eigenständigkeit. Entwicklungsgebiet Floridsdorf-Ost, Wien 21

Das Bearbeitungsgebiet liegt im 21. Wiener Gemeindebezirk zwischen den dicht verbauten Stadtteilen von Floridsdorf im Westen und einem geplanten regionalen Grünzug im Osten. Die südliche Begrenzung bildet der Erholungsraum der Alten Donau. Das Gebiet ist Teil einer Stadtentwicklungszone zwischen den Ortszentren Floridsdorf und Kagran mit einer Ausdehnung von ca. 4 km². Das Donaufeld, ein ursprünglich von Flußarmen durchzogenes Augebiet, wird derzeit überwiegend erwerbsgärtnerisch genutzt.

Ein neuer Stadtteil kann hier aufgrund der guten Verkehrslage und der Nähe zum Erholungs- und Freizeitgebiet der Alten Donau auf eine hohe Standortqualität aufbauen und sollte daher für eine differenzierte Entwicklung, insbesondere auch hinsichtlich hochwertiger, betrieblicher Nutzung geeignet sein. Die Hauptzentren Floridsdorf und Kagran sollen nicht konkurrenziert, sondern ergänzt und damit bestehende Defizite (Arbeitsplätze, Erholungsräume etc.) ausgeglichen werden.

Im Nordwesten des Gebietes ist als Modellversuch eine autofreie Mustersiedlung mit ca. 250 Wohnungen vorgesehen. Der Grünzug entlang der Alten Donau bildet das Rückrat eines überregionalen Grünraumsystems.

Das aus einem Expertenverfahren hervorgegangene Leitprojekt für den Teilbereich Floridsdorf Ost für etwa 3.500 Wohnungen und 1.500 Arbeitsplätze, ist Grundlage für die Erarbeitung eines Flächenwidmungs- und Bebauungsplans. Dabei sind Festlegungen über die Gestaltung und Nutzung des öffentlichen Raumes zu treffen, die weiterführende, konkrete Vorstellungen und Konzepte erfordern.

The city's internal growth – supplementation and independence. Development area Floridsdorf-East, Vienna 21

The development area is located in Vienna's 21st municipal district between the densely built area of Floridsdorf in the west and a planned, regional green stretch in the East. In the south the area borders the recreational area of the Alte Donau (Old Danube). The area is part of a city development zone between the local centres of Floridsdorf and Kagran with an expansion of 4 km² and an assumed development potential of a population of up to 24,000 people and 8,000 jobs. The Donaufeld, originally pastural land crossed by various river arms, is currently primarily used for commercial gardening.

Due to the favourable transport situation and the vicinity of the recreational and leisure area of the Alte Donau, any new city quarter will enjoy a high situational quality from the start, and should therefore be suited for differentiated development, in particular also in terms of high-level, industrial utilizations. The aim is not to create a competitive situation with the main centres of Floridsdorf and Kagran, but rather to supplement them and to make up for any existing deficits (jobs, recreational areas, etc.).

A car-free model zone of approximately 220 flats is planned in the northwest of the area as a pilot experiment. The green stretch along the Alte Donau constitutes the backbone of a transregional green belt.

The master project based on a study for the planning area Floridsdorf Ost, comprising approximately 3.500 flats and 4.500 jobs, serves as basis for the elaboration of a zoning and development plan. For this purpose decisions must be taken on the design and the use of the public space which require continuing, concrete ideas and concepts.

Entwicklungsgebiet Floridsdorf Ost, Wien 21

Vielschichtig verwobene Sequenzen

Der öffentliche Raum

Öffentlicher Raum ist nicht leicht zu bestimmen. Ein zeigender Finger trifft eine Telefonkabine, ein freies Parkfeld, abgesenkte Trottoirkanten – wie aber den öffentlichen Raum? Freilich kennen wir die allgemein bekannten, auf Postkarten abbildbaren und versendbaren Innenansichten alter Städte. Jedoch können ArchitektInnen mit diesen Bildern wenig Konkretes anfangen: in schnell wuchernden neuen Vorstädten, in den verkehrstechnisch einst zukunftsträchtig wie architektonisch trostlos wiederaufgebauten Innenstädten, in Stadtquartieren, in denen nach Feierabend kein Fenster mehr leuchtet. Man kann vielerorts in den Städten einen Mangel öffentlicher Räume wahrnehmen. Den, der sich noch zum letzten Rest der Befürworter urbaner Lebensweise zählt, wird dies schmerzen, den Architekten ganz besonders – ein Schmerz, der halb so schlimm wäre, wenn nicht gleichzeitig eine Ohnmacht bestünde, die aus der eigenen Ratlosigkeit im Umgang mit öffentlichem Raum hervorginge.

Multi—layered interwoven sequences

Public space

Public space is a term difficult to define. You may point your finger at a telephone booth, a free parking lot, at a lowered pavement edge – but how can you point it at public space? We are all familiar with the pictures of inner-city views on postcards. But these remote views are of no particular interest to architects: in today's mushrooming new suburbs, in architectonically dull reconstructed inner cities that once bore the hopes of traffic planners, in urban quarters where no light can be seen at the windows after working hours. There is, indeed, in many cities a lack of public space. For those who see themselves as the few remaining advocates of urban life, this is painful, especially for architects. The pain, however, would not be half as lacerating if it weren't for the powerlessness emanating from their own perplexity towards the issue of public space.

Aus dieser Situation stellt sich für uns die Frage: Wie entwirft man öffentlichen Raum? Hier tritt erneut die Frage nach der Bestimmbarkeit, der Faßbarkeit öffentlichen Raumes auf.

Das Material, das uns zur Klärung dieser Fragen zur Verfügung steht, ist die Summe aller öffentlicher Räume in unseren Städten und in unseren Erinnerungen. Wir üben uns in der Kunst des Beobachtens, des Wahrnehmens. Weniger eine Erfindungsgabe, als eine Entdeckungsgabe ist dazu notwendig.

Wir können nicht davon ausgehen, allgemein gültige Kriterien für die Qualität öffentlicher Räume zu finden und sichere Methoden zu deren Generierung entwickeln zu können. Zu ungeordnet sind die städtischen Entwicklungen, zu unvorhersehbar lokale Vorgänge. Das „großzügige" zur Verfügung stellen von Zonen für eine Gemeinschaft innerhalb einer (geplanten) städtischen Struktur, in denen sich öffentliche Räume dann ganz von selbst entwickeln sollen, reicht aber auch nicht aus. Öffentliche Räume sind zu sehr Teil des komplexen Organismus einer Stadt, als daß sie sich als Option für bereitgestellte Bereiche vorsehen lassen.

Über die Qualität öffentlicher Räume läßt sich vor Ort durch Beobachtung und Wahrnehmung ein Bild machen. Je mehr Räume man kennt, umso größer ist das Wissen, das die Grundlage der eigenen Arbeit darstellt. Als Architekten entwickeln wir konkrete Vorschläge öffentlicher Räume, wir weisen nicht bloße Zonen aus. Konkrete Entwürfe vermitteln Bilder, sie stellen Ideen vor, treffen architektonische Aussagen. Dadurch bieten sie Angriffsfläche für Kritik und entziehen sich einer beliebig interpretierbaren Vieldeutigkeit. Hinter dieser Art des Einbringens von Vorschlägen steckt immer ein Quantum Idealismus, Idealismus, der auch Wissen um die Möglichkeit des Scheiterns neben den kühnen Erwartungen mitträgt. Allerdings können konkrete Entwürfe für öffentliche Räume ohne weiteres zu gräßlichen Fehlplanungen führen: Stadtlandschaften, die wie zu groß geratene Modelleisenbahnanlagen modelliert sind, Fußgängerzonen, die die funktionale Fröhlichkeit von Kaufhausabteilungen aufweisen, gastronomiebetriebene Altstadtkulissen, die eine Disneywelt aus Hexenhäuschen zwischen Hochhäusern schaffen.

Öffentliche Räume sind von Bedingungen auf vielen architektonischen Ebenen abhängig: vom Kleinen, der Materialität einer Sitzbank, bis zum Großen, der Fassadenfront der angrenzenden Bebauung an einen innerstädtischen Großpark. Farbe, Licht und Geräuschwelt können ebenso eine Rolle spielen wie Ausblick, Einsehbarkeit, Abgegrenztheit oder Integration.

Wir Architekten vertreten die These, daß öffentlicher Raum in großem Maße abhängig von seinen Eigenschaften als Raum ist. Wenn wir öffentliche Räume unter dem Aspekt der vohandenen (architektonischen) Räumlichkeit anschauen, wird dies deutlich. Auch wenn innerstädtische Plätze, umgeben von dichter Bebauung, bekannt sind, fassen wir den Begriff der Räumlichkeit öffentlicher Räume weiter. Bereits Tische und Bänke unter Obstbäumen schaffen auf präzise Weise Raum inmitten offener Landschaft.

This situation raises another issue: how do you design public space?
The issue of defining, of grasping public space comes up again.

The material to be used for answering this question consists in the total of all public spaces in our cities, in our memories and the places we have access to as concrete examples. It is an exercise in the art of observation, of perception. It takes a spirit of exploration rather than inventive faculty to undertake this.

We cannot expect to find general, everlasting criteria for evaluating the quality of public spaces, nor can we develop unmistakable methods for developing such spaces. Urban developments are too chaotic, local processes too unpredictable for such an undertaking. "Generously" providing certain zones for a community within a (planned) urban environment in which public spaces are to develop through their own momentum isn't enough either.

We know examples of successful public space designs, of architecture that, in a sense, generates public space.
The quality of public space can only be judged through on-site observation and perception. The more public spaces you know, the larger the knowledge upon which you can base your own work. We architects develop concrete concepts of public spaces; we do not simply identify zones. Concrete concepts convey pictures, they present ideas, make architectural statements. In this manner, they expose themselves to criticism, thus avoiding ambiguity through a multitude of possible interpretations. Behind this presentation of concepts there is always a portion of idealism. An idealism which, next to bold expectations, is well aware of the prospect of failure. Nevertheless, concrete concepts for public spaces may just as well lead to appalling monstrosities: urban landscapes that look like oversized toy railways, pedestrian areas as joyful as supermarket departments, old inner cities crowded with restaurants resembling a Disneyworld of witches' houses amidst scysrapers.

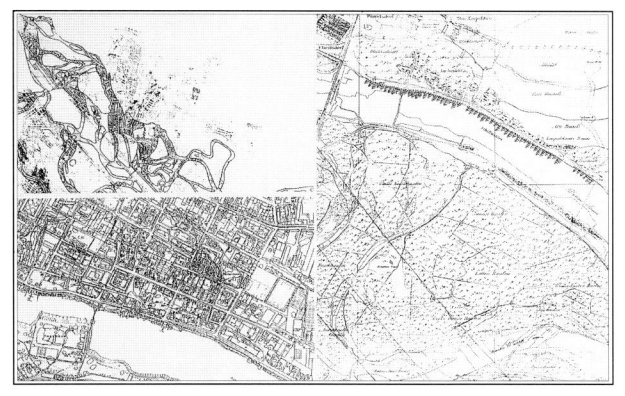

**Donauverlauf vor der Regulierung, ehemaliger Donau Hauptarm mit Schiffmühlen /
Course of the Danube before the regulation. Former main course of the Danube with shipmills**

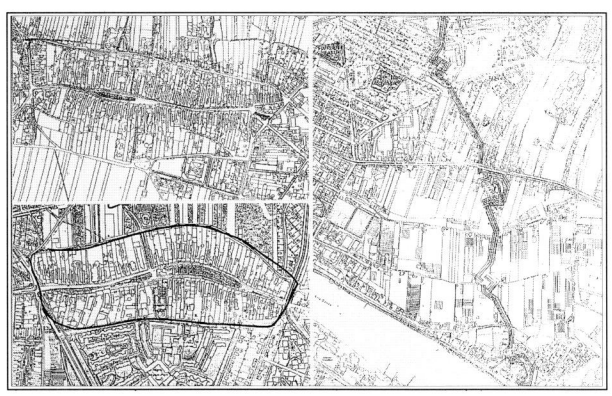

Public spaces depend on conditions at several architectural levels: from the small scale, i.e. a park bench, to the large one, i.e. the facade of buildings adjacent to a large inner-city park. Color, light, or sounds can play a role just as important as view, purpose, isolation, or integration.

We support the thesis that public space is to a considerable extent dependent on its qualities as space. This becomes obvious when we observe public spaces from the point of view of the existing (architectural) spatiality. We are all familiar with inner-city spaces, surrounded by dense chains of buildings. But in defining the spatiality of public spaces, however, we go beyond that. In such spaces, even tables or benches under fruit trees create space amidst an open landscape in a most precise way.

**Anger Stammersdorf, Anger Leopoldau, alte Wehranlage /
villages Stammersdorf and Leopoldau, old fortification project**

Das Entwerfen

Ausgehend von der These, daß öffentlicher Raum vor allem von seinen Qualitäten als architektonischer Raum lebt, stellt sich die Frage: Was gibt es für öffentliche Räume? Worin liegt ihre Spezifität, ihre Öffentlichkeit? Begriffe wie Platz, Straße, Hof können als Teile eines Grundgerüsts dienen. In einem weiteren Schritt wird untersucht, welche öffentlichen Räume untereinander in Beziehung stehen und wie diese in das urbane Geflecht der Stadt integriert sind. Welche Beziehung hat die Wohnung (der Arbeitsplatz) zum öffentlichen Raum? Wir sprechen hier von Raumfolgen.

Beispiel einer solchen Raumfolge (oder Raumsequenz) kann sein: die Raumfolge Zimmer – Hinterhof – Straßenraum - Platz. Zur Beschreibung von Raumfolgen wird versucht, sowohl die architektonischen Kriterien zu erkennen, nach denen öffentliche Räume in Beziehung gesetzt eine Sequenz bilden können, als auch die architektonischen Mittel auszumachen, mit denen die Räume solcher Raumfolgen verbunden werden – also „Schnittstellen". Wir verstehen dabei die Stadt nicht als eine Ansammlung einzelner, funktional verknüpfter Bauten inmitten eines „fließenden Raumes", sondern als Netz von Räumen differenzierter Öffentlichkeit – einen Verbund von kleinst- bis größtmaßstäblicher Architektur in Form von vielschichtig verwobenen Sequenzen.

Wir haben uns entschieden, das Gebiet von Floridsdorf-Ost zu bearbeiten, weil es eine relativ weitreichende Verknüpfung mit der Struktur der Stadt Wien erlaubt. Es steht im Gegensatz zu anderen Entwicklungsgebieten, die weitab, isoliert von der Stadt, bestenfalls Siedlungsbau zulassen. Floridsdorf verfügt bereits über eine relativ hohe urbane Qualität und historische Dichte. Der Stadtteil ist durchzogen mit dörflichen Siedlungsstrukturen aus früherer Zeit. Es besteht eine städtische Bebauung, die sich durch Wiens Stadterweiterung entwickelte. Blockrandbauten der 30er Jahre grenzen direkt an den Gebietsperimeter. Neben der möglichen Anknüpfung an die Urbanität Floridsdorfs bietet die unmittelbare Nachbarschaft der alten Donau und des geplanten Grünzugs als Erholungsräume für Wien weitere Kriterien, die uns bestärkt haben, hier die Entwicklung eines dichten, städtischen Quartiers zu formulieren.

Alle Teilnehmer des Seminars stellten einen individuellen Vorschlag einer städtischen Erweiterung von Floridsdorf mittels einer Sequenz von öffentlichen Räumen vor. Die wichtigsten Utensilien, um städtische Räume zu entwerfen, sind existierende, vertraute, alltägliche Stadträume und Formen des kulturellen Umfeldes – mit der Maßgabe, die geschichtlichen Sedimente ortsspezifische Eigenheiten als Erinnerung zu bewahren. Durch Wiederentdeckung, Neuinterpretation, kritische Bearbeitung, Transformation und Verfremdung wird mit diesem Material ein dem geplanten Stadtteil eigener Charakter gefunden und geprägt. Die Lösung zeichnet sich dadurch aus, daß sie Spezifisches des Ortes ebenso wie Eigentliches der Stadt in sich birgt. Die Sequenz der öffentlichen Räume wird mit perspektivischen Plänen gezeigt: diese Darstellung ist die geraffte Form des Raumes, knapp und zugleich präzise. Licht, Größen, Materialien, Vegetation und Umgebung stellen sicher, daß der Raum sich nicht in Abstraktion verliert. Menschliche Figuren sind in den Zeichnungen nicht enthalten, aber ihre Präsenz ist evoziert durch Form, Maß und Ausbildung der Räume.

Die Entwurfsarbeit beginnt mit der Besichtigung, der Begehung des Grundstücks. Historische Karten und städtebauliche Pläne helfen bei der Entwurfsarbeit. Öffentliche Räume werden in der ganzen Stadt gesucht, photographiert und ausgewertet nach Maßgabe des zu entwerfenden Ortes. Mittels Skizzen und Fotocollagen wird konkret entworfen. Raum wird eingefangen. Anstatt das Quartier auf der architektonisch und räumlich nicht faßbaren Maßstabsebene von 1:5000 integral entwickeln zu wollen, werden punktuell einzelne Räume des Stadtteils entworfen. Die Räume sind Orte unterschiedlichen städtischen Maßstabs, die, in Beziehung gesetzt, das Bild der Stadt prägen. So wie sich in der Erinnerung eine Stadt durch ein Netz von charakteristischen Orten darstellt.

The design

Based on the theory that a public space's raison d' être are its qualities as architectural space, one may pose the question: what kinds of public spaces do exist? What makes up their specificity, their public character? Terms such as square, street, yard may serve as parts of a basic scaffolding. In a further stage we will study the public spaces that stand in relation to each other and the way in which these are integrated in the urban fabric of a city. What is the relationship between the apartment (the work) and the public space? We speak of space sequences.

The following are examples of such a space sequence: room–yard–street–square. In order to describe space sequences, we will try to identify the architectural criteria according to which public spaces can form a sequence when put into relation with each other. Moreover, it means detecting the architectural means with which such spaces are put together into sequences, the "interfaces". We do not see the city as a mere collection of individuals, functionally linked constructions amidst a "flowing space", but rather as a fabric of spaces of differentiated publicity – an association of the smallest to the largest pieces of architecture intertwined in manifold sequences.

We decided to concentrate our work on the area of Floridsdorf-Ost because it allows a relatively broad association with the structure of the city of Vienna. It is different from other developing areas that, isolated from the city, only allow the construction of settlements. Floridsdorf already presents a high degree of urban quality and historic density. This part of the city is full of village settlement structures from earlier times. There exists an urban housing project which developed in the expansion of the city of Vienna, and large housing complexes from the thirties directly adjacent to the areas periphery. Apart from the possible linkage to the urbanity of Floridsdorf, the immediate adjacency of the Alte Donau and the planned green areas as recreational spaces for Vienna provide further criteria to convince us that the development of a dense urban quarter is in the making.

Each participant of the seminar presents his or her own concept of an urban expansion of Floridsdorf, using a sequence of public spaces. The most important requisites consist of existing, familiar, everyday urban spaces and forms of cultural surroundings - the condition being to preserve historical sediments as a reminiscence, as local particularities. Through rediscovery, re-interpretation, critical study, transformation, and detachment, this material will help find and define the individual character of this part of the city. This solution is extraordinary because it bears both the specificity of the area and the characteristics of the city. The sequence of public spaces is made visible with perspective drawings: this form of display is the compressed shape of space, brief yet precise. Light, size, materials, vegetation, and surroundings guarantee that the space will not go down in abstraction. Human shapes do not appear in these drawings, yet their presence is evoked by the shape, mass, and formation of the spaces.

The architect begins his design by observing, by walking on the future building site. Historical maps and urban design plans help with the design work. Then follows a quest for public spaces in the entire city. These are taken pictures of and evaluated according to the object to be designed. Using sketches and collages, the architect begins with the actual design. Space is captured. Instead of trying to develop the area integrally on a scale of 1:5000, unconceivable from a spatial or architectural point of view, individual spaces of the city section are singled out and designed. The spaces are sites of different urban scale, that, when combined with each other, leave their traces on the appearance of the city. Just as a city presents itself in one's memory: as a fabric of distinguished sites.

Beispiele der Studentenarbeiten:

Irene Jauma Maragall

Das Quartier wird durchzogen und gegliedert durch zwei zentrale Grünstreifen – Angern von Nachbardörfern ähnlich. Diese entstanden durch Ausweitung der beiden, parallel zur alten Donau verlaufenden Landstraßen. Ihr Geländeprofil verstärkt topografische Eigenheiten, die Spuren der mäandrierenden Donau. Die Hinterhaus- und Hofstruktur spiegeln Parzellierung und landwirtschaftliche Nutzung wider. Ein weiteres raumbildendes Element stellen die orts-typischen Pappelreihen dar.

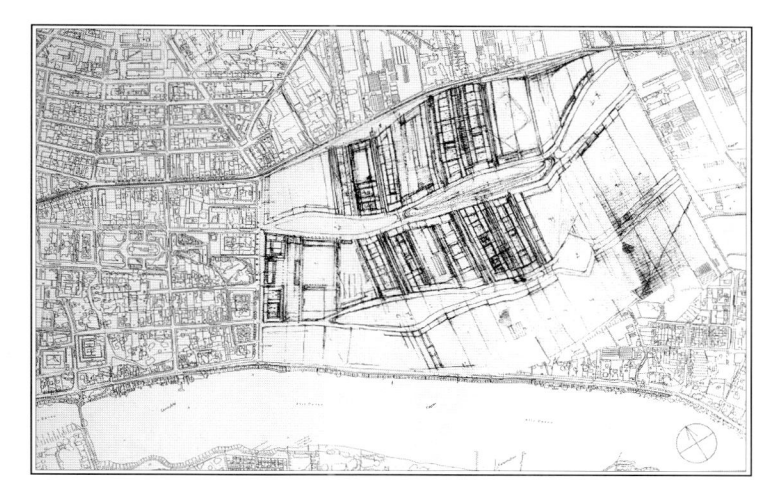

Examples of the student works:

Irene Jauma Maragall

The quarter is divided by two central green corridors running through it, which resemble the meadows of the neighbouring villages and which emerged from the expansion of the two motorways parallel to the Alte Donau. Its terrain profile intensifies local topograhical features, the traits of the Danube's serpent-like course. The structure of the back buildings and yards reflects the parcelled landscape and its agricultural use. The poplar rows, a typical characteristic of the area, constitute a further spatial element.

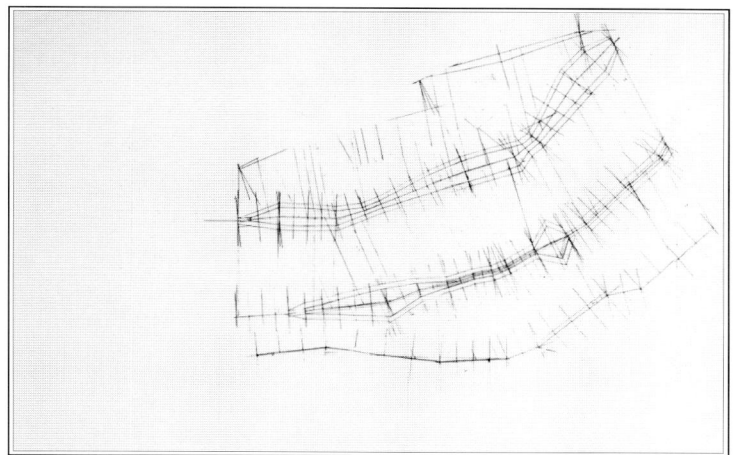

Irene Jauma Maragall

Henrike Laue

Entwicklung eines Quartiers mit Hauptstraßen, die entlang der alten Feldwege führen. Die parallel zur Straße verlaufende, dichte Bebauung weist gemischte Nutzungen auf: Gewerbe, Büros, Wohnungen. Die Nebenstraßen sind quer dazu angelegt, leicht abfallend zur alten Donau. Innerhalb der Blöcke liegen Wohn- und Gewerbeinnenhöfe. Längs der Donau erstreckt sich eine Uferpromenade.

Henrike Laue

Development of a quarter with main streets running along the old field paths. The dense building structure directed towards the street was conceived for multiple use: Shops, offices, apartments. The side streets are situated across the structure, slightly descending towards the Alte Donau. Within these blocks are residential and commercial inner courts. Along the Danube is a promenade.

Henrike Laue

Branko Milošević Berlič

Anknüpfung an den kleinen Grünpark am Rande Floridsdorfs, welcher im „Tal" eines alten Donauseitenarms auf tieferem Niveau liegt, durch die Formulierung eines angrenzenden „harten" Platzes, der Baumbestand aufweist und innerhalb eines dicht bebauten Gebietes liegt. Anlegung eines Landschaftsparks im Osten des Grundstücks als Teil des regionalen Grünzugs.

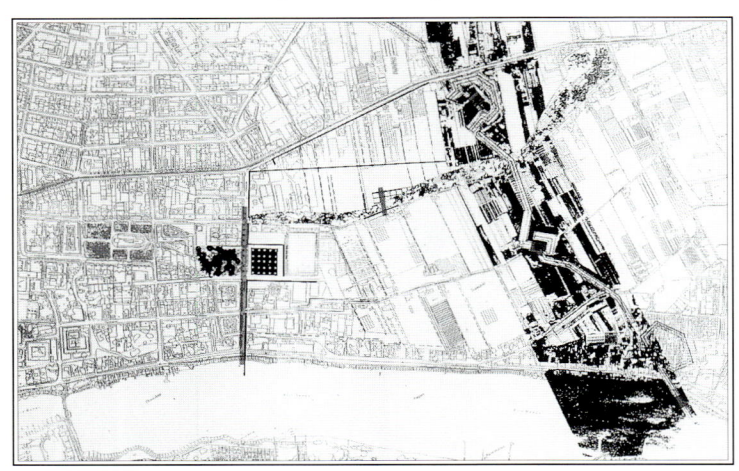

Branko Milošević Berlič

Linkage to the small park at the rim of Floridsdorf which lies in the "valley" of an old lateral branch of the Danube at a lower level, by creating an adjacent "hard" square with trees, amidst dense buildings. Creation of a landscape park on the east side of the location as a part of the regional green zone.

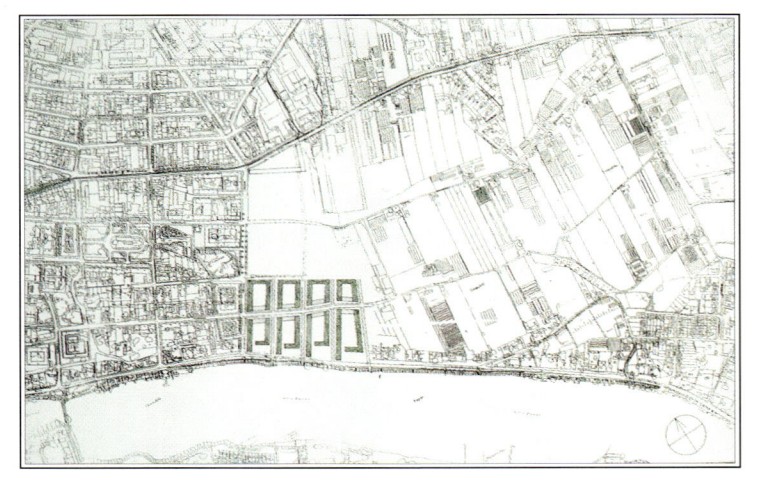

Branko Milošević Berlič

Gabriela Bojalil Rèbora

Das neue Quartier wird bestimmt durch einen großen zentralen Platz, teils offen, teils mit Bäumen bepflanzt, mit einer Hochbahn als Sekante. Seitlich davon gibt es eine Haltestelle. Unterhalb der Bahn liegt ein gewerblich mehrfach genutzter Gebäudeflügel. Der Platz wird eingerahmt und bestimmt durch eine anschließende, vier- bis fünfgeschoßige Bebauung sowie der Querstraße.

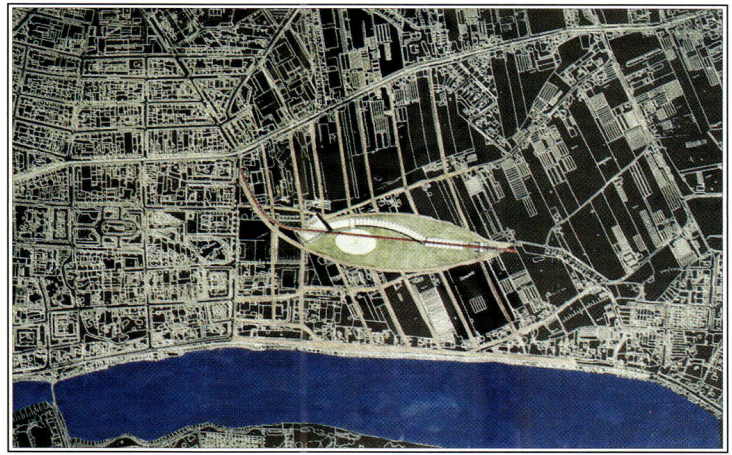

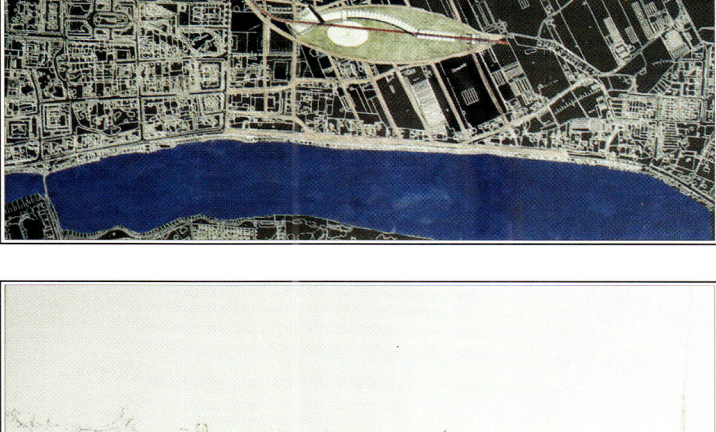

Gabriela Bojalil Rèbora

The new quarter is dominated by a large central square, partially open, partially covered with trees, featuring a raised tramway line serving as a secant. On the side is a tramway stop. Underneath the tramway line is a building section for several commercial uses. The square is surrounded and defined by the adjacent four- to five-storied buildings and the street crossing.

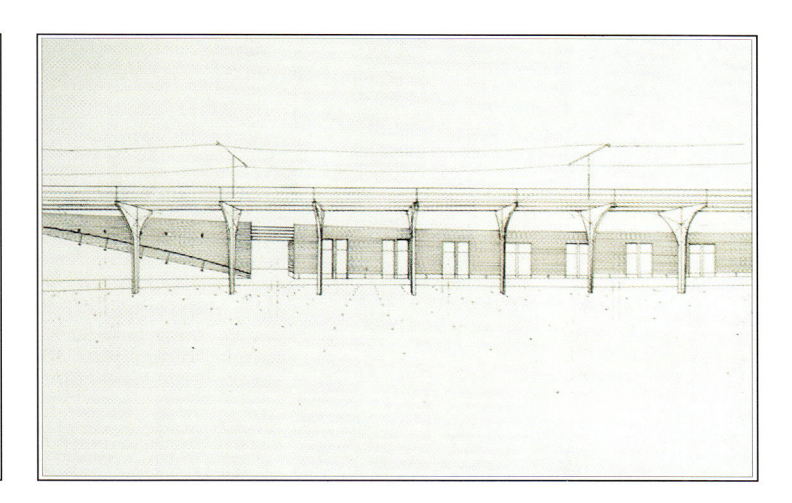

Gabriela Bojalil Rèbora

**Projektgruppe / Projectgroup
Dagmar Richter**

Assistent Keith Sidley

Maren Behler

Roland Bondzio

Damjan Bradac

Arne Erichson

Michael Filser

Isabel von Fournier

Sona Kazemi

Karin Lischke

Hartmut Lissak

Anna-Marija Meniga

David Pareras

Nico Wallner

Claudia Maria Walther

Thomas Willemeit

Kresimir Zmijanovic

**Projektgruppe / Projectgroup
Dagmar Richter**

Dagmar Richter Los Angeles

1955 born in Ludwigshafen, Germany
1982 M.A. in Architecture from the Royal Art Academy, School of Architecture, Copenhagen, Denmark
1984–86 postgraduate studies with Peter Cook at the Staatliche Hochschule für bildende Künste, Städelschule, Frankfurt / Main

Teaching positions
1986–87 Adjunct Professor of Architecture, Rhode Island School of Design, Providence
1986–88 Visiting Professor of Architecture, Irwin S. Chanin School of Architecture, New York
1987–88 Design Critic in Architecture, Graduate School of Design, Harvard University, Cambridge, Massachusetts
1988–89 Assistent Professor, Graduate School of Design, Harvard University
1996 Associate Professor, Graduate School of Architecture and Urban Planning, UCLA, Los Angeles
External Examiner, School of Architecture, Oslo

Selection of work
1991 Folding table, finished prototype, exhibited, published
1990–91 Design of a temporary playhouse in the Pacific Palisades
1991–93 Two story addition to a building in Westwood
1990–93 House addition to a Neutra building

Major exhibitions
1984 UIFA and IBA, Berlin
1988 Gallery ROM, Oslo and Gallery Skala, Copenhagen
1988 Kunsthalle Berlin
1989 Harvard University
1990 Gallerie Fenster, Frankfurt am Main
1991 MIT Museum, Boston
1992 Royal Institute of British Architects, London
1992 Storefront Gallery, New York
1993 GSAUP Gallery at UCLA, Los Angeles
1995 Contemporary Architect Exhibition, Nara, Japan
1995 Technische Universität Berlin

Publications among others
1990 A+U, #233
1991 Assemblage, #14
1992 Journal of Philosophy and the Visual Arts, #2
1992 Theory and Experimentation; ed. Andreas Papadakis
1994 Zodiac, #11
1994 World Cities: Los Angeles; ed. Maggie Toy, Academy Editions

Prizes / Awards
1984 First Prize, National UNESCO Competition for a dwelling of the Future in Denmark
1987 Second Prize, Central Glass Shinkenchiku-sha Interntional Architectural Design Competition, Tokyo
1988 Third Prize, International West Coast Gateway Competition in Los Angeles
1993 Second Prize, International Architectural and Urban Design Competition for the Royal Library in Copenhagen
1994 First Prize, International 9th Membrane Design Competition '94, Tokyo

The art of copying — Manifesto of an ex-centric subject Dagmar Richter

"...and I would say that women's handwriting fighting to escape the language police should slip through the translations, should be quicker than translation. (Let us finish for today for this is all actually a question of practical work and not of theory.)" [1]

Since the 70s a great variety of groups have existed within the postmodern discussion that exploited the critical analysis of poststructuralists in order to politically analyze the role of the author in the process of cultural production. Three major groups made up of numerous sub-groups play a vital role in this context. One of the groups includes postmodern feminists. Theoretically this group works with the constitution and production of modern and postmodern culture and its understanding of an author. On a literary level this group works with possible writing processes that attempt to achieve female writing. The other two groups work both theoretically and practically with the cultural definition of racial minorities as well as homosexuals and their possibilities of creating culture reflecting their experience. Since the inclusion of all tendencies would be beyond the scope of this article, I would like to discuss the feminist theory, which together with the other groups characterizes a major part of the cultural debate in the USA. Rosemarie Tong defined eight feminist movements in her book "Feminist Thought" [2] I do not wish to discuss all different groups in detail. I will attempt to elucidate one of these movements. Postmodern feminism, also called French feminism, is concerned with authorship and probably has the most complex and ambivalent relationship to biologically determined feminism. Postmodern feminists discuss and work on the female author issue. They believe that for the female author who writes and designs, the question of how she actually can produce culture never finds a comfortable answer. How can you assert yourself as a subject and author, how do you develop as a self, vis-à-vis the object, considering that this other has been defined as the second sex and the third world in the course of history? How does the female and male author become part of the chain of cultural descriptions in which they are represented as objects, serving as cultural supports, and described as natural, exotic, beautiful, primitive, erotic, secret, and in a way not available? This has become a major issue in numerous cultural productions especially in the USA where educated women have more possibilities to develop, where a stronger homosexual lobby is active than in Central Europe, which sees itself as the destination for immigrants from many non-Western cultures. In the USA a part of the population that is generally considered a cultural minority has become established in the academic, intellectual, and art world. For many, this new position of being established and the orientation towards the great, golden, western patriarchal past is becoming increasingly difficult.

I wish to discuss the cultural production in architecture in order to make clear certain techniques and methods which attempt to critically analyze the way authors see themselves in our postmodern age.

In my practical work, feminist cultural criticism, which runs parallel or outside of political and economic discussions, is the most interesting since this criticism deliberately deals with the production of culture as a political phenomenon.

Century City, Model – rereading

[1] Helene Cixous
[2] Rosemarie Tong; Feminist Thought; A Comprehensive Introduction Westview Press, Boulder and San Francisco, 1989

Perspektiven / Perspectives: Royal Library

man sich also als Subjekt und Autor behaupten, wie stellt man sich dem Objekt gegenüber, wenn dieses Andere im Laufe der Geschichte als „schwaches Geschlecht" und „dritte Welt" definiert wurde? Wie wird eine Autorin oder ein Autor Teil der Kette kultureller Beschreibungen, in der sie und er nur Objekt ist, als kulturelle Unterlage dienen und natürlich, exotisch, schön, primitiv, erotisch, geheimnisvoll und unnahbar gelten? Diese Frage ist vor allem in den USA in den Vordergrund zahlreicher Kulturproduktionen gerückt. Dort haben gebildete Frauen weitaus mehr Entfaltungsmöglichkeiten, dort ist eine stärkere Homosexuellen-Lobby aktiv als in Zentraleuropa, das sich als Einwanderungsland vieler nicht-westlicher Kulturen sieht. In den USA hat sich ein Teil der Bevölkerung, die kulturellen Minderheiten, in akademischen, künstlerischen und intellektuellen Kreisen etabliert. Für viele dieser neu Etablierten wird es immer schwieriger, sich blindlings an die große, goldene, westlich patriarchalische Vergangenheit zu orientieren, an der sie nicht beteiligt waren.

Ich möchte mich nun mit der Kulturproduktion im Rahmen der Architektur auseinandersetzen, um gewisse Techniken und Verfahrensweisen aufzuzeigen, die sich kritisch mit dem Autorenverständnis in unserer postmodernen Zeit auseinandersetzen.

In meiner Praxis ist die feministische Kulturkritik, die neben oder außerhalb der politisch-ökonomischen Diskussion stattfindet, am interessantesten, da diese Kritik sich bewußt mit der Kulturproduktion als politisches Phänomen auseinandersetzt. Dem Autor wird in diesem Arbeitsprozeß das Recht auf „Unschuld" ebenso versagt, wie einer Kulturproduktion ihre Neutralität, die den Autor durch bestimmte Schreib- und Entwurfsprozesse zu eliminieren versucht. Der Entwurfsprozeß in der Architektur wird in dieser „anderen Praxis" näher untersucht und geprüft.

Das Faktum, daß im Zuge der Definition und des Aufbaus unserer gesamten Kultur das Subjekt und der Autor – derjenige, der aktiv repräsentierte, beschrieb, eroberte, benannte, einvernahm und produzierte – männlich, westlich, weiß, heterosexuell und bürgerlich war, wird heute in den USA und anderen Ländern als Ausgangspunkt genommen, um neue Benennungsexperimente zu starten. Dementsprechend wird versucht, mit anderen Konzepten zu sprechen, zu schreiben und zu produzieren, mit Konzepten, die diese ideologisch fragwürdige Praxis in Frage stellen. „Wir müssen Poesie politisieren"[3] war in diesem Zusammenhang eine grundlegende Forderung von Cixous für die heutige Kulturproduktion. Es muß hier der Deutlichkeit halber hinzugefügt werden, daß diese Fragen und Forderungen heute nicht nur für weibliche Künstler-

Ansicht / Elevation: Royal Library Copenhagen

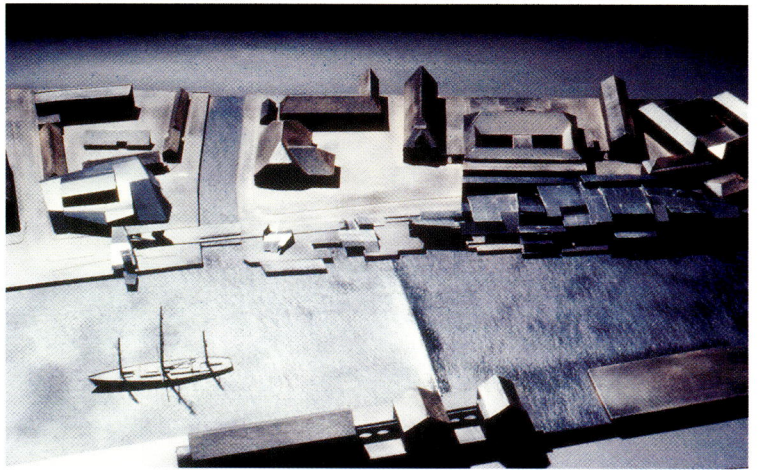

Modell / Model: Royal Library Copenhagen

The author has no right to "innocence" in this work process, just as cultural production has no right to the neutrality the author attempts to eliminate through certain writing and designing processes. The designing process in architecture is closely examined and tested in this "other practical work".

The fact that when our culture was being defined and built the subject and author – the one who actively represents, describes, conquers, names, interrogates and produces – was male, western, white, heterosexual, and bourgeois is used as a basis in the USA and other countries to begin with new experiments of naming. Attempts are being made to speak, write and produce with other concepts that question this ideologically questionable practical process. In this context, Cixous' "We must politicize poetics"[3] was a fundamental demand for today's cultural production. For the sake of clarity I must add that these questions and demands do not only concern female artists, the so-called "inferior" authors and homosexual architects - it has become a question of cultural production as a whole, since the humanist claim has actually been taken seriously. In this sense, aesthetics and language are linked to politics.

Architecture and its representations were shown to the consuming mass as a product of an (any) author who, endowed by the female muse with the gift of a genius, was in general considered to be a humanist who is neutral and names space with the best of intentions. This cultural text, however, has been tarnished and has become ideologically questionable. I would like to quote Adolf Loos as one of the fathers of modernism, as an example of the so-called neutral and objective advocates, who strove to make our environment hygienic. We can read the following in his theoretical text on the objectives of modernism: "The ornament woman basically corresponds to the savage, it has an erotic significance..." and then: "But the human today is a criminal, a degenerate... What is natural for the inhabitant of Papua and a child is an expression of degeneration for modern man ...The evolution of culture is the elimination of the ornament"[4].

The one solution – i.e. that a subject can no longer exist, only a self-reflexibility of the text as such – was tested by the "nouvel roman" and certain deconstructivist architects. They attempted to use discontinuity, fissures, and autorepresentation and refused to represent any universal pretentious truth, which is always false. This resulted in a cultural production that augured the accidental beginning (in architecture a found pattern, a genetic structure, or a

---

[3] Helene Cixous; „Poesie und Politik - Ist Poesie Politik?" Kapitel in Weiblichkeit in der Schrift „Wir brauchen eine poetische Praxis innerhalb/als politische Praxis. Wir müssen die Poesie politisieren." Seite 7

[3] Helene Cixous; „Poesie und Politik - Ist Poesie Politik?" Chapter in Weiblichkeit in der Schrift „Wir brauchen eine poetische Praxis innerhalb/als politische Praxis. Wir müssen die Poesie politisieren." page 7

[4] Adolf Loos; chapter „Ornament und Erziehung" in Trotzdem 1900-1930; 1931 Brenner Verlag, Innsbruck, page 82

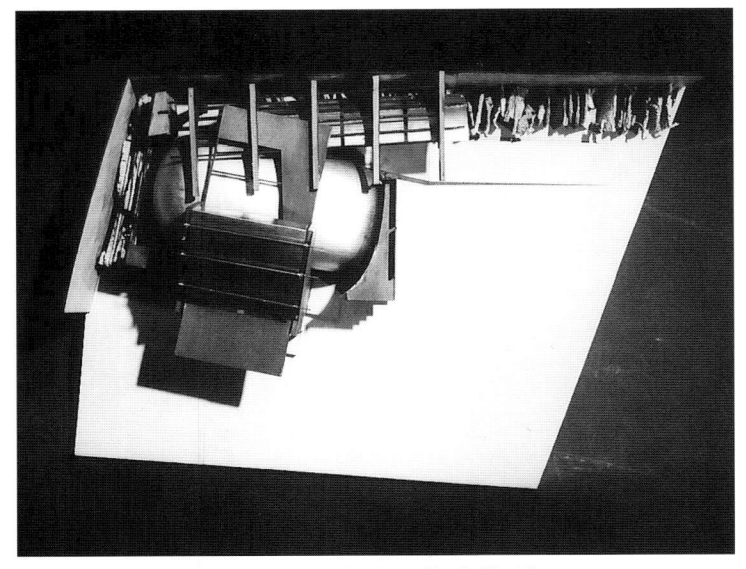

**Modell: eine bewohnbare Maschine – Gästehaus für ein Kind /
Model: A machine to live in – guesthouse for a child**

innen, sogenannte rassisch „minderwertige" Schriftsteller und homosexuelle Architekten gelten – wenn man den humanistischen Anspruch wirklich ernst nimmt, sind sie zu einer Frage der gesamten Kulturproduktion geworden. Ästhetik und Sprache sind in diesem Sinne mit Politik verbunden.

Architektur und deren Repräsentation wurde der konsumierenden Masse als Produkt eines (jeglichen) Autors vorgestellt, der von der weiblichen Muse die Gabe des Genies erhalten hatte. Er galt im Allgemeinen als Humanist, der neutral, mit den besten Absichten für alle Raum benannte. Dieser bestehende Kulturtext ist jedoch heute belastet und ideologisch fragwürdig. Ich möchte hier Adolf Loos, einen der Väter des Modernismus, als Beispiel eines sogenannten neutralen und objektiven Verfechters der Hygienisierung unserer Umwelt zitieren. In seinem theoretischen Text über die Ziele des Modernismus sagt er: „Das Ornament der Frau entspricht im Grunde dem der Wilden, es hat erotische Bedeutung..." und weiter: „Aber der Mensch unserer Zeit, der aus innerem Drange die Wände mit erotischen Symbolen beschmiert, ist ein Verbrecher, ein Degenerierter...Was aber beim Papua und dem Kinde natürlich ist, ist beim modernen Menschen eine Degenerationserscheinung... Evolution der Kultur ist gleichbedeutend mit dem Entfernen des Ornaments." [4]

Die eine Lösung – daß es kein Subjekt mehr geben kann, sondern nur eine Selbstreflexibilität des Textes an sich – wurde vom „nouvel roman" und gewissen dekonstruktivistischen Architekten durchexerziert. Diese versuchten beim Schreiben oder Repräsentieren, Diskontinuität, Riß und Autorenpräsentation anzuwenden. Sie weigerten sich eine universell anmaßende Wahrheit zu repräsentieren, die sich immer als eine falsche Wahrheit erweist. Daraus entstand Kulturproduktion, die den zufälligen Beginn und die Weiterführung der Logik des Entstehungsprozesses als das einzig mögliche heraufbeschwor (in der Architektur ein gefundenes Muster, eine Genstruktur oder eine Nähmaschine).

Wie werden nun in der Textproduktion zum Beispiel alternative Möglichkeiten der Subjektivität geschaffen, wenn man davon ausgeht, daß die Subjektivität des Autors an Bedeutung zunimmt und entgegen der Gepflogenheiten der Strukturalisten und Poststrukturalisten Codes, Texte, Bilder und andere kulturelle Artefakte, Subjektivität sind und eben nicht Subjektivität widerspiegeln?[5] Wie stellt sich das weibliche Subjekt heute und welche Möglichkeiten sehen die Theoretikerinnen, um diese Neukonstitution zu ermöglichen?

Ich werde hier versuchen, einige Konzepte vorzustellen, sie sich in meiner Studioarbeit als wirkungsvoll und hilfreich entpuppt haben.

[4] Adolf Loos; Kapitel „Ornament und Erziehung" aus Trotzdem 1900-1930; 1931 Brenner Verlag, Innsbruck, Seite 82
[5] Andreas Huyssen ibid.

sewing machine) and its further elaboration of the logic of the process of origin (be it positive, negative, rotation, or reflection) as the only possibility. In her analysis of Robbes-Grillet or the work of the surrealists

How are alternative possibilities to subjectivity construed in text production if we assume that the subjectivity of the author becomes significant and in contrast to the habit of structuralists and poststructuralists is made up of codes, texts, images, and other cultural artifacts and does not reflect subjectivity.[5] What is the female subject today and what possibilities are provided by the theoreticians to make this new constitution possible. I will attempt to present some concepts that have proven to be effective and helpful in studio work.

Translation with resistance – a choir song

If we assume that the myth of invention and the continuously resulting new has reached its limits in architecture and should be regarded as an attempt to appropriate that which has already been with the signature of the author, entirely new designing methods could be developed.

Claudine Herrmann calls the female author "les voleuses de langue"[6], the thief of language. Not must the language of architecture must stolen, appropriation can also take place with translation. In this context we can use Benjamin's term "above naming" for translation, since in cultural production,

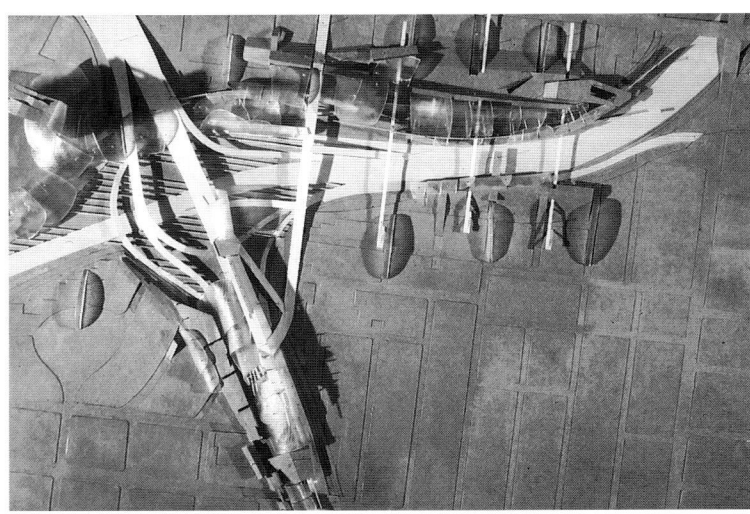

**Lagemodell Electric Highway /
Site model Electric Highway**

be it literature or architecture, only the language that describes all the "others" exists. Donna Haraway described the following method of writing in her "Manifesto for Cyborgs"; "The tools are often stories, retold stories, versions that reverse and displace the hierarchical dualisms of naturalized identities. In retelling origin stories, cyborg authors subvert the central myths of origin of Western culture..." She describes the method as cyborg writing: "Cyborg writing is about the power to survive not on the basis of original innocence, but on the basis of seizing the tools to mark the work that marked them as other[7]." This resistance to translation which evolves in the copy of the found space for example, can be provoked with irony, parody, perversion, laughing, carnival, and fun. Systematic disobedience and rebellious humor has been used in text production, in art and in mass media of cultural minorities for a long time (see Barbara Kruger, The Gorilla Girls, Pulp Fiction etc.). The theory and history of architecture have for years been using the feminist definition of the author in the designing process[8].

[5] Andreas Huyssen
[6] Claudine Herrmann, Les Voleuses de langue Paris: Editions des Femmes, 1976
[7] Donna Harraway: Manifesto of Cyborgs" in Feminism/Postmodernism published by Linda J. Nicholson; Routledge, New York and London, 1990; page 217
[8] see Ann Bergren, Beatrice Colomina, Catherine Ingraham, Jennifer Bloomer and many others

Übersetzung mit Widerstand – ein Chorgesang

Geht man davon aus, daß in der Architektur der Mythos der Erfindung und des daraus resultierenden ewig Neuen an seine Grenzen gestoßen ist und eher als ein Versuch zu verstehen ist, sich das schon immer Dagewesene durch die Signatur des Autors anzueignen, können völlig andere Entwurfstechniken entwickelt werden.

Claude Herrmann nennt die weibliche Autorin „les voleuses de langue"[6], die Diebin der Sprache. Es muß jedoch nicht nur die Architektursprache gestohlen werden, sondern Aneignung kann nur durch einen Übersetzungsakt geschehen. In diesem Zusammenhang kann man, da es in der Kulturproduktion, sei es in der Literatur oder Architektur, eben nur jene Sprache gibt, die alles „andere" beschreibt, den Begriff des Überbenennens von Benjamin für Übersetzung aktiv verwenden. Donna Haraway beschrieb in ihrem „manifesto for Cyborgs" die folgende Schreibtechnik: „The tools are often stories, retold stories, versions that reverse and displace the hierarchical dualisms of naturalized identities. In retelling origin stories, Cyborg authors subvert the central myths of origin of Western culture..." Sie beschreibt die Technik als Cyborg Writing: „Cyborg writing is about the power to survive not on the basis of original innocence, but on the basis of seizing the tools to mark the world that marked them as other."[7] Dieser Übersetzungswiderstand, der beispielsweise beim Kopieren des gefundenen Raums entsteht, kann bewußt durch die Anwendung von Ironie, Parodie, Perversion, Gelächter, Karneval und Spaß hervorgerufen werden.

Systematischer Ungehorsam und rebellischer Humor wird schon seit langem in der Textproduktion, in der Kunst und in den Massenmedien von Kulturminderheiten (siehe Barbara Kruger, The Gorilla Girls, Pulp Fiction usw.) praktiziert. In der Architekturtheorie und -geschichte wird seit Jahren mit der feministischen Definition des Autors im Entwurfsprozeß gearbeitet.[8]

„L'ecriture feminine" statt Literatur bedeutet eine Art von Leseübung, die sich zuerst im Kritzeln, Federkratzen und Notieren ausdrückt. Schreiben beginnt dann als lustvolle und spielerische Aktivität. Das neue Subjekt ist nur in einer komplexen Weise narzißtisch abgesichert. Die Mitglieder in meinem Studio zum Beispiel tauschen während des Entwurfsprozesses permanent die Zeichnungen und Arbeitsmodelle untereinander aus. Diese Technik kann als „ein Versuch im Chor zu sprechen" angesehen werden. „Originale", die einer Signatur entsprechen, gibt es immer nur für einen begrenzten Zeitraum. Es ist für das neu konstituierte Subjekt im Studio nur noch das Überbenennen möglich. Das bedeutet, daß der Autor gefundenen Raum durch ein „Kontinuum von Verwandlungen" mittels einer Übersetzung von einem zum anderen langsam transformiert. Diese gefundenen Räume sind kartographisch und fotografisch dargestellt oder besitzen erst einmal keinen Maßstab. Architektur ist in dieser Hinsicht ein besonders interessantes Feld, da wir schon zu Beginn erklärt haben, daß sie sich durch ihre Übersetzbarkeit definiert. In diesem Sinne wurden, um eine andere Praxis zu ermöglichen, in meinem Studio seit etwa zehn Jahren verschiedene Entwurfsexperimente durchgeführt. Wir nehmen meist internationale offene Wettbewerbe als Experimentierfeld, um mit vorgefundenem Material neue Techniken zu entwickeln. Die Entwurfsprozesse, die entstehen, werden aufgezeichnet und intensiv diskutiert. Die Dualität Theorie und Praxis, Landschaft und Architektur, Rationalität und Emotionalität, Kopie und Original hat sich im Zuge der verschiedenen Entwurfsprozesse weitgehend aufgelöst.

"L'ecriture feminine" instead of literature means a kind of reading exercise that is expressed by scribbling, feather scratching and noting down. Writing begins afterwards as a fun and play-like activity. The new subject is only secured narcissistically in a complex way. The members in my studio, for example, continuously exchange drawings and working models during the design process with each other. This method can be regarded as "an attempt to speak as a choir". "Originals" that are a signature can only exist for a limited period of time. The newly created subject can only use the method of above naming. This means that the author gradually transforms found space which is defined by cartographic and photographic representations or found spaces, which at the beginning do not possess a scale, by a "continuum of transformation", by the translation from one to the other. From this point of view architecture is an especially interesting field since, as we already explained at the beginning, architecture is defined by its translatability. With this in mind, various design experiments that allow a different practical approach have been carried out in my studio in the last ten years. In most cases, we take international open competitions as experimental fields to develop new techniques from the material provided. The design processes that evolve are recorded and discussed at depth. The duality of theory and practical work, landscape and architecture, rationality and emotionality, copy and original has to a large part dissipated in the course of various design processes.

[6] Claudine Herrmann, Les Voleuses de langue Paris: Editions des Femmes, 1976
[7] Donna Haraway: „Manifesto of Cyborgs" in Feminism/Postmodernism herausgegeben von Linda J. Nicholson; Routledge, New York und London, 1990; Seite 217
[8] siehe Ann Bergren, Beatrice Colomina, Catherine Ingraham, Jennifer Bloomer und viele andere

Stadträumlicher Strukturwandel – Entwicklungsträger öffentlicher Verkehr. U-Bahnstation Hybler Park, Wien 11

Im Rahmen der Planungen der Stadt Wien für den Ausbau des öffentlichen Verkehrs werden derzeit Vorbereitungen für die Verlängerung der U-Bahnlinie 3 in den 11. Bezirk getroffen.
Die Verlängerung der U3 wird mit drei neuen Stationen ein ausgedehntes Industrie- und Gewerbegebiet sowie dichtbebaute Wohnviertel unterschiedlichen Alters an der Simmeringer Hauptstraße, einer lokalen Geschäftsstraße, erschließen.
Der Bezirk Simmering entwickelte sich an einer historisch bedeutenden Südostverbindung. Sein Hauptsiedlungsgebiet entlang der Achse der Simmeringer Hauptstraße liegt topographisch auf einer Terrasse, die etwa im Bereich des geplanten Nordaufganges der künftigen U-Bahnstation Hyblerpark mit einer markanten Geländekante zum ebenen Stromland des Erdberger Mais abbricht.
Das Erdberger Mais, einstmals Teil der Aulandschaft der Donau, bezeichnet ein ausgedehntes Betriebsgebiet mit dem Erscheinungsbild einer zerteilten, suburbanen Zone. Vier historische Gasometergebäude, für die neue, hochwertige Nutzungen angestrebt werden, bilden eine raumprägende städtebauliche Dominante. Eine stark belastete Stadtautobahn (Südost-Tangente) durchquert den nordwestlichen Teil des Gebietes. Vom bestehenden Anschlußknoten soll eine mehrspurige Straße in West-Ost Richtung durch das Gebiet geführt werden und eine direkte Verbindung zur Flughafenautobahn herstellen. Im Zuge der Strukturanpassungen und Modernisierungen werden Flächen für neue Nutzungen frei. Damit eröffnen sich Möglichkeiten einer der Lagegunst des Gebietes entsprechenden Enwicklung.

Hyblerpark, Erdberger Mais, Wien 11

Urban structural change – development through public transport. Underground station Hybler Park, Vienna 11

Currently preparations are under way for prolonging undergroud line U3 into the 11th district as part of the City of Vienna´s plans to further develop the public transport system.
The extention of underground line U3 by three stations will provide access for an extensive industrial and commercial area as well as densely built residential quarters of varying ages along Simmeringer Hauptstraße, a local shopping street.
The district of Simmering developed along a historically important south-east link. In terms of topography its main settlement area along the axis of Simmeringer Hauptstraße is situated on a terrace, dropping sharply to the flat river country of the Erdberger Mais, approximately at the planned northern exit of the future undergroud station of Hyblerpark.
The Erdberger Mais, once part of the Danube pastures, constitutes an extensive industrial area of a divided, suburban zone. Four historical gasometer buildings, intended for new, high profile usages, represent a dominant architectural element. A very busy urban motorway (Südost-Tangente) crosses the northwest part of the area. Plans exists for the construction of a new street, leading from the existing junction through the area in a west-east direction, constituting a direct link to the airport motorway. Plots are vacated for new uses as part of the structural adaptions and modernizations, thus opening up possibilities for a development in accordance with the favourable location of the area.

Experimente zur adäquaten Raumfindung im öffentlichen Raum

Autor und Autorität

Die meisten Räume, die wir antreffen, sind willkürlich und zufällig. Einige werden bewußt formuliert, meist sind sie jedoch Ergebnisse des Zufalls. Wir sind mit zahlreichen Ebenen und Schichten des visuellen Textes und der physischen Erfahrung konfrontiert, wovon nur ein geringer Teil das Ergebnis einer bewußten architektonischen Handlung ist.
Daraus ergibt sich, daß unser Arbeitsbereich sich auf Oberflächen beschränkt hat, die uns ermöglichen, verschiedene Schichten der physischen Information gleichzeitig zu lesen, ganz gleich, ob es sich um Architektur handelt oder nicht.
Im untersuchten Planungsprozeß kann die Rauminformation, die durch einen Leseprozeß gesammelt wird, in jedem Raum, ungeachtet seiner Größe, gefunden werden. Der Raum muß aus diesem Grund in eine architektonische Sprache übersetzt werden, die sowohl Maßstab, Nutzung, Konstruktion als auch Projektion der Materialien darstellt.
Der Leseakt wird durch einen Prozeß der Wiederdarstellung der Darstellung manifest - gefundenes Material wird kopiert - womit im Idealfall neue Möglichkeiten aufgedeckt werden, um die verborgene Ordnung des heutigen Raums kritisch verstehen zu lernen.
Die Frage, wie Architekten sich die Autorität aneignen können, um Änderungen für einen Ort vorzuschlagen, von dem sie nur wenig wissen und der dem interessierten Leser nur langsam seine Fein-

Experiments for creating adequate space in the public sphere

Author and authority

Most of the spaces we experience are random and circumstantial, some of it consciously formulated, most of it the product of chance. We are confronted with numerous levels and layers of visual text and physical experience, much of which is not a product of any conscious architectural act.
As a result, our site of operation have been surfaces which let us read different layers of physical information simultaneously, independently of its definition as architecture or non architecture.
In the design process investigated, the spatial information obtained through a reading process can be found in any space independent of size. They have therefore to be translated into an architectural language, which includes scale, use, construction and projection of materials.
The act of reading manifests itself through a process of rerepresentation of representation - the act of copying from found material - which will ideally shed some light on new possibilities for understanding in critical terms the hidden orders of contemporary space.
How to gain authority to propose changes for a place which the architect barely knows, and which only slowly reveals its intricacies and peculiarities to the interested reader, was always in the forefront. A long tradition of statistics, two dimensional simple geometrical patterns, grand ideas from suppo-

heiten und Eigenheiten preisgibt, war schon immer von größter Bedeutung. Eine lange Tradition der Statistik, der zweidimensionalen, einfachen geometrischen Muster, großer Ideen seitens vermeintlich objektiver genialer Autoren und manipulierte Wünsche von unbekannten Nutzern haben bei städtischen Planern und Architekten ein Selbstbewußtsein erweckt, um die Schaffung einer neuen Ordnung und räumlichen Anordnung auf der ganzen Welt zu ermöglichen.

Natürlich liegt dem Ganzen die Schaffung von öffentlichem Raum zugrunde. Die Frage drängt sich dort auf, wo die Autoritätsfrage am dringendsten ist. Wie kann der Planer ohne ein kritisches Selbstverständnis seiner Rolle und Autorität für die Öffentlichkeit entscheiden und gestalten? Bisher wurde das Recht für die Masse zu entscheiden durch die Geschichte begründet und von den Entwerfern und Architekten und ihren Erben übernommen. Jahrhundertelang war es eine Selbstverständlichkeit, daß der Entscheidungsträger ein heterosexueller Mann sein sollte. Alle Fragen nach Geschmack, Anständigkeit, Schönheit, Ordnung und Logik wurden nur peripher tangiert und von einer eher kleineren Gruppe von Vertretern beantwortet, die automatisch das Recht für sich in Anspruch nahm, im Namen aller zu sprechen. Heute funktioniert diese automatische Autorität, die durch eine lange Tradition getragen wird, dort nicht mehr, wo sich das Muster grundlegend geändert hat. Um die Möglichkeiten der Formschaffung für die neu etablierten Autoren, die heute aus ebenso vielen Frauen wie Männern, ganz gleich welcher Hautfarbe oder sexueller Orientierung bestehen, zu erweitern, hat die Theorie neue Möglichkeiten der kritischen Formschaffung in den Raum gestellt. Literatur- und Kunstwissenschaft vertreten die Meinung, daß ein neues Verständnis für die Rolle der Autoren im Prozeß der Schaffung von kulturellen Artefakten notwendig ist. Der Planer soll nicht als großer Künstler betrachtet werden, der stets etwas Neues schafft und dem Ort seine neuen Erfindungen als reine Struktur aufdrängt, da dies so oft destruktive Tabula-Rasa-Bedingungen schafft. Ich erlaube mir vorzuschlagen, daß der Ort als aktive Kraft im Planungsprozeß verstanden werden soll, in dem Autorengruppen allmählich und bewußt Pläne schaffen, die die Möglichkeit anerkennen, das Bestehende, das von außen kommt, und neue Ideen seitens der anderen Gruppenmitglieder als aktiven Fluß, der visuell und räumlich reflektiert wird, zu respektieren. Die neue Arbeitsmethode könnte offene Prozesse schaffen, bei denen für die Beantwortung der Fragen nach Geometrie, Ordnung und Schönheit ein Spielraum besteht und die formell empfänglich ist für eine Unmenge von Einflüssen.

Vorgangsweise

Beim Wiener Seminar experimentierte man mit kartographischen Begriffen, wobei man die Autorität der Objektivität einer herkömmlichen zweidimensionalen Landkarte physischer Strukturen, die man vor Ort an einem gegebenen Datum vorfand, in Frage stellte. Die erste Aufgabe der Gruppe bestand also darin, mit der Interpretation der vom Autor gefundenen Information zu experimentieren. Die Informationsquelle, aus der der Autor schöpfen durfte, wurde erweitert, so daß man Landkarten aus früheren Zeitperioden, Fakten, die man entweder sah oder hörte und als wichtig betrachtete, sowie alles für den Autor relevante in den Prozeß der Formfindung miteinbezog. Jedes Gruppenmitglied war also mit unbearbeitetem visuellen Material konfrontiert, über

sedly objective genius authors and manipulated wishes from unknown users has given the urban designer and architect a self-confidence in order to impose new orders and spatial arrangements into any place anywhere in the world.

Certainly the issue of the making of public space lies at the bottom of this all. It is there, where the question of authority is most prevalent. How can the designer decide and form for the public without a critical self understanding of his or her role and authority? Up to now this authority to decide for the many was established through tradition which was carried on by the designer and architect and his inheritors. For many centuries it was certainly never questioned that the decision maker was supposed to be a heterosexual male. All questions of taste, propriety, beauty, order, and logic were only referred to, and answered by, a rather small group of representatives who automatically assumed the right to speak for everyone. Now, where this pattern has changed substantially, the automatic authority established through tradition cannot work any longer. In order to further the possibilities of form making for the newly established author which nowadays involves as many woman as men, independent of sexual orientation and even race, theory has been able to suggest new possibilities of critical form making. Literary and art theory suggests that a new understanding of the author's role in the process of creating cultural artifacts is necessary at this point. The designer is not to be understood as a great artist inventing the always new and imposing his new invention as a pure structure onto the site which so often results in destructive tabula rasa conditions. I would like to propose that the site could be read as an active force in the design process where groups of authors slowly and consciously produce design which recognizes the possibility of respecting all involved forces from existing, given from the outside and new ideas from different group members as an active flow which will be visually and spatially reflected. This new working method could create open processes, where the question of geometry, order, and beauty stays negotiable, and is formally receptive to multiple influences.

Working processes

The seminar in Vienna experimented with notions of mapping, where the authority of the objectivity of a traditional two dimensional map of physical structures found on the site at a established date were questioned. The first objective for the group was therefore to experiment with the author's reading of found information. The pool of information which the author was allowed to use was expanded towards a larger framework where maps from former time periods, things seen or heard and deemed as important and the authors own found relevance were allowed to be integrated in the process of form finding. Every member of the group was therefore confronted with unedited visual material over which she in the first place had very little control. This situation created unexpected by chance encounters designed to break up habits which have very little theoretical or conceptual base. The student had to engage in an active reading process of the found site's representations irrespective of the original date

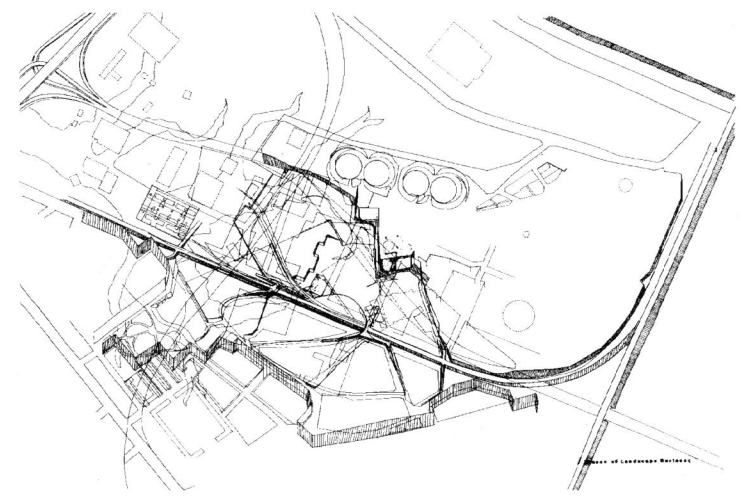

Verschiedene Teilnehmer mehrerer Gruppen studierten Landschaftsformationen und deren Möglichkeiten, das Planungsgebiet zu bereichern (Sona Kazemi) / Different members of several groups studying landscape formations and their possibilities to enrich the site. (Sona Kazemi)

das es anfangs wenig Kontrolle ausübte. Diese Situation brachte unerwartete Begegnungen mit sich, die Gewohnheiten mit geringerer theoretischer oder konzeptueller Grundlage abschaffen sollten. Der Student mußte ungeachtet des Originaldatums der Dokumente eine aktive Interpretation der Darstellungen des gewählten Ortes vornehmen und Implantate aus gewählten Darstellungen von öffentlichen Räumen anderer Kulturen einfügen. Diese Technik kann man als einen ersten Schritt in Richtung einer aktiven Interpretation betrachten, bei der das Land, seine Geschichte und andere entdeckte räumliche Muster in einem Prozeß umgestaltender Betrachtung zum Einsatz kommen. Der einzelne Autor sollte argumentieren, welche Information in den Formfindungsprozeß einbezogen werden sollten. Seine Argumentation war den Reaktionen und Ideen der anderen Gruppenmitglieder ausgesetzt, wobei der gesamten Gruppe willkürlich eine Repräsentationstechnik zugeordnet wurde, um die sich daraus ergebenden Zeichnungen und Modelle von Autor zu Autor austauschbar zu machen.

Die Gruppe sollte die Grundlage ihre Autorität im laufenden Entwurfsprozeß definieren, wobei Fragen zu Geschmack, Schönheit, Objektivität und Willkür permanent untersucht wurden. Die Studenten wurden verstärkt aufgefordert, den Begriff des willkürlichen Geschmacks eines einzelnen Autors als Grundlage für die Schaffung von Modellen abzuschaffen.

Die verschiedenen Zeichnungen und Modelle sind das Ergebnis eines Interpretationsprozesses der ortsbezogenen Kräfte, die durch die Wahrnehmung einer deutenden Gemeinschaft gefiltert und mit den Darstellungen öffentlicher Räume anderer Kulturen konfrontiert wurden. Die verschiedenen Zeichnungen zeigen Ansätze einer möglichen räumlichen Identität, die über einfache euklidische geometrische Muster hinaus die Vorherrschaft einer überlegenen Hochkultur darstellt. Ihre neue Sensibilität läßt neue mögliche Raumdefinitionen zu, welche die Besonderheit und Komplexität dieses marginalisierten Raums zu integrieren vermögen. Im folgenden Projekt wurde eine Methode entwickelt, die auf der Kunst zu kopieren basiert. Einige der von uns erfahrenen Räume sind bewußt definiert, die meisten sind jedoch ein Produkt des Zufalls. Ständig werden wir mit zahlreichen Ebenen und Schichten sichtbaren Textes und physischer Berührungen konfrontiert, wobei die meisten kein Produkt von beabsichtigter architektonischer Kunst sind. Als Ergebnis bot sich unser Arbeitsgebiet als Oberfläche, die uns viele verschiedene Schichten physischer Information entziffern ließ, unabhängig von ihrer architektonischen Bestimmung oder Nichtbestimmung.

of the documents as well as insert grafts of chosen representations of other cultures public space. This technique can be seen as a first step towards an active reading where the land, its history and other found spatial patterns are used in a process of transformative reading. The individual author was to establish the argument transformative reading. The individual author was to establish the argument for which set of information was to be integrated in the form finding process which was permanently confronted with other author´s reactions and ideas, whereas the entire group was arbitrarily assigned a representational technique in order to make the resulting drawings and models exchangeable from author to author.

The group was confronted with the task to define their base of authority in the on going design process, where questions of taste, beauty, objectivity and arbitrariness were permanently under investigation. Students were highly encouraged to break up the notion of a single author´s arbitrary taste as the base of pattern making.

The different working drawings and models are the outcome of a reading process of the site's forces, filtered through the minds of an interpretative community and confronted with other cultures representations of public space. The different drawings begin to suggest possible spatial indentites beyond simple eucledic geometrical patterns representing the dominance of a superior high culture. Their new sensiblilities leave new possiblilities of space definitions which are able to integrate the peculiarities and complexities of this maginalized space.

The following research projects were used to establish a methodology based on the art of copy. Most of the spaces we experience are random and circumstantial, some of it consciously formulated, most of it the product of chance. We are confronted with numerous levels and layers of visual text and physical experience, much of which is not a product of any conscious architectural act. As a result, our sites of operation have been surfaces which let us read different layers of physical information simultaneously independently of its definition as architecture or non architecture.

Modell: Verbindung von örtlichen Elementen und Raum durch eine 1:1 Plastik in der Remise / Model combining site traces and the space by a 1:1 sculpture in the studio

Projektgruppe:
Roland Bondzio, Thomas Willemeit

Roland Bondzio
Sichtlinien und Beobachtungspunkte werden geortet und gewertet. Diese Korridore wurden genutzt um öffentlichen Raum zu schaffen. Der Plan zeigt, wie in der Vergangenheit Straßen und Gebäude wieder und wieder auf angehobenen Plattformen gebaut wurden.
Roland verwendete die von der Gruppe gebaute Holzinstallation für sein Projekt. Die räumliche Form repräsentierte die „Andersartigkeit" in der Halle: die des Arbeitsprozesses und die der Gruppe Richter im Seminar selbst. Roland überlagerte diese Form auf die Autobahn und die Donau und entwickelte neue räumliche Beziehungen entlang dieser dominanten Verbindungen.

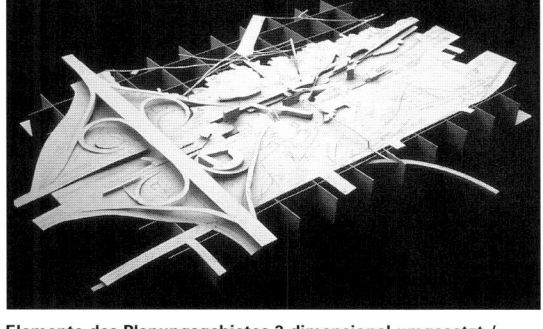

Elemente des Planungsgebietes 3-dimensional umgesetzt / Site traces translated into three dimensions

Project group:
Roland Bondzio, Thomas Willemeit

Roland Bondzio
Sight lines and observation points are located and prioritized. These corridors were to be used to develop public space on the site. The drawing demonstrates how, historically, roads and buildings have been consistently constructed on elevated platforms or berms.
Roland used the wooden spatial form the group constructed within the hall to develop his project. The spatial form acted as the "otherness" within the hall, and the otherness of the process as well as the Richter group at the seminar. Roland overlaid this form on the freeway and Donau and developed a new reading and spatial relationship along these dominant Viennese throughfares.

Thomas Willemeit
Dissonante Musiknoten von bestimmten Choralstücken, die eine Reise ins Paradies beschreiben, werden in den Plan und Bauplatz übersetzt und verwoben. Dieser Plan wird dann durch das Modell ersetzt, wo eine Serie von öffentlichen Räumen einen parallelen Weg/Reise von der städtischen Dichte zu der Parklandschaft/Paradies über der Donau formt.

Thomas Willemeit
Dissonant music notation from a specific choral piece describing the journey to paradise is translated into plan und woven into the site. This plan is transferred to model where a series of urban public spaces begin to form a parallel pathway/journey from the urban density to the parklands/paradiso across the Donau.

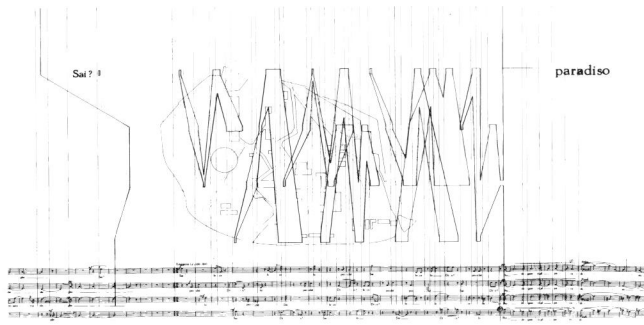

Gebietselemente mit überlagerten Musikfragmenten / Traces from the site plus a music draft copied onto it

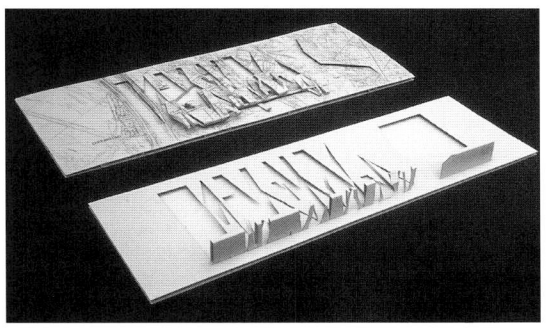

Arbeitsmodell / Work model

Projektgruppe:
Bradac Damjan, Anna Maria Menig, Nico Wallner

Das Fischernetz wurde analog zum Stadtraster als zusammengefallener Raster interpretiert. Die Ordnung der Stadt versagt in diesem vergessenen Segment der Stadt. Die verschiedenen Dichten des kollabierten Rasters werden für bestimmte öffentliche Räume und Aktivitäten genutzt. Eine Serie von historischen Spuren – Kanalsystem, Wasserleitungen und der ursprüngliche Verlauf der Donau sind im Standort zusammengefallen.

Project group:
Bradac Damjan, Anna Maria Menig, Nico Wallner

The fishing net was seen as a collapsed grid analogous to the city grid. The order of the city fails at this forgotten segment of the Viennese Landscape. The differing densities of the collapsed grid are used for specified public space and activity. A series of historic traces, from the sewer system, fresh water distribution, and the original location of the Donau are collapsed into the site of the net.

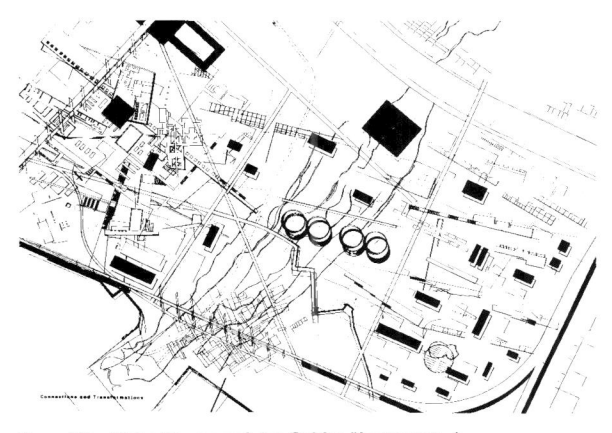

Neue öffentliche Räume auf das Gebiet übertragen / New public spaces, scanned onto site

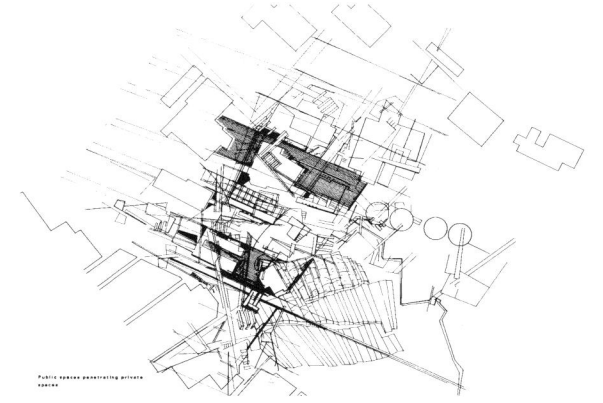

Chinesische Gärten auf das Gebiet übertragen / Chinese Gardens scanned onto site

Dynamische Wellen - der Donau und der Netzwerke / Dynamic waves – of Donau and networks

Projektgruppe:
Isabel von Furnier, Sona Kazemi, Kesmir Zimisanouic

Project group:
Isabel von Furnier, Sona Kazemi, Kesmir Zimisanouic

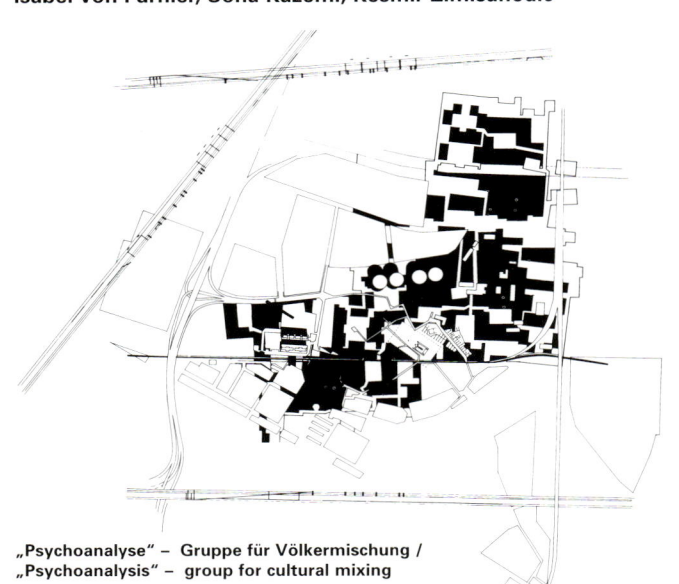

„Psychoanalyse" – Gruppe für Völkermischung /
„Psychoanalysis" – group for cultural mixing

Model / modell

Projekt Gruppe: Bradac Damjan, Anna Maria Menig,
Nico Wallner, Maren Behler, Arne Erichson, Karen Lischke

Project group: Bradac Damjan, Anna Maria Menig,
Nico Wallner, Maren Behler, Arne Erichson, Karen Lischke

Schnitte durch das Gebiet wurden mit einem chinesischen Garten überlagert. Diese Schnitte wurden beim Bau einer Modellbox als Seiten verwendet. Von den Schnitten aus wurde Licht auf den dreidimensionalen Bodenplan projeziert um neue Interpretationsmöglichkeiten des Gebietes und des Raumes zu finden.

Sections cut through the site were overlaid with a Chinese garden.
A box model was constructed using these sections as sides. Light was projected on these sections onto a three dimensional floor plan in order to find a new reading of site and space.

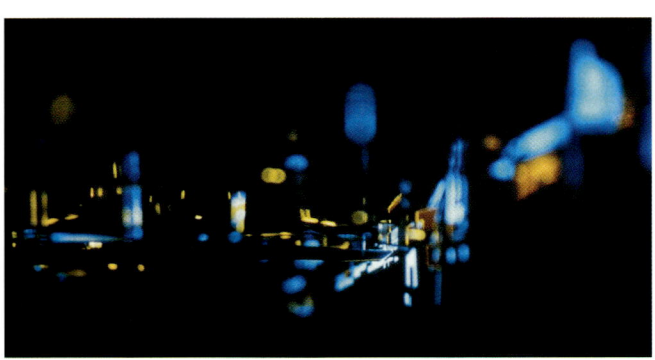

Black Box

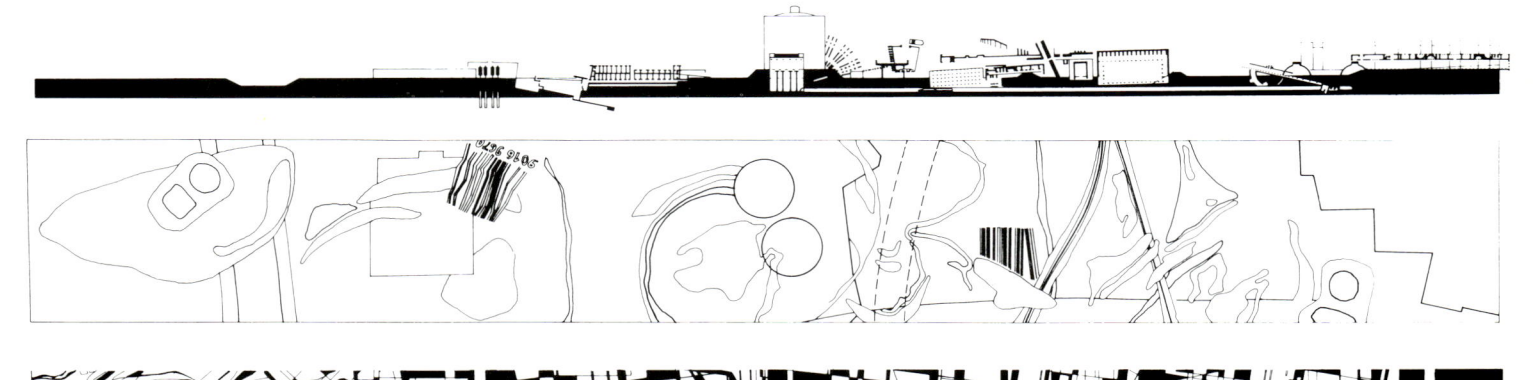

Beleuchtetes Modell – jeder Teilnehmer gestaltete eine Seite der Black Box. Die Verschmelzung aller drei Seiten im Modell wird durch das Licht bewirkt /
Lit model – is a result of each author building on one side of a black box. The melting of all three sides is done in the model through light

Projektgruppe:
Michael Filser, David Pareras, Claudia Maria Walther

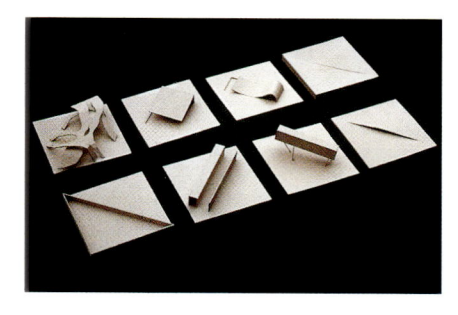

Die Donau hat in der Geschichte verschiedenste Spuren hinterlassen. Diese Spuren wurden zusammen mit der räumlichen Form in das Gebiet zurückgeführt. Unter Verwendung dieser Information als Generator hat die Gruppe einen interimen öffentlichen Raum entlang der vorgeschlagenen U-Bahn-Verlängerung geplant.

Project group:
Michael Filser, David Pareras, Claudia Maria Walther

Various traces were made of the Donau at specific moments through history. These traces were relocated and rescaled on the site together with the "spatial form" in the studio. Using this information as the generator, the group constructed an intermediate transitional public space along the route of the proposed subway extension.

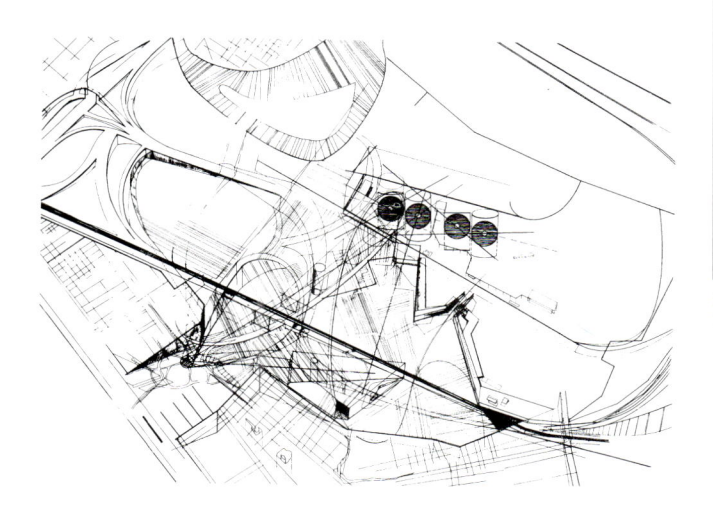

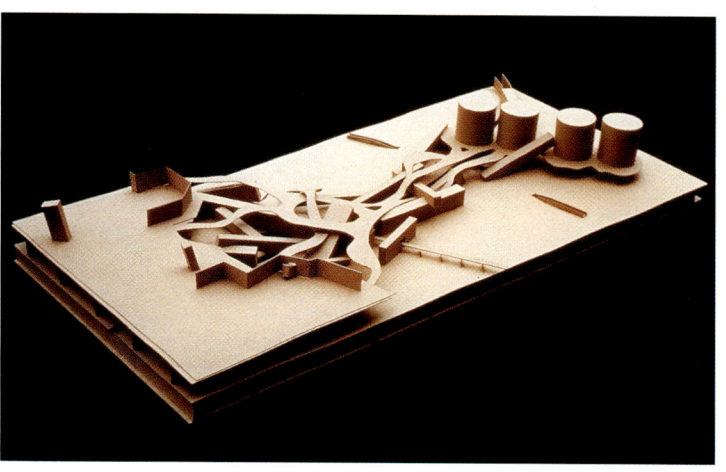

Spuren und Kopien von Autobahnschleifen und Flußwellen /
Traces and copy of highway loops and river waves

Projektgruppe: Kresimir Zmijanovic

Strategie: Dezentralisierte Fragmente
Bestehende urbane räumliche Situationen werden getrennt und dem Arbeitsgebiet überlagert. Das Gebiet kann nun als Überrest einer Explosion betrachtet werden. Unter Verwendung bestehender, jedoch umpositionierter und umgestalteter Räume entstand auf dem Arbeitsgebiet ein neuer öffentlicher Raum. Diese neuen Knoten haben sich innerhalb der bestehenden landwirtschaftlichen Flächen und der Verbindungen zu den dichten Wohngebieten zu einer neuen öffentlichen Architektur entwickelt.

Project Group: Kresimir Zmijanovic

Strategy: Decentralized Fragment
Pre–existing urban spatial conditions are cut, relocated and overlaid on the existing site. The site is now viewed as the remnants or shrapnel from an explosion. A new public space is formed by using existing but repositioned and rescaled spaces on the existing ground plane. These new nodes within the existing farmland and the connections to the dense residential areas are developed into a new public architecture.

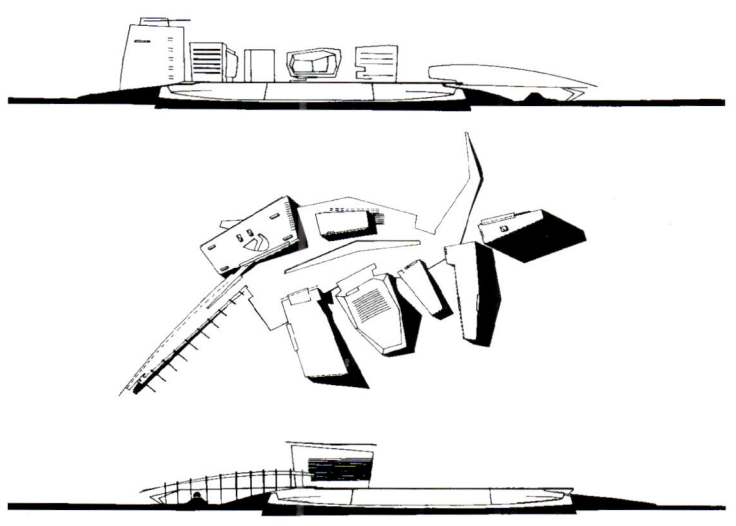

Detailstudie eines Raumelementes /
Detail study of one compressed space fragment

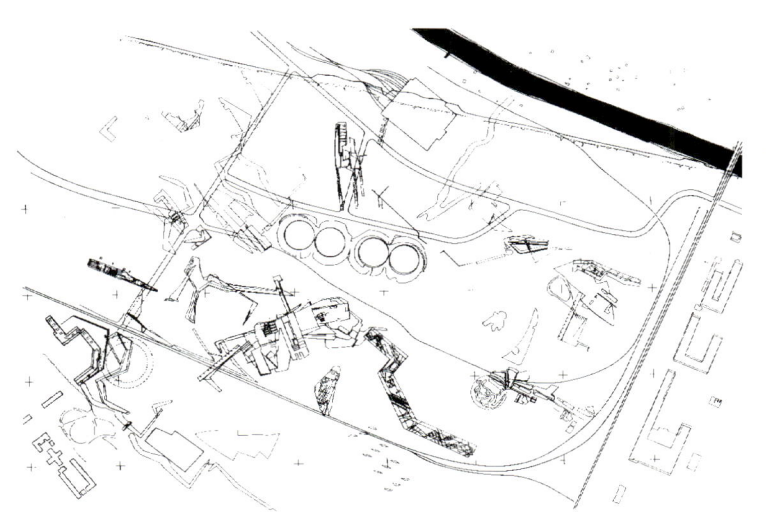

Gegenüberstellung Arbeitsgebiet – Raumfragmente /
Site confrontated with space fragments

Alle Architektur ist öffentlich Thomas Held

Es ist sicher nicht ganz einzusehen, weshalb dieses bedeutende Symposium ausgerechnet mit einem Bericht aus Luzern eröffnet werden soll, einer Stadt etwa von der Größe St. Pöltens, eher bekannt für die Nähe zu den Wilhelm Tell'schen Gefilden und für die schönen Schiffe und schönen Berge als für architektonische Denkmäler. Lassen Sie mich deshalb dem Luzerner Beispiel einige allgemeine Bemerkungen zur aktuellen Situation des Bauens und der Architektur vorausschicken, Bemerkungen, die für zahlreiche Städte in Westeuropa gelten dürften.

Zunächst muß betont werden, daß jedes Projekt öffentlich ist und zwar ganz unabhängig davon, ob ein privater Bauherr oder die öffentliche Hand baut – wer heute ein größeres Bauvorhaben realisieren will, muß sich, unabhängig von der Rechtslage, intensiv mit der Öffentlichkeit auseinandersetzen. Legitimation kann heute jederzeit durch Betroffenheit hergestellt werden. Damit man an einem öffentlichen, sogar förmlichen Diskurs teilnehmen kann, genügt die einfache Erklärung, daß man vom Projekt betroffen ist. Entsprechend haben in den letzten Jahrzehnten die Einspracherechte von Individuen und Kollektiven stark zugenommen. Einzelpersonen können heute ein Projekt ohne großen Aufwand und praktisch ohne Risiko verhindern.

Als Folge dieser Entwicklungen gilt für die Realisierung großer Bauprojekte nicht mehr das „anything goes" der 70er und 80er Jahre, sondern – zumindest in der Schweiz – eher „rien ne va plus". In Zürich prägte ein Mitglied der Stadtregierung das geflügelte Wort: „Die Stadt ist gebaut" und zwar durchaus im normativen Sinn: es soll nichts mehr „Großes" gebaut werden, ein für alle Male. Vorlaufszeiten von 15 bis 20 Jahren für größere Bauprojekte sind keine Seltenheit mehr. Dies führt zwangsläufig zu immer mehr Planungsritualismus. Zwar wird sehr viel Geld in Planungen gesteckt, dieses dient aber letztlich nicht der Realisierung von Projekten, sondern der Ruhigstellung von Planern und Architekten. Entsteht trotzdem irgendwo ein großer Wurf, eine greifbare Vision, wird zu den klassischen Nivellierungsabhilfen gegriffen: Es werden „offene Planungen" als großes Jekami organisiert, es werden Symposien veranstaltet, bei denen aber doch sehr selten die eigentlichen Bauprojekte im Zentrum stehen. Kommt es trotz aller dieser Komplizierungen und Einebnungen einmal doch zur Realisierung, sorgen jede Menge Kommissionen für eine weitere Vereinnahmung der schöpferischen Planung und Architektur.

In Luzern hat man, haben wir, einen anderen Weg gewählt, den ich hier kurz beschreiben möchte. Am Schluß dieses Weges stand eine Volksabstimmung, bei der zwei Drittel der Luzerner Stimmbürgerinnen und Stimmbürger diesem „verrückten" Projekt von Jean Nouvel zugestimmt haben, einem Bauwerk, für das der See teilweise ausgebaggert, das Ufer angetastet, Bäume gefällt und 94 Millionen Franken ausgegeben werden müssen, der größte je für ein Bauvorhaben bewilligte Kredit in der Geschichte der Stadt Luzern.

Wie ist es zu diesem „kulturpolitischen Lichtblick" gekommen, wie die Neue Zürcher Zeitung die Abstimmung am 12. Juni 1994 definiert hat?

Meiner Ansicht nach gibt es fünf Gründe dafür, daß dieses für die Schweiz und für das „Moratoriumszeitalter" so außerordentliche Projekt verwirklicht werden kann, und diese fünf Gründe lassen sich bis zu einem gewissen Grad generalisieren. Ein Projekt muß erstens, einer objektiven Notwendigkeit entsprechen, ein gewissermaßen „historisches" Bedürfnis befriedigen. Diese Notwendigkeit variiert natürlich von Ort zu Ort. In Luzern ergibt sie sich aus der überragenden wirtschaftlichen Bedeutung des Tourismus, der mehr als 50% zum Bruttosozialprodukt der Stadt beiträgt. Die Infrastruktur dafür – die großen Hotels, die Bergbahnen, die Raddampfer – wurde im wesentlichen von den „Gründern" um die Jahrhundertwende geschaffen, in den letzten zwei bis drei Generationen sind wesentliche Investitionen ausgeblieben, es war und ist höchste Zeit für neue Impulse.

All architecture is public Thomas Held

It may come as a bit of a surprise that this important symposium should begin with a report from Lucerne of all places, a town about the size of St. Pölten and better known for its vicinity to William Tell's pastures or its lovely boats and lovely mountains than for architectural monuments. For this reason, I would like to venture a few general remarks on the current situation of building and architecture before going into detail about Lucerne. Remarks which I believe may be applied to many Western European cities in general.

First of all, we must emphasize that every project is public, irrespective of whether the building owner is a private individual or a government body – whoever nowadays wants to implement a major construction project has to enter into an intensive contact with the general public, no matter what the legal situation is like. Today, the legitimacy of intervention can be easily constructed on the basis of feeling concerned: to enter into a public, even formal discourse on a project, it is sufficient to state that one is concerned by it. Correspondingly, the rights of intervention of individuals and collectives have strongly increased over the past few decades. Today, individuals have the power to prevent a project without much effort and practically without risk.

As a result of this development, the motto for the implementation of large-scale construction projects is no longer "anything goes", as in the 1970s and 1980s, but rather - at least in Switzerland - "rien ne va plus". In Zurich, a member of the city government coined the phrase, "The city has already been built", meaning it clearly in the normative sense: no "big" projects were to be built anymore, once and for all. Preparatory periods of 15 to 20 years for large-scale projects are no rarity in our time. In due course, this entails an increased ritualization of the planning process. A lot of money is invested into planning; however, this does not serve to implement projects but is meant to tranquilize urban planners and architects. If despite all this one large-scale success, one tangible vision becomes reality somewhere, the classic devices of levelling-down are employed: "open planning processes" are organized as big pow-wows, symposiums are held (which, however, rarely focus on the actual construction projects). If a project is implemented after all, in the face of all these complications and toning-down measures, a welter of committees further monopolize the creative work of planners and architects.

We in Lucerne have selected a different approach which I would like to describe now. At the end of this road, there was a referendum in which two thirds of the Lucerne citizens and voters approved the "crazy" project by Jean Nouvel, a building for which part of the lake was dredged, the lakeside modified and trees cut down. A total of 94 million Swiss Francs will be spent – the biggest credit ever granted for a construction project in the history of the City of Lucerne.

How did this "ray of hope in cultural policy" come about, as the Neuer Zürcher Zeitung defined the referendum on 12 June, 1994?

In my opinion, there are five reasons why this project, so extraordinary both for Switzerland and the "age of wait-and-see", can be implemented, and these five reasons may be generalized to a certain degree. First of all, any project must meet a certain necessity, must satisfy a "historic" need, as it were. Of course, this necessity varies from place to place. In Lucerne, it results from the overwhelming economic significance of tourism, which contributes more than 50% to the gross municipal product of the city. The required infrastructure – the big hotels, the mountain railways, the paddle-steamers – were created around the turn of the century; the last two or three generations made no extensive investments - the time for new impulses had and has in fact arrived.

The second precondition for the success of a large-scale public construction project lies in the commitment of private citizens. For the concert-hall, which with the sole exception of the Birmingham Symphony Hall is unique in Europe for its acoustic specification and design, approximately 40 million Swiss Francs, were collected from private donors. This enabled a modern, mixed-economy-style funding scheme and an extremely flexible project organization independent of the municipal administration. Although roughly half of the investment costs are borne by the City of Lucerne, the massive public commitment has completely changed political discourse. No politician wanted to decline this offer of considerable and definitely earmarked funds, whose handing-over was, however, tied to such prior commitments by the authorities as e.g. a legal building permit.

The third reason for the success of the Lucerne project is due to its quality and correct scale. Quality is not only something that can be objectively defined by a jury. For big, potentially controversial projects that require the approval of the general public, one needs "stars", big names that can be sold and convey the feeling that something extraordinary is in the making. Without the reputation of Jean Nouvel, it would have been impossible to push the project through in Lucerne. The second "star" that contributed to its acceptance was Russell Johnson from New York, one of the best acoustics experts in the world – certainly one of the most successful with orchestra conductors and musicians. However, above all, the project per se must have qualities that are visible and can be discussed. To present these qualities to a broad public, we first had an urban integration model (scale 1:500 000). This model enabled us to demonstrate to a broad public that Nouvel's project on the one hand fits strictly into the rectangular grid of the railway station zone, yet on the other hand is not swallowed up by it, but projects from the existing structures by virtue of its large roof.

Another, decisive factor for the success of the project was the broad support it received. Projects must never become the pawn of individual interests; it must offer something important to very many. An example: in addition to the big concert-hall, the Cultural and Conference Centre Lucerne also contains a normal, multifunctional, medium-size hall. Since this hall can be used by local clubs and associations, the interests of these groups were taken note of in the course of numerous semi-official talks at the beginning of the planning work. In this way, we found out that for most associations the key feature lay not in scenographic, aesthetic or material-related issues but the need for simple, i.e. cheap, catering: put succinctly, they wanted to be able to boil their sausages on their own. And so the building plan provided a kitchen, which was interpreted as evidence of the balanced character of the project and resulted in hundreds of "Yes" votes.

The heart of the new Cultural and Conference Centre is the big concert-hall, which had to be specially presented to the citizens. Objectively, the hall, with its extreme specifications in almost every respect, is a luxury item for a city with only 50,000 inhabitants. It was and still is to be justified only by the fact that the music festivals held in Lucerne are regarded as Number 2 in Europe after Salzburg – quite a few Lucerne citizens think that it is in fact the other way round. We tried to kindle the citizens' pride in having such a precious concert-hall by advertising, whenever possible, the sophistication of the technical equipment; as a result, every child in Lucerne today knows the meaning of "echo chamber" or "sound ceiling". Apart from conveying this impression of exclusiveness, we let the beauty of the models and the artistic quality of the sections and façade drawings by Jean Nouvel speak for themselves. And not only in the context of architectural exhibitions, but in places where we were able to reach a mass public: for example, in a specially erected tent at the Lucerne Autumn Fair,

aber ästhetisch einwandfrei präsentiert. Oder in den Malls der großen Shoppingcenters der Region, ergänzt durch mobile, von Kindern benützbare Elemente.

Um eine breite Abstützung in der Öffentlichkeit und bei den Stimmbürgern zu erreichen, ist eine besondere Form der Öffentlichkeitsarbeit notwendig. Wie ich schon erwähnt habe, muß zunächst alles, was vorgebracht wird, ernst genommen werden. Es besteht die große Gefahr, daß von den Initiatoren eines Projektes ein kultureller, rein architektonisch-städtebaulicher Diskurs geführt wird und gewisse Anliegen von vornherein als nicht legitim oder als intellektuell-ästhetisch nicht adäquat ausgeschlossen werden. Eine solche Haltung wird aber von der Boulevardpresse oder vom Stimmvolk bestraft. Man muß jedes Anliegen ernst nehmen, das heißt einen echten „runden Tisch" institutionalisieren, Legitimation durch Verfahren schaffen. Als Gegengewicht zum runden Tisch, der natürlich zum Palaver neigt, braucht es aber auch eine starke, konkrete Vision. Ohne die Vision führt der „runde Tisch" zur bekannten mittleren Unzufriedenheit, zu Durchschnittsprojekten, denen man politisch-rational zustimmt, für die sich aber niemand begeistert. Visionen kann man aber nur am Leben erhalten, wenn Projekte rasch verwirklicht werden. Wir haben bei diesem Projekt alles daran gesetzt, Planung und Ausführung zu beschleunigen. Die Tatsache, daß Mäzene – die bekanntlich fast per definitionem zu den älteren Herrschaften gehören – 40 Millionen Franken gespendet haben, und daß diese Persönlichkeiten die Eröffnung des Hauses gerne miterleben möchten, hat mitgeholfen, bei den Politikern und auch bei der Verwaltung den nötigen Druck zu schaffen.

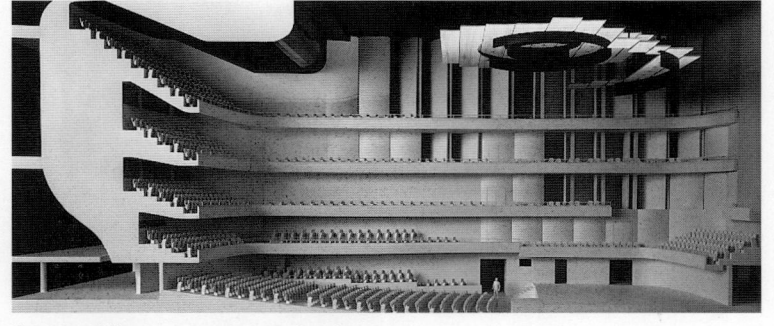

Kultur- und Kongeresszentum am See, Luzern

Um eine solche Beschleunigung durchziehen zu können, braucht es für das Projektmanagement zwei Voraussetzungen. Zum einen braucht es eine Art Verschwörergruppe, die das Projekt jenseits aller politischen Dimensionen, gewissermaßen als „existentielle" Aufgabe zu Ende führen wollen. Zum anderen ist aber auch ein hoher Grad an Neutralität und Unabhängigkeit der Verantwortlichen nötig, nicht nur parteipolitisch und im Spannungsfeld der Stadt- oder Landespolitik, sondern auch im gesellschaftlichen Sinn. Bei unserem Team war dies der Fall. Wir konnten sagen: „Wenn ihr den Nouvel nicht wollt, dann müssen wir leider auch weggehen." Es braucht diesen Druck bisweilen, das totale Commitment, die Mobilisierung, die ständige Aufregung, um etwas verwirklichen zu können.
Die kommunikative Umsetzung dieser Projektmanagement-Strategie läßt sich unter die simple, aber mit Bedacht gewählte These subsumieren: „Die Öffentlichkeit ist die Öffentlichkeit", gemeint ist, daß Projekte dieser Art – weil es sich im öffentlichen Raum abspielt – öffentlich und damit auch politisch sind. Die Werbung und ihre Methoden sind deshalb falsche Modelle, um Zustimmung zu gewinnen. Angebracht ist vielmehr das Modell des Politikers, der in die Arena steigen und eine Wahl gewinnen muß. Das Nouvel-Projekt konnte nur dank einer Art permanentem Wahlkampf realisiert werden, einem „Wahlkampf" mit rund 200 Vorträgen in Sälen und Hinterzimmern, Restaurants und Kneipen, an Parteiversammlungen und Quartiervereinen, vor 500 und vor 15 Personen. In der heißen Phase mußte auch der Pariser Jean Nouvel an die Front im luzernischen Dorf, eine interessante

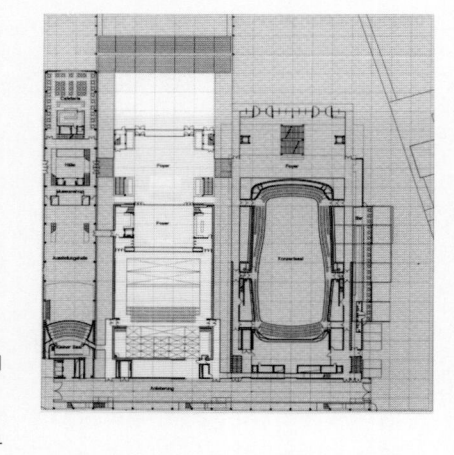

amidst the stands and stalls of a popular agricultural show, yet aesthetically immaculate. Or in the big shopping malls of the region, supplemented by mobile elements that could be used by the children.

To achieve a broad public support of voters, a special form of public relations work is called for. As I have already mentioned, the first thing is to take every argument seriously. There is a great danger that the initiators of a project conduct a cultural, purely architectural or urbanist discourse, thereby excluding certain concerns in advance as being unjustified or intellectually/aesthetically inadequate. But such an attitude is punished by the tabloid press or the voters. Every concern must be taken seriously, which implies providing for a genuine "round table", creating legitimacy through procedures. As a counterweight at the round table, which of course tends to lose itself in talk, one also needs a strong, concrete vision. Without this vision, the "round table" only entails the well-known average dissatisfaction, middling projects which are politically/rationally approved but which inspire nobody, incite no-one's passion. However, visions can only be kept alive if projects are quickly implemented. In this project, we did our utmost to accelerate planning and execution. The fact that patrons – which almost by definition are mostly elderly people – donated nearly 40 million Francs and that these gentlemen and ladies would like to live to see the inauguration of the building contributed to generating the necessary pressure on politicians and administrators.

To be able to push through this accelerated process, two preconditions of project management are required. The first necessary resource is a kind of conspiratorial society which has the intention to complete the project beyond all political dimensions, as a sort of "existential" task. Secondly, a high degree of neutrality and independence of those in charge is required – not only in the context of party politics or in the minefield between municipal and regional policies, but also in the social sense. This was the case with our team. We could really say, "If you don't want this guy Nouvel, then we're afraid we'll have to go, too." To make a project reality, you sometimes need this pressure, this total commitment, this mobilization, this permanent excitement.
The communicative implementation of this project management strategy may be summarized with a simple but carefully chosen motto: "The public is the public", by which I mean that every project of this kind is public – because it happens in the public sphere – and hence political in nature. Advertising and its methods as well as PR work are therefore the wrong models to win approval. Rather, what is needed is the model of a politician who has to step into the arena to win an election.
Nouvel's project could only be implemented due to a sort of permanent election campaign, which included about 200 lectures in halls and backrooms, restaurants and pubs, party rallies and neighbourhood meetings, before an audience of 500 or of 15 persons. In the "hot phase", Jean Nouvel also had to

Erfahrung in direkter Demokratie für den Vertreter der „Grande Nation". Ein solcher „Wahlkampf" ist nötig, damit die Leute sehen, wer das Projekt lanciert, wer dafür verantwortlich ist. Sowenig ein Firmenchef die zentrale Kommunikationsaufgabe an irgendwelche „Sprecher" delegieren kann, sowenig kann diese „Wahlkampf"-Aufgabe an Werbe- oder PR-Agenturen delegiert werden. Es braucht eine persönliche Identität des Projektes, die nur über die Identität des Architekten, des Akustikers, der Projektleitung, eben dieser „Verschwörergruppe", aufzubauen ist.

Eine letzte Bemerkungen zur Kommunikation: Es ist heute nicht mehr möglich zu warten, bis von irgendwoher Kritik aufkommt, bis irgendein Problem entsteht. Ich nenne Ihnen ein Beispiel: Hobby-Ingenieure, die es wie die Hobby-Architekten überall in großer Zahl gibt, haben uns gesagt: „Wenn der Föhnsturm kommt – Sie erinnern sich sicher an die entsprechende Szene in „Wilhelm Tell", dann wird dieses große Dach von Nouvel wegfliegen." Darauf haben wir diese Leute mit den richtigen Ingenieuren von Elektrowatt zusammengebracht, haben Ihnen Fotos aus den Windkanalstudien gezeigt, die einem spezialisierten Institut in Kanada, Ontario, durchgeführt worden waren. Die Hobby-Ingenieure konnten sehen, wie der Rauch um das Dach herumwirbelt, waren beeindruckt – und setzten ihre Hobbyingenieurtätigkeit als nunmehr unsere „Experten" in den Luzerner Kneipen fort.

Nicht alles, was hier konstitutiv für die Realisierung eines großen Architekturprojektes aufgezählt wurde, kann generalisiert werden. Luzern ist eine kleine Stadt, ein Kultur- und Kongreßzentrum ist weder eine Bank, noch ein Verwaltungsgebäude, und Nouvel ist auch nicht irgendein Schweizer Architekt. Generalisierbar ist hingegen, daß alle, die ein solches Projekt betreuen, immer aggressiv und mutig sein müssen: „In Gefahr und größter Not bringt der Mittelweg den Tod!", hat uns schon Christian Fürchtegott Gellert gelehrt. Wir müssen gegen die nivellierenden Tendenzen ankämpfen, wir müssen eine hohe Qualität, eine Radikalität der Architektur anstreben und bewahren, um Zustimmung zu erreichen. Denn die politisch und finanziell letztlich entscheidende Zustimmung kommt nicht nur aus dem „Kopf", sondern eben auch aus dem Bauch. Und nur dank dieser breiten Zustimmung – in unserem Fall die einer Zweidrittelmehrheit in der Politik und 40 Millionen Schweizer Franken Cash aus den Schatullen der Donatoren – läuft die behördliche Maschinerie rund, gibt es Spezialbewilligungen, funktioniert der Markt. All dies so gut, daß nun der Bau um etwa 2 Jahre beschleunigt werden konnte. Und so wird in Luzern bereits am 19. August 1998 Stardirigent Claudio Abbado für das Eröffnungskonzert mit den Berliner Philharmonikern den Taktstock heben.

Thomas Held
Vortrag zum Symposion
„Der öffentliche Raum"
(gekürzte Fassung)

come from Paris to fight at the Lucerne village front – an interesting experience of direct democracy for this representative of the "Grande Nation". Such an "election campaign" is necessary to make the people see who is launching the project, who is responsible for it. Just as the boss of a corporation cannot delegate the central tasks of communication to whatever "spokesperson", the "election campaign" task cannot be shunted onto advertising or PR agencies. What is required is the personal identity of the projects, and this can only be developed through the identity of the architect, the acoustics expert, the project managers, i.e. the abovementioned "conspiratorial society".

A last remark concerning communication: today, it is impossible to wait for criticism, to wait for problems to emerge. I will give you an example: leisure-time engineers, who - like leisure-time architects – are numerous, told us, "When we have a really heavy storm – you will certainly remember the scene in "William Tell" – this big roof by Nouvel will fly away." So we made these people meet the responsible engineers of Elektrowatt, we showed them pictures from the wind-tunnel studies developed by a specialized institute in Ontario, Canada; and so these leisure-time engineers saw the smoke swirling around the roof, were impressed and continued their leisure-time engineering in the pubs of Lucerne – but this time as our "experts".

Not everything that I have mentioned here as constitutive for the implementation of a large-scale architectural project may be generalized. Lucerne is a small city; a cultural and conference centre is not a bank or administrative building; and Nouvel is not just some Swiss architect. However, one thing applies in any case, namely that those who handle such a project must always be aggressive and courageous: "In danger and emergencies, the middle road spells destruction!", as Christian Fürchtegott Gellert has written. We must fight the levelling-down, we must strive for, and preserve, high quality, a radical architecture in order to win approval. For the final politically and financially decisive approval is never made by the head but from the guts. Only with this broad support – in our case, it was a two-thirds majority on the political scene and 40 million Swiss Francs paid in cash from the coffers of the donors – will the government machine run smoothly, special permits be granted – and all this so efficiently that the construction works are two years ahead of schedule. And thus star conductor Claudio Abbado will raise his baton for the inaugural concert with the Berlin Philharmonic already on 19 August, 1998.

Thomas Held
Lecture given at the symposion „The Public Space"
(shortened version)

Zwei Strategien für die Neugestaltung des öffentlichen Raumes Jos Bosmann

Die Herausforderung

„Die Gestaltung der Stadtentwicklung und des städtischen Raumes gemäß vorgegebenen, fixen Formen ist sicherlich anachronistisch. Dies entspricht dem Begriffs des Sonnensystems vor Kopernikus und der Sicht des Bewußtseins vor Freud." Martin Pawley

Es ist wahrlich eine große Herausforderung, sich die Stadt als einen Spiegel des Universums und des menschlichen Geistes vorzustellen. Man könnte diese Herausforderung als eine der gesamten Menschheit im Städtebau verallgemeinern: das höchste und subtilste Streben liegt hinter dem Ausdruck jedes Stadtbildes, das aus „irgendeinem" Grund beeindruckt. Diese Herausforderung ist auch für die profundeste Einstellung, die jeder Architekt gegenüber der Stadt entwickeln kann, maßgeblich. Aufgrund der schizophrenen Zustands, der während der 20. Jahrhunderts in die urbane Kultur eindrang, ist es jedoch fraglich, ob das Anstreben des Spiegelns als Vision des öffentlichen Raumes heute noch sinnvoll ist: ein modernistischer Schwerpunkt macht übergroße Teile des urbanen Gefüges bloß zu einer glanzlosen Demonstration funktionaler Mobilität zwischen Wohngebieten und Arbeitsgebieten – diese beanspruchen auf der Weltkarte mehr Platz als das ältere Gefüge, das in vergangenen Jahrhunderten geformt wurde –, während das postmoderne Interesse am Hedonismus neue Orte für reine Unterhaltung und aufregendes Vergnügen hervorbrachte. Die Realität unserer Städte ist eine willkürliche Mischung solcher Erfahrungswelten und, wenn diese überhaupt etwas widerspiegeln, dann scheint es, daß dies nur eine Mutation eines ziemlich primitiven, mechanistischen Verständnis des Kosmos und des Geistes sein kann. Dringt man allerdings in die Hintergründe der beiden getrennten Begriffe der funktionellen Moderne und der hedonistischen Postmoderne ein, erkennt man, daß es hier eigentlich nicht durch einen Primitivismus zu einem Problem kommt, sondern durch die Frage der Vereinbarkeit: Hinter dem Zugang der Moderne zur Stadt steht die – vielleicht weniger bekannte und – ziemlich kurzlebige Vorstellung von der Stadt als Ausdruck des Universums. Und hinter der banalen postmodernen Sicht der Stadt gibt es sehr spezifische Vorstellungen von der Stadt als Spiegel des Geistes – die meisten von ihnen sind in den frühen Ideen der Moderne verwurzelt, wie zum Beispiel bei Walter Benjamin und Paul Valéry. Somit hat die Schizophrenie des 20. Jahrhunderts in bezug auf den Begriff des öffentlichen Raums offensichtlich eine Spaltung zwischen einem möglichen Spiegel des Universums einerseits und einem des Geistes andererseits herbeigeführt.

Die Stadt und ihr öffentlicher Raum als Spiegel des Universums wurde in diesem Jahrhundert zu einem modernistischen Konzept mit Hinblick auf die Verlagerung als urbanem Faktor. Der Kunsthistoriker Sigfried Giedion (1888 – 1968) definierte diesen Begriff in seinem Buch Space, Time and Architecture als die Faszination über die Autobahn als neue, private Möglichkeit zum Erleben des öffentlichen Raumes. Gegen Ende seines Lebens hat Giedion noch die Erfahrung des Fußgängers, der sich zwischen den freistehenden, skulpturartigen Gebäuden bewegt, als ein Schlüsselerlebnis in der Neuen Umwelt eingearbeitet. Diese Gebäude werden zu einem Pendant von Stonehenge (einer wahrlich kosmischen Vision), was andeutet, daß extrem alte kosmische Visionen jene überlagern und überlappen, die in modernen Gemälden und Skulpturen sichtbar werden. Giedions Ansicht ist als Teil der Diskussion über die Stadt dann sinnvoll, wenn man sie unter dem Gesichtspunkt sich wandelnder Meinungen sieht, die als spezifische Formeln für die Stadtgestaltung definiert wurden, wobei es lange dauerte, bis diese in gestalterischer Hinsicht verstanden wurde.

Daß Räume für die Öffentlichkeit den dualen Aufbau des Geistes widerspiegeln könnten, steht eher in Beziehung zu postmodernen Optionen. Das Unbewußte als urbaner Faktor wurde insbesondere von Rem Koolhaas in seinem Buch „Delirious New York" eingehend behandelt, wo er die neuen Arten von Räumen zur Befriedigung einzelner Wünsche als Teil von kollektiven Erfahrungen erläuterte (die super-kapitalistische Stadt als endgültiger gesellschaftlicher

Two strategies for re-designing public space Jos Bosmann

The challenge

"A design of city development and urban spaces. In accordance with set and fixed forms is certainly anachronistic. It corresponds to the pre-copernican concept of the solar system and the pre-freudian perception of Alwa Reness."
Martin Pawley

Indeed it is quite a challenge to think of the city as a mirror of the universe and the human mind. One could generalize this challenge as one of making cities, being the most primal and the most refined aspiration behind the expression of every cityscape that impresses for "some" reason; a challenge determining as well the most profound attitude every architect may develop towards the city. It is the question, however, if the efforts of mirroring still make sense as a vision of public space today, because of the state of schiziphrenia that entered urban culture during the twentieth century: a modernist focus making extra-large pieces of urban fabric only a dull demonstration of functional mobility between areas for living and and areas for working – and these occupy on the worldmap more surface as compared to the older fabric formed in former centuries-, whereas a postmodernist interest in hedonism has added the new spots of pure entertainment and spoiling excitement. The reality of our cities is an arbitrary mixture of such experiential givings, and if these mirror something, it seems that it may only be a mutation of a rather primitive mechanistic understanding of cosmos and mind. However, if one explores the backgrounds of the two split notions – of functional modernism and hedonistic postmodernism –, one realises that it is in fact not primitivism of the city there is the – maybe less known and – rather ephermal idea of the city as an expression of the universe. And beyond the banal postmodernist view of the city there exist very specific ideas of the city as a mirror of the mind – most of them rooted in early modern ideas, as those of Walter Benjamin and Paul Valery. Apparently 20th century schizophrenia has, in relation to the notion of public space, evoked a split between a possible mirror of the universe at one hand and one of the mind at the other.

The city and its public space as a mirror of the universe has become, in this century, a modernist conception related to the notion of displacement as an urban factor. The art historian Sigried Giedion (1888-1968) defined this notion in his book Space, Time and Architecture as a fascination with the highway as a new private possibility of experiencing public space. Towards the end of his life Giedion added the experience of the pedestrian, walking amidst of freestanding sculpture-like buildings as an equally crucial experience of the New Environment - where it becomes a pendant of Stonehenge (a cosmic vision indeed), suggesting that extremely old cosmic visions do interfere and overlap with those that became visualised in modern painting and sculpture. Giedion´s point of view makes sense as part of a discussion on the city, when one sees it in the perspective of changing opinions, that were defined as specific formulas for urban design, which took a long time to be understood in design terms.

That spaces for the public might mirror the dual construction of the mind is rather related to postmodern options. The unconciousness as an urban factor has been especially elaborated by Rem Koolhaas. In his book "Delirious New York", in which he has explained the new type of spaces for satisfying individual desires as part of collective experiences (the ultimate social condensator of the super capitalist city). Also Koolhaas´ effort operates in the line of an effort to open another understanding of the city. Aldo van Eyck had, as an attack of dogmatic functionalism, argued that architecture has also a "nightside"; but first the Situationists had made of drifting a tool to experience the city in a new way.

Jos Bosmann

Kondensator). Auch Koolhaas strebt mit seinen Bemühungen ein anderes Verständnis der Stadt an. Als Angriff auf den dogmatischen Funktionalismus argumentierte Aldo van Eyck, daß die Architektur auch eine „geheimnisvolle Seite" hat; aber zunächst machten die Situationisten das Driften zu einem Instrument, das es ermöglichte, die Stadt neu zu erleben.

Das Problem der Kompatibilität kann nun wie folgt umformuliert werden: Wie bekommt man das moderne und postmoderne Verständnis der Stadt unter einen Hut? Oder, in dem Versuch das implizite Dilemma durch eine möglichst neuzeitliche Formulierung zu umgehen: Kann ein Begriff des postmodernen Zustands des menschlichen Geistes mit dem neuesten Verständnis des Universums verbunden werden?

Charles Jencks hat solche Ansprüche in seinem Buch „The Architecture of the Jumping Universe" aufgegriffen, wobei er die jüngsten Erkenntnisse der Komplexitätswissenschaft als mögliche Inspirationsleitbilder für die architektonische Gestaltung anwendet. Die von ihm gewählten Beispiele werfen jedoch sofort die Frage auf, ob das angeführte Argument nicht zu leicht einer gezwungenen Annahme über die Kompatibilität zwischen zeitgenössischen "Erkenntnissen" und dem architektonischen „Äußeren" der Dinge entspringt.

Das Interessante an Jencks' Beitrag bleibt sein Ziel – wie bei vielen seiner früheren Schriften – eine Theorie der Imagination zu formulieren. Jencks hat ein sehr gutes Gespür für die neuen Phänomene und ist eigentlich einer der wenigen schreibenden Architekten, die in ihrem Ehrgeiz zu theoretisieren die von Mark Jones als grundlegend angeführten Kriterien einer Theorie der Imagination erfüllen: 1. Prototypische Kategorisierung, 2. Bildschemata, 3. Metaphorische Projektionen, 4. Metonymie und 5. Erzählstruktur[1]. Das Problem liegt hier nicht im Potential der Theorie sondern in ihrer Anwendbarkeit auf ein zeitgenössisches Verständnis des öffentlichen Raumes als Spiegel des Kosmos und des Geistes, der im Teil 3 des Buchs als kosmogene Architektur definiert wird. Was hier gezeigt wird, kann dann nur als Erforschung der Gestaltungsmöglichkeiten in einem bestimmten formalen Vokabular verstanden werden, während die Merkmale des öffentlichen Raumes der "Heteropolis", wie Jencks sie in einem früheren Buch nannte, die Ausbreitung einer bestimmten stilistischen Ansicht eher verhindern würden. Auch hier stoßen wir wieder auf die Dichotomie des modernen/postmodernen Verständnisses, wobei ersteres auf eine konsequente, kettenartige Idee ("vom Stuhl zur Stadt") abzielt, die in einer spezifischen und kohärenten formalen Sprache zum Ausdruck kommt, während letzteres die ideologischen Verknüpfungen solcher Ebenen beiseite läßt und sie als möglichst unabhängig und beziehungslos betrachtet. Wir haben hier zwei theoretische Ansätze, die einander blockieren und die von einem mehrschichtigen Gesichtspunkt aus in Frage gestellt werden müssen.

Der Begriff des „Lebensstils" ermöglicht es, das Design von Möbeln / Häusern / Autos / Vierteln / öffentlichen Räumen / Städten / Regionen als interaktiv zu sehen. Kleine, mittlere, große und übergroße Objekte können als fluktuierende „Fenster" zueinander in Beziehung treten, die einander auf unerwartete Weise formen, je nachdem wie die Phantasie des Betrachters der Interpretation irgendeiner „realen" oder künstlichen Intelligenz entspricht. Auf diese Weise werden Objekte als Ausdruck von Zuneigung und Konkurrenz zueinander in Beziehung gesetzt, unabhängig von der kunsthistorischen Bestimmung eines eventuellen Stils. Eine Reihe von stilistisch völlig heterogenen Artefakten können Teil eines Lebensstils sein, der mit einem anderen konkurriert. Insbesondere ein Ghostwriter wie Rem Koolhaas kann eine Ära konvergierender Kräfte zwischen von Grund auf verschiedenen Optionen und Formen als kollektives Streben vorschlagen, das als Lebensstil erkennbar wird („Delirious New York", „Generic City"). In seiner eigenen Arbeit als Architekt versucht er, dem Dilemma des Stils zu entrinnen; er betrachtet sein Streben, „den Platz der öffentlichen Architektur" zu definieren, als ein stilloses Werk.

[1] Siehe Mark Johnson „The Nature of a Complete Theory of Imagination" In: The Body in the Mind (Chikago und London, 1987)

The problem of compatibility can now be rephrased as the following: How to get a modernist and a postmodernist understanding of the city under one hat? Or, to formulate the question in another way- trying to avoid, by being as contemporary as possible, the implied dilemma-: May a notion of the post-modern condition of the human mind be affiliatied with the most recent understanding of the universe?

Charles Jencks has very evidently taken up such aspiration in his book. The Architecture of the Jumping Universe, applying the most recent insights of complexity science as possible inspirational guidelines for architectural design. His choice of examples, however, raises immediately the question if the given argument does not spring too easily from a forced assumption about the compatibility between the most contemporary "insight" and the architectural "outside" of things.

The interesting contribution of Jencks remains his aim – as in a lot of his former writing – to formulate a Theory of Imagination. Jencks senses the new phenomena very well and in fact he is one of the few writing architects who fulfills in their ambition to theorize the criteria that Mark Jones has indicated as the basic ones for a theory of imagination: 1. prototypical categorization, 2. image schemata, 3. metaphorical projections, 4. metonymy and 5. narrative structure[1]. The problem here is not the potentioal of the theory, but its applicability for a contemporary understanding of public space as a mirror of cosmos and mind, defined in part three of the book as cosmogenic architecture. What is shown here may not otherwise be understood then as an exploration into possibilities of designing in a certain formal vocubulary, where as the characteristics of the public space of "Heteropolis", as Jencks called it in an earlier book, would rather avoid the profilation of one specific stylistic outlook. Again we bump here into the dichotomy of modernist/postmodernist understanding, the first aiming at a consequent chainlike "from-chair-to-city" idea expressed in a specific and coherent formal language, the second leaving the ideological linkages of such levels and considering them as independent and unrelated as possible. We have two theoretical approaches here that block one another and that need to become questioned from a more hybrid point of view.

It is the notion "lifestyle" that allows the design of furniture / house / car / neighbourhood / public space / city / region to be understood as interactive. Small, medium, large and extra-large sized objects may relate as fluctuating "windows", that may frame one another in unexpected manners, depending on how the imagination of the onlooker meets the interpretation of sime "real" of artificial intelligence. In this manner objects are related as expressions of affection and competition, independent from the art historical determinations of a possible style. A series of stylistically completely heterogeneous artifacts may be part of one lifestyle that competes with another one. Especially a ghostwriter as Rem Koolhaas is able to suggest an era of converging forces in between essentially different options and forms as a collective ambition, becoming recognisable ás lifestyle ("Delirious New York", "Generic City"). In his own work as an architect he tries to escape the dilemma of style; he considers his efforts to define "the place of public architecture" as a work with no-style.

In order to become more precise about the role of architectural design in public space, we better speak of strategy than of style. Also thinking of public space in a possible relationship with universe and mind has mainly to do with strategy. And the challenge to see the Chinese boxes of mind-in-public-space-in-universe blurred into one another may even be given a name as a strategy of redesigning public space today, being "superposition".

[1] See Mark Johnson "The Nature of a Complete Theory of Imagination" in: The Body in the Mind (Chicago and London, 1987)

Um präzisere Aussagen über die Rolle der architektonischen Gestaltung im öffentlichen Raum treffen zu können, sollten wir besser von Strategien als von Stilen sprechen. Auch die Betrachtung des öffentlichen Raumes in einer möglichen Beziehung zum Universum und zum Geist hat vorwiegend mit Strategien zu tun. Und die Herausforderung, die ineinander passenden Schachteln des Geistes im öffentlichem Raum im Universum als ineinander verschwimmend zu sehen, könnte heute als Strategie zur Umgestaltung des öffentlichen Raumes die Bezeichnung „Überlagerung" erhalten.

Ein möglicher Weg: Überlagerung

Kapitel XIV in Jencks' Buch trägt den Titel „Überlagerung – kann man für eine bestimmte Zeit bauen?". Als wichtiges Beispiel wird hier der von Koolhaas eingereichte Beitrag für den Parc de la Villette angeführt, „der fünf verschiedene Systeme, ohne eines dem anderen vorzuziehen, überlagerte". Jencks gibt uns Einblick in Insiderinformationen: „Der Grund, aus dem Eisenman und andere diesen Vorschlag so hoch schätzen, ist, daß seine komplexe Ordnung aus der nicht-linearen Dynamik der Bestandteile selbst von innen hervorzugehen scheint, und nicht von außen aufgedrückt wird." Tatsächlich kam bei mehreren Weltausstellungen nach dem zweiten Weltkrieg eine derartige Faszination zum Ausdruck, wobei die neuzeitliche Welt als eine neue und unmittelbare Konfrontation mit dem Aufbau des Universums betrachtet wurde. Dabei wurden oft riesige Kugeln zur Darstellung der Planeten verwendet. Manchmal ging man allerdings auch in die entgegengesetzte Richtung, hin zum Unsichtbaren, wie beim Atomium in Brüssel, wo die über begehbare Brücken verbundenen Kugeln ein Atommodell darstellen. In der alltäglichen Vorstellungswelt haben diese Eindrücke ihren Platz, wie Darstellungen von Comics Strips. Und exakt auf dieselbe Weise wie Hervé überraschte Koolhaas die Architekturszene mit dem Vorschlag einer planetären Vision als Teil seines Entwurfes für den Parc de la Villette. Insgesamt kann dieser Entwurf als eine Landschaft des menschlichen Geistes gesehen werden, wie ihn die Surrealisten bei mehreren Gelegenheiten „kartiert" haben.

Es sind aber weniger diese Inhalte sondern vielmehr die Art, wie die visuellen Bestandteile in diesem Entwurf von Koolhaas gezeigt werden, die Jencks als „Überlagerung" bezeichnet und die er auch in Koolhaas' Grand Palais in Lille erkennt. Das Prinzip wäre grundverschieden von Bernard Tschumis Begriff der „Superimposition", bei der ein Stadtplan dadurch entsteht, daß ein Organisationstyp auf der bestehenden Basis placiert wird, gefolgt von einem weiteren und noch einem."

Das „Mehr", das zu „entstehendem Verhalten" führt, kann anscheinend sowohl durch Überlagerung als auch durch Superimposition realisiert werden. In Lille hat der nicht verwirklichte Entwurf von Shinohara für ein Hotel dieses „Potential gezeigt" [2]; man könnte es als vertikale Montage in der Art von Koolhaas' Entwurf für den Parc de la Villette bezeichnen, als aufeinandergeschichtete Überlagerung: „Es wäre das bedeutendste japanische Bauwerk in Europa geworden." Und es war die Praxis der Stadtgestaltung in den USA, die eine mögliche Faszination des Austauschs von Schichtungen aufzeigte: „Was ich an amerikanischen Städten erstaunlich finde, ist die Tatsache, daß eine Stadt ihr Konzept, ihr Erscheinungsbild in Intervallen von zehn Jahren völlig ändert. Sie wandelt sich buchstäblich über Nacht (...)." [3]

Ein anderer Weg: teilweise Umgestaltung

Anstelle eines Aufstapelns in Form einer komplexen Akkumulation als Strategie für die urbane Umgestaltung versuchte ich gemeinsam mit meinen Studenten an den Instituten für Technologie in Newark und Delft einen anderen möglichen Ansatz zu entwickeln. Unsere Strategie konzentrierte sich auf räumliche Flügel und programmatische Nähte im städtischen Gefüge, um davon ausgehend eine Umgestaltung zu erreichen. Dieses Programm umfaßte zwei Grundstücke in der Randstad und drei in Manhattan mit einem

[2] S, M, L, XL; S. 1190
[4] Koolhaas während eines Seminars an der Rice University; in: Sanford Kwinter (Hrsg.), Rem Koolhaas – Conversation with Students.

One way to do it: Superposition

Chapter XIV in Jencks' book is titled "Superpostition – can one build in time?" As a major example is presented here the competition entry for Parc de la Vilette by Koolhaas "which superposed five different systems, not favouring one over another". Jencks provides us with the inside-information that "The reason Eisenman and others hold this proposal in such high regard is that its complex order would seem to emerge from within the nonlinear dynamics of the ingredients themselves, not imposed from without." In fact several of the world exhibitions after the Second World War have explored such a fascination to see the expression of the modern world as a new and immeditate confrontation with the construction of the universe, often as giant balls representing planets, sometimes going into the other scale-direction of the unseen, as in the case of the Atomium in Bruxelles, where balls linked by passage bridges represent an atom model. In every day imagination these impressions have got a place in the way they are represented in comic strips. And it is exactly in the manner of Herve, that Koolhaas surprised the architectural scene by proposing such planetary vision as part of his design for Parc de la Vilette. As a whole that design can be seen as a landscape of the human mind, in the way the surrealists have "mapped" it an several occasions.

However: it is not so much these contents, but rather the type of display of the visual ingredients in this design by Koolhaas that is labeled by Jencks as "superposition", and that he recognises as well in Koolhaas` Grand Palais in Lille. The principle would be essentially different as compared to "Bernard Tschumi´s notion of `superimpostion`, making a city plan out of placing an organizational type on top of the existing ground, followed by another and another".

The "more" that leads to "emergent behaviour" may apparently be realised both by superposition as well as by superimposition: In Lille the not realised design by Shinohara for a hotel "demonstrated the potential" [2]; one could call it a vertical assemblage in the kind of Koolhaas Parc de la Vilette design. Imposed superposition: "it would have been the most important Japanese building in Europe". And it was the practice of making cities in the United States, that had indicated a possible fascination for an exchange of impositions: "One thing that I find astonishing in American cities is that, in an interval of ten years, a city completely changes its concept, its visual aspect.
It literally changes overnight (...)" [3]

Another way to do it: Fractional re-design

Instead of piling up in the form of complex accumulation as a strategy for urban redesign I have tried to imagine another possible approach together with my students at the Institutes of Technology of Newark and Delft. Our strategy focussed on spatial wigs and programmatic seams in the urban fabric, in order to redesign from there. The program included two sites in the Randstad and three sites in Manhattan, all three a modernist type of housing that denies the old practice of the urban block in favour of an urban ensemble.

Such examples may be found all over the world, clearly asking for a strategy of interpretation. Also here a usefull reference may be a new understanding of "modern universe" that once intended to replace the "authentic spirit" of the old city. One of our sites was one of the most exemplaric in the world: the University Housing complex immediately bordering to Soho. Here the intention "to take over" these borders remained visible and became felt like a treat since the 1970´s. The point is that this tension may become appreciated in the 1990´s as the notion of a transitional phase between two different imageries, two different "stages" next to one another.

[2] S,M,L,XL; p.1190
[3] Koolhaas during a seminar at Rice University; in: Sanford Kwinter (ed.), Rem Koolhaas - conversation with students.

modernistischen Wohnhaustyp, der die alte Praxis der urbanen Blockbauweise zugunsten eines städtischen Ensembles verwarf.

Solche Beispiele, die eindeutig eine Interpretationsstrategie fordern, können überall auf der Welt gefunden werden. Auch hier könnte ein neues Verständnis des „neuzeitlichen Universums", das einmal beabsichtigte, den „authentischen Geist" der alten Stadt zu ersetzen, hilfreich sein. Eines unserer Grundstücke ist eines der beispielhaftesten weltweit: der University-Housing-Komplex direkt an der Grenze zu Soho. Hier blieb die Absicht, diese Grenzen „zu übernehmen", sichtbar und wurde ab den siebziger Jahren wie eine Bedrohung empfunden. Der springende Punkt ist, daß diese Spannung in den neunziger Jahren als Konzept einer Übergangsphase zwischen zwei unterschiedlichen Vorstellungen, zwei nebeneinander liegenden, unterschiedlichen „Stadien", geschätzt werden könnte.

Bei den drei Grundstücken in Manhattan entdeckten wir, daß insbesondere dann der Eindruck der Stummheit und Distanz entsteht, wenn man auf dem Bodenniveau des modernen Komplexes steht. Wir sahen es als Herausforderung an, ihn so subtil wie möglich umzugestalten, wobei die Erfahrung eines enormen leeren Raumes inmitten der Metropole so in ein Gefühl umgewandelt wird, daß durch eine Ausrichtung und ein Programm der Erdgeschoßbereich einen gewissen Anreiz zur Besitznahme bietet. Es ist in der Tat unglaublich, wie eine an La Défense erinnernde Atmosphäre zwischen zwei Plätzen – Washington Square und Soho –, die als Teil des Manhattaner Straßenlebens während des Wochenendes höchst populär sind, aufrecht erhalten werden kann. Wir dachten, daß die Zeit für die Entdeckung der „Eisigkeit" des dazwischen liegenden Gebiets als pure Attraktion reif sei. Die nächste Frage lautete: Wie kann es in Besitz genommen werden?

Das Potential für eine architektonische Strategie zu unserer Absicht, diese Gebiete umzuarbeiten, ergab sich aus einer Spannung von einem historischen Standpunkt aus: Eine Betrachtung der 60er Jahre mit ihrer Überbewertung der formalen Artikulation einerseits, wie es im Werk von Scarpa der Fall war und deren völliger Abwesenheit bei der durchschnittlichen Massenproduktion von Wohnraum andererseits. Stellt man sich eine Möglichkeit zur Überwindung dieser Dichotomie vor, könnte man von einer Verflüchtigung der raffinierter Kleinheit hin zu dummer Größe sprechen.

Um zu veranschaulichen, was bei unserer Übung herauskam, möchte ich Ihnen ein Beispiel zeigen: den Vorschlag von Dario Zini für die Umgestaltung der Chatham Towers in Manhattan. Zur Umgestaltung des Bodenniveaus, das im derzeitigen Zustand eine ziemlich banale Zufahrt zu Parkplätzen darstellt, konzipierte er, wie auch alle anderen Studenten, eine Möglichkeit zur Intensivierung der Erfahrung der Ebene zwischen den Türmen, wobei er der emotional-wirtschaftlichen Versuchung widerstand, zwischen oder um die bestehenden Türme herum Volumina einzufügen. Wir beschlossen, daß man von China Town aus, das an das Grundstück angrenzt, das Gelände durch eine ambivalente Art von Gefüge prägen können sollte, sodaß es erfahrbar wird und die städtischen Kräfte hier nicht in vertikaler Richtung ansteigen (was ein vor kurzem errichtetes Gerichtsgebäude neben den Türmen durch seine Höhe vortäuscht), sondern ebenso stark entlang der horizontalen Ebene einer windreichen Verkehrslandschaft auslaufen. Zini fand durch den Einsatz von Rissen eine Lösung. Das Ergebnis erinnert an Eisschollen. Die Inspiration für die Artikulation durch verschiedene Materialien stammt eindeutig von dem von Scarpa entworfenen Eingang zur Architekturschule in Venedig. Aber im vorgeschlagenen Maßstab und an dem vorgeschlagenen Ort gewinnt der Vokabular meiner Meinung nach als ein Übergangsobjekt zwischen verschiedenen Realitäten stark an Bedeutung, insbesondere da der Eingang in Venedig stillen, symbolischen Charakter hat wie der eines Friedhofes, während dies bei dem Vorschlag für Manhattan zu einem belebten Symbolismus wird: Eine Art skulpturartiger Raum mit innerer Erfahrung und äußerer Wirkung.
Die Bezugnahme auf dieses spezifische Beispiel von Scarpa kann

We discovered in the case of the three sites in Manhattan that it is especially standing on the ground level of the modern complex where the impression of dumbness and distance is produced. We saw it as a challenge to rework it as subtely as possible, turning the experience of an enormous empty space in the middle of the metropolis into a sensation, with some notion of direction and program that would give the ground-level area a bit of incentive to occupy it. In fact it is incredible how a La Défence-like atmosphere be maintained between two places that are most popular as part of Manhattan street life during the weekends: Washington Square and Soho. We thought that time is ripe to discover the "icyness" of the area in between as pure attraction. The next question was: how may it be occupied?

The potential for an architectural strategy for our intention to rework these areas was derived from a tension in a historical perspective, looking at the 1960´s, with a over concern of formal articulation at one hand, as it was the case in the work of Scarpa, and a total lack of it in the average massproduction of housing. Imagining a way to overcome this dichotomy, one could speak of a possible evaporation of refined Smallness into dumb Bigness.

As a demonstration of what came out of our exercizes I show you one example: a proposal by Dario Zini for redesigning the Chatham Towers in Manhattan. In order to redesign the ground level area of the towers, that is in the present state a rather banal entrance to a parking, he, like all the other students, imagined a way of intensifying the experience of the plane between the towers, resisting the emotional-economical temptation to add volumes in between or around the existing towers. From China Town, that borders the site, one should, we decided, be able to inscribe the territory through an ambivalent type of fabric that makes it experential, that the metropolitan forces do not only jump here in a vertical direction (what a recently added court building next to the towers is pretending with its height), but as much strongly wave out along the horizontal plane of a windy traffic landscape. Mr. Zini found a solution working with cracks. The result reminds of Ice-flois. The articulation in different materials is clearly inspired on the entrance of the Venice school of architecture, designed by Scarpa. But in the proposed scale and on the proposed spot this vocabulary gains, in designed by Scarpa. But in the proposed scale and on the proposed spot this vocabulary gains, in my opinion. a lot of meaning as an object of transition between different realities mainly because the Venice entrance is of a silent symbolic kind, like heat of the cemetary, while in the proposal for Manhattan it becomes inhabited symbolism: a type of sculptured space that has an inside experience and an outside effect.

The reference to the specific Scarpa example may even learn more: that this was in its time already an interpretation of the brute "superposition" of the church into the neighbouring buildings. And what was abstracted as a formal vocabulary in the lesson of Learning from Venice at the time, may today be brought into action for a program for bodies inscribing space, as is demonstrated with the example of how to redesign the Chatham Towers.

Conclusion

By taking serious the possibility of an anewed and contemporary analogy of the city with the universe and the mind, as once suggested by Martin Pawley in a rather ironical way, we have been able to verify a little better some current readings and strategies for public space. To the mentioned projects in which an imagery of universe and mind are combined may be added some realised building complexes like Isozaki´s Disney

sogar noch mehr aussagen: Zu seiner Zeit war es bereits eine Interpretation der rohen „Überlagerung" der Kirche auf die benachbarten Gebäude. Was in der von Venedig gelernten Lektion damals als formales Vokabular abstrahiert wurde, kann heute für ein Programm eingesetzt werden, bei dem Körper den Raum beschreiben, wie dies durch das Beispiel über die Umgestaltung der Chatham Towers gezeigt wird.

Schlußfolgerung

Indem wir die Möglichkeit einer erneuten und zeitgenössischen Analogie der Stadt mit dem Universum und dem Geist, wie sie von Martin Pawley auf eher ironische Weise vorgeschlagen wurde, ernst nahmen, konnten wir einige heutige Auffassungen und Strategien für den öffentlichen Raum etwas besser prüfen. Die angeführten Projekte, bei denen das Bild des Universums und des Geistes kombiniert werden, kann man durch einige realisierte Gebäudekomplexe, wie zum Beispiel das Disney Hauptquartier in Florida von Isozaki und Mendinis Museum in Groningen ergänzen. Diese weisen eine Aura der Unterhaltung in der Art der Universal Studios auf. In dieser Eigenschaft scheint es, daß sie sich auf den narrativen Teil einer möglichen Aussage über Hypermodernität konzentrieren. Aber es ist die Frage, ob ein Objekt seine Geschichte wirklich so wörtlich „erzählen" sollte. Das Kunstmuseum in Groningen geht auf intelligente Weise mit dem Konflikt zwischen der Typologie der alten/älteren Stadt und den Auswirkungen der modernistischen Fragmentierung um. Das Objekt selbst wird zu einer Verbindung in der Stadt, die viele Menschen durchqueren; gleichzeitig thematisiert das Gebäude den erwähnten Konflikt architektonisch. Der öffentliche Raum vieler Städte ist durch einen sehr ähnlichen Konflikt gekennzeichnet, aber es ist die Frage, zumindest eine, die ich stelle, ob eine ähnliche Lösung das Versprechen eines möglichen Areals einlösen könnte, wo ein Verständnis des Überganges spezifische neue Erfahrungsqualitäten erreichen kann. In Städten, wo eine Spannung zwischen der ältesten und neuesten Substanz offensichtlich ist – um nicht zu sagen schmerzlich, wie zum Beispiel in Barcelona – könnte gerade in diesen sehr spezifischen Bereichen der bewußte Ausdruck eines Sprungs in ein neues Jahrtausend mit Hinblick auf eine Architektur des öffentlichen Raumes entwickelt werden.

Es waren die Situationisten in den fünfziger Jahren, die die Möglichkeit des „Driftens" im alten Stadtzentrum entdeckten – eine moderne Interpretation der bestehenden alten Substanz –, und in den neunziger Jahren wurde der Begriff der kosmogenen Architektur als Antwort auf die Peripherie geprägt – eine postmoderne Interpretation der modernistischen Substanz. Als Schema für die Stadt waren Geist/Zentrum und Universum/Peripherie dazu verurteilt, eine physisch bestimmte Distanz zueinander zu halten. Während des 20. Jahrhunderts war der Stadtbegriff nichts als die wiederholte Bestätigung eines derartigen Schemas. Als Phänomen der Wahrnehmung und der Erfahrung hat der öffentliche Raum überall in der zeitgenössischen Stadt einige der schwer faßbaren Merkmale eines terrain vague angenommen. Und in diesem Sinne gibt es viele potentielle Gebiete, in denen die Erfahrung des Zentrums und der Peripherie bereits unschlüssig vereint sind. Dies gilt insbesondere dort, wo eine der widersprüchlichen Strategien zur Auslöschung des Alten oder zur Wiederbesetzung des Neuen abgeschlossen werden könnte und wo im wesentlichen unterschiedliche Stadtblöcke nun als Teil einer Stadt (wie in unserem Beispiel von Manhattan) zur Koexistenz gezwungen werden. Die Einsicht, daß das Kräftefeld dieser gemischten Gebiete als ein bewußteres Potential für den öffentlichen Raum zu sehen ist, wird die Herausforderung der nächsten Jahre auf dem Weg ins nächste Jahrtausend sein.

Jos Bosman
Vortrag, gehalten zum Symposium „Der öffentliche Raum"
(gekürzte Fassung)

Headquarters in Florida and Mendini´s museum in Groningen. These possess an aura of entertainment, of the Universal Studios type. As such, it seems, they focus on the narrative part of possible statement about hypermodernity. But it is the question if an object should "tell" the story so literally. The Groningen Art Museum deals in an intelligent way with the conflict between the typology of the old(er) city and the effects of modernist fragmentation. The object itself becomes a link in the city, that many people cross; at the same time the building thematizes the mentioned conflict architectonically. The public space of many cities is characterized by a very similar conflict, but it is the question, anyway an understanding of transition may attain specific new experiential qualities. In cities where the tension between oldest and newest substance is evident – not to say painfull, such as in Barcelona – it will be exactly in those very specific areas that the concious expression of a jump into a new millenium may become developed in terms of an architecture of public space.

It was the Situationists in the 1950´s that discovered the possibility of "drifting" in the old city centre – a modern interpretation of the existing old substance - and in the 1990´s it is a concept of Cosmogenic Architecture, that has been formulated as an answer to the periphery – a postmodern interpretation of modernist substance. Mind/centre and Universe/periphery are, as a scheme of the city, doomed to stay at a physical determined distance from each other. The city-notion during the twentieth century has been nothing but the repeated confirmation of such a scheme. As a perceptual and experiential phenomenon, however, public space has attained everywhere in the contemporary city some of the nondescript characteristics of a terrain vague. And in that sense there are plenty of potential areas in which the experience of centre and periphery are already inconclusively united. Especially there, where neither of the contradicting strategies to erase the old or to reoccupy the new could become completed and where essentially different city blocks are forced now to coexist as a part of one city (as in our examples from Manhattan). The intelligence to read the force field of these mixed areas as a more concious potential for public space will be a challenge for the coming years, at ending the advent of the next millenium.

Jos Bosman
Lecture given at the symposion "The Public Space"
(shortened version)

Architecture on the datahighway   Kay Friedrichs
WebWorld / Mainland / SinCity

At the end of the 20th century, city, public space and architecture are in the defense.

Past urban structures have clear, legible model functions. Digital technologies and global networks, with the help of which "Global Cities" such as London, New York or Tokyo exert their power, confront us with the task of representing architecture and city planning on a new and incomparably more abstract level. The few on-going urban and architectural projects are notoriously over-evaluated by politicians, city planners, and architects. However, the truly significant and profitable projects e.g. World Wide Web, Big and Little LEOs, Pay-TV, Tele Shopping, POP Music, M25, Networking, Global-Banking, Smart Cards, and CyberMoney, etc. no longer have much to do with city or architecture. In contrast to the general decay of urban public space and the merging of metropoles through anonymous suburbs, the so-called sprawl, we are witnessing how user interfaces in computer networks are based on architectural and city planning patterns to facilitate navigation in the boundless data worlds. One of the "side effects" bound to appear in the wake of these trends is the loss of meaning for "real built environment".

The industrial city

The city planning model of modernism, the city zoned according to functions, is a symptom that goes hand in hand with the industrial revolution and also of concomitant Fordism at the beginning of our century. One of Henry Ford's fundamental achievements was the discovery of the worker as consumer. You could think that under the influence of this large-scale influx of labor, mass articles and their consumption, the city would be subjugated to comparable categories as an extended instrument of rigid mass fabrication. According to Ford's production logistics they were zoned into working, living and leisure areas. Fordism seems to have had a great influence under the banner of electro-mechanic industrialisation in that organizational principles of manufacturing were translated into the public domain. The spatial zoning of the factory according to scientifically optimized rules in certain production spaces and surfaces, their maintenance and disposal using complex logistics and the temporal organization of working processes in chronological "labor beats" corresponded to a new city model of the functional city - the zoned city. This model of modernism

sowohl in der Wohnung, als auch in der Stadt, bis auf die Ebene der legislativen Bau- und Städtebauvorschriften durch. Sie bedingte eine Zerstörung des bürgerlichen Ideals von öffentlichem Raum, den der Promenaden, den des Flaneurs und der bürgerlichen Kaffeestuben und ersetzte ihn durch fragmentarische „Bewegungs- und Ruhezonen".

Das Prinzip der Zonierung wird zur expliziten Ordnungskategorie, es besetzt die wichtigsten Fachtermini und durchdringt in einigen europäischen Ländern das gesetzliche Planungsinstrumentarium.

has gained significance in Europe since the 20s when the various areas of living both in the apartment as well as in the city and in the legislation for construction and city planning were separated. This destroyed the civil idea of public space represented by the promenade, stroller and the bourgeois coffee house and replaced it with fragmentary "movement and rest zones".

The principle of zoning develops into an explicit category of order, it uses the most important technical terminology and in some European countries it permeates the legal planning instruments.

Die „Post Fordistische Stadt"

Unter dem Druck der ersten ökonomischen Krisen, der damit einhergehenden Verarmung der öffentlichen Hand und der Restaurierung politisch konservativer Deregulierungsstrategien versagte dieses, zumindest in einigen europäischen Kernländern etablierte Instrumentarium. Dieser institutionelle Bankrott des „öffentlichen, demokratisch kontrollierten Souveräns" als Bauherrn vollzieht sich parallel zu weltweiten Modernisierungsschüben.

Nach Henckel u.a. befinden sich die modernen Industriegesellschaften und die sog. Schwellenländer am Ende des 4. Innovationsschubes. Die alten, zumeist güterverarbeitenden Industrienationen generieren zu informationsverarbeitenden Dienstleistungsgesellschaften, deren technologischer Kern in der Anwendung und Diffusion der Mikroelektronik und einer internationalen Vernetzung der neuen Technologien besteht. Die internationale Vernetzung der I+K - Technologien setzt sie aber darüberhinaus in eine globale Konkurrenz um Dienstleistungen und kognitive Prozesse, bei der die gut ausgebildeten Eliten der sogenannten Schwellenländer, z.B. Indien, zu den globalen Gewinnern gehören. Die neuen integrierten Fertigungsmethoden führen im Verbund mit den Informationstechnologien zu einer international verschärften Konkurrenz um Standorte, Dienstleistungen und Finanzierungen, von Produktion und Distribution, die immer häufiger an den traditionsreichen Kernstädten vorbeigeht. Die räumliche Logik der Dienstleistungsgesellschaft besagt, daß die Orte der Leitfunktionen (Planung, Management, Finanzierung etc.) und die der Distribution nicht mit den Produktionsorten übereinstimmen müssen. Sie werden räumlich und zeitlich entkoppelt und durch die neuen Technologien vernetzt. Der logistische Aufwand für die Gütertransporte wächst exponential, da die Fertigung der Einzelkomponenten und die Endmontage ebenfalls global entkoppelt wird. Produziert und montiert wird an der jeweils kostengünstigsten Stelle, verkauft

The "post-Fordian city"

Under the pressure of the first economic crises, the concomitant pauperization of the state and the restoration of politically conservative deregulation strategies, this instrument that had become standard in some European core countries failed. This institutional bankruptcy of the „publicly, democratically controlled sovereignty", the building master, goes hand in hand with the global modernization phases.

According to Henckel and others, modern industrial society and the so-called threshold economies are experiencing the last leg of the 4th innovation phase. The old, mostly goods-processing industries are changing into information-processing service societies whose technological core is the application and diffusion of micro-electronics and an international networking of new technologies. International networking of information and communication technologies, however, places them into global competition for services and cognitive processes, making the well-educated elites of the so-called threshold economies such as India into the global winners. The new integrated manufacturing methods, together with the information technologies are leading to an internationally stronger competition for location, services and financing as well as products and distribution, which increasingly keep out of the traditional city centers. The spatial logic of service companies says that sites of the main business functions (planning, management, financing, etc.) and sites of distribution do not need to be identical with the production sites. They are spatially and temporally separated and linked using the new technologies. The logistics for goods transport is increasing exponentially since the manufacture of single components and of final installation are also being uncoupled. Production and installation is carried

dort, wo das Einkommensniveau und die Nachfrage am erfolgversprechendsten ausgeprägt sind. Die materielle und zunehmend die informelle Logistik wird zu einer entscheidenden Größe der Industrieproduktion und ihrer zeitsensiblen internationalen Verzahnung. Schon diese Entwicklungen haben einige zentrale Stadtfunktionen überflüssig gemacht. Räumliche Indikatoren für diese Effekte in den Städten sind wachsende Leerstände in klassischen Poduktionsbereichen und bei Büroflächen.

Zu Beginn des 5. Innovationsschubes werden die informationstechnischen, die elektrooptischen, die gentechnischen und die biochemischen Schlüsseltechnologien der „Global Player" die notwendigen strukturellen Veränderungen im Weltmaßstab in Angriff nehmen. Unter der räumlichen Logik der Informationsgesellschaft bildet sich ein neuer Weltmarkt für kognitive Prozesse heraus, der sich an keinem geographischen Ort festmachen läßt und die technischen Eliten in eine instabile, weltweite Konkurrenz um Arbeit treten läßt. Die bislang statische räumliche Zonierung in der Fläche und die linearen repetitiven Zeittakte der fordistischen Produktion entwickeln sich unter den neuen Modernisierungsschüben in Richtung räumlicher und zeitlicher Flexibilität, mehrdimensionaler Funktionsfaltung und -überlagerung. Dem Leitbild der rigide zonierten, „funktionalen" Stadt und der Stadt als monostrukturiertem Dienstleitungs- und Distributionszentrum folgt nun das Leitbild einer räumlich indifferenten Informationsgesellschaft ohne Zentrum. Stattdessen gleichen die mit „weichen" Standortvorteilen ausgestatteten Sprawls einer polyzentrischen Region für das 21. Jahrhundert. Kleinere Städte und das Umland großer Ballungsgebiete können gegenüber den alten Stadtzentren von den räumlichen Wirkungen dieses 5. Innovationsschubes profitieren.

Die Vision einer „vernetzten Region" entspräche für die entwickelten Industrieländer in frappierender Weise den Anforderungen einer beschleunigten, weltweit verteilten Entwicklung und Produktion unter dem Banner einer globalen Informationslogistik. Dieser Trend verlangt von den postindustriellen Gesellschaften in erster Linie die strategische Erstellung und Kontrolle von Software. Die Produktion von klassischen Investitionsgütern (Hardware) bleibt für sie, gemessen an dem Exportausstoß des 20. Jahrhunderts, eine marginale ökonomische Nische, in der mit kleineren, flexibel organisierten dezentralen Entwicklungseinheiten geringer Fertigungstiefe, kleine Serien von hochqualitativen Produkten produziert werden. Dabei wird die weltweite Lagerhaltung auf Flughäfen, die öffentlich finanzierten Straßen und Bahntrassen oder auf die kleinen Zulieferer abgeschoben. Die logistische Abhängigkeit von Zulieferern und Abnehmern wächst. Ein Innovationszirkel („Teufelskreis") schließt sich.

„EuroSprawl"

Mit einer räumlichen und zeitlichen Dezentralisierung und Flexibilisierung, bei ungleich größerer internationaler Verzahnung der Produktion, werden die I+K-Technologien zu strategischen Schlüsseltechnologien. Neben dem „militärischen Komplex" waren es vor allem die Banken, die international agierenden Versicherungs-, Kapital- und Börsenbroker, die sozusagen als „Avantgarde" durch die konsequente Umsetzung neuer Arbeitsstrukturen, die durch die Telekommunikation möglich wurden, auch gleichzeitig demonstriert

out wherever it is most cost-efficient, and products are sold wherever the income level and the demand are most promising. Material and increasingly also informal logistics are developing into a major factor of industrial production and its time-sensitive international interlinkage. These developments have made some of the central city functions superfluous. Spatial indicators for these effects in the cities are the growing number of empty offices and classical production plants.

At the beginning of the 5th innovation phase, information technology, electro-optics, genetic engineering, and key biochemical technologies of the "global player" will take on the necessary structural changes on a global scale. A new global market for cognitive processes is developing with this new spatial logic of the information society. This world market is not bound to any geography and gets the technological elite to enter an unstable, global competition. The static spatial zoning of surfaces and linear, repetitive temporal beats in line with Fordism is now developing spatial and temporal flexibility with this new phase of modernization. It relies on multidimensional overlapping and streamlining of functions. The model of the rigid zoned "functional" city and the city as a monostructuralized service and distribution center is being replaced by a model of a spatially indifferent information society without a center. The sprawls with their "soft" location advantages are turning into the polycentric region of the 21st century. In contrast to old city centers, small towns and the surroundings of large conurbations can profit from the effects the 5th innovation phase has on space.

For the developed industrial countries the vision of an "interlinked region" corresponds astonishingly to the demands of an accelerated, globally distributed development and production represented by global information logistics. This trend demands the strategic creation and control of software on the part of the post-industrialized countries. The production of classical investment goods (hardware) remains a marginal economic niche (compared to the exports of the 20th century), in which production is carried out with smaller, flexibly organized decentralized development units with less manufacturing depth and smaller series of high quality products. Global stocks will be kept at airports, on publicly financed streets and rails or small sub-contractors. Logistical dependance on sub-contractors and customers is growing. An innovation circle ("viscious circle") is closing.

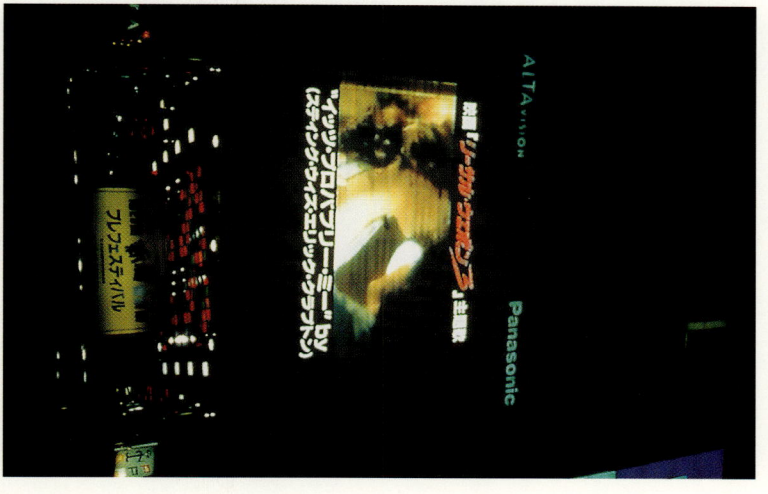

"EuroSprawl"

With both spatial and temporal decentralization and increasing flexibility together with enhanced interlinkage in production, information and communication technologies are becoming strategic key technologies. Apart from the "military complex" banks, it was the internationally active insurance, capital and stock brokers, playing the role of an avant-garde, who demonstrated that these technologies are effective in architecture and city planning as well, if they are applied in production and services by persistently pulling through new work structures made possible by telecommunications. The dominating

haben, daß diese Technologien stadträumlich und architektonisch wirksam werden, wenn sie in der Breite der Produktion und Dienstleistung angewandt werden. Die dominierende Funktion einiger globaler Finanzmetropolen, nach Sassen sogenannten "Global Cities", bedingt ein fein gestaffeltes Umfeld aus untergeordneten "Intelligent Cities" und „vernetzten, ungegliederten Sprawls", verstreuten „Intelligent Buildings" und „Smart Homes", die alle nur aus diesem sehr weit fortgeschrittenen Stadium der Diffusion von Arbeitsstrukturen mit den neuen Technologien anschaulich beschrieben werden können. Die überkommenen, funktionalen und begrifflichen Trennungen in „Arbeit und Wohnen" und auf anderer Ebene in „Stadt und Land" sind seit längerem in Auflösung begriffen. Zentralistische territoriale Macht, wie sie z.B. die Hauptstadt alten Typs repräsentiert, sind obsolet. Koolhaas, Rogers, Pawley u.a. sprechen – was die wirtschaftlich kompaktesten Regionen Europas betrifft – von einer bewußt schwammig definierten Intensitätszone, die sich als transnationale „Entwicklungs-Banane" von London, über Nordfrankreich, die Benelux-Länder, das Rhein-Main- und das Rhein-Neckar - Gebiet, Straßburg, die Schweiz und die Alpen bis nach Turin und Mailand erstreckt. Dieses Gebiet wächst zu einem durchgehenden, polyzentrischen Netz städtischer Entwicklungsstreifen und -knoten zusammen, zu einer Art „EuroSprawl".

function of some global financial metropoles, "global cities" according to Sassen, necessitates a finely woven hierarchical environment consisting of subordinate "intelligent cities" and "netted, unstructured sprawls", dispersed "intelligent buildings" and "smart homes" that can only be described from this highly advanced stage of the diffusion of work structures with the new technologies. The functional and terminological separation into "working and living" and at another level into "city and countryside" is becoming more and more obsolete. Centralist territorial power, as represented by the capital in the traditional sense of the word, is obsolete. Koolhaas, Rogers, Pawley etc. speak of - referring to the most compact of regions in Europe from the economic point of view - an intensity zone that is deliberately vaguely defined and runs like a transnational "development banana" through London, North Africa, the Benelux countries, the Rhine Main and Rhine Neckar area, Switzerland and the Alps all the way to Turin and Milan. This area is growing into a contiguous, polycentric network of city development zones and nods to form a kind of "EuroSprawl".

Software schlägt Hardware

Die „blinden Flecken" der Architektur sind Bewegung und Schnelligkeit (die vierte Dimension) und die räumliche Wirksamkeit der neuen Technologien. Abseits der augenblicklich die Architekturdebatte dominierenden, albernen Stildiskussion, ob nun Glas, Stahl- oder Steintapeten vor identische Ingenieurbauwerke gehängt werden sollen, können diese strategischen Ausblicke natürlich für die Architekten und ihre Vorstellungen von gebauter Umwelt wesentlich existenzieller sein. Wenn doch die bisher statischen Hüllen und Nutzungsprozesse zunehmend dynamisiert werden, die Arbeits- und Wohnverhältnisse durch die technischen Inovationen mobilisiert und deprivatisiert, Schein und Wirklichkeit zusammenfallen, warum dann überhaupt noch in diesem optimierten Ausmaß „real gebaute Umwelt".

Gefangene werden nicht mehr in kostspieligen Gefängnissen ruhig gestellt, sondern verbunden mit einem "Global Position System", jederzeit auffindbar sein, wenn sie unerlaubterweise nicht ihren „Hausarrest" einhalten. Kranke werden durch Ferndiagnose und telematische chirurgische Eingriffe in lokalen chirurgischen Stadtteilzentren behandelt, ohne teure Krankenhausaufenthalte in Universitätsklinken in Anspruch nehmen zu müssen.

Am Ende des 16. Jahrhunderts wurde in Florenz das erste Bürogebäude gebaut, Giorgio Vasari´s Uffizien. Ein spezialisierter Arbeitsplatz, an dem schriftliche und bildliche Informationen auf Papier gehortet, abgelegt und manchmal neu zusammengesetzt wurden. Am Ende des 20. Jahrhunderts ist dieser Arbeitsprozeß mutiert zu einem Chaos aus alten und neuen Medien, als Einzel-, Gruppen- und Großraumbüros, mit Konferenzräumen, Verkehrsflächen, Postein- und -ausgängen etc etc. In diesem ganzen Durcheinander wird der Information (ökonomisch gesehen) ein Wert zugeschlagen. Die Masse der Informationen ist unüberschaubar geworden, ihre Aktualität muß sich jede Sekunde aufs Neue beweisen.

Software beats hardware

The "blind spots" of architecture are movement and speed (the fourth dimension) and the spatial effectiveness of the new technologies. Away from the dominating, silly discussion on style taking place in architecture at the moment, pondering on whether glass and steel or stone wall lining should be hung in front of identical engineer buildings, these strategic approaches can of course be much more essential for the life of an architect and his ideas of a world of buildings. If the hitherto static shells and utilization processes are becoming more and more dynamic, labor and living conditions are becoming increasingly mobilized and de-privatized thanks to technical innovations while appearance and reality coincide, why then "real built environment" to this optimized extent?

Prisoners will no longer be kept quiet in costly prisons, but in combination with a "global position system" they will be accessible at all times if they infringe upon their "house arrest". The sick will be treated after a distance diagnosis and telematically operated in local municipal surgery centers, expensive stays in university hospitals will not be necessary.

In the late 16th century the first office building was built in Florence, Giorgio Vasari's Uffizi. A specialized workplace at which written material and pictures on paper were stockpiled, filed and sometimes put together in new combinations. Now, at the end of the 20th century this work process has mutated to a chaos consisting of old and new media, of single, group and large-scale offices with conference halls, roads, postal entrances and exits, etc. The mass of information has become too immense, it must prove its value every second or two.

Virtuelle Strukturen

Bei diesen Beispielen geht es zuerst darum, die Datenelemente mit möglichst natürlichen Rezeptoren, Verhalten und Aussehen auszustatten. Virtuelle Strukturen sind auf der Ebene der naiven Interfaces von Spezialisten und Computerlaien gleichermaßen nutzbar und insofern prädestiniert für eine partizipative gesellschaftliche Anteilnahme. Die Möglichkeiten der Virtuellen Strukturen werden in den nächsten Jahren zu Modellen einer digitalen Bibliothek, eines digitalen Büros, einer digitalen Fabrik oder einer digitalisierten Region führen und von vielen Gruppen visualisiert werden.

Und die Architektur?

Natürlich ist eine Stadt- und Gebäudekultur, die über mehrere tausend Jahre gewachsen ist, der größte gesellschaftliche und kulturelle Reichtum, der von Menschen geschaffen wurde. Solange Architekten und Stadtplaner davon ausgehen konnten, daß Gebäude die notwendigen Hüllen und die bauliche Repräsentanz, öffentliche Plätze den Aufenthaltsort für lokale, gesellschaftliche Nutzungen bilden, konnten sie jedem technologischen Inovationsschub und jeder sozialen oder politischen Umwälzung gelassen entgegensehen. Die Architektur paßt sich gleich einem Chamäleon (auch das zeigt die Architekturgeschichte) jeder Änderung innerhalb kürzester Zeit an und dienten neuen Herren und Notwendigkeiten. Diese ambivalente Zweckheirat scheint allerdings aufgekündigt in einer Zeit, da die Industriegesellschaften zu informellen Dienstleistungsgesellschaften mutieren und alle Mobilien, abgesehen von den elementaren Lebensbedürfnissen, prinzipiell ubiquitär geplant, erstellt und verteilt werden können. Für die Architekten ergibt sich am Anfang des 21. Jahrhunderts die Chance einer radikalen Neuorientierung, die zu einer Erweiterung des Architekurbegriffes führen muß, wollen sie mit den augenblicklichen Innovationsschüben Schritt halten. So wie einst der mechanische Aufzug dazu führte, daß die „Belle Etage" beliebig oft in die Höhe multipliziert werden konnte und das Penthouse für Reiche die abgelegenen Mansardenwohnung für die Bediensteten verdrängte, so sollten sich die Architekten heute darum bemühen, die Möglichkeiten der neuen Technologien mit der gebauten Umwelt zu kombinieren, wo es sinnvoll und möglich ist. Das erfordert gesteigerte Anforderungen an die Hilfsmittel der Planung und innovative Vorschläge für neue Bauaufgaben oder intelligente Umnutzungen des Bestehenden. Wo die neuen Technologien Funktionen übernehmen, die bisher untrennbar mit Gebäuden verknüpft waren, müssen Planer an der Gestaltung der neuen virtuellen Arbeitsumgebungen verantwortlich mitarbeiten, z.B. bei der Gestaltung des „virtuellen öffentlichen Raums". Hier wird eine Diskussion angerissen, die weitreichender ist, als die Raum- und Architekturwirksamkeit neuer Technologien. Die Debatte um die Zukunft der kognitiven Arbeit unter den Rahmenbedingungen einer globalen informellen Vernetzung wird die nächsten Jahre dominieren. Dabei sollten wir uns nicht von Software-Propagandisten wie dem Milliardär Bill Gates verblöden lassen, der über die schöne neue Com@Welt. schrieb: „Wird einem der Arbeitsplatz wegrationalisiert, bekommt man die Möglichkeit etwas anderes zu tun." (Bill Gates, Der Weg nach vorn, 1995)

Kay Friedrichs
Vortrag, gehalten zum Symosion „Der öffentliche Raum"
(gekürzte Fassung)

Virtual structures

These examples intend to equip the data elements with the most natural receptors, comportment and appearance. Virtual structures can be used at the naive interfaces by specialist and computer fans alike and are thus predestined to cause the participation of society as a whole. The possibilities of virtual structures will give rise to models of digital libraries, digital offices, digital factories or digitized regions and be visualized by many groups in the next few years.

And architecture?

Of course, a culture of cities and buildings that has developed in the course of more than a thousand years is the largest social and cultural achievement of mankind. As long as architects and city designers believe that buildings are the necessary shell and that built representations and public spaces are the venue of local and social life, they can meet all social and political change without fear. Architecture quickly adapts to any changes like chameleons (as proven by the history of architecture) and serve new masters and necessities. This ambivalent marriage of convenience seems to be ending in a time when industrial society is mutating to an informal service society and, except for the elementary necessities of life, all movables are planned, created and distributed ubiquitously. With the dawning of the 21st century, architects will have the opportunity to radically reorientate themselves, inevitably leading to a broader definition of the term architecture if they want to keep pace with the innovation phases. Just as the mechanical lift allowed the height of the "belle étage" to be multiplied as many times as necessary and the penthouse for the rich replaced the remote mansard for servants, architects should strive to combine the possibilities of the new technologies with the built environment wherever useful and possible. This demands more from the tools used in planning and innovative proposals for new building tasks or intelligently changing the utility of the existing structures. Wherever the new technologies take on functions that to date have been inseparable from buildings, planners must contribute in designing the new virtual work environment, e.g. creating "virtual public space".
This touches on a discussion that goes far beyond the spatial and architectural effectiveness of new technologies. The discussion on the future of cognitive work against the backdrop of a global informal interlinkage will dominate the years to come. We should not allow ourselves to be stultified by software propagandists such as the billionaire Bill Gates who writes about the nice new Com@world, "If your job is streamlined, you will have the opportunity of doing something else." (Bill Gates, ..., 1995).

Kay Friedrichs
Lecture given at the symposion "The Public Space"
(shortened version)

On public spaces Mariano Bayon

Unity and anatomy

Open space, public space, private space. Architecture, empty spaces, the city, the tools, the activities...
All is the same. The same origin and the same destiny.
The sixth symposium on architecture in Vienna looks at public space in the city that is defined as the place "between objects" and accordingly investigated.

I would like to take this opportunity to express my deepest conviction that "unity" may be the strongest field of power in which all human activities have ever taken and still take place.
Unity is claimed by all our activities, not only by architecture.
For the medieval Scholastics, the function of art and all human work was to create a context within which we grasp the universality of the knowledge of life and uniformly achieve an immediate and sensual perception of life.
This vision is still valid today.
Unity is the perceptible conviction that all is the same and that the link with all other aspects and facets of the same thing becomes effective.
Through this unity the architecture of an era for example can be recognized in even the smallest imaginable particle of its environment.

Nothing can be detached. This order is necessarily linked to the other orders or power fields of our activities. Architecture is impossible without industry, no industry without art, no art without science, no science without a common frame that carries and spreads it and vice versa.
Architecture is impossible without structure, without infrastructure, without hydraulics.
Structure in the broadest sense of the word, infrastructure in the broadest sense of the word.
The relation between energies that go hand in hand with building, even of the mechanical means, the relation between cost and realization, the harmony in production and use of the urban environment, the inner relation between the systems and forms of life, and between these and architecture.

Architecture is all. Everything is all. All is everything.

This vision of unity dissolves all distances and also the term public space, open space becomes meaningless just as its separation from built space.
In practice, public space is not limited to open space and the city acts as an expandable and variable (in space and time) container for public and private spaces.
Often a disco will be more of a public space than a square, a train station more than a park, a lecture hall more than a street.
In order to be able to shape open spaces, one must first comprehend the closed space, the extensive nature of a city.
A city becomes manifest in its dynamic surface, in a spectrogram in relative movement as are ocean waves, superficial, although as with the ocean, a balanced structure of its purest nature can be made out beneath the troubled surface.
According to Mondrian all things change, all things flow. At the bottom of variable things one comes upon the invariable that is without time and reveals itself as pure creative beauty.
This sensation of unity invites to talk about architecture, architecture understood as uniform.
To understand that public space, opened space or limited space must be planned from the same point of view.
All this is the same architecture.

The city is born from an infinite number of experimental projects not realized.
They are united by the illusion of solidarity and the certainty of intellectual continuity.
The sum of the built and empty objects in their anonymity is more than its individual parts. Architecture stands over man's doings with its own behavior.

Öffentlicher Raum, geöffneter Raum und begrenzter Raum sind vom selben Ausgangspunkt zu planen.
All das ist dieselbe Architektur.

Die Stadt entsteht durch eine unbegrenzte Anzahl von nicht verwirklichten und experimentellen Vorhaben.
Sie werden durch die Illusion der Solidarität und die Gewißheit der geistigen Kontinuität vereint.
Die Summe der verbauten und leeren Objekte in ihrer Anonymität ist mehr als ihre Einzelteile. Über dem Treiben des Menschen steht die Architektur mit ihrer eigenen Verhaltensweise.
Sie besitzt darüber hinaus prophetische Kraft, die weit und nachhaltig in die Zukunft wirkt.
Die Gestaltung der Stadt ist entweder unausweichlich oder unmöglich. Man benötigt viel Zeit zur Formulierung eines Stückes Stadt, man benögtigt viel Zeit zur Formulierung der Architektur. Aber wenn der Zeitpunkt gekommen ist, ist die Architektur der Stadt unausweichlich.
Nach Kandinsky erreichen die Notwendigkeiten ihre Reife wenn ihre Zeit gekommen ist.

Überlegungen über die Architektur anzustellen, ist eher ein Erforschen der Bedingungen für ihr Zustandekommen. Ein Prüfen des Reifens der Notwendigkeit, ein Fühlen des Unausweichlichen. Nach Kandinsky sind die authentischen Werke daran erkennbar, daß sie aus der inneren Notwendigkeit ihres Schöpfers entstehen. Im entgegengesetzten Fall, meint er, entstehen sie aus äußerer Notwendigkeit. Das heißt aus Ehrgeiz und Gier.

Eines vorab: wenn ich von Architektur spreche, beziehe ich mich nie auf jene Architektur von Architekten für Architekten, losgelöst und selbstgefällig, angespornt vom heutigen Konsumrausch: Moden, Trends, Schlagwörter, Überschriften. Nur schnell konsumieren. Der Einsatz leicht durchschaubarer grimassierender Oberflächlichkeit zur Sicherung eines kurzfristigen Einflusses. Der Einsatz falscher Theorien zur Stützung des Unhaltbaren.

All dies sind Auswüchse einer wahrhaft lärmenden Welt, wenn doch die authentische Theorie Grundlage konstruktiven Wissens und Denkens sein sollte.
Gegenüber einer Architektur, die nur dem persönlcihen Ausdruck ihrer Uhrheber dient, kann ich nur mein Desinteresse und meine Distanzierung anmelden.
Ein müßiges Unterfangen. Schlußendlich wird sie etwas anderes sein: ebenfalls unausweichlich.
Architektur entsteht in vielen Fällen sogar trotz der Architekten.
Die Architektur gehört uns nicht. Sie besteht in sich selbst.
Architektur kann man nicht machen.

Es ist notwendig, positiv und beharrlich Übereinkünfte zu sammeln, um die Bedingungen für das notwendige und einmütige Entstehen von Architektur zu erkunden.
Zuerst bedarf es der Liebe zu dieser notwendigen und einmütigen Architektur und dann in einem Akt der Reflexion, der Fähigkeit, sie zu erkennen. Namenlos. Wie es der spanische Dichter Gabriel Celaya formulierte: „Das Notwendigste besitzt keinen Namen".
Die Architektur entsteht aus einem architektonisch jungfräulichem „Zustand". Aus einem latenten Zustand. Aus einem Zustand des Offensichtlichen – wie jegliche menschliche Aktivität oder Idee.
Und was wir Architektur nennen, soll sich niemals auf eine persönliche, exhibitionistische Zurschaustellung mit persönlichen Formen beziehen, noch auf einen krampfhaften Kampf, sondern vielmehr auf eine stille, freudige und prächtige Entschleierung des Verborgenen, eine Erhellung des Unsichtbaren, aber tatsächlich Vorhanden, als Wegzehrung und Erleuchtung für den Geist aller Zeiten. Die Architektur entsteht, bevor sie ist.

Um sie zu erkennen und wahrzunehmen, benötigen wir einen entsprechenden Empfänger, der sie unserem Gehör zugänglich macht. Diese zarte Membran, empfänglich für die Strahlen des

Moreover architecture possesses prophetic power that reaches far into the future with sustainable effects. Much time is needed to formulate a part of a city, much time is needed to formulate architecture.
Shaping the city is either inevitable or impossible.
According to Kandinsky necessities reach maturity when their time has come.

Reflecting upon architecture is rather an investigation of the conditions for its materialization. A testing of the maturation of necessities, a sensing of the inevitable.
According to Kandinsky, authentic works can always be recognized because they develop from a necessity innate in their author. In the opposite case, according to him, they develop from an external necessity. Meaning from ambition and greed.

To begin with: When I speak of architecture, I never refer to architecture for architects, remote and smug, spurred on by the modern consumer's society, fashions, trends, slogans, headings. Aspiring only to hasty consumption. Applying grimacing superficiality that is easily exposed, desperately straining to secure but temporary influence. Applying false theories to sustain the untenable.

A truly clamorous world, despite that authentic theory should be the foundation of constructive knowledge and thinking.
As regarding architecture limited to the author's mere personal expression, I can but disassociate myself and voice my disinterest.
An idle venture. In the end it will be something else: inevitable, too.
In many cases architecture develops even in spite of architects.
We do not possess architecture. Architecture exists within itself.
Architecture can not be made.

It is necessary to positively and assiduously collect agreements, even without design, to investigate the necessary and harmonious genesis of architecture.
First comes the love for this necessary and harmonious architecture, then in an act of reflection follows the capability to recognize it. Nameless. As the Spanish poet Gabriel Celava put it: "The most necessary carries no name."
Architecture springs from an architectural 'condition' of virginity. From a latent condition. From a condition of the obvious. As do all human activities and ideas.
And what we call architecture should never refer to a personal exhibitionist display of personal shapes, nor to a desperate battle, rather it should refer to a quiet, joyful, and magnificent unveiling of the secluded, illumination of the invisible yet actually existing, to feed and enlighten the spirit of the times along its journey. Architecture is born before it is.
There are all manner of invisible and inaudible vibrations in every space, yet that actually exist, actually are.
To recognize them we require an appropriate receiver that makes them audible to our hearing. It is this delicate membrane, subtle and permeable, sensitive to the aura of the authentic that makes the architect, the artist, the scientist, the inventor.
Saint Thomas said: "Beauty is the brilliance of truth."
Necessary and harmonious architecture emerges from anonymity and so naturally and without difficulty recedes back into anonymity. Light, light bulb, and the switch we throw do not bring Edison to mind.
And both, the light bulb and the switch have an inventor, without us believing this is really so.
Architecture, as everything brought forth by man, reaches beyond the author, the user, and people.
It contains, as does the electric current, something non-human exceeding the construction or design.

Now as in the past.

Authentischen, macht den Architekten, den Künstler, den Wissenschaftler, den Erfinder aus. Der Hl. Thomas sagte: „Die Schönheit ist der Glanz der Wahrheit".
Die notwendige und einmütige Architektur kommt aus der Anonymität und taucht deshalb mit Leichtigkeit, mit Natürlichkeit in die Anonymität ein. Weder das Licht, noch die Glühbirne oder der Schalter, den wir betätigen, erinnern uns an Edison.
Und doch haben Glühbirne und Schalter einen Erfinder, ohne daß wir glauben, das sei tatsächlich so.
Die Architektur reicht, wie jede menschliche Hervorbringung, über ihre Schöpfer, über ihre Benützer, über die Menschen hinaus.
In ihr ist, wie beim elektrischen Strom, etwas nicht-menschliches vorhanden, das über den Bau, über den Entwurf hinausgeht.

Heute wie gestern.

Wenn wir einen Teil der tatsächlichen Stadt, verbaut oder leer, näher betrachten oder sogar das Stockwerk eines geplanten oder bestehenden Wohnhauses, können wir wie in einem Labor die Veränderungen beobachten, die das tatsächliche Leben bewirkt hat und weiterhin unaufhörlich bewirkt.
Die gegenwärtigen Bilder, die Kommunikationsmittel, wechselnde Nutzung, die Schichtungen der Aktivität, die Leerräume, die Gliederungen der Elemente, die unsichtbaren Spannungen, die unterschiedlichen räumlichen und psychologischen Maßstäbe, neue Möglichkeiten und Materialien, die Summen subtiler und unsichtbarer Kräfte sind heute die neuen Abstraktionen, die unser Empfindungsvermögen beeinflussen.
Wir bemerken sie zwar, setzen uns aber nicht besonders mit ihnen auseinander.
Die Architektur erscheint nach einem abstrakten Aufpfropfen in uns selbst.
In unserem Inneren findet sich alles notwendige Wissen.
Der wahre Künstler kann nicht außerhalb seiner selbst sein.
Die Suche im Äußeren ist daher einzustellen. Das System der inneren Suche gründet sich auf die Auswahl, nicht auf die Anhäufung.
Ich greife auf die vergessenen Worte von Mies van der Rohe zurück: „Wir lehnen jede ästhetische Spekulation, jedes Dogma und jeden Formalismus ab. Die Form, ausgehend vom Kern des Problems mit den Mitteln unserer Zeit zu schaffen, das sind unsere Aufgaben. Wir müssen die innere Ordnung unseres Wesens Wirklichkeit werden lassen".

When we look more closely at a part of the city, be it built or empty, or even a certain floor of a projected or existing apartment building, as in a laboratory we can observe the changes that have been and are incessantly brought on by actual life.
The present images, the means of communication, changing uses, the stratification of activities, the vacant spaces, the arrangement of the elements, the invisible tensions, the various measures of space and psychology, new possibilities and materials, the sums of subtle and invisible powers are the new abstractions that influence our faculty of perception today.
We may notice them, but we do not particularly bother to deal with them.
Architecture appears within us following an abstract grafting.
All necessary knowledge lies within us. The true artist cannot be outside of himself.
Therefore the search among things exterior must be brought to an end. The system of the inner search is based on the choice not on amassment.
I quote the long forgotten words of Mies van der Rohe,: "We reject all aesthetic speculation, all dogma and all formalism. Creating the form based on the core of the problem with the means of our time is our mission. We must allow the inner order of our nature to come true".

Mariano Bayón
Vortrag, gehalten zum Symosion „Der öffentliche Raum"

Mariano Bayón
Lecture given at the symposion "The Public Space"